Plato and Demosthenes

Plato and Demosthenes

Recovering the Old Academy

William H. F. Altman

LEXINGTON BOOKS
Lanham • Boulder • New York • London

Published by Lexington Books
An imprint of The Rowman & Littlefield Publishing Group, Inc.
4501 Forbes Boulevard, Suite 200, Lanham, Maryland 20706
www.rowman.com

86-90 Paul Street, London EC2A 4NE

Copyright © 2023 by The Rowman & Littlefield Publishing Group, Inc.

All rights reserved. No part of this book may be reproduced in any form or by any electronic or mechanical means, including information storage and retrieval systems, without written permission from the publisher, except by a reviewer who may quote passages in a review

British Library Cataloguing in Publication Information Available

Library of Congress Cataloging-in-Publication Data

Names: Altman, William H. F., 1955- author.
Title: Plato and Demosthenes : recovering the old academy / William H.F. Altman.
Description: Lanham : Lexington Books, [2023] | Includes bibliographical references and index.
Identifiers: LCCN 2022033543 (print) | LCCN 2022033544 (ebook) | ISBN 9781666920055 (cloth) | ISBN 9781666920079 (paper) | ISBN 9781666920062 (ebook)
Subjects: LCSH: Plato. | Demosthenes.
Classification: LCC B395 .A5554 2023 (print) | LCC B395 (ebook) | DDC 184—dc23/eng/20220909
LC record available at https://lccn.loc.gov/2022033543
LC ebook record available at https://lccn.loc.gov/2022033544

Is it possible to mistake the connection between the political attitude of the greatest and most popular orator who, with all the convincing rhetoric at his disposal, hammered into the Greek brain and heart again and again the thesis: royal rule is slavery, only democracy is freedom; and the theory of government of the leading philosopher of the time, who maintained royal rule to be diametrically opposed to a rulership over slaves, the latter to be rather—as all perverted constitutions are—democracy. Aristotle's doctrine of government is not without its political background. It can be understood only by remembering the direct opposition in which it stood to the political system, which obtained its living expression in the orations of Demosthenes.

Hans Kelsen (1881–1973)[1]

---

1. Hans Kelsen, "The Philosophy of Aristotle and the Hellenic-Macedonian Policy." *International Journal of Ethics* 48, no. 1 (October 1937), 1-64, on 20.

Contents

Acknowledgments	ix
Preface	xi
Abbreviations for Writings of Plato and Demosthenes	xxxi
Chronology	xxxiii
Introduction	1
1 The End of the Old Academy	21
2 Five Other Students of Plato	43
3 Plato the Teacher	65
4 Demosthenes	85
5 Suppressions	111
Notes	139
Bibliography	213
Index	231
About the Author	245

Acknowledgments

This book's purpose to validate the ancient evidence that Demosthenes and other patriotic fourth-century Athenian statesmen were Plato's students, thus providing external evidence for a reading of the Platonic dialogues presented in a series of five volumes already published by Lexington Books, an imprint of Rowman & Littlefield. Based on the hypothesis that Plato's dialogues constituted the original curriculum of the Academy, *Plato the Teacher* and its companions broke with tradition by presenting Plato as more like a high school teacher than a university professor or think-tank director, writing entertaining and accessible dialogues for the betterment of the youth. Through studying these challenging dialogues, young Athenians between the ages of fourteen and eighteen would acquire the kind of civic and selfless virtue that would that would ultimately benefit Athens and preserve the freedom to philosophize that the city dedicated to the goddess of wisdom had made possible. If this was Plato's goal, he fulfilled it primarily through the eloquent Demosthenes, last great defender of Athenian democracy in the face of Macedonian tyranny. At the center of this Athens-centric conception of both the Old Academy and its first students stands the Allegory of the Cave in Plato's *Republic*, the most famous and frequently excerpted passage from the dialogues. Beginning with *Plato the Teacher*, I presented the Cave Allegory as a summons, challenging philosophers to return to the dangers of a political life in a democratic city. Since these books were written by a public high school teacher who lacked the elite credentials and customary advantages of a university affiliation, it required an act of faith on the part of the professionals at Rowman

& Littlefield to publish them, and now, in an extension of that faith, to publish this book, dependent as it is on views developed at length elsewhere. It is difficult to imagine that any other press would be willing to publish such a book and it is therefore a pleasure and a privilege for me to express profound gratitude for a working relationship that began more than a decade ago. In particular, thanks are due to Jana Hodges-Kluck, Julie Kirsch, Nicolette Amstutz, and Lexington's editorial board.

It is also a pleasure to acknowledge the help I received from important and highly credentialed scholars. Harold Tarrant provided necessary encouragement at the very beginning, and early conversations with Matthias Haake helped me focus the project. Laurent Pernot, Kai Trampedach, and Irene Giaquinta made their books available to me, and Judson Herrmann taught me how to read Demosthenic Greek. Ryan Balot, David Konstan, Tony Preus, and an anonymous reader also made valuable contributions. But since writing this book required connecting Plato's dialogues to fourth-century events, I was in desperate need of guidance from scholars with an expertise in ancient history, and I was fortunate enough to find it. Profound gratitude is therefore due as well to Anthony Natoli and Robin Waterfield, both of whom were kind enough to read the whole manuscript, making hundreds of suggestions, comments and corrections; their generosity has been exemplary and deserves both praise and imitation. Naturally the errors and instances of intemperance that remain are neither their responsibility nor anyone else's other than mine.

As usual, I have considerable debts to my family. To begin with, this book was written while my beloved sister, Leslie Rescorla (1945-2020), was struggling with cancer; her courage in the face of pain and death inspired me. At the other end of the life cycle, my grandchildren, Eliza and James, are a daily source of delight, and I am grateful to their parents, Erin Rafferty and my son Philip, for making me an important part of their precious young lives. From my son Elias, I continue to receive not only familial but also technological support; his advice and courage have been indispensable and inspirational. But first and foremost, as the daily source of my inspiration, and the spiritual as well as physical basis of my life as a scholar, stands my beloved wife, Zoraide: your bright-eyed delight, passion, caution, and loving support command my respect, gratitude, and love as always. For everything you have done to make this book and its companions possible, my darling, there are no unsung words.

Florianópolis
March 14, 2022

Preface

What Dionysius of Halicarnassus Didn't Say about Plato and Demosthenes

Commenting on a passage in Cicero's dialogue *Brutus* where Demosthenes is said to have read Plato with care and to have been his auditor, A. E. Douglas remarked that the connection between Demosthenes as student and Plato as his teacher is "as consistently denied by modern scholars as it is asserted by ancient sources."[1] This book will strengthen the case for reconnecting Demosthenes and Plato, and thus it aims to restore the ancient view at the expense of the modern consensus. As such, it must draw heavily on the methods of philology, intellectual history, and reception studies, particularly with a view to explaining not only how the ancient consensus came about in the first place but also how it came to be overruled in modernity. Since the modern consensus depends on the view that Demosthenes was not Plato's student, moderns who take the question seriously must explain why some ancients fabricated evidence for a connection that had in truth never existed. But it is far easier for a defender of the ancient view to show how this same evidence was rather suppressed than fabricated, for rejected, denied, and suppressed in modernity it unquestionably has been. In addition to being necessary for reestablishing the connection between Demosthenes and Plato, the suppression-fabrication dynamic in play here is at once a complex historical phenomenon and an intrinsically fascinating one, and it might easily be mistaken as the book's principal subject. Although understandable, this would be an error.

---

1. A. E. Douglas (ed.), *M. Tulli Ciceronis* Brutus (Oxford: Clarendon Press, 1966), 100 (on 121, *audivisse*).

This study is ancillary to a larger project devoted to Plato, and more specifically to "Plato the Teacher."[2] That project is based on a new way of reading the Platonic dialogues. By illuminating their many interconnections, it challenges a historicist approach that searches the dialogues for indications of Plato's intellectual development, offering instead a student-oriented alternative. When read in a pedagogically plausible order indicated or established by highlighting the many dramatic interconnections between them, the dialogues are shown to constitute a well-constructed and progressive curriculum. History reenters the story with the following claim: once arranged and ordered in accordance with Plato's hints, the dialogues as a whole constituted the Academy's curriculum.[3] We know next to nothing about how or what Plato taught in the Academy; the purpose of *Plato the Teacher* was to fill this gap on the basis of the evidence that survives: Plato's eminently teachable dialogues. In defending this approach, modern readers, beginning with the author, were treated as Plato's intended students, and recurring once again to a profoundly ahistorical approach, the dialogues were read as constituting "the eternal curriculum of the Academy." In the present book, history will return with a vengeance: in place of an amorphous and historically underdetermined "student," the young Demosthenes will here become the necessary correlate of "Plato the Teacher."

In short, having collected *internal* evidence of what Plato taught in the Academy from the dialogues themselves, the author now seeks to corroborate those findings with *external* evidence from fourth-century history. Although Demosthenes is not the only student of Plato who will be considered here, he will be presented as archetypical. To state the obvious first, Demosthenes was an Athenian and the Academy was located in Athens. Thanks above all to Aristotle, traditionally taken to be Plato's student par excellence, it has become easy to imagine that Plato's typical student was a foreigner. It is more plausible that at the start, all of Plato's students were Athenians and that only gradually did foreigners journey to Athens in order to study at the Academy. More importantly, Demosthenes provides external evidence for the claim at the center of *Plato the Teacher* that the Allegory of the Cave contains the internal core of what

---

2. Although the title of only one of them, *Plato the Teacher* is best understood as the umbrella term for a five-volume study that includes: *Ascent to the Beautiful: Plato the Teacher and the Pre-Republic Dialogues from* Protagoras *to* Symposium (Lanham, MD: Lexington Books, 2020), *Ascent to the Good: The Reading Order of Plato's Dialogues from* Symposium *to* Republic (Lanham, MD: Lexington Books, 2018), *Plato the Teacher: The Crisis of the* Republic (Lanham, MD: Lexington Books, 2012), *The Guardians in Action: Plato the Teacher and the Post-Republic Dialogues from* Timaeus *to* Theaetetus (Lanham, MD: Lexington Books, 2016), and *The Guardians on Trial: The Reading Order of Plato's Dialogues from* Euthyphro *to* Phaedo (Lanham, MD: Lexington Books, 2016).

3. For a more nuanced version of this claim, see *Ascent to the Beautiful*, preface.

Plato taught: the philosopher's obligation to return to the dangerous shadows of political life. It is no accident that Cicero, in his *Brutus* and elsewhere, was the principal defender of the view that Demosthenes was Plato's student. He did so for the exact same reason that he considered himself to be Plato's student as well: both returned to the Cave and mastered the rhetorical tools required for resisting the inevitable slide of their city's democracy into tyranny.[4]

It is in the light of this larger purpose that the fabrication-suppression dynamic should be understood: it is principally *for Plato's sake* that the ancient view that Demosthenes was his student is being revived here. As complex and fascinating as the philological question may be, and as necessary as it unquestionably is to revisit that question, it is rather the teacher-student and internal-external dynamics that will remain central in what follows. First of all, "Plato the Teacher" could never be fully understood without considering his students. Consider next the obvious historical facts: although Plato's dialogues are set in the fifth-century, his school was founded, his dialogues were written, and the majority of his life was lived in the fourth. If the dialogues are our best *internal* evidence of what Plato taught, this book will show that events of the fourth century, clustering around Demosthenes, provide *external* evidence that corroborates previous findings based on the dialogues alone. But if the ancient evidence that Demosthenes *was* Plato's student illuminates what Plato taught, the modern consensus that he *wasn't* must do much the same thing in a different and indeed opposite manner. This contrast must remain central, because it is primarily our understanding of Plato, not of Demosthenes, that is at stake here. The modern view that the ancient evidence that Demosthenes was Plato's student is incompatible with what we now know to have been Plato's purpose is inseparable from the author's antithetical claim that we can gain a clearer view of his purpose by revisiting that evidence as well as by reading the dialogues themselves without modern preconceptions about the order in which he wrote them.

Demosthenes was not the only Athenian politician of the fourth century who was said to have been Plato's student. In his *Reply to Colotes*, Plutarch mentions that both Chabrias and Phocion left the Academy to address the Assembly,[5] and his *Life of Phocion*, which reinforces the claim,[6] is likewise a principal source for the political activities not only of Demosthenes but of (the Athenian) Lycurgus and Hyperides as well.[7] Along with Demosthenes' principal antagonist Aeschines, the trio of Hyperides, Lycurgus,

---

4. See the author's *The Revival of Platonism in Cicero's Late Philosophy: Platonis aemulus and the Invention of "Cicero"* (Lanham, MD: Lexington Books, 2016).
5. Plutarch, *Reply to Colotes*, 1126c.
6. See Plutarch, *Life of Phocion*, 4.1 and 6.1.
7. See especially Plutarch, *Life of Phocion*, 17.2.

and Demosthenes are all said to have been Plato's students in *Lives of the Ten Orators*,[8] and a few comments on this treatise will serve to illustrate the suppression/fabrication dynamic while introducing the philological complexities involved.[9] To begin with, four of the ten orators it describes are identified there as Plato's students; his rival schoolteacher Isocrates is a fifth; all five are Athenians. Since only one of Lycurgus' speeches survives, *Lives of the Ten Orators* is also the principal source for our information about the fourth century politician whom it is easiest to link with a conventional understanding of Plato's purposes.[10] Counterbalancing all of this is the denial that Plutarch wrote the treatise, and it is currently ascribed to "Pseudo-Plutarch" or "[Plut.]."[11] Whatever the philological merits of this re-assignment, the important thing is that the case could only be a modern one. Nor should it come as a surprise that Arnold Schaefer (1819-1883),[12] the great German scholar primarily responsible for creating the modern consensus that Demosthenes was not Plato's student in the Academy, is generally recognized as being primarily responsible for attributing *Lives of the Ten Orators* to Pseudo-Plutarch.[13]

---

8. See most recently Joseph Roisman and Ian Worthington (eds.) with Robin Waterfield (trans.), *Lives of the Attic Orators: Texts from Pseudo-Plutarch, Photius, and the Suda* (Oxford: Oxford University Press, 2015), 53 (840b) on Aeschines, 55 (841b) on Lycurgus, 60 (844b-c) on Demosthenes, 67 (848d) on Hyperides.

9. For the results of these, to be discussed in the introduction, see especially Kai Trampedach, *Platon, die Akademie und die zeitgenössische Politik* (Stuttgart: Franz Steiner, 1994).

10. Robert F. Renehan, "The Platonism of Lycurgus." *Greek, Roman & Byzantine Studies* 11, no. 3 (1970), 219-231; the more recent work of Danielle Allen will be considered in chapter 2.

11. See Roisman and Worthington, *Lives*, 10-14.

12. See Arnold Schaefer, *Demosthenes und seine Zeit*, three volumes (Leipzig: Teubner, 1856-58).

13. See, for examples, Andrea Wörle, *Die politische Tätigkeit der Schüler Platons* (Darmstadt: Kümmerle, 1981), 50, and Roisman and Worthington, *Lives*, 11 ("as Schaefer has demonstrated"). In fact, doubts about the authenticity of *Lives of the Ten Orators* long predate Arnold Schaefer, *Commentatio de libro vitarum decem oratorum* (Dresden: Blochmann, 1844) as proved by Anton Westermann (ed.), *Plutarchi vitae decem oratorum* (Quedlinburg and Leipzig: Becker, 1833), iii, and "De auctore et auctoritate libri qui inscribitur vitae decem oratorum commentatio" in the same volume, 1; following A. G. Becker, Westermann's goal was to restore to Plutarch what had been already stolen from him, and it was to refute this recent restoration that Schaefer directed his attention to the Catalogue of Lamprias (see 2-27). See Albert Gerhard Becker, "Über die Schrift des Plutarchos, *Leben der zehn Redner*" in Becker, *Andokides, übersetzt und erklärt*, 111-132 (Quedlinburg and Leipzig: Becker, 1833), which, while presuming the authenticity of the Lamprias Catalogue (113-14), explained the various contradictions between a late *Lives of the Ten Orators* and what Plutarch had written earlier on the same subjects elsewhere—these contradictions provided the older basis for doubt, Becker supplied and Westermann endorsed a developmental or chronological explanation—by regarding the text as a collection of notes, gathered by thorough research, but neither yet incorporated into a single finished work, nor used to inform or correct what Plutarch had written elsewhere (see especially 129-32). Becker applies this thesis to Demosthenes in particular on 130: "But what speaks even more for regarding Plutarch as the collector of these materials is the

As the last note is intended to illustrate, the philological issues are complex, and since a consideration of those complexities is inescapably required for advancing the claim that Demosthenes was Plato's student, it will be necessary to burden the reader with them beginning in the introduction, starting with a passage from Plutarch's *Life of Demosthenes*. As a general rule, an Introduction is hardly the place for such complexities, but here there is no help for it; it is necessary to begin with the way modern scholars rejected the evidence for this study's preliminary claim. But the way the word "suppression" has already been used and will be used there must be clearly understood. The introduction will begin with the evidence that modern scholars found it easiest to invalidate and it will consider the historical and philological arguments they used while invalidating it. A defender of the relationship that this evidence validated must illuminate the weakness of the arguments on which the modern consensus originally depended. Having done so, the introduction moves from the initial claim that this evidence was valueless to the deeper question of its origin, and this is where "fabrication" enters: once universally recognized as false, the existence of this evidence now needed to be explained. It is in explicit opposition to the hypothesis that this evidence was fabricated that my use of "suppression" applies, not to the original invalidation, through philology, of that evidence. Only in retrospect is there evidence that the teacher-student relationship was suppressed rather than fabricated, but the more important matter, to be considered in the five chapters that follow the introduction, is how that relationship, once revisited with fresh eyes, can help us to understand Plato better and thus to recover the Academy in its original form, which I am calling "the Old Academy."

It is therefore a far less complex piece of invalidating evidence and one that depends primarily on a certain understanding of Plato that this preface will consider. It is clearly stated in a recent commentary on [Plutarch], *Lives of the Ten Orators*, attached to the following statement about Demosthenes: "He took as his models Thucydides and the philosopher Plato who some say was his main teacher."[14] Ian Worthington comments: "That Demosthenes was taught by Plato is almost certainly erroneous

---

circumstance that in the life of Demosthenes found here much is incorporated from the earlier biography [sc. Plutarch's *Life of Demosthenes*] in a correcting manner, which presents its investigative criticism as more trustworthy, or at least as more likely, than what is found in the first *Life*." Becker's approach is most highly developed in Westermann's "De auctore et auctoritate,"12-14. For a recent approach to such problems—positing an evolving text with multiple authors—see Gunther Martin, "Interpreting Instability: Considerations on the *Lives of the Ten Orators*." *Classical Quarterly* 64, no. 1 (2014), 321-336.

14. Roisman and Worthington, *Lives*, 60 ([Plutarch], *Lives of the Ten Orators*, 844b).

given Plato's contempt for rhetoric."[15] Here, a certain view of Plato is taken as interpretive bedrock, and presumably on the basis of *Gorgias*, a contemporary scholar discovers nothing objectionable about negating the testimony of Pseudo-Plutarch on the grounds that rhetoric's avowed enemy could not possibly have taught the most eloquent of Greek orators.[16] This is not the kind of "evidence" that led nineteenth-century German philologists to create the modern consensus: it is rather the logical result of that consensus's triumph. It currently requires no argument, as when Brad Cook writes in the 2020 *Oxford Handbook to Demosthenes*: "Did Demosthenes study with Plato? If he had, we might then read his assembly speeches differently; but his tutelage under Plato seems wholly implausible." And in Worthington's contribution to this state-of-the art volume, he once again makes his characteristic claim: "Plato's dislike of rhetoric makes him an unlikely teacher of the subject."[17]

To this kind of argument, Cicero offered the classic response when Crassus, the leading character in his *De oratore* observed at 1.47 (except where otherwise noted, all translations will be mine): "I read *Gorgias* with great care, in which book I admired Plato especially for this: because in ridiculing orators, he himself seemed to me to be the greatest orator."[18] It is universally admitted that Socrates was ironic; scholars have been slower to admit that Plato habitually practiced irony as well.[19] Cicero recognized that Plato's eloquent speeches against rhetoric scarcely proved his antagonism to eloquence or his lack of rhetorical skill; he is unlikely to have been the first to do so despite the fact that he is first to provide evidence that he did. Once identified as Platonic practice, ironies of this kind abound, as when Plato imitates Socrates making the case against imitation, or allows him to make long speeches in favor of brevity, crafting poetic speeches against the craft of poetry, and erroneous arguments in favor of the proposition that no one errs voluntarily.[20] All this is not to say that Plato's irony indicates the absence of a serious purpose, or that it was the ironic Plato who influenced Demosthenes. But it is intended to prove that the eloquent Plato's apparent opposition to rhetoric does not *ipso facto* justify the claim that Demosthenes could not have been his student.

---

15. Roisman and Worthington, *Lives*, 215 (on "He took as his models . . . teacher"). Confirmed in private correspondence, see also Ian Worthington, *Demosthenes of Athens and the Fall of Classical Greece* (Oxford: Oxford University Press, 2013), 19, for the claim that Worthington is responsible.

16. Cf. Helen F. North, "Combing and Curling: *Orator Summus Plato.*" *Illinois Classical Studies* 16, no. 1/2 (Spring/Fall 1991), 201-219.

17. See Gunter Martin (ed.), *The Oxford Handbook of Demosthenes* (Oxford and New York: Oxford University Press, 2019), 298 (Cook) and 403 (Worthington).

18. Cicero, *De oratore* 1.47; except where otherwise noted, all translations will be mine.

19. For an exception that proves the rule, see G. R. F. Ferrari, "Socratic Irony as Pretense." *Oxford Studies in Ancient Philosophy* 34 (2008), 1-33.

20. See *Ascent to the Beautiful*, beginning with xi.

Unlike Cicero, Demosthenes never wrote a philosophical dialogue, and therefore never made use of Platonic irony. Indeed his most ostentatiously Platonic production—so Platonic, indeed, that its authenticity is disputed—is a thoroughly un-ironic version of the great erotic speech in *Phaedrus* (cf. 61.1 and *Phdr.* 227b4).[21] Like Aristotle, Demosthenes seems to have lacked Plato's sense of humor, and it is because Cicero clearly had such a sense that his writings are more obviously Platonic. But despite his sense of humor and use of irony, Cicero understood Plato's serious purpose and captured it perfectly in his "Dream of Scipio," the culmination of his own *Republic*.[22] While recognizing the superiority of celestial contemplation, Scipio honors his civic obligations and returns from "the highest heaven of invention" to be murdered in defense of the Republic.[23] It is therefore not primarily Cicero's literary ironies or his oratorical skill that proves him to be a Platonist but the life he lived and the death he died in faithful service to his native city, teetering as it was on the brink of tyranny. It is at the intersection of rhetoric and the Cave's Idea-based dualism that Cicero situated his Platonism in *Orator*: "He calls these forms of things ἰδέαι, that most serious authority and master not of understanding only but also of speaking: Plato [*ille non intellegendi solum sed etiam dicendi gravissimus auctor et magister Plato*]."[24]

Cicero's praise for Plato as his *magister dicendi* is matched by his admiration for Demosthenes, and for those who regard Plato as rhetoric's enemy, Cicero's choice of these two role models appears to be confused and incoherent.[25] Cicero requires those who would understand him to recognize what made his admiration for both coherent: only when guided by philosophy is perfect eloquence possible.[26] It was as the orator who

---

21. I will cite the sixty-one speeches preserved under Demosthenes' name in the text by number and section in parenthesis, as here the *Erotic Essay*, in accordance with S. H. Butcher and W. Rennie (eds.), *Demosthenis Orationes*, three volumes (Oxford: Clarendon Press, 1903-31). Plato's dialogues (*Phaedrus* here) will likewise be cited in parentheses in the text, using abbreviations in accordance with Henry George Liddell and Robert Scott, *A Greek-English Lexicon* [hereafter "LSJ"], revised and augmented throughout by Sir Henry Stuart Jones with the assistance of Roderick MacKenzie and with the co-operation of many scholars, with a Supplement (Oxford: Clarendon Press, 1968 [first edition in 1843]), xxxiii. All citations of the dialogues will be based on John Burnet (ed.), *Platonis Opera*, volumes 2-5 (Oxford: Clarendon Press, 1901-1907), E. A. Duke, et al. (eds.), *Platonis Opera*, volume 1 (Oxford: Clarendon Press, 1995), and S. R. Slings (ed.), *Platonis Rempublicam* (Oxford: Clarendon Press, 2003).
22. See J. G. F. Powell (ed.), *M. Tulli Ciceronis, De re publica*, etc. (Oxford: Clarendon Press, 2006), 135-47 (6.13-33).
23. See Altman, *Revival of Platonism*,
24. Cicero, *Orator* 10; for discussion, see Altman, *Revival of Platonism*, xvii and 265-68.
25. In addition to Caroline Bishop, *Cicero, Greek Learning, and the Making of a Roman Classic* (Oxford and New York: Oxford University Press, 2019), chapters 2 and 4, see her "Roman Plato or Roman Demosthenes? The Bifurcation of Cicero in Ancient Scholarship" in Altman (ed.), *Brill's Companion to the Reception of Cicero*, 283-306 (Leiden and Boston: Brill, 2015).
26. With Cicero, *De oratore*, 1.5, see also *Orator* 7-14, culminating with: *sine philosophia non posse effici quem quaerimus eloquentem*. Cf. Qintilan, Institutio

came closest to achieving perfect eloquence that Cicero praised Demosthenes, and his praise took the highest possible form: imitation. A treatise about "the best kind of oratory" would have culminated with a translation of Demosthenes' *On the Crown*,[27] and his late *Philippics* make his admiration even more obvious and sincere.[28] The fact that Cicero was writing *De officiis* at the same time he was delivering the *Philippics* is an outward sign that he regarded philosophy and rhetoric as compatible and complimentary,[29] and throughout his career, this compatibility constitutes the core of Cicero's thought. But the historical basis for his own practice was Cicero's well-documented certainty that Demosthenes was Plato's student:[30] only through philosophy could rhetoric reach its peak.

On the theoretical plane, Cicero justified his admiration for Demosthenes on the basis of the distinction between Attic and Asiatic oratory, and it was likewise on this basis that Dionysius of Halicarnassus would second and confirm Cicero's choice: Demosthenes was the unsurpassed master of "the middle style" that combined rhetorical fullness with Attic austerity, powerful simplicity with emotion-stirring immediacy.[31] Arriving in Rome only a few years after Cicero's murder, Dionysius would repeatedly advance his predecessor's case for Demosthenes' superiority, particularly in the studies that created the literary model for *Lives of the Ten Orators*. Dionysius wrote perceptive and retrospectively canonical accounts for at least five of them, and from what we have of *On the Ancient Orators*, it is obvious that its purpose was to defend Demosthenes as not only unsurpassed but unsurpassable. It is therefore striking that Dionysius, despite providing abundant evidence of his familiarity with Cicero's writings,[32] never mentions Cicero himself, least of all as the Roman orator who came closest to surpassing his Greek role model.

By far the longest of Dionysius' treatises *On the Ancient Orators* is *On the Style of Demosthenes*, and its most striking feature is a detailed comparison of Demosthenes and Plato *as orators* staged as a contest between them in the middle of the work. To begin with, this juxtaposition is

---

27. Cicero, *De optimo genere oratorum*.
28. Cicero, *Ad Brutum*, 2.4.
29. See Altman, *Revival of Platonism*, chapter 10.
30. Cicero, *De oratore* 1.89, *Brutus* 121, *Orator* 15, and *De officiis* 1.4.
31. For relevant background, see George A. Kennedy, *The Art of Rhetoric in the Roman World: 300 B.C.-A.D. 300* (Princeton, NJ: Princeton University Press, 1972), 342-363.
32. Cf. Kennedy, *Art of Rhetoric*, 353: "We know that Dionysius acquired a good knowledge of Latin (*Rom. Ant.* 1.7.2); his thought is often close to that of Cicero and the possibility cannot be ruled out that he had read *De oratore* and *Brutus*, and *Orator*. At very least he had talked to Romans who had read them and were interested in the topics they discuss." See also Cecil W. Wooten, *Hermogenes' On Types of Style* (Chapel Hill and London: University of North Carolina Press, 1987), 131 ("may have been influenced by Cicero") and 132. Better is Emilio Gabba, "Political and Cultural Aspects of the Classicistic Revival in the Augustan Age." *Classical Antiquity* 1, no. 1 (April 1982, 43-65, on 48. b

relevant to the simple as opposed to the complex evidence that Demosthenes could not have been Plato's student because Plato was opposed to rhetoric: Dionysius says nothing about this alleged opposition and is exclusively concerned to show that Plato's eloquence, though considerable and worthy of praise, is nevertheless surpassed by that of Demosthenes.[33] Naturally Dionysius must also demonstrate Demosthenes' superiority to other authors, and *On the Style of Demosthenes* contains lengthy comparisons with Thucydides (9-10),[34] Lysias (11-13), and Isocrates (16-22) as well. But the comparison with Plato is the longest of these (23-32), and it occupies the center of the essay as a whole (1-58), long after Dionysius has already attacked as tasteless and inappropriate the overly dithyrambic style of Socrates' Great Speech in *Phaedrus* (5-7). Dionysius was sufficiently proud of this passage that he quotes it in full in his *Letter to Pompeius*, but it is what he writes immediately after it that deserves to occupy the center of this preface:

> Such, then, was the political style that Demosthenes inherited, and having come upon it—altered as it had been so variously [ποικίλως] by so many practitioners— of no one of them did he become the emulator, neither of a character nor a man, believing all to be something halfway done and incomplete; rather, selecting from all of them such things as were best [κράτιστα] and most useful, he was weaving them together [συνύφαινε], and completing one dialect out of many [μίαν ἐκ πολλῶν διάλεκτον]—proud and prayerful, extraordinary and plain, uncommon yet familiar, ostentatious yet genuine, austere yet merry, tense yet relaxed, both sweet and bitter, both ethical and pathetic—differing in no way from Proteus, storied among the ancient poets, who took on every kind [ἰδέαν] of shape effortlessly, whether it was as a god or something divine that he was leading astray [παρακρουόμενος] the vision of men, or it was a varied kind of discourse [διαλέκτου ποικίλον τι χρῆμα] in a wise man, deceptive [ἀπατηλόν] to every ear, which one might consider more likely since it is pious to attribute base and unseemly sights neither to gods nor to what's divine. Such is the kind of opinion I hold of Demosthenes' style, and I attribute to it this character: it is a mixture of every form [ἐξ ἁπάσης μικτὸν ἰδέας].[35]

In this amazing passage, Dionysius demonstrates his familiarity with Plato's vocabulary, refers specifically to passages in *Republic* (on the impiety of attributing deceptive appearances to the gods) and *Phaedrus* (on making one out of many), and applies to Demosthenes a poetic and

---
33. See *Ascent to the Beautiful*, 345-46.
34. Otherwise unidentified parenthetical citations in the remainder of the Preface are to *On the Style of Demosthenes*, easily accessible in Dionysius of Halicarnassus, *The Critical Essays in Two Volumes*, translated by Stephen Usher (Cambridge, MA: Harvard University Press, 1974 and 1985).
35. Dionysius, *On the Style of Demosthenes*, 8.

oxymoronic description of his style's teeming variety (as in ποικίλον and ποικίλως), to which the Platonic dialogues clearly have a far greater claim,[36] and he does all of this immediately after telling us: "I will leave Plato behind and will proceed to Demosthenes [Πλάτωνα μὲν ἐάσω, πορεύσομαι δ᾽ ἐπὶ τὸν Δημοσθένην]" (8). To recur to the question of Platonic irony, Dionysius here demonstrates a greater awareness of it than Demosthenes ever will. But it is not for his irony that Dionysius is praising Demosthenes but rather for being a literary Proteus, and thus the master of a varied type of discourse (διαλέκτου ποικίλον τι χρῆμα). Since Demosthenes wrote speeches for others to deliver, the ability to do so in a variety of characters was a requisite skill; it is also striking that Dionysius emphasizes the deceptive (ἀπατηλόν) character of his speech, and its capacity "to lead astray [παρακρούεσθαι]." This will give the reader some idea of the kind of "new evidence" this book will use to prove that Demosthenes was Plato's student once the older "complex evidence" has been considered in the introduction, and its "simple" counterpart—never mentioned by Dionysius, and antithetical to his purpose—is rejected here in the preface.

Aside from Cicero's discovery of Platonic irony in *De oratore*, the principal basis for rejecting that evidence is Dionysius of Halicarnassus's unblushing determination to compare Demosthenes and Plato as rhetoricians in *On the Style of Demosthenes*,[37] a comparison that undermines the view that rhetoric's foe could not possibly have taught rhetoric's master. The passage just quoted follows a preliminary skirmish based on *Phaedrus*; others have noted that blaming Plato for the rhetorical excesses of Socrates' speech in *Phaedrus* is both unfair and tone deaf since Socrates himself draws attention to its excess.[38] The main event comes later, and takes the form of a comparison or rather contest between Plato's *Menexenus* and the greatest passage from Demosthenes' greatest speech (14) rather than with his *Funeral Oration* (60.1-37), the authenticity of which Dionysius was the first critic to deny (23 and 44). The unfairness involved is equally obvious,[39] especially since Dionysius is determined to compare both Isocrates and Plato to Demosthenes on the basis of what seem to be their best speeches (16), and he expressly rejects

---

36. Plato's dialogues have an *equal* claim to ποικιλία at Dionysius, *De compositione verborum*, 19.
37. For useful observations on this comparison, see North, "*Summus Orator Plato*," 214-15.
38. See W. Rhys Roberts (ed.), *Dionysius of Halicarnassus, The Three Literary Letters* (Cambridge, UK: At the University Press, 1901), 30: "he [sc. Dionysius] seems sometimes to show himself blind to the fine irony and other subtle qualities for which Plato is so remarkable."
39. For early critical comment, see François Arnaud, "Sur le Style de Platon, en general; et en particulier, sur l'objet que ce philosophe s'est propose dans son dialogue intitulé Ion" (1769) in *Oeuvres completes de l'Abbé Arnaud*, volume 2, 157-94 (Paris: L. Collin, 1808), on 163-67.

the opposite approach as unfair (23 and 33). With respect to *Menexenus*, Dionysius, while apostrophizing the loser, does select "the passage in this speech which seems, Plato [apostrophizing him], to be most beautiful" (30), and although it would be silly to rank Aspasia's Funeral Oration—and Dionysius never mentions her or the possibility that Plato is once again writing with tongue in cheek—among the best speeches in Plato, the paradoxical relationship between defeat and victory in its finest passage (*Mx.* 247a4-6) will reappear in *On the Crown*.

As if to insure Demosthenes' victory, Dionysius quotes Plato first (30), and after doing so, prepares for the victor's speech as follows (30-31):

> This passage seems to be for Plato the most beautiful in this speech; indeed it's done for the most part beautifully—"for it does not seem best to lie"—except that the form of it is just political, not fitted for competition. Let us examine in comparison with this, then, taking a passage from Demosthenes's speech *On behalf of Ctesiphon*. It is not a summoning [παράκλησις] of the Athenians to the beautiful and virtue [ἐπὶ τὸ καλὸν καὶ τὴν ἀρετήν], as in Plato, but an encomium of the city because it regards all other things to be inferior to honor and reputation, which beautiful actions [καλαὶ πράξεις] bring with them even if someone might not succeed with them.

Since it unquestionably praises καλαὶ πράξεις and celebrates his countrymen both for imitating those who have done them in the distant past and for recently having done them themselves, *On the Crown* is better understood as itself an inspiring παράκλησις, once again aimed ἐπὶ τὸ καλὸν καὶ τὴν ἀρετήν.[40] In any case, after quoting it (31), Dionysius announces the inevitable decision with which he is sure the reader will concur (32):

> There is no one who would not agree if only he might have a measured perception concerning speeches and might be neither a sorcerer nor some kind of crank that the passage just quoted differs from the earlier one to the same extent that weapons of war differ from their ceremonial stand-ins, and as true spectacles do from illusions, as bodies nourished in the sunlight and by hard work differ from those pursuing shade and a lazy rest.

On Platonic terms, this judgment is hardly unjust: *On the Crown* is delivered "as if in battle" (*R.* 534c1), deep in the shadows of the Cave, while the context of Plato's *Menexenus* is thoroughly educational as opposed to practical: Menexenus is a young man interested in speeches (*Mx.* 234b5-6; cf. 52 on Demosthenes as a youth) and Socrates knows the

---

40. The related verb, παρακαλεῖν (LSJ: "call; call in, send for, summon") will play an important role in chapter 4 below, and it should be noted.

speech of Aspasia by heart precisely because she is teaching him rhetoric (*Mx.* 235e3-236c1).

As Aspasia is to Socrates, as Socrates is to Menexenus, as *Menexenus* is to *On the Crown*, as lazy rest in the shade is to hard work in the sunlight, so too is Plato to Demosthenes.[41] Dionysius never offers the obvious solution, and although obvious, it must be spelled out here: he never explains Demosthenes' superiority to Plato in terms of Plato's best student surpassing his teacher in the capacity to activate a Platonic παράκλησις outside of the Academy, to inspire καλαὶ πράξεις, and to summon (παρακαλεῖν) others ἐπὶ τὸ καλὸν καὶ τὴν ἀρετήν. The curious contest between Plato and Demosthenes points to it, the Proteus passage implies it, numerous passages in *On the Style of Demosthenes* suggest it, and Dionysius states that Demosthenes studied the speeches of both Plato and Isocrates with care (14, 16, and especially 51; cf. 8), but he never states that Plato was Demosthenes' teacher. Why not?

To begin with, his failure to do so needs to be understood in relation to Cicero, who had repeatedly joined Plato and Demosthenes as teacher and student. The fact that Dionysius did not do so admits of two explanations: his silence either meant that he rejected Cicero's claim that Demosthenes was Plato's student, and thus was the first to do so, or that his silence on the question is better explained in relation to the curious fact that he never mentions Cicero.

The proof that there is no easy way out of this conundrum is that Dionysius was clearly interested in the question of who had taught Demosthenes. In his *First Letter to Ammaeus*, he convincingly refuted some unnamed Peripatetic's claim that it was due to Aristotle's *Rhetoric* that Demosthenes "became greatest [κράτιστος] of all the orators."[42] Although supplying little information about his own dates,[43] Dionysius employs an

---

41. Cf. Hermogenes (second century AD) in Wooten, *Hermogenes' On Types of Style*, 112-13 (section 386): "The most beautiful of panegyric styles in prose is surely that of Plato. I do not mean panegyric passages in practical cases, but pure panegyric, which perhaps would not even be called practical oratory. And just as we said that the most beautiful kind of practical oratory is synonymous with that of Demosthenes, so we could say here that the most beautiful kind of panegyric oratory is synonymous with the style of Plato. Just as in the case of practical oratory the style of Demosthenes is interchangeable with the best practical style, the same is true with panegyric oratory and Plato. For the most beautiful of panegyric styles is that of Plato, and the style of Plato is the most beautiful of panegyric styles in prose." For comment, see North, "*Summus Orator Plato*," 216-17.

42. Dionysius, *First Letter to Ammaeus* 1; for the letter, see volume 2 of Dionysius of Halicarnassus, *Critical Essays*, 301-344.

43. For Dionysius's dates, see Earnest Carey, "Introduction" to *The Roman Antiquities of Dionysius of Halicarnassus*, seven volumes (Cambridge, MA: Harvard University Press, 1937), 1.vii-xi, beginning with: "He also informs us ([Book I] chapter 7) that he had come to Italy at the time when Augustus Caesar had put an end to the Civil War in the middle of the 187th Olympiad (late in 30 B.C. or in 29)." He thus arrived in Rome when Augustus was κράτιστος.

annalist's expertise in comparative chronology to demonstrate the impossibility of the Stagirite's influence on the Athenian, and his accounting is off only to the extent that he makes Demosthenes three years younger than Aristotle, whereas they were in fact both born in 384.[44] Once again, Dionysius neither confirms nor denies the claim already made by Cicero that Demosthenes was Plato's student; his purpose in the letter is to prove that he *wasn't* Aristotle's, and in proving this point, Dionysius does not discuss the unnamed Peripatetic's purpose for claiming that he was. But he does emphasize from the start that his first reaction to the Peripatetic's claim about Aristotle's influence, so clearly aimed at glorifying his school, was that above all it was a paradox.[45] He does not tell us *why* he regarded it as paradoxical.

The fact that Dionysius does not name this Peripatetic is the least significant of three other silences noticeable in the *First Letter to Ammaeus* beginning with his failure to mention Cicero here or anywhere else in his writings. In addition, he does not mention the political gulf that divided the author of the *Philippics* from the tutor of Philip's son Alexander (see epigraphy). Finally, there is the silence of highest concern in this preface: neither here nor anywhere else—and this despite the fact that he will compare them frequently and at length, especially in *On the Style of Demosthenes*—does Dionysius discuss the possibility that Plato was Demosthenes' teacher.[46] Since Cicero champions the view that he was, it seems reasonable to link two of these silences. Could it be that it was dangerous for a learned Greek who knew the ways of Rome to do so for political reasons in the aftermath of Augustus' quadruple triumph (30 BC)? At a time when Octavian had only recently become κράτιστος in the strongest sense, was it politically inexpedient for Dionysius to link his hero Demosthenes to Cicero, the eloquent champion of republican Rome for whom ties to both Demosthenes and Plato were foundational to what is currently called "his self-fashioning"?[47] It's possible, of course, that he simply rejected the connection, but there is no good reason for why he would not have stated his rejection had he done so; there is, however, a political reason why he may have chosen not to endorse the connection publicly even if he did so privately.

---

44. For full discussion of the date of Demosthenes' birth, see Douglas M. MacDowell (ed.), *Demosthenes, Against Meidias; Edited with Introduction, Translation and Commentary* (Oxford: Oxford University Press, 1990), 370-71.

45. Dionysius, *First Letter to Ammaeus*, 1.

46. As pseudo-Plutarch would do thereafter in *Lives of the Ten Orators*, and this may well explain his anonymity. For useful observations on other but relevant differences between Dionysius and Pseudo-Plutarch, see L. V. Pitcher, "Narrative Technique in the *Lives of the Ten Orators*." *Classical Quarterly* 55, no. 1 (2005), 217-234, on 228-29.

47. Following John Dugan, *Making a New Man: Ciceronian Self-Fashioning in the Rhetorical Works* (Oxford: Oxford University Press, 2005).

This "between the lines" reading gains strength from the following passage in his *First Letter to Ammianus*:

> "Not true is this speech," my dear Ammaeus, nor out of the technical precepts [τέχναι] of Aristotle—these having been published later—have the speeches [λόγοι] of Demosthenes been put together, but down from certain other introductions [εἰσαγωγαί] on behalf of which [ὑπὲρ ὧν] I will clarify in a separate (or private?) writing [ἰδίᾳ γραφῇ] the things that seem to me [τὰ δοκοῦντά μοι]. The account [λόγος] concerning them [περὶ αὐτῶν] being ample, it would not be fitting [καλῶς ἔχειν] to make it the mere addendum [πάρεργον] of another writing [γραφή].[48]

It is unfortunate that there are no learned commentaries to consult on this remarkably subtle passage,[49] although if there were any, the scholarly consensus would probably be that the ἰδία γραφή to which Dionysius refers here is his *Concerning the Style of Demosthenes*. But it is what makes this passage subtle that vitiates this solution, for it depends on making the λόγοι of Demosthenes rather than the εἰσαγωγαί that really influenced him—as the τέχναι of Aristotle clearly did not—the antecedent of both ὑπὲρ ὧν and περὶ αὐτῶν. While possible, this construction is by no means certain. Neither is it certain that what caused Dionysius to regard a claim about Aristotle's guidance as paradoxical was the fact that he regarded Plato's dialogues as the εἰσαγωγαί from which Demosthenes learned, but it is possible that it was. One thing is certain: Dionysius is at present unwilling to offer Ammaeus—nor did he ever offer anyone else—an additional γραφή devoted to a λόγος that would go beyond refuting the claim that it was the τέχναι of Aristotle that constituted the εἰσαγωγαί from which Demosthenes' supreme eloquence derived.

Here then is an early example of the dialectic between "fabrication" and "suppression." Instead of accepting as a given the possibility that Cicero retailed fabricated evidence that Demosthenes was Plato's student in order to support his theoretical views about rhetoric and philosophy, it is also possible that Dionysius was suppressing the claim. Among the reasons that the second possibility should not be rejected out of hand is that Dionysius by no means suppresses *the evidence* for their teacher-student connection, only the claim itself. By this I mean that a specific comparison of the passages from *On the Crown* and *Menexenus* that Dionysius selects creates a plausible way to support the general claim.

---

48. Dionysius, *First Letter to Ammaeus*, 3. In bracketing the Greek, I will generally convert inflected forms of nouns and adjectives to the nominative case, verbs to the infinitive form.

49. Although the editions of W. Rhys Roberts remain valuable, he did not comment on *The Style of Demosthenes*; somebody should do so. See his *Dionysius of Halicarnassus*, On Literary Composition; Being the Greek Text of De compositione verborum, *edited with Introduction, Translation, Notes, Glossary, and Appendices* (London: Macmillan, 1910).

Despite withholding that claim, Dionysius may well have indicated his actual attitude toward it not only by what he writes *but by what he doesn't*.[50] The refusal to reject the claim, the decision not to mention Cicero, and the mere intimation of a missing treatise are examples of the latter; the explicit rejection of Aristotle's influence, the Proteus passage, and the comparison between *Menexenus* and *On the Crown* are examples of the former. Likewise supporting this conception of "suppression" is that by the time they are willing to give Cicero the praise he is due, both Tacitus and Quintilian will endorse the view that Demosthenes was Plato's student.[51]

With the fabrication/suppression dialectic having been introduced, it now becomes possible to explain this book's subtitle. Scholars typically apply the term "the Old Academy" indiscriminately to Plato's time and to the Academy as it continued under the first scholarchs who followed him—Speusippus and Xenocrates—through Crates or Polemo;[52] here it will be reserved for *Plato's* Academy strictly speaking. Consider the following hypothetical analogy: Just as the victory of Augustus temporarily made it inexpedient to praise Cicero, the eloquent philosopher he had betrayed and caused to be murdered, so also was it politically inexpedient for the post-Plato Academy to lay claim to Demosthenes, author of the *Philippics*, after the victory of Macedon. This book will develop this hypothetical analogy, and locate the origin of the phenomenon I am calling "suppression" in the response of Plato's immediate successor to Philip's growing influence and eventual hegemony. Plato died in 347 and Philip's victory at Chaeronea occurred in 338; Demosthenes met his death in 323. Somewhere between the deaths of Plato and Demosthenes, with Chaeronea as perhaps the most obvious turning point, "the Old Academy" came to an end, and this book is an effort to *recover* it, using external evidence to confirm the only unimpeachably Platonic evidence: the Platonic dialogues themselves. The external evidence in question will

---

50. Cf. Dionysius of Halicarnassus, *The Ancient Orators* 1 (Stephen Usher translation): "In the epoch proceeding our own, the old philosophic rhetoric [ἡ ἀρχαία καὶ φιλόσοφος ῥητορική] was so grossly misused and maltreated that it fell into decline. From the death of Alexander of Macedon [sc. 324] it began to lose its spirit [Demosthenes died in 322] and gradually faded away, and in our generation had reached a state of almost total extinction." Without mentioning Cicero, and making no clear statement as to the responsible agency, Dionysius goes on to claim at 2: "the ancient, sober Rhetoric has thereby been restored to her former place of honor." For perceptive discussion, including Dionysius's connection to Cicero (46n12 and 48), see Gabba, "Classicistic Revival," 44-50.

51. Tacitus, *Dialogus* 32, and Quintillian, *Institutio Oratoria* 12.2.22 (quoted in chapter 4).

52. The standard authority is John Dillon, *The Heirs of Plato: A Study of the Old Academy (347-274 BC)* (Oxford: Oxford University Press, 2003). There, Dillon quotes and discusses the list of Plato's students in Diogenes Laertius, *Lives of the Eminent Philosophers*, 3.46 as far as Dicaearchus on 13 (13-15 is relevant to much of what follows in this book); he does not quote Chaemaeleon on Hyperides, or 3.47, which names Lycurgus and Demosthenes (this passage will be quoted in chapter 5).

identify Demosthenes as Plato's student and even more pointedly as the representative student of "the Old Academy." By contrast, Speusippus, Xenocrates, and above all Aristotle are responsible for our current conceptions of Plato's intentions, his primary philosophical concerns, and the Academy's original purpose.

Following the introduction, chapter 1 will make the case for bifurcating the Academy along these lines. Whether the Academy was anti- or pro-Macedonian was the subject of a spirited nineteenth-century debate, and after reviewing it, the first chapter will resolve the question along historical lines by distinguishing "the Old Academy" as the former, "the post-Plato Academy" as the latter. It will identify Speusippus, Plato's first successor, as the turning point in this transformation by focusing on the letter he wrote to Philip in 342, five years after Plato's death in 347. Taking Anthony Natoli's study as the basis for this letter's authenticity and purpose,[53] the chapter will break new ground by integrating Demosthenes into the story by considering his visit to Philip's court in 346 as part of what is called "the First Embassy." Our only source for his interaction with Philip comes from his enemy Aeschines,[54] and although scholars have often emphasized the possible or even likely unreliability of this evidence,[55] here it will be interpreted with a currently unfashionable sympathy for Demosthenes. Although Aeschines claimed that Demosthenes' speech to Philip about Amphipolis was a failure,[56] the hypothesis that it was really a success helps to explain why it became necessary for Speusippus to present the Academy as pro-Macedonian in his letter to Philip.

Beginning with Aeschines, the second chapter will consider five men other than Demosthenes who were said to have been Plato's students in "the Old Academy." Our source for the disputed but early claim that Aeschines was Plato's student is Demetrius of Phaleron, and the immediate aftermath of his pro-Macedonian regime (318-307) will bring the historical account to an end, advancing as far as the deaths of Demosthenes, Aristotle, and Phocion. By characterizing Aeschines and Aristotle as broadly pro-Macedonian, the chapter places Phocion in the central and apparently neutral place dividing them from the two anti-Macedonian politicians Hyperides and Lycurgus. Thanks to the work of Danielle

---

53. Anthony Francis Natoli, *The Letter of Speusippus to Philip II: Introduction, Text, Translation and Commentary* (Stuttgart: Franz Steiner, 2004).
54. See Aeschines, *On the Embassy*, 20-39.
55. And so must be answered by Edward M. Harris, *Aeschines and Athenian Politics* (Oxford and New York: Oxford University Press, 1995), 57-60, climaxing with: "Granting that Aeschines may have exaggerated certain details for the sake of dramatic effect, it would be wrong to question the essentials of his account." This makes me wrong.
56. Aeschines, *On the Embassy*, 34-35.

Allen,[57] the level of cooperation between Lycurgus and Demosthenes has recently become a matter of scholarly dispute; here they will be presented as allies, united by the Academy and its original ends. Indeed it will be partly on the basis of his connections to Lycurgus and Hyperides on the one hand and his opposition to Aeschines on the other that I will be advancing the claim that Demosthenes, rather than Aristotle, best represents the aims and ideals of Plato's Academy.

The primary basis for this claim is naturally Plato himself, and the book's middle chapter is devoted to him. Having elsewhere defended a reading of Plato's dialogues that detaches them from the way Aristotle's accounts of Socrates and Plato have traditionally caused them to be read,[58] I will here summarize the results of that defense. What I call "the Curricular Hypothesis" stands at the center of a reconstruction of the Academy's purpose that depends entirely on the dialogues,[59] that is, the hypothesis that the dialogues themselves constituted the Academy's curriculum and that it was constructed with an adolescent audience of young Athenians in mind.[60] The tradition has been overly influenced by the view that it was those who stayed on at the Academy, as Aristotle famously did, who most deserve to be considered Plato's best students; a Cave-centric reading of the dialogues suggests instead that those who stayed on for years had missed Plato's point. The claim that Demosthenes, along with Aeschines, Phocion, Hyperides, and Lycurgus, were Plato's students in the Academy is not only compatible with the view that they departed from it for civic life in Athens at the age of eighteen, it is constitutive of that claim. And since *reading* Plato's dialogues is what I am claiming Plato's students did in the Academy, it is completely unnecessary to reserve that status for those whose principal concerns gravitated more toward *Timaeus* than *Republic*.

The fourth chapter, on Demosthenes, naturally begins with his youth, and it follows Dionysius of Halicarnassus by taking Isaeus to be an early influence if not the earliest or most important one, that is, the place this book reserves for Plato. Emphasizing the passage from *On the Crown* that Dionysius used to prove Demosthenes' rhetorical superiority to Plato, the chapter situates him as both the heir of the Athenian heritage and as the last best representative of a free, proud, and democratic Athens, the violet-crowned city of Marathon. Quintilian regarded "the Marathon Oath" as sufficient proof that Demosthenes was Plato's student, and I will

---

57. See especially Danielle S. Allen, *Why Plato Wrote* (Chichester: Blackwell, 2010).
58. See *Ascent to the Good*, introduction.
59. Cf. Dillon, *Heirs of Plato*, 16-18, beginning with "one must resolve to look beyond the dialogues." This is exactly what I have resolved *not* to do in "recovering the Old Academy" although I am going to use Demosthenes and Co. to help me do so.
60. See *Ascent to the Beautiful*, preface and epilogue.

defend his claim; I will also explain why the idealized Athens of Demosthenes is the functional equivalent of the ideal city in Plato's *Republic*, particularly with regard to the Guardian's duty to participate in politics. The argument will proceed on two tracks, and I will break some new ground by considering the *Exordia* as Demosthenes's most Platonic text. But the principal track takes its start from Plato's dialogues, and will show that his variety (particularly with respect to characters), his deliberate use of deception (and thus the means to detect it), and above all his ability to make the just and beautiful appear to be advantageous, continued to guide Demosthenes throughout all his works. The book's structure precludes considering every one of them, of course, and the reader should keep in mind that while its purpose with respect to Plato is confirmatory, it is merely prefatory with respect to the study Demosthenes.

The fifth chapter will revisit the fabrication-suppression dynamic introduced in this preface and associated with Laurent Pernot in the introduction.[61] It will center on three Greek texts: Lucian's or rather pseudo-Lucian's *Encomium of Demosthenes*, the anonymous and apocryphal *Letters of Chion of Heracleia*, and the *Platonic Orations* of Aelius Aristides. All three are broadly speaking products of the Second Sophistic,[62] and none of them make the express claim that Demosthenes was Plato's student. Nevertheless, each manages to capture what this author regards as important aspects of that claim's truth, and they do so in a manner that will strengthen the case, introduced here, for a post-Cicero "suppression." Like Dionysius of Halicarnassus, Aelius Aristides juxtaposes Plato and Demosthenes in a manner that suggests his awareness of their more intimate connection;[63] by focusing his attention on *Gorgias*, he also completes an edifice already begun in chapters 3 and 4. The other two texts recall the problem of *Lives of the Ten Orators*, the single most important secondary source connecting Demosthenes, Lycurgus, and Hyperides to Plato. Only if written anonymously could this important text be wrongly attributed to Plutarch, so if Plutarch didn't write it, why did its author choose to conceal his authority?[64] Meanwhile,

---

61. Laurent Pernot, *L'Ombre du Tigre: Recherches sur la reception de Démosthène* (Naples: M. DiAuria, 2006).

62. See generally Tim Whitmarsh, *The Second Sophistic* (Cambridge, UK: Cambridge University Press, 2005). For *Chion of Heracleia* as a product of the Second Sophistic, see Simon Swain, *Hellenism and Empire: Language, Classicism, and Power in the Greek World AD 50-250* (Oxford: Clarendon Press, 1996), 93n72.

63. See North, "*Summus Orator Plato*," 203.

64. Schaefer had argued for a single author, writing shortly after Dionysius of Haricarnassus (*Commentatio*, 37). While upholding this preference for a single author (11-12), Roisman and Worthington, *Lives*, 13-14, points to a much later, early third century date, for pseudo-Plutarch's composition; see also 25-26 for an illuminating discussion of his or her interest in monuments, the basis for this dating. Note that the three decrees appended by pseudo-Plutarch to Lives of the Ten Orators (269-77) regard Demosthenes and

the skill and ingenuity that produced the *Encomium for Demosthenes* argue for its authenticity,[65] but if Lucian didn't write this playfully Platonic homage to Demosthenes, then [Lucian] evidently preferred anonymity to literary glory just as [Plutarch] must have done, both making the same choice that the author of *Chion of Heracleia* unquestionably made. In the last chapter, these choices will be considered in the context of a Roman or imperial "wave of suppression," one of three waves that include a more ancient Macedonian suppression, and the modern one, accomplished by nineteenth-century philologists, to whom the introduction will now turn.

Lycurgus, making the latter "a role model for present day leaders to gain rewards during their lifetime and after death" (277n15), the theme of Demosthenes' speech *Against Leptines*, to be considered in Platonic context in chapter 4.

65. See Brad L. Cook, "The *Encomium of Demosthenes*: A Dialogue Worthy of Lucian." Paper delivered to the American Philological Association in Chicago (January 4, 2014).

Abbreviations for Writings of Plato and Demosthenes

Alc.1	*Alcibiades Major*	D1	*First Olynthian*
Ap.	*Apology of Socrates*	D2	*Second Olynthian*
Cri.	*Crito*	D3	*Third Olynthian*
Criti.	*Critias*	D4	*First Philippic*
Clt.	*Clitophon*	D5	*On the Peace*
Cra.	*Cratylus*	D6	*Second Philippic*
Ep.	*Letters*	D7	*On Halonnesus*
Epin.	*Epinomis*	D8	*On the Chersonese*
Euthd.	*Euthydemus*	D9	*Third Philippic*
Grg.	*Gorgias*	D10	*Fourth Philippic*
La.	*Laches*	D11	*Reply to Philip*
Lg.	*Laws*	D12	*Philip's Letter*
Men.	*Meno*	D13	*On the Symmories*
Mx.	*Menexenus*	D14	*On the Navy*
Phd.	*Phaedo*	D15	*On the Liberty of the Rhodians*
Phdr.	*Phaedrus*	D16	*For the Megalopolitans*
Phlb.	*Philebus*	D17	*On the Accession of Alexander*
Prm.	*Parmenides*	D18	*On the Crown*
Prt.	*Protagoras*	D19	*On the False Embassy*
Plt.	*Statesman*	D20	*Response to Leptines*
R.	*Republic*	D21	*Against Meidias*
Smp.	*Symposium*	D22	*Against Androtion*
Sph.	*Sophist*	D23	*Against Aristocrates*
Thg.	*Theages*	D24	*Against Timocrates*
Tht.	*Theaetetus*	D25	*Against Aristogeiton I*
Ti.	*Timaeus*	D26	*Against Aristogeiton II*

D27	Against Aphobus I	D45	Against Stephanus I
D28	Against Aphobus II	D46	Against Stephanus II
D29	Response to Aphobus	D47	Against Euergus and Mnesibulus
D30	Response to Onetor I		
D31	Response to Onetor II	D48	Response to Olympiodorus
D32	Response to Zenothemis	D49	Response to Timotheus
D33	Response to Apaturius	D50	Response to Polycles
D34	Response to Phormio	D51	On the Trierarchic Crown
D35	Response to Lacritus	D52	Against Callippus
D36	On Behalf of Phormio	D53	Response to Nicostratus
D37	Response to Pantaenetus	D54	Against Conon
D38	Response to Nausimachus and Xenopeithes	D55	Response to Callicles
		D56	Against Dionysodorus
D39	Response to Boeotus I	D57	Response to Eubulides
D40	Against Boeotus II	D58	Against Theocrines
D41	Response to Spudias	D59	Against Neaira
D42	Response to Phaenippus	D60	Funeral Oration
D43	Response to Macartatus	D61	Erotic Essay
D44	Response to Leochares		

Chronology

393: Speusippus is fourteen
388: Phocion is fourteen
388–87: Dion is Plato's student
387: Academy opens
386: King's Peace
386: Plato's *Menexenus*
384: Births of Demosthenes and Aristotle
383: Aeschines is fourteen
376: Lycurgus is fourteen
373: Hyperides is fourteen
370: Demosthenes is fourteen
367–66: Plato's second visit to Syracuse
367: Aristotle enters Academy at seventeen
366: Oropos Trial: Speech of Callistratus
363-62: Demosthenes' inheritance speeches
356: Birth of Alexander
355: *Against Leptines*
355: Xenophon's *Ways and Means*
355: Death of Xenophon
348: Fall of Olynthus
347: Aristotle leaves Athens with Xenocrates
347: Death of Plato
347: *Against Meidias*
347: Speusippus becomes head of Academy
346: First Embassy to Philip

346: Peace of Philocles
346: *Philippus* of Isocrates
343: Letter of Speusippus to Philip
343: *On the False Embassy*
343–42: Aristotle comes to Philip's court.
342: Alexander is fourteen
339: Death of Speusippus
339: Xenocrates becomes head of Academy
338: Battle of Chaeronea
338: *Funeral Oration* of Demosthenes
338: Death of Isocrates
336: Death of Philip
336: Demetrius of Phaleron is fourteen
335: Alexander destroys Thebes
335: Aristotle returns to Athens
330: *On the Crown*
325–24: Death of Lycurgus
323: Harpalus Affair; Demosthenes leaves Athens
323: Death of Alexander
323: Aristotle flees Athens
323: Demosthenes returns to Athens
322: Battle of Crannion
322: *Funeral Oration* of Hyperides
322: Antipater demands surrender of Demosthenes and Hyperides
322: Demosthenes and Hyperides flee Athens
322: Murder of Hyperides
322: Deaths of Demosthenes and Aristotle
318: Death of Phocion
318: Demetrius of Phaleron governor of Athens
314: Death of Xenocrates
314: Polemo becomes head of Academy
307: Demetrius flees Athens
307: Speech of Demochares

Introduction

Fabrication or Suppression?

The complex story begins with Plutarch's *Life of Demosthenes* or rather with Hermippus, the named source of information about the unnamed memoranda in which it was recorded that Demosthenes had not only studied with Plato but had gained the most from him "with respect to speeches [πρὸς τοὺς λόγους]."

> As a result of this [ὅθεν], having left behind remaining studies [μαθήματα] and the youthful concerns [διατριβὰς], he [sc. Demosthenes] practiced himself [αὐτὸς αὑτὸν ἤσκει] and worked hard in those practices by which he himself [αὐτὸς] would be among those speaking. He made use also of Isaeus as a guide in speech [πρὸς τὸν λόγον] even though Isocrates was then lecturing [σχολάζοντος], either (as some say) being unable to pay the requisite fee of ten minas on account of his being orphaned [διὰ τὴν ὀρφανίαν] or rather embracing the speech [τὸν λόγον] of Isaeus as wicked effective [ὡς δραστήριον καὶ πανοῦργον] for the purpose [ἐπὶ τήν χρείαν]. And Hermippus claims to have come upon anonymous memoranda in which it was written that Demosthenes had studied with and benefitted most from Plato in making speeches [πρὸς τοὺς λόγους] and he cites Ctesibius saying that from Callias of Syracuse and certain others Demosthenes obtained in secret the technical precepts [τέχναι] of Isocrates and Alcidamus.[1]

In reading this complex passage, readers should keep in mind: (1) that they are encountering a story midstream, and will therefore not fully understand it until they learn the referent of that initial ὅθεν; (2) that whatever it was to which that ὅθεν points, Demosthenes' initial impulse, having abandoned his prior μαθήματα, was to exercise *himself* as an autodidact; (3) that since Isaeus specialized in inheritance law and Demosthenes was being robbed of his διὰ τὴν ὀρφανίαν, there were *two* good reasons why Isaeus was more suitable for Demosthenes' needs than Isocrates, (4) that by relying on an unnamed source for the influence of Plato, Isocrates' rival, Hermippus was rather implying its improbability than upholding its veracity; and (5) that Hermippus, via a named and thus more reliable source this time, shows how Demosthenes may nevertheless have been *secretly* instructed through the τέχναι of Isocrates after all. Since Plutarch is our oldest *surviving* source, and Hermippus is Plutarch's source for the Plato-Demosthenes connection, the modern story takes its start from the unreliability of Hermippus, and as my fourth and fifth points are intended to suggest, this should be easy: he seems more interested in establishing a connection between Demosthenes and Isocrates than in inventing a story to the effect that Demosthenes learned the most πρὸς τοὺς λόγους from Plato.

In turning now to the referent of ὅθεν, it is convenient to switch over to Plutarch's admirer and contemporary Aulus Gellius,[2] whose version of the story has the great advantage of identifying Hermippus as its source and by quoting his words:

> Hermippus has left behind this text: Demosthenes, while still an adolescent, frequented the Academy and was accustomed to hear [*audire*] Plato. "And this Demosthenes," he says, "having left home as was his custom, while he was en route to Plato, and was seeing many people running in one direction, he asks the cause of this thing and learns they are running so that Callistratus could be heard [*auditum*]. This Callistratus was an orator in the Athenian polity one of those whom they call demagogues [δημαγωγοί]. It seemed best to turn aside briefly and to determine whether hearing him was worthy of the great zeal of those rushing ahead. He arrives," he said, "and hears Callistratus speaking that noble speech *The case concerning Oropus* [ἡ περὶ Ὠρωποῦ δίκη], and he was so moved, delighted, and captivated, that from then on he began to follow Callistratus, and he left the Academy along with Plato."[3]

It will be observed that when Plutarch tells the same story,[4] his version is more vivid and imaginative but it mentions neither Hermippus nor Plato. Since Demosthenes both mentions and praises Callistratus (18.219, 19.297, 24.135, 49.9-13, and 59.27),[5] and more importantly since ἡ περὶ Ὠρωποῦ δίκη was delivered in 366 when Demosthenes was eighteen, there is nothing inherently implausible about the tale, either from the traditional perspective or from mine. With respect to the latter, if the remaining μαθήματα he then abandoned were the dialogues Plato had written for eighteen-year-olds,[6] Demosthenes had already read through most of the Academy's curriculum in accordance with the Curricular Hypothesis (see preface). As for the former perspective, neither has the tradition doubted that Hermippus is Plutarch's source for his version of the story (even though he does not cite him), nor that the information Plutarch does attribute to Hermippus (on the basis of the anonymous memoranda) comes from the same source.[7] But it is Plutarch's failure to follow Hermippus in identifying the young man's reaction to Callistratus as responsible for causing him to leave Plato and the Academy that now requires critical comment.

The reason the modern consensus that Demosthenes was not Plato's student always begins with Hermippus is because he is the oldest source for the claim that he was *for us*, and therefore if *his* reliability is dubious,[8] the connection can be denied. The principal basis for denying his authority in the present case is that Hermippus is late, with a *floruit* in the third century,[9] and therefore more than a hundred years after the speech of Callistratus. But here's the interesting thing: while modern scholars have generally accepted that the speech of Callistratus made a deep impact on the young Demosthenes,[10] it is rather the claim that this impact caused him to desert the Academy that has been not so much denied as simply ignored. Rather, the evidence upon which the consensus has fastened is the unreliability, at once late and anonymous, of those memoranda. What gets overlooked is that Hermippus could not possibly be the oldest source of the information that Demosthenes was Plato's student at the Academy for the simple reason that the story about the speech of Callistratus, quoted verbatim by Aulus Gellius, *presupposes* the fact that Demosthenes was already Plato's student and was already known to be. Hermippus' purpose was not to fabricate evidence, where none had existed before, that Demosthenes learned from Plato. Instead, it was his purpose to use the story of Callistratus to create *distance* between Demosthenes and Plato, and thus to create a connection between Demosthenes and Isocrates.[11]

There have been two modern studies devoted exclusively to Hermippus aside from the chapter in Felix Jacoby's *Fragmente der griechischen Historiker*:[12] Fritz Wehrli calls him "Hermippus the Callimachean"[13] and Jan Bollansée calls him "Hermippus of Smyrna."[14] But as the inclusion of *Hermippos der Kallimacheer* in Wehrli's series on "The School of Aristotle" indicates, his name was attached to a third and more revealing epithet: "Hermippus the Peripatetic."[15] Quite apart from the fact that an Aristotelian might well be motivated to deny that Plato was the teacher of the most eloquent Athenian orator—and here, the unnamed Peripatetic refuted by Dionysius comes to mind (see preface)— Wehrli, Bollansée, and Jacoby identify the source of Hermippus' account of Demosthenes as a treatise entitled *On the Students of Isocrates*.[16] This is a crucial point. Considered in the light of this origin,[17] the peculiar features of the Callistratus story become more intelligible: since Isaeus was said to be the student of Isocrates,[18] and since Demosthenes ultimately if stealthily gained direct access to the τέχναι of Isocrates, Hermippus was using the story of Callistratus to explain not only how Demosthenes turned away from Plato but more importantly to justify the thesis to which his book was devoted: that Demosthenes turned away from Plato toward Isocrates. It was not the anonymous memoranda on which Hermippus relied for connecting Plato and Demosthenes as teacher to student—the story about Callistratus already presupposed that connection—but rather the claim he wanted very much to undermine: that it was from Plato that Demosthenes learned the most πρὸς τοὺς λόγους. Whether he did so for the sake of Isocrates or Aristotle or both must remain unclear.

The modern consensus builds on Plutarch and Hermippus, but it might be said to begin with Arnold Schaefer's magisterial *Demosthenes und seine Zeit* (1856–1858). First comes the crucial link: "Since Hermippus, and thus since the end of the third century B. C., the belief that Demosthenes had been Plato's student had taken root, and among the Romans [by 'the Romans,' of course, Schaefer has primarily Cicero in mind], it is from the start a foregone conclusion."[19] Schaefer then mentions two other pieces of evidence for the same claim: Diogenes Laertius, whose value as a source, like Plutarch's, is undermined by the unreliability of *his* sources[20]; and then Demosthenes' own *Fifth Letter*,[21] which Schaefer regards as fabricated (*ein gefälschtes Zeugniss*).[22] Schaefer can dismiss this evidence briefly and breezily because he relies on "the learned treatise" of K. H. Funkhänel (1808–1874),[23] citing as dispositive his *Dissertatio de Demosthene Platonis discipulo* (1836).[24] In it, Funkhänel promptly made the crucial claim: by citing the anonymous memoranda discovered by Hermippus, Plutarch proved that no better evidence for the connection existed, and thus the claim was unworthy of faith.[25] Three other points are worthy of note: (1) Funkhänel cites Schaefer's work on *Lives of the Ten Orators* to establish the worthlessness of "Pseudoplutarchus,"[26] (2) it is still necessary for him to debate the question with a learned defender of the connection,[27] and (3) he elsewhere argues that Isocrates was the decisive influence on Demosthenes.[28] Naturally Funkhänel never indicates that this was Hermippus' purpose as well.

Although he relied on Funkhänel's philological arguments, Schaefer must be considered the creator of the modern consensus. Once again, three points are decisive for proving this: (1) Friedrich Blass (1843–1907), whose influence was arguably just as great, dedicated his *Die attische Beredsamkeit* to Schaefer and follows him on the question,[29] (2) it is Schaefer whom Karl Steinhart cites in his 1873 biography of Plato,[30] where the consensus that Demosthenes had not been Plato's student spread to Platonic studies; and (3) Schaefer's willingness to rely on Funkhänel did not prevent him from further justifying the separation of Demosthenes from Plato on what may broadly be called philosophical grounds. He did the latter in a lengthy, learned, and rhetorically powerful paragraph.³¹ While allowing at the end of the paragraph that Demosthenes *may have read and even studied* Plato's dialogues, Schaefer is most eloquent when contrasting Plato's concern for the ideal ("Plato lives in the world of Ideas") with Demosthenes:

> Demosthenes, by contrast, stands on the ground of the given: as little as he mistakes the ailments of the Athenian polity, so distant is he on that basis to despair of it, and it is not through overturning established relations but rather only from a moral regeneration that he awaits salvation [*das Heil*]; he undertakes to rejuvenate [*zu verjüngen*] his people through the spirit in which their forefathers lived, and it is to a second battle for the freedom and independence of every Greek that he summons them.³²

It is with the proponent of establishing on earth the ideal City that Schaefer is contrasting Demosthenes, not with the teacher who taught adolescents in the Academy. The *Republic*-centered reading of the dialogues defended in *Plato the Teacher* is incompatible with Schaefer's.

From the origins of the consensus, then, two parallel tracks are visible. The first is a philological case that relies of source-criticism or *Quellenforschung*, the crown jewel of the historical approach as established by German scholars in the nineteenth-century, although the rejection of selected ancient texts as inauthentic or *Echtheitskritik* is an arguably equally important and in any case closely related phenomenon.³³ The second is a more broadly philosophical case that must necessarily rely on a certain *Platonbild* or "conception of Plato," and more specifically on a conception of his ideals and intentions that will justify separating him from Demosthenes not only as a matter of historical fact, but also on a theoretical basis. To hammer the point already made in the preface, it is this second track that is this book's focus; hence the need to consider the first track here, in the introduction. But quite apart from the fact that keeping these two tracks apart is antithetical to my purpose— it is for the sake of justifying a new *Platonbild* based on the dialogues that I am concerned with Demosthenes—even here in the introduction they can't be separated for reasons that have nothing to do with my concerns. Beginning with Schaefer, the two tracks, the philological and the more broadly interpretive, were intertwined, and they remain so. Consider the fact that Kai Trampedach's 1994 study of the relations between Plato's Academy and the political realities of its time is divided into an empirical part, where the Academy's impact on contemporary politics is marginalized on a historical basis, and what he calls its "Hermeneutic Part," which is devoted to Plato's writings and climaxes with a reading of the *Seventh Letter*, tending in the aggregate to justify his lack of concern with political reality.³⁴

Although antithetical in its conclusions, Trampedach's impressive book is nevertheless indispensible to my project in a dialectical sense, and not only because it coordinates a marginalization of the same evidence, I must now defend with a conception of Plato that I have already challenged in print. In introducing Trampedach, the place to begin is with his *Doktorvater*, H.-J. Gehrke, whose book on Phocion and article on Demetrius of Phaleron will also be cited with some frequency in what follows.[35] Passed on to both Trampedach and Matthias Haake, another of his students,[36] Gehrke's project is to reveal the flimsy historical basis on which claims about what may broadly be called a Plato-inspired "philosophical statesmanship" depend. In the case of Phocion, for instance, Plutarch's testimony is more difficult to reject, and Gehrke does not reject it. But even though Phocion was Plato's student in the Academy, this does not prove what Gehrke denies: that *his political views or actions* are meaningfully interpreted as Platonic. With respect to Demetrius of Phaeron, it is rather a case of self-presentation, and despite the fact that Demetrius clearly wished to be understood as "a philosophical statesmen" in the Platonic tradition, Gehrke has no difficulty in puncturing that pose. But it is with Haake that the theoretical basis of the school's empirical findings becomes most clearly visible: the incompatibility in principle of politics and philosophy.[37] Whether this incompatibility claim should be called a principle or a prejudice, it is usefully antithetical to a Cave-centric conception of Plato that can find a Platonist in Cicero not in spite of his political activity but rather because of it.

Trampedach devotes the last chapter of seven in the first part to "the Academy in Athenian politics." He subdivides this chapter into sections on orators, generals, and philosophers.[38] Phocion is discussed in the middle section along with Chabrias and Timotheus:

> In contrast with Chabrias and Timotheus, Phocion entered the Academy early as a young man and he remained in connection with it until the end of his life. Yet [*dennoch*] it is unknown how long he took part continuously in the Academy's instruction. In any case [*jedenfalls*], he did not dedicate himself to the life of contemplation [βίος θεωρετικός] but rather began a political career early in the wake of Chabrias, with whom he possibly [*vielleicht*] came into contact through the Academy. [n. 84][39]

Obviously the most significant thing here is Trampedach's suggestion that since Phocion did not pursue the βίος θεωρετικός but pursued a political career instead, we are therefore entitled to doubt how much "the Academy's instruction" affected him; even in the "empirical part" of his study, then, Trampedach's conception of Plato's purpose informs his analysis. Three other points deserve notice: (1) Trampedach cites Gehrke in n. 84, (2) he is a skillful writer, and uses *dennoch, jedenfalls,* and *vielleicht* in an effectively deflating manner, and (3) his use of *vielleicht* is especially clever given that it is rather likely (*wahrscheinlich*) that his abandonment of the βίος θεωρετικός was conducted under the auspices of Chabrias, linked with Phocion as products of the Academy in Plutarch's *Reply to Colotes*.[40]

Naturally it is Trampedach's discussion of Demosthenes in the "orators" section of the chapter that is of most concern, and on the basis of the Callistratus-story as told by Aulus Gellius, he correctly identifies its purpose: "Here the calling of Demosthenes to be an orator is presented as his abandonment of philosophy."[41] What Trampedach fails to consider is that the way he has just told the story of Phocion and Chabrias is configured for a similar purpose: to illustrate Phocion's rejection of philosophy for politics. Moreover, as Trampedach is well aware, Chabrias was also linked to Callistratus by the Oropus trial in which they were both defendants.[42] This creates an interesting parallel between Phocion and Demosthenes, one that suggests that in neither case was the Academy left so very far behind quite apart from the ongoing claim that Plato's purpose was to persuade promising young Athenians (in Schaefer's apt phrase) "to rejuvenate his people through the spirit in which their forefathers lived." Not only does Diogenes Laertius preserve an anecdote that Plato came to the defense of Chabrias in the Oropus-trial,[43] but thanks the connection between Chabrias and Callistratus, Demosthenes' decision to follow the latter, like Phocion's to follow the former, plausibly—somewhere between Trampedach's *viellecht* and my *wahrscheinlich*—did not constitute a rejection of the Academy but rather was more like a post-graduate apprenticeship, and fully consistent with the Academy's original purpose.[44]

Trampedach appears to consider Demosthenes first among the orators, and it is certainly true that the five paragraphs he devotes to him precede the shorter sections on Aeschines, Lycurgus, and Hyperides. The first paragraph begins as follows: "For the tradition [*Überlieferung*] of the relationship between Plato and Demosthenes, obviously Hermippus once again [*wieder einmal*] plays the central role."[45] It is true that "Hermippus of Smyrna" has already appeared in Trampedach's book, but his most important appearance there is found in the short paragraph that immediately precedes this *wieder einmal*:

> Greek biography, ever since its initial shaping through Aristoxenus of Tarentum, is characterized by a mixture of real and fictional elements. Our guarantors Idomeneus and Hermippus are typical representatives of the genre: they not only have shown an extraordinary interest in scandalous stories and malign gossip, but one can also rely on them for a conscious fabrication [*Fabrikation*] of details.[46]

Even before mentioning Plutarch or Aulus Gellius, then, Trampedach has already used a more acceptable kind of "malign gossip" to render Hermippus, the central "guarantor" of the relationship, unreliable and ridiculous if not odious. The remainder of the first paragraph identifies the anecdote as part of an ongoing conflict between Rhetoric and Philosophy,[47] a perceptive claim, on which more will be said below.

It is necessary to be crystal clear regarding my own approach to the allegedly central importance of Hermippus' testimony in "the tradition of the relationship between Plato and Demosthenes." The source-critics start from the hypothesis that Demosthenes was not Plato's student, and therefore must show the flimsiness of the ancient evidence that he was. By contrast, I regard the best basis for confirming the opposite hypothesis is what the two men said, wrote, and did, not on what, when, and why others, necessarily less well informed, wrote about them. The testimony of Hermippus offers a perfect example of this difference: for the nineteenth-century source-critics who practiced *Quellenforschung*, it is the earliest evidence of the connection, and its unreliability—whether as a factor of when he lived (late), who he was (a purveyor of gossip), or why he wrote (to glorify Rhetoric at the expense of Philosophy)—tells against the connection's existence; for me, the story presupposes it. To hammer the point: although no doubt staged as the rejection of Plato, the fuller version of the Callistratus-story that survives in Aulus Gellius depends entirely on what must have been the then-current view that Demosthenes was originally Plato's student. The pre-existence of this view does not prove that it was true but it does contribute to disproving the hypothesis that Hermippus fabricated it.

It would give a misleading impression to pass over in silence those modern scholars who have upheld the connection between Demosthenes and Plato, and among them, Andrea Wörle deserves particular notice for her 1981 study of the political activity of Plato's students.[48] In the section on Demosthenes, she begins by listing all of the evidence for the connection—and there is, of course, a substantial amount of it—thus creating a very different prejudice from the one Trampedach is able to create through Hermippus, and she concludes: "On the basis of the foregoing ancient testimonies, one must consider it possible and even likely [*wahrscheinlich*] that Demosthenes belonged to the auditors of Plato even though his political actions indicate no detectable traces of Platonic conceptions."[49] This caveat can naturally be turned against the connection, as it was by Schaefer and by P. A. Brunt following Eduard Zeller (1814–1908)[50]; for my purposes, by contrast, it is not so much *what* those political actions were but the fact that Plato's students left the Academy *to do them* that is relevant, as aptly observed by C. W. Müller: "Leaving the Academy is part of Returning to the Cave."[51] But it is necessary to give

Trampedach his due, and his dismissal of Wörle in a footnote is likewise worth quoting, partly because it is attached to his claim that "no verifiable influence of Plato on them [sc. Demosthenes and Aeschines] has been discovered," but most of all because he would probably apply his criticism to my approach as well:

> As opposed to mere faith-based creeds [*Glaubesbekenntnisse*], as by Egerman [Franz Egerman, *Von attischen Menschenbild* (Munich: Filser, 1952), 59: "Demosthenes, who otherwise reveals himself to be on the side of the new conception of man [*Menschenbild*] did not remain unaffected by the spiritual power that Plato represented so well. Plato's philosophy called forth a new form of life, of political life as well." I recognize in this the high-spirited tone of "New Humanism," but no argument. Similar is Wörle, *Platonschüler*, in her respective chapters on Demosthenes, Aeschines, Lycurgus, and Hyperides.[52]

Finally, there is Trampedach's own *Platonbild* to be considered, the subject of his hard-nosed study's "Hermeneutic Part." With a chapter on the *Seventh Letter* as its fourth and last—naturally he can use it to complete the case for distancing Plato from Athenian politics—the other three are "Political Psychology" (based on the tripartite soul of *Republic* 4), "Political Metaphysics" (with emphasis on *Statesman*, and climaxing with a section on "The Salvation of Theory"), and "Philosophical Lawgiving" (with emphasis on *Laws*). He naturally emphasizes turning Kings into Philosophers rather than turning Philosophers into "leaders and kings in the hive" (R. 520b6–7) by sending them back down into the Cave,[53] an obligation to return to which he can find only in the Ideal City, a restriction on which he comments: "Herein lies a clear rejection of any form of political activity."[54] But it is in his discussion of "the *Theaetetus* Digression" (*Tht.* 172b8–177c2) in "Das Heil der Theorie" that he states this claim must clearly in the text:

> In *Theaetetus*, Socrates admittedly reveals absolutely no political ambitions; on the contrary, there is scarcely any other text in the History of Western Philosophy that contains so radical a rejection of politics [*eine radikale Ablehnung der Politik*]. Socrates proposes instead the apotheosis of the βίος θεωρετικός. Necessarily wandering under the domain of evil, mortal nature is what one must escape as quickly as possible. But this Flight takes the form of Assimilation with God (ὁμοίωσις θεῷ, 176b1) to the extent possible.[55]

Naturally Trampedach sees no reason to distinguish the fleeing Philosopher of the Digression from either Socrates (cf. *Tht.* 173d6–9 and 144c5–8) or Plato,[56] for if he did, his case that the Academy's last word was βίος θεωρετικός—and thus *eine radikale Ablehnung der Politik*—would be leveled with the dust.

As important as Trampedach's book clearly is, the modern study that plays the central role in this introduction and in what follows is Laurent Pernot's "In the Shadow of the Tiger; Investigations in the Reception of Demosthenes."[57] The forty pages of its first chapter ("À l'école de Platon") are devoted exclusively to the relationship between Plato and Demosthenes, and as useful as Trampedach is in a dialectical sense, Pernot is more so. This point deserves emphasis: although both of their findings are antithetical to mine—for both uphold the modern consensus—the antithesis is useful for illuminating my own position by contrast, hence the adjective "dialectical." In Trampedach's case, it is the two tracks that appeared first in Schaefer that creates the useful dialectical friction. As his emphasis on the ὁμοίωσις θεῷ has just revealed, Trampedach's case for disjoining Demosthenes from Plato rests not only on philology or *Quellenforschung*, but just as much on a conception of the Academy that renders the connection of philosopher and orator virtually unthinkable. Since this resolutely apolitical conception is antithetical to a Cave-centric and dialogues-based Academic curriculum, Trampedach's book is of critical importance to the second and more important track. What entitles Pernot's to the central place in this introduction is that his approach is more applicable and hence more useful in a dialectical sense to the first track.

In the background of Pernot's opening chapter are almost sixty pages of *testimonia*,[58] including all of the ancient evidence regarding the connection between Demosthenes and Plato.[59] Unlike Wörle, Pernot does not begin by allowing the sheer volume of this evidence to speak for itself but it is there, at the end of his book, for all to see. Instead, the first chapter proceeds through this evidence in a thoughtful and provocative manner, as I will try to show, and indeed it is not difficult to do so. Naturally the first texts he discusses—the relevant passages from Plutarch and Aulus Gellius—derive from Hermippus, but he situates them brilliantly. His section on "the Sources" begins with a statement that is as simple and true as it is ultimately misleading and complex ("the idea that Demosthenes was a student of Plato's figures in neither Demosthenes nor in Plato") and he ends the paragraph that begins with this observation as follows: "The existence of a relationship of a scholarly nature between the two men is intelligence [*renseignement*] furnished from outside, by different authors who range from the third century B.C. until the Byzantine epoch."[60] Only then does he state another fact both simple and true, likewise tending to dissipate the value of the testimony he is yet to mention: "This history begins with two lost authors, Hermippus of Smyrna and Mnestratus of Thasos."[61] The primary sources for a connection of which there is no trace in either Plato or Demosthenes are thus not only late but lost.

Why our author pairs Hermippus with Mnesistratus must be clearly understood since it implicates, however subtly, Pernot's thesis. As Pernot observes, we know nothing about Mnesistratus except what we find in Diogenes Laertius, who adds this to his list of Plato's students: "Sabinus adds Demosthenes, citing Mnesistratus of Thasos as his authority in the fourth book of his *Collected Meditations*. And this is likely [εἰκός]."[62] With respect to source-criticism, this εἰκός is conveniently ignored: what does it matter if Diogenes thought that it was likely (*wahrscheinlich*) and not merely possible that Demosthenes was Plato's student? But it had already required re-punctuating and emending the received text in order to make Mnesistratus the source—with the earlier punctuation, Polemo had appeared to be, and Mnesitratus merely another one of Plato's students[63]—and even though this guess proved to have been a lucky one,[64] the source-critics still couldn't know for sure whether this Mnesistratus was early or late.[65] To this extent, joining Hermippus to Mnesistratus still remains risky: since the latter is completely lost, he may even, unlike Hermippus, be early. Pernot cites the relevant evidence regarding the attempts, just detailed in the notes, to render this evidence both late and valueless in a footnote.[66]

What makes Pernot so important is that his chapter's thesis is that philosophers who were hostile to rhetoric and sophistic proceeded to fabricate evidence that Demosthenes was Plato's student as part of an ongoing war, aiming to show the radical insufficiency of Rhetoric when unguided and undisciplined by Philosophy.[67] It is in the light of this thesis—obviously of supreme importance with respect to what was called "the fabrication-suppression dynamic" in the preface—that Pernot's decision to displace Hermippus from the initial place to which source-criticism from Funkhänel to Trampedach via Schaefer and Blass had uniformly accorded him becomes intelligible and even necessary. By "displacement," I mean only that Hermippus appears on the scene *with* Mnesistratus, and it should be noted that this displacement is merely partial: he first demonstrates that Hermippus is late before suggesting that Mnesistratus is likely to be late as well. Nevertheless, we are dealing from the start with *two* lost authors, and this tends to minimize rather than accentuate the importance of Hermippus from the start. When he revisits the subject later in the chapter in the context of presenting "the Callimachean" Hermippus as "a lover of curiosities as well as a fabricator [*un affabulateur*],"[68] he will not conceal the fact that the Callistratus-story appeared in *On the Students of Isocrates*,[69] but he will not revisit this fact when he returns to Hermippus a second time after introducing his thesis,[70] and that for the simple reason that it contradicts it: an anecdote that depicted Demosthenes abandoning Philosophy for Rhetoric could not possibly be the point of origin for intelligence (*renseignement*) that was fabricated for the purpose of subjecting Rhetoric to the guidance of Philosophy.

If it were not also necessary, Pernot's attempt to avoid this conundrum would be ingenious, but even if the solution itself—distinguishing Plutarch's version of the story from Aulus Gellius's, and then suggesting that the latter may not be either the original or the more reliable one—was required, the way Pernot insinuates it is not only ingenious but a rhetorical *tour de force*. Having postulated an ongoing Quarrel between Rhetoric and Philosophy,[71] the easy route would have been to identify Hermippus as a proponent of Rhetoric, as indeed it seems obvious that the author of *On the Students of Isocrates* actually was. But Pernot sees with great clarity the cross-purposes of the anecdote, and he is correct to point out in the first sentence of the crucial paragraph that "the passage raises multiple problems."[72] In its most important sentence, he must admit the possibility on which I have insisted: that the anecdote presupposed the relationship between Demosthenes and Plato, and could not have invented it:

> In admitting that the testimony of Aulus Gellius is worthy of faith, and that the tale of conversion figured in Hermippus, we are nevertheless still ignorant if Hermippus was the inventor of the tale or if he found it in this form among his predecessors, for example in the anonymous memoranda to which he was referring.[73]

And he ends it with all the important questions about Hermippus unanswered—I will insert my own answers to them in brackets—and is apodictic only about the zero-sum conflict his thesis demands:

> Was the anecdote in his eyes unfavorable to Plato, revealing him to be an inadequate teacher? [Yes]. Or was it unfavorable to Demosthenes, making him look like a defector from philosophy? [No]. The testimony of Hermippus preserves an element of mystery. But what is certain is that the version transmitted by Aulus Gellius opposes Philosophy and Rhetoric as two distinct biographical moments and as two commitments, two choices of life that are incompatible with each other.[74]

Since Cicero is the source of multiple *testimonia* (T2, T3, T4, and T5),[75] Pernot naturally will have a great deal to say about him but the incompatibility claim just quoted should give the reader a clear idea of how he will fare.[76] To be clear, it is antithetical to Pernot's thesis to demonstrate the compatibility of Rhetoric and Philosophy that was (1) the guiding principle of Cicero's life and of many of his books, (2) the essence of his Cave-based Platonism, and (3) the reason he attached so much importance to the parallel student-teacher relationship between Demosthenes and Plato. Although there is a certain dialectical necessity that motivates a critical stand to Pernot, before continuing in that vein it is necessary to make perfectly clear that his work has been invaluable to me to such an extent that I am building on his foundation. To take a comparatively insignificant example of my dependence on his lead, consider the first chapter's second section, entitled "A Historiographical Debate."[77] Here he usefully divides modern scholarship into three camps: (1) those who reject the relationship between Plato and Demosthenes entirely (a list that begins with Funkhänel), (2) those who reject the possibility that Demosthenes was Plato's student in a formal sense but admit the possibility that he was familiar with his writings and thus conversant with his ideas (a list that begins with Schaefer), and (3) those who embrace the tradition (a shorter list that ends with Wörle). Pernot's erudite catalogue is a most impressive and valuable achievement.

It is true that his brief animadversions on what I have called "the second track" leave much to be desired, but it is the "first" not the "second" that makes his chapter stimulating even in its starkest antitheses. Nevertheless, the relevant passage must be quoted:

> If it is necessary to compare Plato and Demosthenes, it is better to be sensible of all that separates them. Demosthenes believed in democracy, he demonstrated no sympathy for Sparta, he devoted his life to political activity, from day to day, with realism, and he relied on eloquence; all these take us very far away from the author of *Gorgias* and *Republic*.[78]

Although this is a considerably less sophisticated approach than Trampedach's[79]—it would have been more convincing to cite *Theaetetus*, *Statesman*, *Laws*, and the *Seventh Letter*—this list has its dialectical value as well, and with the exclusion of Sparta-based difference—Demosthenes says nothing revealing on the subject[80]—I will hereafter refer to (1) Plato's alleged hostility to Democracy, (2) his alleged rejection of politics for the sake of the βίος θεωρετικός, and (3) his alleged lack of reliance on eloquence, as "Pernot's Triad" despite the fact that the third dominated the preface and the second figured prominently in the discussion of Trampedach.

But it is neither Pernot's clarity nor erudition that makes him so valuable in a dialectical sense: it is the sincerity of his defense of Rhetoric and the sinuous subtlety that defending it repeatedly requires him to demonstrate. Consider in this connection his reading of Lucian's *Encomium of Demosthenes*, a text that will receive attention in chapter 5. With respect to its evidentiary value, it can be dismissed quite apart from the fact that its authenticity has been denied. But it leaves little room for doubt that its author's intention to praise Demosthenes is sincere even if the distortions of history required for praising him indicate Lucian's customary playfulness. It is, of course, almost as absurd to claim that Demosthenes was taught by Plato, Xenocrates, and Aristotle as it is to place the most over-the-top praise for him in the mouth of Antipater, who was primarily responsible for his death, especially when he narrates a dialogue he had with Philip, Demosthenes' nemesis, in which the way the Macedonian King praises him makes his speeches the most over-the-top aspect of the *Encomium*. Probably inauthentic, but sincere; historically valueless but certainly friendly to a Plato-inspired Demosthenes; such would be the predictable scholarly reactions.

Pernot takes a radically different approach: he redeems Lucian's reputation as a satirist by reading his *Encomium* as satiric and his praise for Demosthenes as thoroughly ironic. He achieves this improbable result thanks to the disingenuous simplicity of his partisanship for Rhetoric—particularly when it is in conflict with Philosophy—and the subtlety of his methods in defending it, already visible in his approach to the versions of Hermippus found in Plutarch and Aulus Gellius. Here Pernot achieves this result by discovering Lucian's true attitude toward Demosthenes in *Teacher of Orators*.[81] Staged as "a Choice of Lives" in the tradition of Xenophon's Prodicus or Plato's Glaucon but to opposite effect, Lucian's "teacher of orators" recommends not the difficult but the easy path, and identifies those who revere Demosthenes with the former:

> These are the things he will say, this imposter—archaic as truly a man of Cronus' time—putting forth ancient corpses to imitate, and demanding you to excavate speeches, buried away long ago, as if they were the greatest good, demanding that you emulate a sword-maker's son [sc. Demosthenes] and another [sc. Aeschines], the son of a certain schoolmaster named Atrometus, and do so in peacetime, with neither a Philip attacking nor an Alexander giving orders—at which time, perhaps, their speeches might have seemed useful—unaware of the kind of quick and easy road that has recently been made a short-cut straight to Rhetoric.[82]

Pernot takes this attack on Demosthenes seriously, and his ability to do so is a product of his sincere commitment to what might be called "Rhetoric Unleashed." Perfectly unconsciously, then, he reveals the ongoing political bite of the *Encomium of Demosthenes* for anyone who still lived by χαλεπὰ τὰ καλά ("noble deeds are difficult") and who could recognize that there were still tyrants, more powerful than ever, to be fought in Lucian's day.

As far as Pernot is concerned, Lucian's purpose was to challenge the intellectual tyranny that the cult of Demosthenes promoted, and he uses *The Teacher of Orators* to support his satiric reading of the *Encomium*:

> Alerted by the hyperbolic character of the encomium, by the unabashed reprise of the most hackneyed aspects, by the improbabilities and the untruths

slipped in here and there, by recourse to the scarcely credible records of the Macedonian royal house, they [sc. more astute interpreters] recognize, with good reason according to us, a satiric intention, directed, one more time, not against Demosthenes, but against [emphasis mine] *the idealization of the figure of Demosthenes* which was current during the imperial epoch, against the legend shaped by it [*contre la légende formée à son sujet*].[83]

I take the referent of Pernot's *la légende* to be the allegedly fabricated tale of Demosthenes' connection to Plato, and instead of his "idealization," the term "Platonizing" would be more accurate. By de-Platonizing Demosthenes, Pernot believes he is defending him, all in the service of Rhetoric Unleashed.

My intent, by contrast, is "to flip Pernot." Where he finds fabrication, I see suppression, and the extent of my debt to him is measured by the dialectical role that the suppression-fabrication dynamic plays in this book. To take the most recent case first, it is in his *Teacher of Orators*, not the *Encomium of Demosthenes*, that Lucian is being satiric. But Pernot is absolutely right to juxtapose the two texts. Particularly because tyranny, no matter how benignly concealed it may temporarily have become, "was current during the imperial era," it was precisely the Platonic Demosthenes, along with the republican Cicero who fashioned himself in his predecessor's image, who kept a principled opposition to tyrants alive. What made this hazardous survival possible was the unquestioned and unquestionable rhetorical supremacy of Demosthenes and Cicero: a mastery that it was easy to separate from philosophically significant and politically dangerous implications, thanks precisely to "the emancipation of rhetoric" from "the tyranny of Platonism." To "flip" Pernot in this case means to recognize that it was the Platonizing of Demosthenes that needed to be suppressed, not *la légende* of their connection that needed to be fabricated.

Consider Pernot's approach to the *Fifth Letter* of Demosthenes (T 26),[84] the one that begins with εὖ πράττειν,[85] the characteristically Platonic greeting and something like the Academy's secret handshake:

> But the *Fifth Letter* raises a grave difficulty since modern scholars [*les savants modernes*] are in agreement that it should be considered apocryphal for a variety of reasons—both of content and of language—that appear solid. It would thus be a forgery of the Hellenistic era. One can imagine that the forger was inspired precisely by the tradition according to which Demosthenes had been a student of Plato's, unless, on the contrary, it was instead the existence of the apocryphal letter which had been the origin of this tradition (supposing that the forgery was ancient enough to have been able to play this role).[86]

Voilà! It was in response to this passage that what I am calling "the fabrication-suppression dynamic" was born. It is necessary to spell out precisely what makes Pernot's argument here so ripe for "flipping." His argument does not establish that the *Fifth Letter* is a forgery: it rather assumes that it is a fabrication on the basis of *les savants modernes*. But the proof that neither he nor anyone else can know that it is a fabrication—and what follows is the endemic problem that surreptitiously undermines all inauthenticity arguments—is that he cannot say who fabricated it, cannot even say, that is, whether it was forged to support a fabricated tradition or to create one. All Pernot knows for sure is that it is forged, and thus that the tradition it either supported or initiated is a product of fabrication. But there is more than one "grave difficulty" that now confronts Pernot and *les savants modernes* on whom he relies: (1) if the letter was forged to prove that Demosthenes was Plato's student, it did so in a clumsy manner, for its author merely takes his addressee to task for behaving in a manner unworthy of Plato and the Academy, in which the addressee, and only by implication the author, was a student. (2) In a distinctly brave but even more distinctly erudite work of scholarship, Irene Giaquinta has recently argued for the authenticity of all six of Demosthenes' *Letters*, including the *Fifth*.[87] (3) Finally, there is far more evidence that the *Fifth Letter* was suppressed than that it was forged.

It is this last point that justifies flipping Pernot with respect to the suppression-fabrication dynamic. As indicated not only by his "either/or" with respect to the date of the alleged forgery but also more subtly by reasons "both of content and of language," the suppression of the *Fifth Letter*, starting with Funkhänel,[88] is the most obvious example of it. Although different scholars have fastened on different ways of demonstrating how, when, and why it was fabricated, it is only the fabrication claim that has remained constant. To secure a hearing from an audience brought up on the tradition's certainty that the legend of Plato and Demosthenes is just that, it was necessary to deal with that tradition's arguments for fabrication first, despite their complexity. While stretching the acceptable and indeed justifiable bounds of what a decent introduction should be, I have attempted to introduce, as clearly as the complexities of the case allows, the weaknesses of both the first and second tracks on which the modern consensus rests. Pernot has brilliantly revealed that the first track ultimately depends on the hypothesis of fabrication, and thanks to his insight that the legend was fabricated for the purpose of subordinating Rhetoric to Philosophy, he has not only made my response intelligible as a dialectical "flip," but more specifically has allowed me to show that source-criticism's emphasis on the testimony of Hermippus—the crucial first step on the first "track"—is ill-suited for proving what *les savants modernes* want it to prove, presupposing as it does a prior connection between Plato and Demosthenes before the latter abandoned the Academy for Rhetoric.[89]

But it may still be possible to make this introduction more properly introductory. Just as "the first track" (the external evidence for the connection that has made it necessary to engage with the source critics here) is of less moment in this book as a whole than the "second track" (the internal evidence of the connection in the words and deeds of Plato and Demosthenes), so too are *both tracks combined* of less moment than a "third track," one that takes its start from the reality of the connection, and uses it to create a new "conception of Plato" or *Platonbild*. It is true that this new *Platonbild* must already inform my approach to "the second track," and first in the preface, then the synopsis of Trampedach's "hermeneutic part," and now with "Pernot's Triad," this new conception has been sketched. But even though it is necessary to justify the existence or plausibility of the connection along "the second track," it is rather to elucidate the *implications* of that connection that is this book's purpose, and it is to this "third track" that what remains of this introduction will be more properly introductory. And just as the dialectical approach advanced in opposition to Trampedach and Pernot has made it easier to explain my approach to the "first" and "second tracks," so also will a contest between Demosthenes and Aristotle for the title of the Old Academy's, and thus Plato's, archetypal student illuminate the "third."

Naturally they have never before been compared in this context:[90] the modern consensus precludes comparing them. But I hope to show in what remains of this introduction that undisputed historical facts indicate that such a comparison is both appropriate and inevitable, as if by design, once the possibility is admitted, if only for the sake of argument, that Demosthenes was Plato's student as well. To begin with, it is worth considering, if only for a moment, how Aristotle's status, not only as "Plato's most genuine disciple,"[91] but even simply as one of Plato's students, would stand up under a grilling based on the same kind of source-criticism that has been applied to Demosthenes,[92] especially since Plato never mentions Aristotle, Aristotle never says expressly that he was Plato's student, and that Hermippus is our earliest source for much more biographical information about Aristotle than about Demosthenes.[93] Naturally it is not my purpose to deny that Aristotle was Plato's student; the comparison with Demosthenes that I am proposing requires both of them to have been his students. But what makes this comparison plausible, and what suggests that it was always somehow inevitable, is the revealing coincidence that both were born in 384 and died in 322.

Consider another date: Plato died in 347. It is well known that Aristotle left the Academy, and found a new if temporary hospice with Hermias, the tyrant of Atarneus. Although it is customary to imagine that it was

Plato's death and the installation of Speusippus as his successor that caused Aristotle and Xenocrates to leave Athens, Diogenes Laertius states that he left while Plato was still alive.[94] Anton-Hermann Chroust links Aristotle's departure from Athens to the fall of Olynthus in 348:

> This incident, together with Demosthenes' fiery and constant denunciations against Philip, led to the outbreak of violent anti-Macedonian sentiments and actions among the Athenians. Aristotle, it must be remembered, was a "Macedonian resident alien" in Athens, who was probably suspected of strong pro-Macedonian leanings or sympathies.[95]

By the time Aristotle left Athens, Demosthenes had already delivered his three *Olynthian Orations* and his *First Philippic*,[96] but it may be even more useful to consider Demosthenes' career as an orator in the context of Plato's death. It was in 347 that Demosthenes wrote but perhaps did not deliver *Against Meidias*, the speech that most revealingly connects—thanks in part to Douglas MacDowell's magisterial commentary—his youthful attempt to regain his inheritance to the political career that would make him famous (21.77–87). And when an earlier and even more impressive Anglophone Demosthenes scholar collected the orator's eight most important public orations in two volumes,[97] Plato's death falls between the speeches covered in the first and those in the second.

If Aristotle's "first flight from Athens" was connected to Demosthenes, so too was his "second," and this time it was Alexander's death in 323 that marked the moment. After leaving the comfort and security of Hermias' hospitality (347–343) for the even more secure and comfortable security of Philip's—he became Alexander's teacher in 342—Aristotle would finally return to Athens in 335, shortly after his pupil destroyed Thebes and enslaved its inhabitants. Chroust comments: "Thus it appears that Aristotle moved back to Athens almost in the van of the conquering Macedonian phalanx—that he, so to speak, came back, or was brought back, by the force of arms."[98] Confirming this appearance is that it was Alexander's death that caused him to leave Athens the second time:

> His close ties with King Philip, Alexander, and later with Antipater of course were suspect in essentially anti-Macedonian Athens. It is hardly surprising, therefore, that he should be suspected of being an enemy of the Athenian patriots and an opponent of all efforts to throw off the Macedonian yoke—a key foe of the anti-Macedonian party (including Demosthenes, Lycourgus, Hypereides, Chares, Charidemus, Ephialtes, Diotimus, Himeraeus, Merocles, and others).[99]

While allowing this passage to speak for itself with respect to comparing Demosthenes and Aristotle, Chroust's use of the word "party" deserves some comment. Despite the efforts of Julius Beloch (1854–1929) to examine the politics of fourth-century Athens in terms of various pro- and anti-Macedonian parties,[100] a concerted effort has been made to disable the distinction by showing that talk of "parties" is anachronistic,[101] as well it might actually be. But despite appearances, this effort has not succeeded nor can it ever succeed in suppressing the fact that Aristotle was pro-Macedonian and Demosthenes was anti-Macedonian, even if neither belonged to anything like "a political party" in the modern sense. Despite the fact that Chroust spells their names differently, both Lycurgus and Hyperides were likewise anti-Macedonian, and if I were inclined to speak of parties—which I am not—it would make more sense to join them with Demosthenes in "the Academy Party," or rather "the party of the Old Academy." More concretely, Alexander's death forced Aristotle to flee Athens just as it allowed Demosthenes to recover from the humiliation of the Harpalus Affair, and even though Aristotle was already too ill to take advantage of the restoration of Macedonian control over Athens in 322,[102] it was that restoration that led to Demosthenes' suicide.

Trampedach used the *Theaetetus* Digression to align a thoroughly theoretical and practically apolitical Plato—and thus the Academy's purpose—with the βίος θεωρετικός and the ὁμοίωσις θεῷ. A careful reading of the dialogue vitiates this approach: the philosopher Socrates describes in the Digression is indifferent to the social, political, and even personal circumstances of his interlocutors (*Tht.* 174b1–4); Socrates not only knows a number of details about young Theaetetus (*Tht.* 144c5-8) but joins with him in dialogue precisely because his interest is confined to Theodorus' most promising *Athenian* students (*Tht.* 143d1–6; note ἡμῖν at d5).[103] The principal point of contrast between Aristotle and Demosthenes is the simplest: one was a foreign metic and the other—despite the efforts of Aeschines with respect to Demosthenes' mother[104]—an Athenian. A question, then: was Plato primarily interested in teaching Athenians or foreigners in the Academy or did he not care? In addition to aligning him with his Socrates on this point, I would likewise align Plato with Demosthenes on the second most important difference between the latter and Aristotle: that one was pro- and the other anti-Macedonian. In *Gorgias*, it is Polus, not Socrates, who admires a rich and powerful Macedonian tyrant (*Grg.* 470d5–471d2); in *Republic* 8, whatever the flaws of Democracy and the Democratic Man may be, both are better by far than their tyrannical counterparts, and just as I would align Plato with Athens rather than Macedon, and democracy rather than tyranny, so also does it make some sense, even at this introductory stage, to align him with Demosthenes rather than Aristotle.

Finally, consider the two in relation to "the Third Wave of Paradox" in *Republic* 5. First with Themison, then with Hermias, and finally, with

Alexander, Aristotle had considerably more success in guiding rulers to Philosophy than Plato did with Dionysius in Syracuse:

> Whatever the reason for Aristotle's new appointment [sc. as Alexander's teacher], it was no doubt accepted joyfully for its own sake. To be educator to a prince was an ambition inherited from Plato which he [sc. Aristotle] never gave up. Some ten years earlier he had addressed a protreptic work to a Cypriot king called Themison, in which he urged on him that philosophy was the most profitable education for a monarch. Next we saw him molding the mind of the tyrant of Atarneus with some success, perhaps because he had relinquished a little of the intransigence of what one might call romantic Platonism. Here it could possibly be significant that his abandonment of belief in the transcendent Forms—Justice and the rest—had occurred in the meantime.[105]

To use the word "romantic" in W. K. C. Guthrie's sense: is it with this post-romantic Platonism that we should align the Old Academy? Was it not precisely the Idea of Justice ("and the rest") that would have prevented true Platonists from simply accommodating themselves, on the basis of a prudent φρόνησις,[106] to the new Macedonian reality as a matter of principle? It was not merely an accident of birth that caused Plato to locate his school in Athens, and the clear lesson of his *Letters* was that he had failed miserably with the easier and more economical route of bringing political power and philosophical virtue together in one man.[107] From the attention-capturing puzzles of the *Protagoras* and the crystal clarity of the *Alcibiades Major* through to the advanced legal training of the *Laws* and "the practice of death" in *Phaedo*, Plato's dialogues as a whole, considered as the Academy's curriculum, align its purpose with turning out a man like Demosthenes—along with Phocion, Lycurgus, and Hyperides—and not like the preceptor of Hermias and Alexander. Naturally we have become comfortable with aligning Plato and the Academy's purpose with Aristotle, but we have done so primarily on the basis of Aristotle's own evidence, and to an extent that makes an alternative conception virtually inconceivable. This inconceivability is a product of *suppression*, emerging in response to Macedonian hegemony, and its power is so enduring that the ample ancient evidence that Macedon's principal Athenian opponent was Plato's student must now be conceived as a *fabrication*.

1

The End of the Old Academy

Plutarch's *Life of Phocion* not only connects Plato and Phocion as teacher and student but also links Phocion's story to Demosthenes, Lycurgus, and Hyperides. It does not, however, provide evidence for an "Old Academy Party" united by anti-Macedonian patriotism, and indeed it is probably better understood as proving just the opposite. Unlike Demosthenes, Lycurgus, and Hyperides, all of whom remain resolutely anti-Macedonian throughout the story, Phocion does not, and the way he does not is at the center of the *Life*. By juxtaposing him vividly with the pro-Macedonian Demades from the start,[1] Plutarch makes it impossible to align Phocion with Macedon in opposition to Demosthenes, Lycurgus, and Hyperides. Phocion's patriotism is never in doubt: he is pro-Athenian and serves his city well. But in comparison with the younger trio of Athenian patriots whose patriotism makes them more or less radically anti-Macedonian, Phocion plays the role in Plutarch's story of the political realist, and to the extent that he accommodates Macedon—to a tragic extent for those who recognize that the trio were likewise students of Plato—he does so because he bows to the inevitable: especially after Chaeronea, continued resistance to Philip is futile. Since Phocion is the only one of the four whom Plutarch identifies as a student of Plato in the *Life*, the fact that his stance is based on political realism and even expediency instead of binding and inflexible "romantic" principle (see introduction, *ad fin.*) makes Plutarch's text of particular interest to his fellow Platonists, especially those who are looking to Athenian history and Athenian politicians for some indications of what Plato really taught in the Academy.

Plutarch pairs Phocion with Cato the Younger, and given the famous remark of Cicero (106-63 BC) about "the sewer of Romulus,"² it would have been difficult to harmonize the inflexible City-based "Platonism" of the one with the political realism and accommodation of the actual Academic. Fortunately, Plutarch makes no effort to do so. His emphasis is rather on what might be called "the crisis of the Republic," for both statesmen had the misfortune of leading "a city in unexpected happenstances."³

> Wherefore, this kind of polity [πολιτεία] is completely precarious, for she ruins together with herself the speaker whose goal is gratification, and ruins beforehand the one who refuses to gratify her.⁴

We therefore expect from the start that Phocion, who famously and indeed hilariously refused to accommodate popular opinion,⁵ will meet an untimely and appropriately Socratic end, as Plutarch makes sure we will recognize:

> But the things done to Phocion reminded the Greeks once again of those done to Socrates, as though this error was most similar to that one, as likewise being a calamity for the city.⁶

Plutarch compares Phocion and Demosthenes as orators,⁷ but not as Academics. Having raised in the introduction the possibility that Demosthenes served a kind of post-graduate apprenticeship with Callistratus,⁸ it is noteworthy that Phocion began his political career under the guidance of Chabrias⁹; if not as a "political party," an Academic association can thus be discerned. In any case, by recording the fact that Phocion was elected general more times than any other,¹⁰ Plutarch makes a useful observation about the distinction between generals and orators:

> Seeing that the public men of his day had divided up as if by lot the work of general and of orator, some of them only speaking in the assembly and proposing decrees, such as Eubulus, Aristophon, Demosthenes, Lycurgus, and Hyperides, and others—men like Diopeithes, Menestheus, Leosthenes, and Chares—advancing themselves by serving as generals and waging war, Phocion wished to resume and restore the πολιτεία of Pericles, Aristides, and Solon, which was equally apportioned to both spheres of action.¹¹

This use of πολιτεία in this context is significant, and it raises the critical question: was the purpose of Plato's Πολιτεία to create an ideal City or rather to inspire young Athenians like Phocion to strive for the kind of synthesis that Plutarch tells us he did here? The same dialogue a skeptic could cite with respect to Pericles also contains Socrates' fulsome praise of Aristides (*Grg.* 526a2–b4); not surprisingly, Demosthenes echoes it

(3.21–26, 23.209, and 26.6–7).¹² And no more than Socrates, Pericles, Solon, Aristides, or Phocion, did Demosthenes aim to gratify the Athenians by telling them what they wanted to hear.

Of course, the more pressing matter is the first mention of Demosthenes, Lycurgus, and Hyperides in Plutarch's *Life of Phocion*; hereafter, those I will call "the Academic Trio" will play an increasingly important part in the story. By the time we encounter this passage, Plutarch has already linked both Phocion and Cato to Plato; he will link Chabrias and Phocion to Plato in the *Reply to Colotes*. But what shall we say about the Platonic credentials of this trio? While nothing in the *Life of Phocion* proves either that they were students of Plato or that Plutarch regarded them as such, there is likewise nothing in it that compels us to conclude that he didn't and that they weren't. It is one thing to claim that Plutarch did not write *Lives of the Ten Orators* but something else entirely to claim on this basis that he would therefore necessarily have been unaware or would even have denied that Demosthenes, Lycurgus, and Hyperides were, like Phocion, Plato's students as well. Given that we cannot be sure about what Plutarch knew or believed about them—apart, that is, from what survives in *Lives of the Ten Orators*, in his shadow if not by his hand—it is best to consider or reconsider this text with an open mind on the question, and my claim is that the reader who does so will see that Plutarch's *Life of Phocion* is best appreciated as a vivid and pathetic tale about "the End of the Old Academy."

In the aftermath of Chaeronea, Phocion thought that it was necessary to accept the policy and embrace the philanthropy of Philip: Plutarch refers to this policy as "the other πολιτεία."¹³ When Philip was assassinated in 336, Demosthenes greeted his death with jubilation, Phocion with prescient realism. After Alexander had razed Thebes to the ground in 335, he demanded that Athens surrender "those around Demosthenes and Lycurgus and Hyperides and Charidemus."¹⁴ Being asked repeatedly in the Assembly to respond to this demand, Phocion finally did so, recommending that it is better "to persuade and beseech the winners, not to fight them." But he began the speech by using his dearest friend Nicocles as a prop:

> "To such a pass," he said, "have these men repeatedly led the city that even if someone should demand Nicocles here, I would order you to give him up. As for me, I would regard it as my good fortune [εὐτυχία] to die on behalf of all of you [τὸ ὑπὲρ ὑμῶν ἁπάντων ἀποθανεῖν]."¹⁵

Given Phocion's character, this claim should not only be regarded as sincere, but more importantly as a challenge that presupposes the Trio's own commitment to Plato's πολιτεία: if they were as Platonic as he is, they too would count it as εὐτυχία "to die on behalf of others [ὑπεραποθνῄσκειν]" (e.g., *Smp.* 179b4).[16] This verb is an important marker for the kind of Platonism that places a higher value on noble action in the light of the Good than on cosmological speculation or the βιός θεωρετικός, and it points to Plato's own ability "to persuade and beseech" his students to sacrifice their own personal good by returning to the Cave, as I am claiming that Phocion and the Academic Trio actually did. For all his realism with respect to Alexander—and of course his counsel is framed in relation to what has just befallen Thebes—Phocion remains committed to this ideal, and his initial reticence to speak suggests that he would have much preferred dying himself to arguing that these others should die.

The Platonic stakes are increased the second time Phocion is forced to make this choice. After the defeat at Crannon in 322, Alexander's regent Antipater marched on Athens; Phocion met him in Thebes, securing his promise to remain there while the terms of Athens' capitulation could be settled. Securing *carte blanche* to negotiate from the Athenians, Phocion's embassy returned to Thebes, this time including "Xenocrates the philosopher."[17] Plutarch does not identify Xenocrates either as Plato's successor or as his student, and the reason he does not do so is that he counts on his audience to know it, just as I am claiming that Plutarch could count on them to recognize the Platonic pathos of Antipater's response to Phocion's plea:

> He replied that there would be friendship with the Athenians and alliance should they hand over Demosthenes and Hyperides, organize themselves politically through "the traditional constitution [ἡ πάτριος πολιτεία]" on the basis of a property qualification, receiving a garrison at Munychia, and further, paying in addition the expenses of the war and a penalty.[18]

Including Demosthenes and Hyperides—Lycurgus was now dead—this sad story revolves around four of Plato's students and one of Aristotle's, for even though Plutarch does not mention the connection here,[19] Antipater was at once Aristotle's executor,[20] his correspondent,[21] and his protector.[22] Antipater demands that the Athenians surrender both Demosthenes and democracy; it is only the demand for a garrison that Phocion initially resists, and his attempt "to persuade and beseech the winners" is here rejected. Both Hyperides and Demosthenes would die as a result, one killed by Antipater's soldiers, the other would kill himself to avoid falling into his hands.

But it is not this aspect of Plutarch's story that would receive the most scholarly attention but rather the role of Xenocrates in this pathetic proceeding. Plutarch claims, to begin with, that Xenocrates was sent by the Athenians in order to secure more generous and merciful terms from Antipater, and although he states that this expectation was based on Xenocrates' reputation for virtue, it is more likely that they counted on his personal connection with Antipater.[23] But whatever it was upon which the Athenians were counting, they were mistaken: in Plutarch, Antipater treated him with contempt, first refusing to greet him, then interrupting his speech and reducing him to silence.[24] No source for the story was cited in the *Life of Phocion*, and although the recently discovered Academic *Index of Philodemus* indicated the presence of a common source,[25] it shed no light on the discrepancy between Plutarch's account of Antipater's rudeness and the briefer account in Diogenes Laertius that depicted the two in friendly conversation later that night.[26] But even without Diogenes, scholarly interest was fully justified by the questions raised by Plutarch's tale itself. Did it indicate Antipater's cruelty in general, his hostility to Xenocrates personally, or his hostility to the Academy, of which, of course, Xenocrates was the head in 322? Certainly nothing the Athenians knew beforehand could have allowed them to anticipate the resulting snub; they would not have added Xenocrates to the embassy if they knew Antipater regarded him with suspicion. On the other hand, was it only on the basis of what their informants in Athens could have reported to them, that first Alexander and now Antipater recognized that Demosthenes, Hyperides, and the now deceased Lycurgus, were particularly inimical to Macedonian interests?

These questions led to the spirited debate between Jacob Bernays (1824–1881) and Theodor Gomperz (1832–1912) about the Academy's relationship with Macedon,[27] and an account of this debate will illuminate this chapter's theme. In an 1881 study published shortly before his death entitled "Phocion and his Recent Critics,"[28] Bernays had argued for the Academy's pro-Macedonian orientation, part of his book's larger claim about the inherent cosmopolitanism of Greek philosophy itself.[29] Ever since Thales had attempted to unite the cities of Ionia, philosophers had ranged themselves against the petty politics of individual cities, Bernays claimed,[30] and therefore welcomed the rise of Macedonian hegemony.[31] Partly because his subject was Phocion—whose Platonic inheritance Bernays tied to Socrates' famous claim in *Gorgias* that it is better to suffer a wrong than to do one[32]—and partly because he needed to implicate the Academy in this drive to the World State, Plutarch's account of Xenocrates' role in the embassy to Antipater was important to his argument.[33] But what made this passage even more important is that it was here that Gomperz focused his criticism.[34] For Bernays, the case for an alliance between Xenocrates and Antipater, mediated by their mutual friend Aristotle, was so obvious that he skimmed over, at least in the text, the rude treatment Antipater had accorded the philosopher in Plutarch, emphasizing instead the story in Diogenes Laertius.[35] Gomperz pounced on an interpretation that forced Bernays to explain Antipater's rudeness to Xenocrates as "a little comedy performed by the two of them, the kind of thing that was only possible between good friends or was something profitable [*erpriesslich*]."³⁶

With respect to Plutarch, Gomperz had the high ground, and in doing so he was not alone: in their reviews of *Phokion und seine neueren Beurtheiler*, some of Germany's foremost classicists endorsed his critique and then added their own.³⁷ With respect to Phocion, Schaefer pointed out that before Chaeronea, the general whom Bernays considered the pro-Macedonian leader of the aristocratic "Peace Party," and thus a principal force in the (praiseworthy) drive to a World State,³⁸ had effectively thwarted Philip's schemes in Euboea and Byzantium,³⁹ the latter, as Blass pointed out, in company with a classmate from the Academy.⁴⁰ In the aggregate, these reviews also had a higher purpose: to liberate "the Academic philosophers, at least Plato and Xenocrates, from the 'stain' of pro-Macedonian sentiment."⁴¹ Yet here, it was Bernays who occupied the higher ground, at least with respect to Xenocrates. In defending this position, Aristotle played the primary role, and only one of Bernays' critics made any effort to deny the Stagirite's "pro-Macedonian sentiment."⁴² Naturally Bernays had a stronger case to make and he had made it:

> Already through his birth as the son of the personal physician of Philip's father Amyntas, he [sc. Aristotle] belonged to the Macedonian royal court, and his subsequent career brought him into the closest intimacy of trust with the three great Macedonian rulers Philip, Alexander, Antipater; to Antipater he bound himself in so strong a personal friendship that he could name this prince as his testamentary executor.⁴³

Had not Xenocrates accompanied Aristotle to Atarneus,⁴⁴ and did not Hermias, their host, occupy a strategic bridgehead for a Macedonian invasion of Asia?⁴⁵ Had not Xenocrates already participated in an embassy to Philip and been offered gifts by Philip?⁴⁶ Had he not had friendly intercourse with Alexander as well, for whom he had written, at the prince's request, a treatise on kingship?⁴⁷ In the light of all this, was it not possible that Bernays was right to suggest that Antipater's conduct toward Xenocrates in 322 was not what Plutarch's account had made it appear to be?

For Bernays, of course, Xenocrates was only one member of a pro-Macedonian philosophical alliance that included Plato, Aristotle, and Hermias,⁴⁸ and which found in Phocion—on whose continued instruction from Xenocrates Plutarch had insisted from the start⁴⁹—a principled and effective ally.⁵⁰ But for obvious reasons, it is Plato's role in this "men's club [*Männerbund*]"⁵¹ that is the crucial matter here. Bernays did his best with Plato's *Fifth Letter*—despite the fact that Euphraeus became a bitter enemy of Philip's and eventually died on behalf of his anti-Macedonian politics (9.62)—and with his *Sixth*, addressed to Hermias, Erastus' and Coriscus,[52] the latter two being young philosophers whose experiences in the Academy made it necessary for them, in Plato's words: "to supplement their knowledge of the Ideas—that noble doctrine—with the knowledge and capacity to protect themselves against wicked and unjust men" (*Ep.* 322d4–e1).[53] Since this advice, even if the letter was genuine, scarcely closed off the possibility that Hermias himself might be one such man,[54] this was weak evidence, at least for the case Bernays was making, especially in the light of Blass' question: "Plato a friend of Macedon, he who in *Gorgias* had made Achelaus the archetype of a criminal favored by good fortune?"[55] On the other hand, did not Aristotle's arrival in the Academy indicate Plato's connection with Macedon?[56]

But before Bernays could align Plato with Hermias, Aristotle, and Xenocrates in a pro-Macedon *Männerbund*, he first needed to detach Plato and the Academy from Athens, and the selective citation of two texts from *Republic* helped him to do so. He used the Third Wave of Paradox to prove that the only way to create a World State was through advising an absolute monarch "since there was currently no prospect that Philosophers would become Kings."[57] Professing the need to take every one of Plato's words seriously—which he did for the sake of using δυνάσται to prove that the Third Wave of Paradox already made reference to Macedon[58]—he quoted the following passage in Greek, deleting the italicized words:

> "Unless either philosophers become kings in our states or those whom we now call our kings and rulers [δυνάσται] take to the pursuit of philosophy seriously and adequately, and there is a conjunction of these two things, political power and philosophic intelligence *while the motley horde of the natures who at present pursue either apart from the other are compulsorily excluded*, there can be no cessation of troubles, *dear Glaucon*, for our cities, I conjecture, nor for the human race."[59]

To be sure Bernays is not alone in deleting or at least ignoring the most paradoxical part of the Paradox—here in italics—but its relevance to an alternative account of the Academy's purpose should be obvious.[60] But just in case it isn't, Plato was using Socrates to tell his students to return to the Cave, however dangerous, and that any philosopher who refused to do "the political things [τὰ πολιτικά]" had misunderstood what he meant by πολιτεία and was thus no true Academic. Bernays quoted and suppressed this passage through ellipsis in a lengthy endnote,[61] but he included in the text his translation of *Republic* VI 496c5–497a7,[62] an account of the dangerous uselessness of engaging in politics that begins immediately after Socrates has just said that it was the Sign that prevented him from doing so, "the divine thing" that prevented him from doing what he intended and was about to do (R. 496c3–5).⁶³ My response to Bernays is that although Plato and Socrates were not active politicians, they both taught their followers "to practice politics [πράττειν τὰ πολιτικά]," and to do so in Athens.⁶⁴

Gomperz responded by attempting to demolish the evidentiary basis for "the pro-Macedonian Academy" Bernays was promoting, and however uncritical he was about Plutarch's account of Xenocrates,⁶⁵ he made what I naturally regard as the crucial point:

> And against Phocion, the head of the Peace Party in Athens, stood Demosthenes, the head of the War Party, whose participation in the Platonic course of instruction [*platonischen Lehrcursen*] is sufficiently attested (*Ztschr. f. öst. Gymn.* 1865, 819ff.), to say nothing of Lycurgus and Hyperides, in regard to whom this same thing appears secured against any contestation.⁶⁶

In the 1865 article Gomperz cites here, he had not only found additional evidence in the recently discovered fragments of Philodemus from Herculaneum that Demosthenes had been Plato's student,⁶⁷ but had defended the connection on the basis of the evidence we had always had,⁶⁸ including a brilliant critique of the way Plutarch's citation of Hermippus in *Life of Demosthenes* had been used by opponents of the connection.⁶⁹ And although Schaefer's student did not follow Gomperz by using Demosthenes for this purpose, Blass did cite both Lycurgus and Hyperides for the same purpose in his review of Bernays while endorsing Gomperz's claims about Xenocrates.⁷⁰ As a result, Blass had reached an apparently unobjectionable conclusion: "The truth is that the Academy in its totality [*in ihrer Gesamtheit*] had no single political direction whereas its members had the most widely divergent ones."⁷¹

The chapter's purpose is to refine this conclusion by giving it a historical dimension, and this refinement is the basis for distinguishing "the Old Academy" in the currently accepted sense from the one on which this book's title is based. In the former sense, the descriptor applies to the Academy (to exploit Blass's term) *in ihrer Gesamtheit*, a chronological completeness that applies "the Old Academy" indiscriminately to both the period of Plato's life and that of his immediate successors Speusippus,⁷² Xenocrates,⁷³ and Polemo. Aristotle's account of Plato's thought in *Metaphysics* A abets and perhaps created this generalizing conception, especially given his description of the rival and arcane views of Speusippus and Xenocrates as described in *Metaphysics* M and N, differing from Plato and between themselves (and of course from Aristotle) primarily about the status of Numbers, whether in relation to, or in substitution for, the Ideas.⁷⁴ For reasons that should be obvious, Aristotle never distinguishes Plato from his successors on the basis of their pro- or anti-Macedonian views; this book's purpose is to do just that. Demosthenes is as archetypically anti-Macedonian as Aristotle was the opposite,[75] and I am using this opposition to distinguish the Academy under Plato from a more chronologically inclusive but politically misleading conception of "the Old Academy."

In describing the debate between Gomperz and Bernays, next to nothing has yet been said about Speusippus,[76] but he will go on to play the central role in this chapter. Before turning to him, however, it is necessary, on the basis of the foregoing, to make my own conclusions about the rival claims of these two modern scholars crystal clear even though it will be impossible at this early stage to do the same for Xenocrates and Phocion. Albeit in a preliminary way to be further explored in chapter 2, I take Phocion to be as fully representative of "the Old Academy" as Demosthenes, Lycurgus, and Hyperides; all four were Athenians, devoted from their youth to the service of Athens, a devotion that it was Plato's intention to instill in them. Phocion believed that Chaeronea had settled the question in a way the others did not. As for Xenocrates, Bernays is a much surer guide to his pro-Macedonian orientation than Gomperz, despite the fact that the latter is closer to the truth in rejecting his rival's claims about the Academy *in ihrer Gesamtheit*. In the following chapter I will offer an explanatory hypothesis for why it was necessary for Antipater and Xenocrates to stage a show that made the latter appear to be anti-Macedonian, but such I believe they did, and had, moreover, good reason to perform it. In short, Gomperz is right about "the Old Academy" while Bernays is right about the Academy after Plato, at least with respect to Xenocrates. This difference marks the high point of their usefulness, but their difference of opinion about Speusippus' *Letter to Philip* can be used to introduce this crucial document, the smoking gun in the story of "the end of the Old Academy."

Without claiming that the *Letter* was genuine,[77] Bernays needed almost all of the information in it to be substantially true because he believed it proved his point that Plato was pro-Macedonian. Overlooking Speusippus' purpose in writing the *Letter*, it was its amazing claim that Philip owed his kingdom to Plato that mattered to Bernays, and in a detailed endnote, he justified the letter's author or "manufacturer [*Verfertiger*]" in claiming that Plato, by having sent Euphraeus to the court of Perdiccas as described in the *Fifth Letter*, had been Philip's ally from the start.[78] No more than Bernays does Gomperz claim the *Letter of Speusippus* is authentic, but even if it were, it would only prove that its writer bent Plato's *Fifth Letter* to an improbable and altogether unwarranted conclusion.[79] Once again, and finally, the debate between Gomperz and Bernays in 1881–82 left critical questions untouched, and what neither of them could know at the time was that scholarly opinion about the authenticity of "Speusippus' Letter to King Philip" was going to shift dramatically in the twentieth century, beginning in 1928.[80] Because both Bernays and Gomperz regarded the *Letter of Speusippus* as a forgery, it was only whatever degree of historical truth it contained that figured in their debate, and on that question, Gomperz was closer to the mark. But once the *Letter of Speusippus* was recognized as authentic, it was now its author's intentions that mattered, not the truth of what he had written, and here Bernays was right to think that it supported his thesis about the pro-Macedonian orientation of the Academy *with respect to Speusippus*.[81]

Given the comparative level of prestige accorded to Oxford University as opposed to the University of Sydney, and the concomitant fact that Michael Frede and Myles Burnyeat have famous names while Anthony Francis Natoli does not, it is perhaps not as unlikely as it should be that the tide of scholarly opinion may yet be reversed by the posthumous publication of Frede's 2001 lectures committed to proving that Plato's *Seventh Letter* is inauthentic.[82] Counting on a prejudice against ancient letter collections as a genre that began with Richard Bentley,[83] Frede needed to deny the authenticity of Speusippus' *Letter* because if he didn't, it would be an example of what the most intractable defenders of the *Seventh Letter* claimed that *it* was: a single authentic letter amid a collection of many other inauthentic ones. More important than the weakness of the ongoing "guilt by association" argument upon which Frede's lectures depend throughout is that although they were published well after Natoli's magisterial study (2004),[84] they were delivered before it appeared, and thus in ignorance of Natoli's findings, approach, and arguments.[85] As ever, it is antithetical views in particular that are of greatest dialectical value, and *The Seventh Letter: A Seminar* will reappear in this book's final chapter. But on the immediately relevant question, Frede's thesis will be ignored, and following Natoli on all but one point, what follows presupposes the authenticity of *The Letter of Speusippus to Philip II*, hereafter simply "the *Letter*."

The *Letter* is of central importance because it is an ancient document that connects the Academy, through its leader, to Macedon, and more specifically to Philip, the infamous nemesis of Demosthenes. It is a friendly letter, to begin with, and thus points to a sharp contrast between Speusippus and Demosthenes with respect to Macedon; the head of the Academy attempts to ingratiate himself with Philip during the same decade during which Demosthenes was delivering the *Philippics*. Despite a difference between Demosthenes and Phocion with respect to *Realpolitik*, even the cursory account of the latter at the beginning of the chapter should be sufficient to indicate that a fascination with, and participation in, debates about Number Theory should not be regarded as the *sine qua non* of what it takes to be regarded as an Academic. This is not to say that such participation and fascination is an insignificant matter, and since I have argued at length elsewhere for the critical importance of the so-called mathematical "Intermediates" for recognizing, understanding, and defending Plato's Ideas,[86] not only are these debates important, but they constitute further proof—if such were needed—that first Speusippus, then Xenocrates, and of course Aristotle, had broken with Plato on matters touching the heart of Platonism.[87] But even closer to its heart was and remains the philosopher's response to the challenge of the Cave, and like Phocion, Demosthenes responded through political action, and more specifically, in opposition to the same Philip that Speusippus sought in the *Letter* to reconcile to the Academy, now under his leadership.[88]

The verb "reconcile" takes us to the heart of the matter, for Speusippus' attempt to placate Philip proves that relations between the Academy and Macedon were frosty when Speusippus wrote the *Letter*, and that Plato's successor was now attempting to improve them. But even before looking more closely at the *Letter*'s timing,[89] and leaving for more detailed analysis its specific purpose and context, the contrast between a pro- and anti-Macedonian political orientation, especially at the time period illuminated for us by the speeches of Demosthenes, is a no less important context for a discussion of Platonism than whether one regards the Ideas as Numbers—whether Intermediate or Ideal—or not. For Bernays, the Platonic philosopher's highest office would be exercised "through an advisory influence on the absolute monarch."[90] While this goal may well have caused Speusippus to write the *Letter*, Aristotle to teach Alexander, and Xenocrates to write a treatise on kingship for the young man,[91] it does not explain why (1) Plato founded the Academy, (2) taught youngsters for free in it, (3) wrote his dialogues, (4) set all of them except *Laws-Epinomis* in democratic Athens, (5) made democracy—despite its obvious faults and weaknesses—preferable to tyranny, (6) referred to the democratic city as "a bazaar of constitutions" and thus the one in which it was appropriate investigate πολιτεία (R. 557c11–d8),[92] and (7) finally preserved for posterity in his *Letters* the embarrassing story of his abject failure to convert a king to Philosophy.[93]

Plato died in 347, and Speusippus writes to Philip in the more immediate context of Isocrates' *To Philip* (346), the most important text mentioned in the *Letter* and the only one that survives intact.[94] As already mentioned, the *Letter* also presupposes the information contained in Plato's *Fifth Letter*, to which it gave a far-fetched twist that Bernays found useful, ignoring the fact that if relations between the Academy and Macedon had been continuously friendly beginning in Plato's time, there would have been no reason for Speusippus to improve or repair them. A third text initially made it conceivable that the *Letter*, alone among the so-called *Socratic Letters* was authentic: in the course of trashing Plato—as he was wont to do,⁹⁵ here for being malicious—Athenaeus (second century AD), quoted a passage from it in his *Sophists at Dinner* that Carystius of Pergamum (second century BC) had cited in a work now lost:

> So too his *Crito* contains an attack on Crito himself, while his *Republic* attacks Sophocles, and his *Gorgias* attacks not just the man who gave the work its title, bit also the Macedonian king Archelaus, who is said not only to be from a quite unsavory family, but to have killed his master. And this is the Plato who, Speusippus claims, was Philip's good friend and was responsible for him becoming king! Carystius of Pergamum, at any rate, writes as follows in his *Historical Commentary*: "When Speusippus heard that Philip was making hostile comments about Plato, he wrote something along the following lines in the letter."⁹⁶

Apart from the fact that the *Letter* attributes these hostile comments to Theopompus, not Philip,⁹⁷ the summary of its argument that follows in Athenaeus is accurate. Finally, an accumulation of details in the *Letter* has allowed scholars to carry on a fact-based debate as to whether it was written in 343 or 342.

Before turning to the *Letter* itself, two observations about Athenaeus and Isocrates are in order, both recalling the earlier discussion of Bernays. With regard to the passage just quoted, it was a critic of Bernays who cited the passage from *Gorgias* to refute the claim that Plato was pro-Macedonian,⁹⁸ and like Athenaeus, Bernays took Speusippus' argument in the *Letter* to be historically accurate.⁹⁹ The result was paradoxical: the same Plato who had insulted the Macedonian monarchy had been responsible and had taken credit for making Philip its King.¹⁰⁰ For Athenaeus, the discrepancy between the passage Bernays takes seriously and the other one that his critics threw in his face, can be explained by Plato's malevolent hypocrisy. Instead of regarding Speusippus' claims as farcical, as defenders of the *Letter*'s authenticity do as well,¹⁰¹ both Athenaeus and Bernays have bad reasons for taking them seriously, the one to prove Plato's hypocrisy, the other his pro-Macedonian political orientation. Naturally my approach takes a different approach to this very real discrepancy, and explains it in relation to "the end of the Old Academy." While the earlier passage from *Gorgias* tells against Plato's affection for Macedon, his successor's *Letter* proves his, thus using chronology to mark a political divide.

And then there's Isocrates, whose dream of uniting Greece against Persia was first announced in his *Panegyricus* (c. 380).¹⁰² In this brilliant text, Isocrates imagined that Athens and Sparta would lead Hellas away from intercity strife to everlasting glory. Now a much older man—he was ninety in 346—Isocrates' dream remains the same, but his last best hope for realizing it has shifted from his native Athens to Macedon, and since Philip's son would finally realize Isocrates' dream, the dreamer must be regarded as prescient if not patriotic. But even if only on the basis of the widely recognized rivalry between two great Athenian schoolteachers—and appreciating the *Letter* depends on this recognition[103]—neither Isocrates nor his dream should be considered Platonic. Once again, Bernays helps us to see things more clearly despite himself: the far more easily documented intellectual impetus behind a World State with the King of Macedon at its top was the school of Isocrates, not the Academy. On the other hand, my purpose is to render this last use of "the Academy" problematic, and it is yet another mark of the end of "the Old Academy" that the immediate context of the *Letter* is that it was Isocrates' *To Philip*, not Plato's *Gorgias*, that had recently been read aloud, discussed, praised, and criticized in the Academy under Speusippus.

Isocrates' text is, however, definitely worthy of criticism, and thanks to its introduction, it gets off to a terrible start. When Isocrates announces in its opening sentence that he expects Philip to be *surprised* that *To Philip* begins with a discourse that is not addressed to him, he probably expected to be praised for this witty example of deliberate self-contradiction; he should have realized that the addressee would be irritated thereby. Assured by the praise of those who have already heard it (Isocrates, 5.4), Isocrates explains the gist of an earlier discourse as if the approbation of a few Athenian flatterers, most likely his own students, would warrant a positive reaction from Philip. Although his goal was to illustrate his neutrality in the war, just terminated by the Peace of Philocrates (346), Isocrates succeeds only in irritating both sides, and at least in comparison with Plato's Socrates, he is unable to prompt another "to reconsider and fight against one's previous opinion [γνωσιμαχεῖν]" (Isocrates, 5.7). But he loves a paradox, and attaches the introduction (Isocrates, 5.1–7) in order to preserve the following one: in the war just ended, you and the Athenians have been fighting "over Amphipolis" (Isocrates, 5.1), the possession of which would be bad for them; thus giving it back to them would be good for you. In short, by giving Amphipolis back to the Athenians, Philip will be benefiting Macedon and harming them. Only someone infatuated with his own wit could have imagined success in this enterprise: Isocrates was telling the victor to return a strategically and economically important city he had just won on the grounds that by doing so, he would at once secure the good will and friendship of the city he had just beaten while at the same time putting it in a bad strategic situation.

Amphipolis was not just any city. Occupying a bend in the Strymon, the widest river in Greece, and thus having the mighty river on both sides of it, the city linked the forests and goldmines upstream to the sea. Pending the return of Xerxes' millions who were thirsty and numerous enough to drink rivers dry,[104] the Strymon prevented western powers like Thessaly and Macedon from reaching the Chersonese, and an invasion from the Asian east from reaching the three fingers of Chalcidice. An Athenian colony established before the Peloponnesian War, Amphipolis not only would play an outsize role in the history of Athens—Socrates fought there, for example (*Ap.* 28e2)—but had in a way created it: Thucydides found the time to write his *History* because the Spartan general Brasidas captured the city in a surprise attack (winter 424) while the son of Olorus was one of two generals in the vicinity responsible for its safety.[105] This passage is an important one not only because Thucydides' readers would naturally be interested in the cause of his exile but also because he took advantage of the fact that the foolish hopes that the Spartan capture of Amphipolis inspired the inhabitants of other cities and northern islands to revolt from Athens:

> For doing so even seemed unhazardous to them, at once deceived about the scope of the Athenian task force that later appeared, as well as relying for the most part on indistinct wishing [βούλησις ἀσαφής] rather than mistake-avoiding foresight [προνοία ἀσφαλής], accustomed as human beings are not only to give themselves up to hope without perspective [ἐλπὶς ἀπερίσκεπτος] for the things they desire but to push aside with sovereign reasoning [λογισμὸς αὐτοκράτωρ] what they don't want.[106]

Between Thucydides and Amphipolis, this is a good place to begin shifting the focus back to Demosthenes. The author of *Lives of the Ten Orators* joined Thucydides to Plato as important influences on the young Demosthenes (see preface), and one could succinctly encapsulate Demosthenes' ongoing political project by contrasting the βούλησις ἀσαφής and ἐλπὶς ἀπερίσκεπτος of the Athenian Assembly with his own προνοία ἀσφαλής and λογισμὸς αὐτοκράτωρ. Zosimus reported that Demosthenes could recite all of Thucydides by heart,[107] and Lucian preserves a story that he copied out Thucydides eight times,[108] but even if he didn't and couldn't, no student of Plato's dialogues can understand half of them without a thorough knowledge of the *History*.[109] Demosthenes was particularly well aware of the importance of Amphipolis, which Philip seized—while initially promising to return it—in 358.[110] Philip didn't return it, of course, and between 356 and 346, there was an undeclared or phony "Amphipolitan War" which Athens lost,[111] and it was during it that Demosthenes stepped up to the podium (the Greek βῆμα) and first became famous for his orations calling for the Athenians to put aside ἐλπὶς ἀπερίσκεπτος and face the fact, endorsed by sovereign reasoning, that Philip was their enemy. But as the opening of the *First Olynthian* makes clear—and in all but one ancient manuscript and in all modern editions, this speech stands first—it is not so much reasoning or foresight that he requires to set his audience straight in 348 but simply their memory of Amphipolis:

> For if, when we had come to the aid of the Euboeans, and the Amphipolitan ambassadors were here on this very βῆμα, telling us to sail and take the city in hand, if we had demonstrated the same eagerness on our own behalf that we did for the sake of Euboea's safety, we would then have held onto Amphipolis, and you would have avoided all the troubles that came afterwards.[112]

Two years later (346), Demosthenes was the youngest of the ambassadors Athens sent north to negotiate a peace and possible alliance with Philip, and although it looks in retrospect like Demosthenes was himself unduly guided by ἐλπὶς ἀπερίσκεπτος, he undertook to gain the same result that Isocrates would still be seeking even after the Peace of Philocrates had ratified Macedonian control of Amphipolis. His enemy and fellow ambassador Aeschines tells us that on the way to Pella, Demosthenes boasted that he could make a compelling case for the return of Amphipolis—one that would "sew Philip's mouth shut" (*On the Embassy*, 2.21)—and he also reported to the Athenians after the embassy had returned that Demosthenes, who had spoken last in Philip's presence, had spoken in defense of Athens' claim to the city between the Strymon (*On the Embassy*, 2.48). What happened in between these two events is the basis for one of the most interesting historical or rather historiographical puzzles arising from an ancient text, for in his defense speech *On the Embassy*, spoken last in his trial of 343, Aeschines told the jury not only that he had already made an eloquent speech proving Athens' right to Amphipolis (*On the Embassy*, 2.25–33) but that when it was Demosthenes' turn to speak last, "he suddenly stopped speaking and stood helpless" after uttering a lame exordium or proem (*On the Embassy*, 2.34). Aeschines also tells us that Philip, while charitable to the tongue-tied orator (*On the Embassy*, 2.35), had rejected the claims of Aeschines point by point while not even mentioning Demosthenes (*On the Embassy*, 2.38), and finally that on the way back to Athens, Demosthenes offered a counterpoint to his boasting on the way up: "And he begged me [sc. Aeschines] earnestly not to fail to tell how Demosthenes also said something in support of our claim to Amphipolis" (*On the Embassy*, 2.43). As already mentioned, Aeschines confirms that he did so (*On the Embassy*, 2.48)

Before sorting out the resulting historiographical puzzle, it is necessary to explain the connection between all this discussion of Amphipolis and the *Letter of Speusippus*. This is easily done: Speusippus not only attacks Isocrates for what he had said about Amphipolis in the introduction of *To Philip* but devotes the bulk of his papyrus to a defense of Philip's absolute and incontestable right to the city, based on Heracles.[113] This (1) odious defense of Philip's interests dovetails with the *Letter*'s two other goals: (2) to introduce a young historian named Antipater of Magnesia, who is the source for the mythic and historical defense of Macedon's irrefragable claim to Amphipolis, and more importantly, (3) to prove that instead of listening to Isocrates and believing the slanders of his student Theopompus against Plato, Philip should honor the Academy's founder as having "laid the foundation for your rule during the reign of Perdiccas,"[114] and welcome the support of his successor, now writing him this useful letter. To integrate the foregoing, we have four speeches about Amphipolis to consider: (i) Isocrates' call for Philip to return it to Athens in *To Philip* for the sake of a higher goal; (ii) the mythological argument now retailed to Philip by Speusippus, asserting his right to the city on the basis of Heracles; (iii) Aeschines' speech, reported by him in detail, which found a mythological basis for Athens' right to Amphipolis in Acamas, son of Theseus; and finally—and ostensibly the least important of the four—(iv) Demosthenes' failed speech on Athens' right to Amphipolis about which Aeschines only allows us to know (a) that it was never delivered, (b) that Demosthenes had boasted earlier that it would make the Athenian case irrefragable, and (c) that in accordance with Demosthenes' entreaties, he had told the Athenians that Demosthenes had spoken in defense of the Athenian claim.

From the foregoing complexities, it should at least be clear that the *Letter* was not only pro-Macedonian but also anti-Athenian: although not to the extent that Demosthenes boasted his speech would be or that Aeschines claimed that his was, Isocrates' *To Philip* looks patriotic in comparison.[115] Of the *Letter*'s three purposes, the first two have an obvious connection to the First Embassy of 346 and thus whatever Aeschines and Demosthenes said or didn't say about Athens' claim to Amphipolis. Only its third is relevant to the Academy, and it is in considering the specific circumstances of this third purpose that Natoli takes a false step. Our difference relates to the following passage from Diogenes Laertius' *Life of Plato*:

> He [sc. Plato] died, in the manner we have related, in the thirteenth year of Philip's reign [347-346], as Favorinus says in the third book of his reminiscences. Theopompus says that Plato was accorded honors [ἐπιτιμηθῆναι] by Philip.[116]

Going against the majority of scholarly opinion,[117] Natoli takes the verb ἐπιτιμηθῆναι to mean that Philip took the opportunity of Plato's death to punish him—a common enough use of the verb ἐπιτιμᾶν, especially in Demosthenes—rather than the more plausible "to award him due honor" in the positive sense.[118] Since the occasion of the *Letter* is that either Philip (in Carystius as cited by Athenaeus) or Theopompus (in the *Letter* itself) has been slandering Philip, and since we know that Theopompus wrote a book attacking Plato, Natoli's is a rather elegant solution, as one would expect from his excellent book. But not only is it possible that Theopompus could both attack Plato and claim that Philip had honored him in the same book but it also seems unlikely that Diogenes would use the beginning of Philip's reign to date Plato's death and then go on to cite evidence that Philip took the opportunity to dishonor him, the kind of tasteless thing that Aeschines tells us that Demosthenes did when Philip died.[119]

If Philip had honored Plato in 347, and was either himself slandering Plato or listening to Theopompus do so before Speusippus wrote the *Letter* in 343–342—so let's say this slandering took place in 343—what explains Philip's change of mind in the interval?[120] It is true that Isocrates had belittled not only popular orators who address their speeches to the Assembly—as of course Demosthenes did and indeed was doing at the time— along with those equally ineffectual kinds of discourses that touch upon "the laws [οἱ νόμοι] and the polities [αἱ πολιτεῖαι] which have been written by the sophists."[121] Speusippus reasonably takes this to be an attack on Plato. But this can't be what caused Philip to change his mind, indeed it is more likely that it was his awareness of Philip's growing distaste for Plato that led Isocrates to dismiss Plato's writings (and of course Νόμοι has often been called the last of these) in *To Philip*, and possibly to write it in the first place (it was the first time he addressed Philip but it would not be the last).[122] Remarkably, the three other possible explanations for this change—a change, I must emphasize, that Natoli sees no reason to explain thanks to his reading of ἐπιτιμηθῆναι—involve Demosthenes.

The first does so only indirectly. In the *Third Philippic* (341), Demosthenes tells us that Euphraeus died combatting Philip's schemes in Euboea (9.59-62); according to Athenaeus, Carystius claimed that Philip so hated Euphraeus that he had him murdered in 342.[123] Demosthenes naturally lionizes Euphraeus for much the same reason that Philip had him murdered, and if both had attended the Academy, Demosthenes had an even stronger motive for doing so, perhaps audible when, after mentioning that Euphraeus, "having lived among us here at one time," fought with Philip's agents for the sake of his countrymen "in order that they will be free and slaves of nobody" (9.59); he concludes the tale with: "this Euphraeus slaughtered himself, having given witness in deed that both justly and purely on behalf of his fellow citizens he had opposed Philip" (9.62). To begin with, the fact that this Euphraeus was the Academy's link to Macedon through Perdiccas and Plato's *Fifth Letter*,[124] combined with the fact that he later emerged as a resolute Philip-hater, might easily have prompted Philip's suspicions of the Academy, and a speech mentioned in *Sophists at Dinner* by Demosthenes' nephew Demochares in 306—more on this speech in the next chapter—may point to an earlier cause of Philip's contempt for Euphraeus on the basis of his ostentatious Platonizing in the court of Perdiccas.[125] But the *Letter* makes it unlikely that Euphraeus could have been the cause of Philip's recent hostility toward Plato: since Speusippus' purpose was to improve relations between Philip and the Academy, it would have been counter-productive for him to give Euphraeus the prominent role that he does if Philip already hated Euphraeus in 343.[126]

But since this chapter is devoted to "the end of the Old Academy," it will not be out of place to consider the last actions of Euphraeus, a freedom-loving patriot as described by Demosthenes, with those of the youngster Plato had introduced to Perdiccas years before, and if possible to contrast that development with two other phenomena: why Isocrates believed the speeches of Demosthenes and the discourses of Plato were equally "useless [ἄκυροι],"[127] and why Speusippus is now attempting to ingratiate himself with Philip. In the context of the Third Wave of Paradox, it is initially tempting to split the young Euphraeus from the old one since the first would be helping a king become a philosopher while the other would lead the anti-Philip resistance in Oreus. But in comparison with both Isocrates and Speusippus, this contrast loses its sharpness: the latter are both unquestionably ingratiating themselves with a king but not for the sake of philosophy; the one aims for the good of his school, the other for the realization of his cherished dream. The reason Isocrates regards the speeches of Plato and Demosthenes as equally ἄκυροι is precisely because they are not addressed to a single man with real power:

> Nevertheless, disregarding all these difficulties, I have become so ambitious in my old age that I have determined by addressing my discourse to you [sc. Philip] at the same time to set an example to my disciples and make it evident to them that to burden our national assemblies with oratory and to address all the people who there throng together is, in reality, to address no one at all; that such speeches are quite as ineffectual [ἄκυροι] as the legal codes [οἱ νόμοι] and the constitutions [αἱ πολιτεῖαι] drawn up by the sophists; and, finally, that those who desire, not to chatter empty nonsense, but to further some practical purpose, and those who think they have hit upon some plan for the common good, must leave it to others to harangue at the public festivals, but must themselves win over someone to champion their cause from among men who are capable not only of speech but of action and who occupy a high position in the world—if, that is to say, they are to command any attention.[128]

It is Isocrates, not Plato, who validates the theories of Bernays. As for Euphraeus, how did he learn to hate Philip's tyranny if not from a combination of what he learned at the Academy and what he experienced in Macedon?[129] Of course Euphraeus the philosopher did not become a king, but he stood up to one, and died opposing him. I regard Euphraeus' life and death as a product of "the Old Academy," Speusippus' *Letter* as a sign of its end.

And the same applies to Demosthenes. Unlike Euphraeus, Demosthenes has not simply "dwelt among us for a time" (9.59), but their goal remains the same: to see to it that their countrymen will remain free and be nobody's slaves. Thanks to Philip, opposed by Demosthenes and flattered by both Isocrates and Speusippus, it becomes possible—on the hypothesis that like Euphraeus (*Ep.* 321c2–322c1), Demosthenes was Plato's student—to separate "the Old Academy" from the one that Speusippus was now leading. And that's not all: thanks to Amphipolis, it is possible to make the contrast even more concrete. If not at Pella during the First Embassy, then elsewhere, repeatedly and eloquently, Demosthenes opposed Philip's seizure of Amphipolis whereas Speusippus contrives to defend Philip's historical right to it. Despite the quarrel with Isocrates, Speusippus is far closer to him than he is to either Euphraeus or Demosthenes, and the point of this book is to learn something about Plato by situating him in relation to this comparative proximity. Despite his contempt for the discourses of the likes of Plato and the speeches of the likes of Demosthenes, Isocrates is an Athenian patriot compared with Speusippus, and it is precisely this fact—which not only made it impossible for Isocrates to assert Philip's right to keep Amphipolis but caused him to recommend returning it—that created an opening for Speusippus to win a race to the bottom.

Having drawn some lessons from Euphraeus in the context of ruling him out as the cause of Philip's change of heart between 347 and 343, it is time to return to the fact of that change, and it is at the intersection of that fact with the absence of a better explanation for it, that the best evidence for what I have called "the first suppression," here in its infancy, can be found. In other words, Philip's discovery that Demosthenes, his foremost detractor in Athens, had been Plato's student, would sufficiently explain his recent hostility to Plato post-mortem, and his willingness to listen to his detractors. Since Demosthenes had delivered his *First Philippic* in 352–351, and the three *Olynthians* in 348, Philip might well have heard of the up-and-coming orator—thirty-seven at the time of Plato's death—long before meeting him in 346, when the First Embassy arrived in Pella. But even if Demosthenes' reputation for anti-Macedonian eloquence proceeded him, it was in 346 that Philip had the best opportunity to discover Demosthenes' connection with the

Academy either first hand or through the other Athenian ambassadors, including Aeschines. And with that possibility, it is finally time to return to the great historiographical puzzle of Demosthenes' speech to Philip during the First Embassy, for which Aeschines is our only source.

Beginning in antiquity, Aeschines' account has most often been believed, and the modern sensibility that professes objectivity on the basis of the principle that "the truth must lie somewhere in between" will necessarily—in the absence of Demosthenes' side of the story—give credit to the lies of his enemy.[130] Quite apart from his alleged affiliation with the Academy, Demosthenes *is* his side of the story, and if he ever responded to Aeschines' account of the First Embassy, those who selected which of his speeches would survive made a wise choice by not including it: only in its absence could they ensure that their students would need to recognize Demosthenes' greatness on their own, for they would now be forced to regard Aeschines as a liar, as Plutarch did in antiquity,[131] and as Schaefer would do in modern times.[132] Demosthenes had faced the raucous Assembly and shouted down the sea (see the cover illustration); he did not falter in the presence of Philip. According to Demosthenes, Aeschines would henceforth be Philip's agent in Athens while Demosthenes had been and would remain his foe. And it is between Aeschines' detailed account of what he had said about recent events in his own speech in comparison with his passing reference to ancient history, that we can perhaps get some idea of what Demosthenes had actually said in his:

> As proof of all my statements, I offered the letters of the persons in question, the decrees of the people, and Callisthenes' treaty of truce. Now the facts about our original acquisition both of the district and of the place [περὶ μὲν οὖν τῆς ἐξ ἀρχῆς κτήσεως τῆς χώρας] called Ennea Hodoi ["('Nine Roads') was the old name of the place colonized by the Athenians in 436 under the name of Amphipolis"] and the story of the sons of Theseus, one of whom, Acamas, is said to have received this district as the dowry of his wife—all this was fitting to the occasion then, and was given with the utmost exactness, but now I suppose I must be brief; but those proofs which rested, not on the ancient legends [ἐν τοῖς ἀρχαίοις μύθοις], but on occurrences of our own time, these also I called to mind.[133]

From our modern perspective, an argument that used myth to trump Philip's right of conquest and possession must be regarded as ineffective and even farcical.[134] The *Letter* shows that this perspective is anachronistic: Speusippus clearly expected Philip to be grateful for the mythological account, now creatively presented to him by Antipater of Magnesia, that tied Macedon's legal and historical claim to Amphipolis to Heracles, who preceded in time, and surpassed in authority, the Athenian Acamas, son of Theseus. I am suggesting, then, that the speech about which Demosthenes boasted on the way to Pella and the one he actually gave there—the speech that provoked the response from Philip that Plutarch described or imagined—was anchored ἐν τοῖς ἀρχαίοις μύθοις, and that its topic was περὶ τῆς ἐξ ἀρχῆς κτήσεως τῆς τῶν καλουμένων Ἐννέα ὁδῶν, i.e., "concerning our ancient founding of Amphipolis." In the *Funeral Oration* he delivered after Chaeronea, Demosthenes revealed himself to be an adept mythologist, and spoke in glowing terms of this same Acamas who faced death for the sake of his mother (60.29),[135] just as Xenophon tells that Antilochus won fame for being willing "to die and behalf of [ὑπεραποθνῄσκειν]" his father.[136] Despite the tenuous thread that must inevitably tie all such speculations together, this one has the merit of solving two problems at once, explaining why Philip had turned against the Academy, and what Demosthenes really said in Pella. The hypothesis on offer here is that it was because Philip discovered that Demosthenes had been Plato's student after his myth-based speech in Pella that Speusippus now needed to use an alternative and Macedon-friendly account of the founding of Amphipolis in order to regain the king's sympathy for the Academy, or rather, for him. Above all, he needed to suppress—for the sake of the Academy's reputation and of course his own—that the eloquent and Philip-hating Demosthenes had been Plato's student.

It was never going to be possible to prove that Demosthenes was Plato's student on the basis of some "new" ancient testimony to that effect on "the first track." The case is necessarily a circumstantial one, and in the following chapter, the relevant circumstances are five others who, like Euphraeus, were said to be Plato's students. Before considering Demosthenes himself in chapter 4, chapter 3 will follow "the second track" in order to illuminate aspects of Plato's dialogues that tend to strengthen the circumstantial case that Demosthenes had read, learned from, and been inspired by them. While remaining on "the first track," the chapter now ending also implicates "the third," and what this means must be clearly understood before closing. If the *Letter of Speusippus* accurately reflects the Old Academy's attitude toward Philip, it is very unlikely that Demosthenes was Plato's student, and in the theories of Bernays, we have found a conception of the Academy that justifies this conclusion. But in juxtaposing Bernays with the opposition his *Phokion* generated, a way of distinguishing Speusippus not only from Phocion, but from other students of Plato, has been introduced: a spiritual difference with a clear-cut and plausible chronological basis, that indicates "the end of the Old Academy." Euphraeus, a well-attested anti-Philip Academic, points in this direction, and prepares the way for recognizing in Demosthenes the archetype of this combination, and thus antithetical to the Academy under Speusippus. In this light, acknowledging that Demosthenes had been Plato's student was inconvenient for Speusippus even before Chaeronea, and would became impossible for his followers after it. Finally, the "new ancient evidence" that Demosthenes really was Plato's student is that it is this hypothesis that best explains what Speusippus found it convenient to say in the *Letter*, and the fact that he needed to say it in 343.

2

Five Other Students of Plato

Considering that three of the five—Aeschines, Hyperides, and Lycurgus—are included among "the Ten Attic Orators," Demosthenes is arguably this chapter's subject despite his titular absence from it, for he is the crown of that canonical list and the probable final cause of its creation. Here it is useful to recall the perspective of Pernot, and as measured by the number of devotees each attracted in antiquity, Rhetoric was victorious in its quarrel with Philosophy. It was Rhetoric's victory that enshrined Demosthenes to such an extent that it immortalized his predecessors, colleagues, and even his enemies, without all of whom his speeches could not be fully appreciated. And without appreciating them, it was believed, one could never become eloquent. Lucian parodied the lazy students (and their useless teachers) who sought to avoid the study that an appreciation of Demosthenes required, including, as already indicated, a considerable knowledge of History. Much of our knowledge of the fourth-century depends on Demosthenes' speeches and the supporting material that allowed students of Rhetoric to appreciate them. Meanwhile, a preliminary discussion of *The Life of Phocion* has already indicated how closely Plutarch connected Phocion with Demosthenes, and the brute though seldom emphasized fact of "384–322"[1] is sufficient to connect him with Aristotle quite apart from the quotations from his speeches found in the *Rhetoric*,[2] and the possibility that he too was Plato's student.

But Aeschines remains the most obvious case: he survives because of Demosthenes and for no other reason. This is easily explained. In an anonymous *Life of Aeschines*, we are told that when he read aloud his speech *Against Ctesiphon*, his auditors expressed disbelief that he could possibly have lost the case; he replied: "because you didn't hear that beast."³ From Homer and Hesiod to Aeschylus and Euripides in the *Frogs* of Aristophanes, it is the contest or ἀγών that repeatedly characterizes Greek Literature if only because a lively competition readily captures the attention of those who would be required to study it. All three of his surviving speeches range him against Demosthenes,⁴ and he was the winner in all but the final contest. But there are other benefits. As indicated in the previous chapter, Demosthenes can't be appreciated without Aeschines and that not only in the obvious way. Quite apart from the historical background his speeches illuminated and the incentives to excellence they offered, even his lies about Demosthenes are necessary for understanding him. So too with the information, likewise found in the anonymous *Life of Aeschines*, that he too was Plato's student,⁵ and the important point is that whether this is true or false, nobody would have claimed that he was if it were not for Demosthenes. In short: everything we know of Aeschines, whether it be true in a historical sense or not, has been preserved for the sake of better understanding the great orator who competed with and surpassed him.

Before considering the source of the claim that Aeschines studied with Plato, it is first useful to consider the evidence Aeschines himself provides on the question. In his speech *Against Timarchus*, a preemptive assault that allowed him to avoid the attack from Demosthenes that would have followed,⁶ he describes his enemy as a hunter of young men (*Against Timarchus*, 1.170) to whom Demosthenes made extravagant promises, and he validates the charge with a list of others he had taught, "having filled them with empty hopes, that straightaway, yes, foremost among the orators would they stand" (*Against Timarchus*, 1.171). In fact, claims Aeschines, while pretending to be a young man's lover and having summoned him to benevolent intimacy, Demosthenes was actually a teacher of evil deeds, and caused his disciple to first mutilate—by cutting off his tongue (a fate that would actually befall Hyperides)—and then to kill one of Demosthenes' detractors, a friend of Meidias (*Against Timarchus*, 1.172).⁷ It is after this grim description that Aeschines compares Demosthenes to Socrates:

> Did you put to death Socrates the sophist [ὁ σοφιστής], fellow citizens, because he was shown to have been the teacher of Critias, one of the Thirty who put down the democracy [δῆμος], and after that, shall Demosthenes succeed in snatching companions [ἑταῖροι] of his own out of your hands, Demosthenes, who takes such vengeance on private citizens and friends of the people [δημοτικοί] for their freedom of speech? At his invitation some of his pupils [τινὲς τῶν μαθητῶν] have come to the lecture [ἐπὶ τὴν ἀκρόασιν]. (1.73 (Adams translation modified))

Like Socrates, Demosthenes too has ἑταῖροι, and τινὲς τῶν μαθητῶν are in attendance in 346–345 just as Plato and others (*Ap.* 33e7–34a2) were in court fifty-three years earlier. But by referring to the crimes of Critias against the δῆμος and those of Demosthenes against the δημοτικοί, Aeschines manages to compare him not only to Socrates the corruptor of youth but to Plato, presumably the most corrupt of his students.

With respect to Aeschines, the relevant question arising from this passage is whether it could possibly have been spoken by one of Plato's students. But it also raises the parallel question about Demosthenes, and on its basis, there is more reason to find an imitator of Plato in Demosthenes than in Aeschines. Calling Socrates ὁ σοφιστής scarcely seems Platonic,[8] and the way Aeschines blames Socrates for Critias suggests the influence of Polycrates rather than Socratics like Xenophon and Plato.[9] But with respect to Demosthenes, the situation is reversed. To begin with, Aeschines is comparing him with Socrates as if that were a bad thing.[10] But he is also comparing him with Plato, and that in a double sense. First of all, both are schoolteachers, and both are teaching young men subjects that might well make them "foremost among the orators." We don't normally imagine "Demosthenes the Teacher" but Aeschines helps us to do so, indeed he suggests that he is presently performing for his students: "For he is promising them, while at your expense doing deals for himself as I am discovering, to escape your notice, having diverted the contest and your attention [μεταλλάξας τὸν ἀγῶνα καὶ τὴν ὑμετέραν ἀκρόασιν]."[11] Exactly as if the indictment of Timarchus for lewd sexual practices were not Aeschines' own attempt to divert the jury's attention from the Peace of Philocrates and "the false embassy" that led to it,[12] Aeschines has managed to compare Demosthenes to both "Plato the Teacher" and Socrates ὁ σοφιστής:

> By no means provide this sophist [ὁ σοφιστής] with laughter and tuition [διατριβή] at your expense, but undertake to see him when he gets home from the courtroom, affecting to put on a grave and solemn air [σεμνυνόμενος] in his school of youngsters [ἐν τῇ τῶν μειρακίων διατριβῇ], and telling how successfully he stole the case away from the jury.[13]

As difficult to imagine that the scene Aeschines is asking us to imagine could have Demosthenes as its central figure, it is even more difficult to imagine Socrates in this role, and the parallel between them depends on the reappearance of ὁ σοφιστής.[14] But what are we to say about Plato? Those who reject the notion that Demosthenes could have been imitating Plato by teaching adolescents rhetoric in his own school—and this passage in Aeschines constitutes our only evidence that he did so— might want to consider the fact, to receive further attention later, that the first subject Aristotle taught on his own in the Academy was likewise rhetoric.¹⁵ There is also an interesting parallel between Aristotle and Aeschines, arising from the interesting fact that three of the ancient biographies of Aristotle make the same impossible claim—that he was first taught by Socrates and then by Plato¹⁶—that we find in this passage from the anonymous *Life of Aeschines*:

> That he became a student [μαθητής], as, on the one hand, Demetrius of Phaleron says of Socrates the philosopher [ὁ φιλόσοφος] and later of Plato, as, on the other, Caecilius and Idomenaeus and Hermippus report, he heard those men not for the sake of learning [μάθησις]. For they say that he preserves nothing of the Platonic character.¹⁷

Here, for a change, I get the chance to play at source criticism, a task made possible—as in the parallel case of Demosthenes albeit *mutatis mutandis*—because I find in *Against Timarchus* compelling evidence that Aeschines was neither the student of Plato nor Plato's Socrates, because if he had been, it is unlikely that he would have referred to Socrates as ὁ σοφιστής but rather as ὁ φιλόσοφος.

So here's how the game can be played to the advantage of Demosthenes for a change: To begin with, on the basis of the same error in the case of Aristotle's biographies, let's dispense with the common dodge that "Socrates" is the corruption of an original "Isocrates."¹⁸ In chronological order, the three sources who regard Aeschines as a bad student of Socrates and Plato are Idomenaeus,¹⁹ Hermippus, and Caecilius,²⁰ so the last two can be ignored making the former the inventor of a way to preserve the fact to which Demetrius of Phaleron testified while undermining its interpretive value. As a result, even though Idomenaeus, author of *On the Followers of Socrates*, is early (c. 325–c. 270) compared to Hermippus and Caecilius, he depends upon the even earlier Demetrius (born c. 350).²¹ The following parallel seems important: while Demetrius is identified in The *Oxford Classical Dictionary* as an "Athenian Peripatetic philosopher (pupil of Theophrastus) and statesman,"²² the same source makes this piquant observation about the author of *On the Followers of Socrates*: "Following the Peripatetic anecdotal method, Idomenaeus reproduced unreliable scandal."²³ In short, by creating the fanciful image of Aeschines as a bad student, Idomenaeus upheld the veracity of Demetrius, the inventor of (what I regard as) the fiction that Aeschines had been Plato's student.

Why did Demetrius of Phaleron do this? As already indicated, his reason for doing so cannot be separated from Demosthenes, and indeed I consider his false claim that Aeschines was Plato's student to be the earliest evidence—apart from the life and writings of Demosthenes himself, that is, and the passages from Aeschines already considered above—that Demosthenes was. Consider the passage from Plutarch's *Life of Demosthenes* that introduces the stories everybody knows: "For his bodily deficiencies he adopted the exercises which I shall describe, as Demetrius of Phaleron tells us, who says he heard about them from Demosthenes himself, now grown old."[24] Fritz Wehrli, who identifies this passage as fragment (fr. 166) of Demetrius, rightly rejects this claim of autopsy[25]; when considering Demetrius' claim that Aeschines was Plato's student (fr. 171) in the same work, the fact that no source is named for it is the basis on which Wehrli suggests that it too is false.[26] But Wehrli does shed some light on the motives of Demetrius when he identifies him as the source for the story in Photius that Demosthenes' teacher in the all-important subject of delivery was an actor (fr. 164) to which I would add the parallel story about the guidance Demosthenes received from Satyrus in Plutarch.[27] On the surface, then, by identifying Plato as the teacher of Aeschines, Demetrius made him more respectable than Demosthenes, at least for those who had forgotten that Aeschines was himself an actor. But Demetrius knew the truth: he attacks both Demosthenes (fr. 163) and Plato (fr. 170) on the same grounds.[28]

As his inclusion in Wehrli's series on *Die Schule des Aristoteles* indicates, Demetrius of Phaleron was a Peripatetic,[29] a student of Theophrastus, who provided Cicero with the opportunity to raise an important question: "Who can readily be found, except this man, that excelled in both careers, so as to be foremost both in the pursuit of learning and in the actual government?"[30] Styled by Lara O'Sullivan as "a philosopher in politics,"[31] and I believe self-styled as one—moreover lionized as such by later Peripatetics—Demetrius was also the quisling, appointed by Antipater's son Cassander, who ruled post-democratic Athens for ten years (317–307). Already mentioned (see introduction) as the founder of the school to which Trampedach and Haake belong, Gehrke takes a diachronic approach to this parody of a philosopher-king: he ruled as a practical politician and only later professed to have done so as a philosopher.[32] In any case, it could only have been after the death of Demosthenes that "the Regime of Demetrius of Phaleron" was possible, and this fact was not lost on Demetrius himself. "In the Peripatetic tradition, beginning with Theophrastus, Demosthenes was contrasted unfavorably to his contemporaries and political rivals both in terms of rhetorical skill and political integrity."[33] As Craig Cooper has shown, Demetrius played a major role in defaming Demosthenes, and I am claiming that falsely identifying Plato as the teacher of his enemy Aeschines is a previously unremarked part of that defamatory project.

Cooper's main interest is the contrast between the more natural, factual, and effortless eloquence of Aeschines and Demades as opposed to the laborious artificiality of Demosthenes: Demetrius tells us about such things as the pebbles, the sea, the cave, and the shaved head in order to highlight this invidious comparison.[34] Although this contrast remained important thanks to the primary place of rhetoric in ancient pedagogy, and although it is clearly relevant to Pernot's concerns—dependence on instruction from Plato would reinforce the artificiality of Demosthenes' eloquence—as well as to the contrast between ease and labor in Lucian's *Teacher of Orators*, it is fourth-century history that reveals the impact of these stories on philosophy. Demades, Aeschines, and Demetrius of Phaleron were all pro-Macedonian, and it is this political difference that should be regarded as the root cause of its merely rhetorical ramification, indicated among other things by the fact that Demetrius did not prefer Aeschines to Demosthenes because he regarded the former as self-taught.[35] On the other hand, rhetoric and philosophy begin to merge in another of Cooper's observations, implicating yet another friend of Macedon: "For Peripatetics, like Demetrius of Phaleron, Demosthenes embodied precisely the kind of corruption that Aristotle talked about in his *Rhetoric*."[36]

The remains of Philodemus' treatise *On Rhetoric* allowed Anton-Hermann Chroust to create a compelling account of Aristotle's earliest writing,[37] and as already mentioned in relation to the portrait of "Demosthenes the Teacher" in *Against Timarchus*, the first subject he seems to have taught in the Academy was rhetoric, and he taught it, at least at the start,[38] in relation to his dialogue *Gryllus*. It was already clear from Quintilian that the subject of *Gryllus* was rhetoric and that it had mentioned Isocrates,[39] and Cicero "had insinuated Aristotle started to teach rhetoric only in order to compete with or, perhaps, to outvie Isocrates."[40] Chroust combined this information with what he learned from Philodemus, beginning with Aristotle's words: "It would be a disgrace to keep silent and let Isocrates speak."[41] It is pleasing to imagine, as Chroust does not, Aristotle's *Gryllus* as a dialogue between Xenophon's son, who fell "before Mantineia" in 362, and Isocrates, with the author placing his own criticisms in his dead friend's mouth on the model of Plato's *Gorgias*, where it is of course Socrates who challenges a famous sophist. But Chroust makes a more interesting point when he imagines the debut of young Aristotle in purely Platonic terms:

> This clash between Aristotle and Isocrates, which in all likelihood was the main theme of the Gryllus, might be reduced to a conflict between an uncompromising "principled philosophy" and a less principled "practical philosophy of life" which takes into account worldly success, practical effectiveness, and the general human condition within an existential rather than ideal world.[42]

Aristotle was probably more Aristotelian from the start than Chroust suggests, and the fact that his first dialogue was about rhetoric, the practical value of which "within an existential rather than a real world" is obvious, strengthens this suspicion. Of course I am claiming that Plato was already teaching rhetoric in his dialogues (see preface), and there was a Platonic necessity for him to do so: only when armed with rhetoric could philosophers influence their fellow Cavemen in accordance with the more difficult of the Third Wave's two paths.[43] A passage about Aristotle preserved by Philodemus, who incidentally recorded the fact that Demosthenes "was said to have studied with Plato and Eubulides,"[44] suggests that if the young Aristotle was not already more inclined to follow the easier and royal path, he had already failed to understand the more difficult one:

> He [sc. Aristotle] alleged many reasons for engaging in politics; first, that one who has no knowledge of what is done in government finds them unfriendly to him; secondly, that a good government will be favorable to the growth of philosophy; thirdly, that he was disgusted with most of the contemporary statesmen [οἱ νῦν τὰ πολιτικὰ πραττόντες] and their continual rivalry for office.[45]

If this was not already a rejection of the longer and harder way, Aristotle had clearly rejected it when he offered his treatise *On Kingship* to Alexander,[46] about which Themistius (fourth century AD) wrote in the specific context of the Third Wave:

> Worthy of admiration is Aristotle, who having slightly altered the words of Plato, made the statement [ὁ λόγος, sc. the Third Wave] truer, stating that it is not necessary, but even rather an obstacle, for the king to philosophize, but on happening upon those philosophizing truly, to be easily persuadable and attentive.[47]

This should be considered not one but two steps removed from Plato's position if the Academy's purpose was to persuade young Athenians—like Phocion, Lycurgus, Hyperides, and Demosthenes—to offer a principled but still democratic alternative to οἱ νῦν τὰ πολιτικὰ πραττόντες. If the self-presentation of Demetrius of Phaleron, however fraudulent, remains one step removed, Aristotle's involvement with Hermias of Atarneus and then Alexander of Macedon represent the truer Peripatetic alternative to "the Old Academy," and when Aristotle returned to Athens in 335, well equipped with the necessary funds, this alternative would be embodied in the Lyceum.[48]

Even under Macedonian protection, teaching the superiority of Monarchy in Athens—naturally carefully distinguished from Tyranny—was a tricky business, but Aristotle found a way to do it.[49] But it is difficult to improve on the comparison drawn by Hans Kelsen in 1937, not least of all because he avoids identifying Aristotle and Demosthenes by name:

> Is it possible to mistake the connection between the political attitude of the greatest and most popular orator who, with all the convincing rhetoric at his disposal, hammered into the Greek brain and heart again and again the thesis: royal rule is slavery, only democracy is freedom; and the theory of government of the leading philosopher of the time, who maintained royal rule to be diametrically opposed to a rulership over slaves, the latter to be rather—as all perverted constitutions are—democracy.[50]

Here the reader will recognize this book's epigraph, selected because it perfectly captures the contrast at its center. Unfortunately, however, Kelsen not only fails to connect Demosthenes to Plato, but also to separate Xenocrates from "the Old Academy,"[51] and as a direct result of these linked errors, he mars his otherwise splendid paper with the same claim Bernays had made:

> Not only Aristotle's school of philosophy but also the Platonic Academy was on the side of the Macedonian party. Extremely instructive of the whole situation is the fact that Alexander ordered from Xenocrates, who was at that time the head of the Academy, a work on monarchy, which meant an apology for this constitution. Macedonian imperialism created for itself in Hellas, partly by consciously directed action, partly without effort, an adequate ideology. Not, of course, without exciting a passionate countermovement. The part played by Demosthenes in this opposition is well known.[52]

Naturally Kelsen emphasizes the passage in *Politics* 3.13–14 in which Aristotle writes that "a certain unique and better man" (1283b21–22) at the head of a kingdom he will call "economic" (1285b31–32) or, more economically παμβασιλεία (1285b36), will "likely be as a god among men" (1284a10–11).[53]

Nor were such thoughts confined to theory: the flattery of Isocrates and the foretaste in Philip culminated in Alexander's politic use of apotheosis.[54] When the divine Alexander died in 323, Aristotle was promptly tried for impiety in Athens on the ostensible basis of a poem he had written celebrating the virtue of Hermias,[55] the conceit of which likewise suggested a willingness to blur the distinction between Man and God.[56] Although Jesus made a quick and tortured exit after being crowned with nothing but thorns, the poisonous solution to "the theological-political problem" that had originated in Egypt, reappeared in Augustus via Athens and Alexandria, and would continue to advance the claims of a Kingdom *that was very much of this world* until "the separation of Church and State" emerged as modernity's alternative and liberal solution to what Leo Strauss would call "*the* theme of my investigations."[57] Thanks to the increasing reliance that later Platonists placed on the ὁμοίωσις θεῷ (see introduction), and already partly visible in the Number Theory of Plato's immediate successors, the post-Plato Academy would offer little resistance to the poisonous and self-divinizing solution to the theological-political problem, and even if Callipolis and Magnesia were intended to test the commitment of his best students to a higher and less earthly Ideal, the fact that Plato had dreamed them into theoretical existence could easily tempt others to deny that he had laid the foundations for the modern and secularizing solution to the problem in antiquity (*Prm.* 134d9–e6). But whether as "the separation of the Forms" on a theoretical level, or as a more practical and difficult willingness to sacrifice worldly existence for the sake of what's higher, Platonism—when and wherever it remains worthy of the name—is Philosophy's oldest and most important alternative to Wittgenstein's famous claim: "The world is all that is the case."[58]

A speech by Demosthenes' nephew Demochares marked "the end of the Old Academy," the process that had begun with the *Letter of Speusippus* some thirty-five years earlier.[59] The speech was made possible when Demetrius Poliocetes overthrew the regime of Demetrius of Phaleron and restored the democracy in 307; the Athenians promptly manifested their degeneracy by bestowing divine honors on their liberator.[60] Seeking the cause of the anti-democratic regime among the intellectual elite, Sophocles of Sunium proposed a decree to the effect that all non-authorized schools of Philosophy should be closed,[61] a measure clearly aimed primarily at the Lyceum and its patron Demetrius of Phaleron.[62] After the Assembly carried it, a student of Theophrastus prosecuted Sophocles for proposing an unconstitutional decree, and Demochares defended him with a speech attacking not only the Lyceum but also the Academy, naming Socrates as a feeble soldier, Plato as a teacher of tyrants, and emphasizing Xenocrates[63] (Polemo had been the Academy's head since 316).[64] This is the evidence that allowed Haake to argue for the radical incompatibility of philosophy and politics,[65] making his impressively erudite work not only the successor of Gehrke's *Phokion* but also the dialectical catalyst for an alternative conception of "the Old Academy." Thanks to his unwillingness to question the school's conventional *Platonbild*,[66] Haake made no more distinction between Plato and Xenocrates on the matters that prompted Demochares' attack on "philosophers" than Demochares had done.[67] While it is possible that Demochares was unaware of his uncle Demosthenes' connection with the Academy, he now had good reason to distinguish what it had been then from what it had become, and given the law's true target,[68] no loyalty to the latter for his uncle's sake was now appropriate. The jury convicted Sophocles, the decree became a dead letter, Demochares went into exile, and the shape of Ancient Philosophy was forever changed as a result.[69] Within seven years, two new schools of philosophy would open in Athens, and both the Garden and the Porch offered equally apolitical responses to the challenge of Plato's Cave.[70]

With both now exiled from Athens, Demetrius of Phaleron and Demochares carried on a literary war that implicated Phocion and Demosthenes as their respective champions. Cooper has ably described this war's rhetorical basis, with Demetrius contrasting the artificial and overly verbose Demosthenes against the pruning knife of Phocion's incisive brevity. Laying the foundations for the future quarrel between Attic and Asiatic oratory, Demetrius also added an ethical dimension:

> The impression from these fragments is of a Demetrius hostile to Demosthenes; he had, as we have seen, charged Demosthenes with corruption and cowardice in direct contrast to Phocion, who was the more able and honest orator. And just as Phocion's honesty was reflected in his speech, so Demosthenes' corruption showed through in his oratory; his extravagant delivery was aimed at pandering to a corrupt Athenian audience.[71]

But it would be shortsighted to ignore the more primordial political dimension of the quarrel, and it seems likely that it was with Demochares' attack on Demetrius as a corrupt Macedonian stooge that the quarrel began, and implicated Demosthenes as a result:

> Demades' and Phocion's complicity with the Macedonians would certainly explain Demochares' hostility toward them. It was their complicity that led directly to Athens' loss of freedom and Demosthenes' death.[72]

Demochares is the likely source for juxtaposing the many examples of Demosthenes' previous support for Phocion with the latter's conduct later,[73] when, as Cornelius Nepos puts it: "He [sc. Phocion] not only failed to defend him in dangers but even betrayed him."[74] And without "Pseudo-Plutarch," we would not know that Demochares was responsible for the decree of 280–79 that allowed Demosthenes to return to Athens in bronze.[75]

Cooper claims that "a casualty of this war was Demosthenes' rhetorical reputation,"[76] but the more important casualty was the Old, that is, Plato's Academy. Demetrius had his own motives for making Aeschines Plato's student while Demochares had his for rejecting the possibility that Demosthenes had been[77]; in antiquity's closest anticipation of the modern consensus, neither mentioned the connection (see preface). In turning the page on Demosthenes' enemies, it is important to realize that Phocion, Lycurgus, and Hyperides, despite sharing, as principled Athenian statesman, an affiliation with the Academy, are probably best understood by ranging them on a spectrum, placing Hyperides on one extreme, Phocion on the other, and Demosthenes and Lycurgus between them. Moreover, I am claiming that Plato influenced all four equally, and must therefore be prepared to show how this is so, while at the same time showing why doing this now seems so difficult. Even without a *soupçon* of Bernays, modern scholars can easily embrace Phocion's connection to the Academy thanks to his aristocratic opposition to the δῆμος, while "Demosthenes the Democrat"[78] must represent the elite Academy's vulgar antithesis. The trajectory of this book will have begun to hit its mark if the reader recognizes in this juxtaposition precisely the Peripatetic and pro-Macedonian perspective, a perspective lethal to "the Old Academy."

To recapitulate the argument of chapter 1, the alternative on offer uses a chronological distinction—with a turning-point somewhere between 347 and 338, and most likely midway between them with Speusippus' *Letter to Philip* (343–42)—to recover "the Old Academy." What justified Demochares' attack on the Academy was that the Academy no longer was what Plato had intended it to be: Speusippus had cultivated Philip, Xenocrates advised Alexander, and Polemo seems to have left Athens along with the Lyceum in 307.[79] A similar distinction applies to Phocion. He had made a choice as a young man to be usefully beneficial to his city, and he did so as Plato's student. Athens rewarded him for making this choice by repeatedly electing him general, and calling him "Phocion ὁ χρηστός" an epithet that means something like "usefully beneficial." He never turned aside from trying to be χρηστός, and clearly regarded being so as compatible with the politics of realism—which probably should be distinguished from *Realpolitik*—even when he ran afoul of a fellow Academic:

> And while Lycurgus was saying many slanderous things to him in the Assembly, and above all that, with Alexander demanding ten of the citizens, he counseled surrendering them, he said: "many things have I counseled, beautiful *and* advantageous for them [καλὰ καὶ συμφέροντα τούτοις] but they have not been persuaded by me."[80]

In comparison with giving advice that was advantageous *for him*, a willingness to break with Lycurgus, Hyperides, and Demosthenes by advising the Athenians to do things that, even if they were no longer καλά, were nevertheless συμφέροντα τούτοις, keeps him on what might be called "the Platonic spectrum."

Perhaps the most interesting error Bernays makes in his *Phokion* is that he uses Plutarch's emphasis on Phocion's loyalty to the most notable claim in *Gorgias*—that it is better to suffer an injustice than to do one (hereafter "the [*Gorgias*] Reversal")—to explain why Socrates' loyalty, and by extension, Plato's loyalty and that of his students, could never be to Athens: "The deeper basis upon which Socrates and his authentic students withheld themselves from the practical politics of their cities rested on their conception of Virtue."[81] As already noticed above, Bernays uses the passage in *Republic* 6—translating it with care and eloquence—to justify philosophers avoiding practical politics because to πράττειν τὰ πολιτικά would lead to their deaths before achieving any good thing for themselves or for others; in preference to this, it is therefore best "to do one's own thing [τὰ αὑτοῦ πράττειν]" (R. 496d6). Introducing this passage in the previous chapter, I called attention to what Socrates had said just before it; this time, consider what happens right after it. Adeimantus responds—for it is not to Glaucon that Socrates is speaking here—that the man who avoids politics, and thus escapes harm to himself, will have accomplished "not the least things [οὐ τὰ ἐλάχιστα]" (R. 497a1), and in response to this Bernays-friendly perspective, Plato allows Socrates to reply: "'Nor, indeed,' I said, 'the greatest things [τά μέγιστα], not having hit on a suitable πολιτεία'" (R. 497a3-4).

The Athenians called Phocion ὁ χρηστός because he chose to do τὰ μέγιστα, not because he was content with οὐ τὰ ἐλάχιστα, and in making this choice of lives, he did exactly what Plato intended to provoke him to do when he wrote this passage. Consider the following typology: those who preferred not to be wronged at any cost accomplished τὰ ἐλάχιστα, while the words οὐ τὰ ἐλάχιστα apply to those who did so while also abstaining from doing wrong; neither lived (and died) in accordance with the *Gorgias* Reversal. Plato, of course, gives the lazy a way out: the challenge of his pedagogy is not addressed to them, and the effete and erudite Adeimantus represents the best of these.[82] In the present case, he allows them and us to take away the comforting message that only in a suitable πολιτεία will the philosopher condescend to πράττειν τὰ πολιτικά; only in the non-existent City will philosophers return to the Cave. Phocion is an example of a student who chose to do something more difficult, not waiting for Athens to became "Plato's πολιτεία" before serving her. Instead, by making himself ὁ χρηστός, he acted throughout in accordance with the Reversal. Naturally we will be told that such is not the essence of Platonism, as if generating a visible cosmos from the One and Indefinite Dyad, even while writing *Concerning Kingship* at royal command, is a stronger basis for being considered a philosopher and a Platonist.

Nor does Phocion's break with the policies of Lycurgus, Demosthenes, and Hyperides demonstrate his failure to practice a rather more pedestrian if also infinitely more difficult kind of Platonism than Xenocrates did. Plutarch, who clearly admires him, breaks with Phocion on the Reversal (*Life of Phocion*, 32.4), and does so as a Platonist. He pairs Phocion and Cato for many reasons, but one of them, not so much stated as shown, is because he wants us to see that their admirable virtues were not always beneficial to the cities they served. I suspect he did so to teach us something about putting Platonism into practice in a way that he, as a Greek subject of omnipotent and imperial Rome, could himself no longer do, except in the context of the municipal offices he held in Chaeronea. Plutarch paired Demosthenes and Cicero to teach a better lesson, but for exactly the same reason. Incidentally, it was by pairing Cicero and Demosthenes that Plutarch expressed his real opinion about whether the latter, like the former, had been Plato's student, not by quoting Hermippus. As he made clear in the introduction to his *Phocion* with respect to pairing it with *Cato*, Plutarch's obvious purpose was to show how two principled men act when they do not have the privilege of "happening upon an appropriate polity," exactly as if it had not been this apparent misfortune that joined Demosthenes and Cicero as well, thus making them a pair of pairs.

It is not the passage about the *Gorgias* Reversal that best conveys Plutarch's estimation of Phocion, but rather his comment, already quoted in chapter 1, about "good fortune [εὐτυχία]."[83] Recall that it appeared in the context of the *Life*'s central crisis: the drama of the Old Academy's disintegration. Phocion clearly believed that "those around Demosthenes and Lycurgus and Hyperides and Charidemus" had led Athens into a disaster, and, as recent scholarly prejudice with regard to Demosthenes proves, he had plausible grounds for doing so. Considered with care, Plutarch's criticism of Phocion at 32.4 echoes Phocion's criticism of Demosthenes and Company: they were upholding their personal probity at the city's cost. In chapter 4, Demosthenes will be given a chance to respond to this charge, but the important point for now is that the original Academic choice for τά μέγιστα rather than οὐ τὰ ἐλάχιστα, and a commitment to act in accordance with the Reversal, had always already implicated a willingness "to die on behalf of all of you [τὸ ὑπὲρ ὑμῶν ἁπάντων ἀποθανεῖν]."[84] In the footsteps of Socrates, this was what "to suffer an injustice" really meant, and that is why Plato allowed Glaucon, not Adeimantus, to explain the horrific consequences of being a Just Man (*R.* 361e4–362a1). While debating whether the Just Man would be happy under torture, the Athenian schools of philosophy that carried on after the demise of "the Old Academy" could understand what they called "happiness [εὐδαιμονία]" but could no longer recognize what Phocion had regarded as εὐτυχία. He was killed in 318.

Plutarch did not write a life of Lycurgus the Athenian but virtually everything we know about him—only one of his speeches survives—comes from *Lives of the Ten Orators*, which ends with a decree of 307 that awarded the son of Lycurgus high honors on the basis of his own but more especially his father's services to Athens. Lycurgus died before "the

Harpalus Affair," which led to, or was the occasion for, a breach between Hyperides and Demosthenes, and the only time "Pseudo-Plutarch" mentions the latter in *Lycurgus* is to record the fact that Demosthenes gained the release of Lycurgus' sons with his *Third Letter*,[85] written from exile in 323 after their father's death in 325/24. In the absence of any explicit ancient statement of a rift between Lycurgus and Demosthenes, Danielle S. Allen has tried to show that there was one, and since Allen's work will be cited frequently in what follows, a list of her most significant claims will prove instructive: (1) she situates Plato in an explicitly political and Athenian context, finding "traces of his influence on the politics of Athens"[86]; (2) central to this influence is the word for "choice [προαίρεσις]" translated by her as "deliberated commitment"[87]; (3) she explains this influence in relation to a "culture war" between 350 and 330 with Plato at its center[88]; (4) she has a particularly strong interest in Lycurgus,[89] whom she regards as Plato's student[90]; and (5) she pits Lycurgus *against* Demosthenes, whom she does not regard as Plato's student,[91] in the "culture war" she describes.[92] It is only with the last of these five claims that I disagree: she never mentions Demosthenes' *Third Letter*, and refers to Alexander's revealing demand that Athens should surrender Lycurgus *and* Demosthenes in 335 only in an endnote.[93]

But the more important basis for this disagreement centers on a 1977 article by Edmund M. Burke, who recognized what he called "political collaboration" between Demosthenes and Lycurgus on the basis of the very same speeches on which Allen's case for a "culture war" between them depends.[94] Her argument is a complicated one, but it depends on the claim that Lycurgus was Plato's student while Demosthenes wasn't, and it may make things simpler to quote her on this more general claim: "My own interpretation of the rhetorical patterns of argument and vocabulary to be found in the orators would confirm pseudo-Plutarch's identification of Lycurgus, Aeschines, and Hyperides as students of Plato while also confirming doubt about the claims that Demosthenes studied with him."[95] With that said, Allen's complex case aligns Lycurgus with Aeschines on the grounds that just as Leocrates fled Athens after Chaeronea, the fighting of which Lycurgus regards as a patriotic duty, so too does Aeschines charge Demosthenes with doing the same, despite the fact that he, even more than Lycurgus, had been the catalyst for fighting that battle in the first place, and that Aeschines had opposed it, thus ranging Aeschines, not Demosthenes, on the side of the unpatriotic and cowardly Leocrates. As to whether it was Demosthenes or Aeschines who caused the latter's prosecution to come before a jury only in 330, no one will ever know, and Allen follows Burke in finding Demosthenes responsible; she breaks with him importantly on who was aligned with whom.[96] Where I differ with Burke is that even though he notes that "on a number of occasions, Lycurgus and Demosthenes worked in consort," and that "both were adamant anti-Macedonians,"[97] he never mentions that either Lycurgus or Demosthenes was a student of Plato, let alone that both of them were.

As it turns out, it is easier to accept that Lycurgus was: in an article on "The Platonism of Lycurgus," Robert Renehan does for Lycurgus what no one has yet dared to do for Demosthenes: he takes seriously the ancient evidence that he was a student of Plato's and then analyzes his only surviving speech for evidence of that influence.[98] Perhaps the most striking feature of Renehan's analysis is his emphasis on *Laws*. In discussing the lengthy quotation from Tyrtaeus in *Against Leocrates*, for example, he remarks that Lycurgus is only the second author who tells us that Tyrtaeus was an Athenian; the first was Plato (*Lg.* 629a4–5).[99] And when Lycurgus observes: "Birds at least, which by nature are best fitted for a swift escape, can be seen to be willing to die for their young [ὑπὲρ τῆς αὐτῶν νεοττιᾶς ἐθέλοντα ἀποθνήσκειν],"[100] he appropriately highlights the bracketed phrase in order to connect it to *Laws* 814b2-4,[101] not to *Symposium*.[102] But when the first and last words of this phrase are combined into the verb ὑπεραποθνήσκειν, it is the speech of Phaedrus at Agathon's victory party that comes to mind: twice he uses this verb (*Smp.* 179b4 and 180a1) before "dis-interesting" it further with ἐπ-αποθνήσκειν at 180a1. When this verb reappears in Socrates' Diotima Discourse (*Smp.* 207b4 and 208d2), it does so in a passage that is so closely connected to Lycurgus that it cannot be understood without him:

> "Are you then imagining," she said, "Alcestis to have died for Admetus, or Achilles to have died after Patroclus, or your own Codrus to have died in advance [προαποθνήσκειν] on behalf of the kingdom of his children [ὑπὲρ τῆς βασιλείας τῶν παίδων], *not* considering a deathless memory of virtue [ἀθάνατος μνήμη ἀρετῆς] to be in store for them which now we have?"[103]

Among such company as Alcestis and Achilles, Codrus is the outlier. Few of us have heard of him, and this is what makes Lycurgus a necessary guide to this passage's meaning: he is our oldest literary source for the story to which Diotima merely alludes here.

Although it is the following chapter that will deal with Plato, an important hermeneutic principle regarding how I read his dialogues will be introduced here, using the two different explanations of ὑπεραποθνήσκειν in *Symposium* as an example.[104] According to Diotima, those who die on behalf of others do so for the sake of securing "an immortal reputation for virue [ἀθάνατος μνήμη ἀρετῆς]"; hence the motive is essentially selfish. According to Phaedrus, by contrast, although the gods subsequently reward Alcestis and Achilles for their virtue (*Smp.* 179c3–d2 and 179e1–2), there is no hint that they were willing to ὑπεραποθνήσκειν for the sake of those rewards.[105] By offering us two different accounts and thus forcing us to choose, Plato employs one of his most characteristic pedagogical devices. Consider the *Gorgias* Reversal in the context of the claim Socrates makes in *Republic* 1, similarly staged in the context of an active and passive version of the same verb: "For any man of sense would prefer to be benefitted than to take the trouble of benefitting others (R. 347d6–8)."[106] Those who are willing to benefit others as long as they suffer no injustice may perhaps be said to have accomplished οὐ τὰ ἐλάχιστα (R. 497a1), while those who are willing to refrain from doing injustice only as long as doing so benefits them have accomplished considerably less; those alone accomplish τὰ μέγιστα who are willing to benefit others even if they suffer injustice for doing so.[107] Plato is perfectly willing to put a false claims in one of his character's mouths if such claims can serve as "stepping stones and incentives" (R. 511b5)—indeed as provocative challenges—to activity in accordance with the Highest Good. In comparison with Phaedrus, Diotima's self-serving account of ὑπεραποθνῄσκειν is an example of one such provocation, and therefore led the great Wilamowitz to confess: "It is to be hoped that this motive for the sacrifice of Alcestis, Achilles, and Codrus is not Plato's actual opinion [*Platons wirkliche Meinung*]; here we would rather uphold the speech of Phaedrus, 179b."[108] This is exactly what Plato wanted Wilamowitz along with all the rest of to prefer,[109] but he leaves the choice (or προαίρεσις) to us.

The pedagogical complexity at play in Diotima's account of ὑπεραποθνῄσκειν is matched by the philological obscurity of her mention of Codrus, and the longest of the ancient Platonic *scholia* is devoted to him.[110] Without Lycurgus, this *scholium* could not have been written, nor the reference explained: *Against Leocrates* is the oldest surviving version of the story of how Plato's relative,[111] the last King of Athens,[112] sacrificed himself by allowing the Spartans to kill him, having been informed by an oracle that if they did, Athens would be saved. Like Plato, his ancestor used deception:

> And so noble [γενναῖοι] were our kings then, gentlemen, that they preferred to die [ἀποθνῄσκειν] on behalf of the safety of those they ruled [ὑπὲρ τῆς τῶν ἀρχομένων σωτηρίας], rather than living, to immigrate to another land. For they say that Codrus, telling the Athenians in advance to take note when he should depart this life, having taken a beggar's clothes so that he might deceive [ἀπατᾶν] their enemies.[113]

Lycurgus shows that he was not deceived: it is *for the safety of his subjects* that Codrus chose to die, not (as Diotima had said) ὑπὲρ τῆς βασιλείας τῶν παίδων.[114] Leaving aside what the tradition's reliance on *Against Leocrates* tells us about the "deathless memory of virtue" that Diotima tells us "we now have,"[115] the more important point now is that Lycurgus is also revealing how *Symposium* influenced him, and thereby showing us how Plato's teaching revealed itself in practice. It is Plato's verb ὑπερἀποθνήσκειν that Lycurgus uses to connect Codrus' choice to die for the benefit of others in preference to being benefitted by them, and it constitutes the link between the two passages in *Symposium* to which Lycurgus refers in *Against Leocrates*, connecting Codrus to Diotima's self-sacrificing birds.

From Phaedrus and Diotima to Socrates and the Cave, ὑπεραποθνήσκειν is the soul of "Plato's Political Theory." To be sure there are good or at least understandable reasons why the reception of Plato has long since proved itself to be more comfortable with imagining him as the proponent of an authoritarian philosopher-king, despising Athens, and concerned only with dreaming up a Kallipolis or Magnesia. Lycurgus points us in a better direction. With his rhetorical skill and political service to Athens, his honest oversight of the city's finances,[116] his concern with public buildings,[117] his many contributions to literature,[118] his patriotic efforts on behalf of the ephebeia,[119] the anti-Macedonian orientation of his politics,[120] and his hatred for Alexander,[121] Lycurgus shows us what going back down into the Cave looked like to the best of Plato's contemporary students.[122] But however impressive may be the achievements of the statesman, we should not forget the devotee of the Muses who played rhapsode in *Against Leocrates*,[123] and presumably fell in love with *Ion* before making the difficult decision to return to the Cave. It is primarily *Symposium* that he is channeling now, and this is why ὑπεραποθνήσκειν reappears when Lycurgus applies the story of Codrus to the cowardly Leocrates, who fled his country and its sacred institutions when the Macedonians had proved themselves unstoppable at Chaeronea:

> Is there any resemblance between Leocrates' love for his country [ἡ πατρίς] and the love of those ancient kings who were choosing, having deceived their enemies, to die on her behalf [ἀποθνήσκειν ὑπὲρ αὐτῆς] and to trade in exchange their own life [ψυχή] for its common security?[124]

It is above all in a funeral oration that such sentiments are most naturally and poignantly expressed,[125] and this brings us to Hyperides,[126] the last of Plato's five students to be considered in this chapter.[127] In tandem with *Against Leocrates*, Hyperides' *Funeral Oration* reveals what might be called "a vocabulary of gallantry,"[128] of which the key words are: "danger [κίνδυνος]" and "to undergo danger [κινδυνεύειν]"[129]—including "to wish to undergo danger [ἐθέλειν κινδυνεύειν]"[130] and even "to be willing to die [ἐθέλειν ἀποθνήσκειν]"[131]—"to remain steadfast [ὑπομενεῖν],"[132] "to run to the aid of [βοηθεῖν],"[133] "endurance [καρτηρία],"[134] "freedom [ἐλευθερία],"[135] and of course both καλόν and καλῶς.[136] In his *Funeral Oration*, Hyperides identifies the purpose of a good education, and thus, tacitly, of his own: "I believe all of us know that it is for this that we educate the youth: that they may become good men, and of those who have become, in time of war, men excelling in virtue [ἀρετή], it is obvious [πρόδηλον] that, being children, they were nobly [καλῶς] educated."[137] Echoing Simonides' epitaph for the dead at Plataea,[138] he adds a Platonic touch by referring to those who are willing to expose *their bodies* to danger[139]; "they have expended life that others live well."[140] With his "the choice they chose [προαιρέσεως ἧς προείλοντο]," he does more than pay tribute to the string of cognate accusatives in Pausanias' speech in *Symposium* (*Smp.* 182e2-183a8),[141] and with his "things worthy of dirges [θρήνων] have they not suffered [πεπόνθασιν] but of fulsome praises [ἐπαίνων] have they done [πεποιήκασιν],"[142] he honors Agathon's favorite (Gorgianic) tricks of ἀντιθέσεις and παρισώσεις, for the use of which Dionysius of Halicarnassus would later take Plato to task.[143] And who can say where rhetoric ends and Platonism begins in the following?

> For if what to others is most painful—death—has become for them the chief author [ἀρχηγός] of great goods, how is it right to judge them unlucky, or how even to have departed from life, but not rather, to have been born [γεγονέναι] from the beginning [ἐξ ἀρχῆς] a nobler birth [γένεσιν] than the actual first?[144]

If we can see the influence of *Symposium* and *Ion* on Lycurgus, it is *Phaedo* and *Menexenus* that seem to have captured Hyperides' youthful admiration. In imagining the reception the dead heroes will receive from the ancients in Hades (*Funeral Oration* 35), Hyperides pays tribute to *Menexenus*, where the dead heroes will only welcome their own children if they too have been heroic (*Mx*. 247c1-4).[145] But it is the paradoxical interplay of defeat and victory—whereby the losers win—that will make Plato's *Menexenus* a critical text for both Hyperides and Demosthenes, and the crucial passage will be quoted here:

> *Socrates*: Every form of knowledge [ἐπιστήμη] when sundered from justice and the rest of virtue is seen to be plain roguery rather than wisdom [σοφία]. On account of these things, both first and last, and through it all, with full devotion, do completely try [καὶ διὰ παντὸς πᾶσαν πάντως προθυμίαν πειρᾶσθε] so to be that, first and foremost, you surpass us and those who went before in good repute, but if not, know that for us, should we defeat you [νικᾶν] in virtue [ἀρετή], that victory [ἡ νίκη] brings shame [αἰσχύνη], but that our defeat [ἡ δὲ ἧττα], if we should be defeated [ἡττᾶσθαι], brings happiness [εὐδαιμονία].[146]

Carefully distinguishing a Socratic commitment to virtue over all other and apparently more "philosophical" kinds of ἐπιστήμη—physics, cosmology, and number theory come to mind—this passage also casts "Socratic eudaemonism" in a new light, here making εὐδαιμονία the posthumous possession of those alone who have been defeated by their sons in a contest for ἀρετή. Replete as it is with downright false statements about

Athenian history, *Menexenus* characteristically allows Aspasia to mix truth with falsehood for the reader's benefit, and does so in three crucial ways: (1) it mixes a deceptive account of Athenian History with the foregoing account of virtue, happiness, and defeat as victory, and (2) it praises Athens for behaving in accordance with selfless and generous virtues it did not possess, in a manner that nevertheless *or rather thereby* emphasizes the excellence of selfless generosity, a theme that reappears when Socrates recites another woman's speech in *Symposium*.

The third raises the most basic question about *Menexenus*: why did Plato write it in the first place? On the basis of the internal evidence provided by Plato's other dialogues, I have elsewhere called for placing it between *Ion* and *Symposium* in a reconstruction of the Platonic "Reading Order"—rhetoric, Athenian History, and "the feminization" of eloquence all play a role—and it is easy to refer the reader to appropriate sections of "Plato the Teacher."[147] But on the basis of the kind of external evidence under consideration here, the funeral orations of Hyperides and Demosthenes may further illuminate the purpose of Aspasia's, making *their* patriotic eloquence in defense of Athens something like the Final Cause of Plato's *Menexenus*; in a word, the genre must always implicate the verb ὑπεραποθνῄσκειν. In addition to illuminating Hyperides' speech in his commentary, Judson Herrman has championed the authenticity of Demosthenes' *Funeral Oration*,[148] building on the work of Johannes Sykutris,[149] so important in bringing *The Letter of Speusippus* back from oblivion. Dionysius of Halicarnassus was the first to deny the authenticity of "the Demosthenic *Funeral Oration*," and doing so allowed him to crown *On the Crown* rather than *Menexenus* (see preface) as the acme of eloquence. Naturally this is not the place to discuss Demosthenes, but the principal reason he is confined to one chapter in this book is that an adequate treatment would require fighting repeated battles over the authenticity of his most obviously Plato-inspired writings, as here. In what follows, I will cite Demosthenes' sixty-one surviving speeches, including the *Funeral Oration*, as I find them; readers can exclude citations as they see fit when they come from speeches or other writings that have been rejected by critics from Dionysius to Blass.

Blass also rejected the evidence that Hyperides was Plato's student,[150] and Trampedach's single paragraph on the subject follows the three he devotes to Lycurgus.[151] Relying on Johannes Engels to have already accomplished the task,[152] Trampedach naturally cannot discover Plato's influence on "the political life of Hyperides" because he does not regard his *choice* or προαίρεσις to live that life as inspired by the Allegory of the Cave. As for Engels, not even Funkhänel (see introduction) managed to exploit the evidence in *Lives of the Ten Orators* that Hyperides was the student of both Plato and Isocrates in a way that maximizes the impact of one while minimizing the other.¹⁵³ Despite "differences in political temperament, way of life, and in general political views" (a necessary caveat given their radical divergence on Macedon), Engels concludes that: "the goals of Isocratean education/παιδεία (cf. βίος πρακτικός) corresponded to the life of Hyperides to a large degree."¹⁵⁴ A fragment from a lost speech that merely mentions Socrates is made to supply evidence of distance between Plato and Hyperides,¹⁵⁵ while the passage in the *Funeral Oration* that echoes Socrates' post-mortem dilemma (*Ap.* 40c6-41a8),¹⁵⁶ forces Engels to follow Schaefer in leaving the door ajar just before slamming it shut: "Beyond a probable acquaintance with Plato's *Apology*, and therefore possibly a reference in the context of the *Funeral Oration*, one should not derive from this parallel any further results of Plato's influence on Hyperides."¹⁵⁷

It is only possible to find evidence for distance between Hyperides and Demosthenes amid the complex opacity of "the Harpalus Affair,"¹⁵⁸ and the conventional view that the more radical Hyperides broke with his fellow anti-Macedonian because Demosthenes embraced a more realistic and cautious approach under Alexander (336–323) follows a pattern already visible in the case of Phocion's break with both Demosthenes and Hyperides after Chaeronea (338).¹⁵⁹ But it is noteworthy that the principal exculpatory evidence regarding not only Demosthenes' motives for diverting some funds (*Against Demosthenes*, 5.13), but also for the Council's motives in making him the scandal's poster-boy (*Against Demosthenes*, 5.14), comes from Hyperides' *Against Demosthenes*.¹⁶⁰ By linking Demosthenes to a pro-Macedonian scoundrel like Demades (*Against Demosthenes*, 5.25, 5.34–35),¹⁶¹ Hyperides may have deliberately gone too far, and his emphasis on Demosthenes' willingness to die (*Against Demosthenes*, 5.1), his over-the-top praise for the "most especially democratic" Areopagus (*Against Demosthenes*, 5.5), the comparative question of 5.6-7, a trio of unanswered questions (*Against Demosthenes*, 5.12), and the truth expressed at 5.14,¹⁶² all point to the possibility that his purpose was different from that of Dinarchus. By way of establishing some source-critical *bona fides*, I follow Demetrius of Magnesia,¹⁶³ Westermann,¹⁶⁴ and the young Schaefer,¹⁶⁵ in rejecting Dinarchus' *Against Demosthenes* as inauthentic,¹⁶⁶ finding in it a rhetorical school exercise in obvious imitation of Aeschines; the fact that the teachers of the real Dinarchus were Theophrastus and Demetrius of Phaleron leaves no doubt as to the specific school in question.¹⁶⁷ Schaefer would only change his mind because he came to regard Dinarchus himself as derivative and unoriginal, taking his inclusion among "the Ten Orators" as a sign of the decline of Attic eloquence.¹⁶⁸ But the survival of Dinarchus, like that of Aeschines, depends entirely on Demosthenes, and it is revealing that the latter's modern critics echo the views of his ancient enemies,¹⁶⁹ especially when it comes to creating distance between him and Hyperides,[170] with Demosthenes' alleged refusal to support Sparta's revolt in 331 being exhibit A.[171]

It is rather the intimate connection and close collaboration between Hyperides and Demosthenes that is the salient phenomenon, recently confirmed yet again by the discovery of the fragmentary *Against Diondas*.[172] Until 2008, all we knew about this speech—apart, that is, from an indication of Hyperides' familiarity with Xenophon's *Hellenica*[173]— depended on the choice comments of Porphyry as preserved by Eusebius to the effect that *Against Diondas* so closely resembled *On the Crown*, that just as it would enhance Hyperides' reputation without diminishing Demosthenes' if it were the earlier work, it would leave Demosthenes' intact but diminish his own if Hyperides' speech had been written later.[174] In an article devoted to "the rhetoric of revolt," Herrman points in a better direction.[175] Using *Against Diondas* as proof, he argues that Demosthenes and Hyperides were so close in their anti-Macedonian aspirations that the suspicion of Libanius—that *On the Treaty with Alexander*, preserved among the speeches of Demosthenes, was really the work of Hyperides— can now be corroborated.[176] In a striking passage, the long-lost speech reveals that the pro-Macedonian Diondas had repeatedly attempted to prosecute Lycurgus, Demosthenes, and Hyperides himself.[177] The discovery of these fragments further confirms perhaps the most amazing fact about Hyperides. Until the nineteenth century, we had none of his speeches; in the memorable phrase of F. G. Kenyon in 1906, "All the Hyperides that we have today we owe to Egypt."[178] Even more fitting than the fact that the most recent discovery confirms the close relationship between Demosthenes and Hyperides is that the latter's *Funeral Oration*, discovered in 1847,[179] "is the last surviving speech we have of an Attic orator."[180]

Engels did his best to minimize the influence of Plato on Hyperides, but it is another passage in the *Funeral Oration* that illustrates the kind of "double action" at the heart of this book. Long before Glenn Most joined forces with André Laks to place Socrates among the sophists,[181] he had challenged Nietzsche's view that Socrates' last words in *Phaedo* proved that he was "a life denier," and owed a rooster to Asclepius (*Phd.* 118a7-8) because life was the disease from which he had now recovered thanks to the hemlock.[182] When Hyperides claimed that death "has become for them the chief author of great goods," and raises the possibility that, so far from having "departed from life," they have now "been born from the beginning a nobler birth than the actual first,"[183] it is *Phaedo* that he echoes. By "double action," then, I mean the following: Hyperides reveals the extent of Plato's influence on him *while at the same time* illuminating Plato's intentions, here confirming that Socrates' last words meant what Most tried to prove that they didn't. So much has been said in this chapter about the verb ὑπεραποθνῄσκειν that the following chapter can focus light elsewhere, but it will remain central throughout, justifying the connection of Demosthenes and Hyperides, both murdered in 322 on Antipater's command,[184] as well as the apparently adventitious fact that the latter's *Funeral Oration* is the last speech, emerging from the desert two millennia later, that we will hear from an Attic orator. In the light of Plato's impact on both, it is possible to see that this fact is not adventitious. Despite appearances, *Menexenus* is not Plato's only contribution to the genre: the dialogues as a whole, climaxing with *Phaedo*, collectively constitute his Funeral Oration for Socrates. Although Aristotle would derive from that immortal dialogue the notion of "the Forms as causes"[185] in a way that made "participation" vulnerable to "the Third Man," at least four of Plato's Athenian students would find in it a different lesson, and as confirmed by "double action," this is what their teacher intended them to find: an inspiring celebration of and an equally inspiring incitement to what in German is called a *Heldentod*: a hero's selfless commitment to benefit others in perfect contempt for death.

3

✛

Plato the Teacher

"Plato" stands first in this book's title for a good reason: its purpose is to use information about Plato's most famous Athenian students to support a dialogue-based conception of the Academy, developed at length elsewhere. This chapter will summarize that conception in a way that prepares the reader for the discussion of Demosthenes in chapter 4. Briefly, my claim is that the Academy's original purpose was to promote, on a philosophical basis, the traditional values of civic obligation and Socratic courage in the face of death, and in the last chapter, the deaths of Phocion, Lycurgus, and Hyperides were used to demonstrate that Plato realized this objective in a number of his students. His influence is not to be detected or sought in specific policies, least of all in a program to institute the utopian reforms announced for pedagogical reasons in the *Republic*. Even if it would ultimately be congenial to his defenders to present him as such, Plato was opposed neither to Athens nor to democracy.[1] In the ideal City, philosophers are compelled by law to return to the Cave; no such obligation applied to Demosthenes, Hyperides, Lycurgus, and Phocion, nor, for that matter, to us. Rather, a free *choice* to practice rhetoric for the city's benefit in the light of a higher and transpersonal Idea of the Good is only possible in a democratic city. With the coming of Macedonian and then Roman hegemony, the Academy remained in operation but its purpose necessarily changed[2]; chapter 1 described the historical circumstances initially responsible for that change. The effects of those changes are still with us, and this explains why it now seems obvious that we can learn more about the Old Academy from Aristotle than from Demosthenes, whose political commitments placed them on opposite sides of the burning political question of the day. But the written record as preserved in the Platonic dialogues tells a different story, and it begins with *Protagoras*.

So often have the words "the Great Speech" been applied to what the elegant sophist says in defense of virtue's teachability in Plato's *Protagoras* that it has become easy to forget that "his" speech is only one small part of a much greater and more lively speech made by Socrates: the delightful story, told to his comrade so that you (plural) too can hear (ἀκούετε at *Prt.* 310a7) of how Socrates overcame Protagoras with pleasure by proving that no such thing is possible.³ Socrates' speech begins with a courageous and intrepid (*Prt.* 310d3) youngster named Hippocrates knocking on his door at dawn, eager to find a guide who can make him speak well (δεινὸς λέγειν at *Prt.* 312d7) and more generally, as Socrates will put it, to become "most capable both to do and say [καὶ πράττειν καὶ λέγειν] the things of the city [τὰ τῆς πόλεως]" (*Prt.* 319a1–2).⁴ Quite apart from all the other things that Plato taught in the Academy, I take this to be an accurate statement of what most of his students initially came there to learn, and this book is emphasizing those students, Athenians all, who were most conspicuous for learning it. The reason it was christened "the Great Speech" is because Plato has portrayed Protagoras with a recognizable sympathy; my claim is that this sympathy's origin is best explained by recognizing that Plato too was teaching "the political art [ἡ πολιτικὴ τέχνη]" (*Prt.* 319a4; cf. *Grg.* 521d6–8) and virtue generally—even while allowing his Socrates to claim that virtue cannot be taught—and was doing so primarily to young Athenians like Hippocrates, whom Plato the Teacher taught to δεινὸς λέγειν *and then some*.⁵

The survival of Isocrates' writings explains why it was necessary for Plato to teach rhetoric as well as all the other things he taught: he had an impressive rival.⁶ In response, the tradition has grown comfortable with framing the contest or ἀγών between two fourth-century Athenian schoolmasters as a zero-sum conflict between the impractical philosophy of the one and the practical political rhetoric of the other, and through Hermippus, this framework has already been shown to have had a decisive impact on how that tradition came to regard the education of Demosthenes.⁷ The "Great Speech" of Protagoras in Plato's *Protagoras* is a good example of how one-sided this framework really is. By allowing Protagoras to advertise his wares (*Prt.* 318d7–319a2)—hence "the announcement I am announcing" (*Prt.* 319a6–7)—Plato is staging the ἀγών with his rival schoolteacher on his own terms, and while there is no doubt that there are parallels between the sophist's well-told myth of political origins and the brilliant passages in Isocrates that celebrate the civilizing influence of rhetoric,⁸ it is Plato who is now proving himself capable of writing such a speech, and doing so eloquently. When his Protagoras twits Hippias for teaching arcane subjects like mathematics, astronomy, and music (*Prt.* 318e2–4), Plato is doing more than indicating his rival's perspective: he is beginning to flesh out what "and then some" is going to look like. Plato's mastery of rhetoric is on full display in both "the Great Speech" of Protagoras and *a fortiori* is the greater one of Socrates that includes it, and it is in the latter that he will show that rhetoric, myth, and personal charm—as practiced by Protagoras or Isocrates or both—are useless in an ἀγών against the characteristic weapon of Socrates, whether it be best described as dialectic or eristic.

A clear indication that the quarrel between Plato and Isocrates should not be oversimplified as the quarrel between rhetoric and philosophy is that Isocrates no more surrenders φιλοσοφία to Plato than Plato surrenders effective instruction in ῥητορική to Isocrates. It is true that Plato appears to reject rhetoric,[9] and more generally, "the sophistic ideal;"[10] he also can and would increasingly be construed as rejecting politics (τὰ τῆς πόλεως or τὰ πολιτικά) for the sake of "the theoretical life," especially on the basis of the ὁμοίωσις θεῷ (*Tht.* 176b1). But the Platonic corpus as a whole belies this appearance: too many of the dialogues are overtly political and even the anti-political digression at the center of *Theaetetus* is staged on the eve of Socrates' greatest public speech. At the very least, Plato's Socrates is what we would call "a public intellectual" and his own self-description as the only true πολιτικός (cf. *Grg.* 521d6–8 and *Men.*100a1–2) goes further. There are three kinds of evidence that point to the Old Academy's original purpose: (1) the dialogues themselves as a whole, considered as the Academy's curriculum, (2) the Athenian students under consideration in this book, Demosthenes in particular, and (3) the survival of Isocrates, Plato's rival. There are, to be sure, profound differences between the two teachers with respect to tuition, method, and philosophy, and among the latter, Isocrates' claim that rhetoric is to be pursued for the orator's benefit stands out.[11] There is also, of course, an important difference regarding Philip of Macedon to be considered.

"Demosthenes is the consummation of the Isocratean ideal." Reviving the position of Hermippus, whom he never mentions, Harry Mortimer Hubbell wrote these words in his 1913 Yale University doctoral dissertation on "The Influence of Isocrates on Cicero, Dionysius, and Aristides."[12] By the time Hubbell turned to Aelius Aristides and "Pseudo-Lucian" in the last chapter of his book—and both will reappear in the last chapter of this one—he had already "traced the revival of the sophistical ideal in Cicero and Dionysius [sc. of Halicarnassus]."[13] as the exemplar of what he now for the first time calls "the Isocratean ideal," Demosthenes enters the story because "the conflict between rhetoric and philosophy is nowhere plainer than in Aristides,"[14] and it still remains a temptation to read Aristides (as well as Dionysius; see preface) as if he were championing Demosthenes *against* Plato.[15] Hubbell's statement of the zero-sum conflict is notable both for his identification of this conflict's cause and the claim that no compromise between rhetoric and philosophy is possible:

> As the opponent of the sophistical ideal we find Socrates as presented in Plato, who rejects the sophistical rhetoric and makes knowledge (ἐπιστήμη) the end of education,—a knowledge which must be the foundation of any true rhetoric. Isocrates and Plato are in this exact opposites. To Plato a political science is possible, and is the necessary antecedent of rhetoric; to Isocrates ἐπιστήμη is impossible; rhetoric is both an end in itself and a means to the acquisition of an accuracy of judgment (δόξα) which is the best guide to all action. The two ideals were diametrically opposite, and anything like a compromise between them was impossible. There sprang up between philosopher and rhetorician the most intense rivalry for the privilege of training the young men.[16]

It is difficult to determine whether this view was dependent on the prior suppression of the ancient evidence that Demosthenes was Plato's student during the nineteenth century or whether that suppression had already depended on the view that Hubbell expresses here.

Not all of Plato's *Protagoras* is a speech of Socrates quite apart from the fact that "the Great Speech of Protagoras" is merely a speech within that speech: the dialogue in "the frame" begins with an erotically charged discussion that begins with Alcibiades. Except for the student who has already been made aware of the information found in either Plato's *Symposium* or Xenophon's, it would be impossible to read the *Protagoras* frame without wondering if the relationship between Socrates and Alcibiades is a sexual one. At first sight, this may not appear to be a question of any deep philosophical significance; this appearance will disappear in Plato's *Symposium*, which will not only answer the question in the negative but will introduce the kind of incorporeal and asexual love we still call "Platonic." Characters who appear as no more than chorus members in *Protagoras* (*Prt.* 315c2–e3) make eloquent and memorable speeches in *Symposium*, and although the priority of the one to the other is conventionally ascribed to which of the two was written first, it is at least equally obvious which of the two *Plato intended his readers to read first*. In addition to preparing the student for the revelation of Platonic Love in the later *Symposium*, the *Protagoras* Frame helps us to better understand the methods and motives of Isocrates' rival schoolteacher. By building the Frame around Alcibiades, Plato put political, moral,[17] and rhetorical malpractice at the center of whatever story he had to tell; had his students been unable to identify with Alcibiades' grandiose ambitions, he would not have told the story of his relationship with Socrates. And the fact that he used a prurient question about their relationship to capture his readers' attention helps us to see Plato's first readers for what they were: adolescents with a natural interest in sex.

Until late antiquity, it remained obvious not only that Plato had written *Alcibiades Major* but that he had intended the neophyte to begin the study of Platonic philosophy with it, and to this extent, they were at a great advantage over those scholars, including us, who followed in Schleiermacher's wake.[18] But whether it was because they were eager to promote their own apolitical reading of the dialogues or simply because they did not read them with the requisite care, the Neoplatonic commentators failed to realize that *Alcibiades Major* presupposed the reader's prior acquaintance with *Protagoras* in much the same way that *Symposium* did. The following facts are significant in this connection: (1) the *Protagoras* Frame draws the reader's attention to Alcibiades from the start; (2) *Alcibiades Major* keeps alive without resolution the prurient question raised by the Frame, as does *Alcibiades Minor* as well; (3) the opening speech of Socrates in *Alcibiades Major* states that Socrates and Alcibiades have never spoken before (*Alc.1* 103a4); (4) despite the fact that Alcibiades repeatedly comes to Socrates' aid in *Protagoras* and that Socrates claims that he repeatedly forgot all about his presence (*Prt.* 309b5-9); the two never actually speak to each other in *Protagoras*; and (5) the smartest thing Alcibiades says in *Alcibiades Major*—he might have learned justice the same way he learned to speak Greek (*Alc.1* 111a1-4)—was said by Protagoras in the Great Speech (*Prt.* 327e3-328a1). One of Schleiermacher's justifications for denying the authenticity of *Alcibiades Major* depended on the claim that it was inconsistent with *Protagoras* because Alcibiades shows himself to be already familiar with his antics.[19] As proved by Xenophon's *Memorabilia*, however, it was standard Socratic practice to make himself known to a young man whom he wished to influence long before speaking directly to the youngster for the first time.[20]

We have no information about the extent to which Plato made himself known in advance to those students who chose to come to the Academy in preference to the far more prestigious and expensive school of Isocrates.[21] Convinced primarily by Aristotle, and then by the testimony of Aristoxenus,[22] we have become habituated to imagine that Plato lectured in his school on the basis of his "unwritten teachings,"[23] and building on this habituation, it has become commonplace to imagine that Plato *published* his dialogues, and did so only or at least primarily as a way of attracting students to the Academy. But apart from a story told by Aristotle and preserved by Themistius (fourth-century AD) about *Gorgias* attracting a Corinthian farmer to become a

Platonist,[24] there is no evidence that the dialogues were published, let alone that they were intended to be advertisements.

It is necessary to emphasize how important otherwise unwarranted assumptions about the publication of the dialogues really are: it is on their basis that scholars from Schaefer to Engels have been able to finesse the ancient evidence that Hyperides and Demosthenes were Plato's students by admitting, and readily, *that they may well have read his dialogues without any formal connection with the Academy*.[25] Instead of imagining the dialogues as published, and hence available to "the reading public," the dialogue-based conception of the Academy's curriculum introduced in *Ascent to the Beautiful* defends the view that reading, hearing, playing, and discussing those brilliant and provocative dialogues *constituted* the remarkably effective education that the Academy provided, and provides us still. Naturally *we* can now read those dialogues without going to Athens, and at a certain point the dialogues clearly did become available to "the reading public." But in response to applying equally unsubstantiated assumptions about publication to the mid-fourth century, I am claiming that very few of Plato's dialogues were anything like published before he founded the Academy,[26] and that none were made public *by him* thereafter.[27] In short, to *read* the dialogues during Plato's lifetime—or at least until the departure of Aristotle, who seems to have taken copies of them with him when he left the Academy, and then made them available to *his* students[28]—was not something that just anyone could do; students came to the Academy to read, study, and perform them. Once again: the ongoing claim of *Plato the Teacher* is that the Platonic dialogues, arranged in a "Reading Order" that began with *Protagoras* and *Alcibiades Major*, constituted the Academy's curriculum *and that reading through* (some portion of) *that curriculum is what* (at first only) *Plato's students did*.

"The Curricular Hypothesis" is the hermeneutic innovation at the center of *Plato the Teacher*, and it can be defended on a logical basis as follows: since we know that the founder of the Academy was a teacher, and since more than two millennia of collective pedagogical experience has demonstrated that the Platonic dialogues are eminently teachable, a conception of the dialogues that builds on these two uncontested truths by treating them as the Academy's curriculum is long overdue.[29] The internal evidence for this hypothesis has now been published, and takes the form of reconstructing the order in which the Platonic dialogues might most effectively be taught. As for those to whom he taught them, my conclusion is that they were youngsters. Halfway between internal and external evidence are the following: the eager young Hippocrates of *Protagoras*, the sexual titillation of that dialogue's frame along with the exciting ἀγών at its center, the distance between the fourteen-year-old Persian princelings and the nineteen-year-old Alcibiades in *Alcibiades*

Major, and finally this brilliant if currently devalued dialogue's pedagogical transparency. This book is intended to provide the *external* evidence for the Curricular Hypothesis by approaching "Plato the Teacher" through those of his Athenian students who have made a mark on history, and exploring the necessarily mutual relationship between what Plato taught through his dialogues and those to whom he taught it. Naturally this chapter is an outlier in the sense that it focuses on the former, but even here Plato's students will not simply disappear.

Consider in this context the much-discussed question of why Plato wrote dialogues. The twinned hypotheses that the dialogues constituted the Academy's curriculum, and that Plato's students were between the ages of fourteen and nineteen years old, makes the decision to teach philosophy and virtue through the lively play of character a natural and indeed a virtually inevitable one. Starting with the great enigma of Socrates himself, the dialogues, and *Protagoras* in particular,[30] are plays, and express a playful pedagogy that not only entertains while it instructs but manages to conceal the progress of instruction through the surfeit of entertainment they provide. Plato is the first dramatist to write a play in prose, and by the time that the erstwhile chorus members of *Protagoras* become the accomplished speakers of *Symposium*, Socrates will increasingly share the spotlight with a varied cast of complex, delightful, and vividly depicted characters. *Symposium* marks a turning point in the play of character: in the *Alcibiades* and *Hippias* dyads that precede it, direct dialogue keeps the dramatic situation simple. But beginning with *Lysis*, *Euthydemus*, and *Charmides*, Plato's decision to combine Socratic narration with the addition of more complex and problematic supporting characters and dramatic frames indicates that philosophical progress is inseparable from pedagogical playfulness in the Platonic dialogues once ordered in accordance with the Curricular Hypothesis.

It is here, in the pre-*Republic* dialogues, that Plato showed himself to be the real Proteus (see preface), assuming the forms of the love-struck Hippothales, the bemused but scarcely detached Ctesippus, the doughty Menexenus, and Lysis the coquette (*Ly.* 211a3). The fact that Plato makes it possible to imagine that he prefers Lysis to Menexenus in *Lysis* (*Ly.* 213d6–8), that he regards Nicias as more Socratic than Laches in *Laches*, that his Ctesippus does more harm than good in *Euthydemus*, and that his portrait of Critias in *Charmides* is a sympathetic one,[31] all testify to his possession of what Dionysius of Halicarnassus called διαλέκτου ποικίλον τι χρῆμα, i.e., a variegated kind of dialectic that has the power to be deceptive (ἀπατηλόν). Plato's dialogues abound in what Cicero called *varietas*,[32] and this Latin word encompasses not only a dramatic ability to make a wide variety of characters believable—and to do so almost entirely through their own words—but the moral and ethical *dissonances* that force students to think for themselves. Long before the distinction between appearance and reality becomes the foundation of *Republic* 1,[33] Plato has not only introduced it on a theoretical level in *Hippias Major* (*Hp. Ma.* 293e11–294e10),[34] but has made it far more intelligible and at the same time fun to observe through the play of character in the dialogues between *Symposium* and *Republic*.

Plato's successors would forget this kind of play after his death, and with it a dialogues-based curriculum passed into oblivion. A modern reader need only compare the traditional way of reading the dialogues—as treatises in which their leading character becomes simply Plato's mouthpiece—and the dialogues themselves. Apart from the way others quickly came and then long continued to read him, there is no good reason to identify Plato simply and resolutely with one or more of his characters: as reflected in his writings, his goal is rather to make us think for ourselves. Neither in its skeptically Socratic nor in its dogmatically cosmological phases did the post-Plato Academy prove itself worthy of these carefully crafted and deliberately puzzling masterpieces of pedagogical art, and the words "as Plato says in the *Timaeus*" marked as precipitous a decline in Platonism as did Plato's death, the defeat of Athens at Chaeronea, and Speusippus' *Letter to Philip*.

Just before introducing the distinction between appearance and reality in *Hippias Major*, Plato writes: "*Socrates*: Let us therefore keep watch lest somehow we be deceived [σκοπώμεθα μή πη ἄρ' ἐξαπατώμεθα] (*Hp. Ma.* 293e9), and deception or ἀπάτη is promptly linked to appearance at 294a7. Although it will not be until *Phaedrus*, and thus after *Republic*,[35] that Plato will name the art or τέχνη that makes both ἀπάτη and its detection possible (*Phdr.* 261d10–262c4), he has been expecting us to detect his own use of deception and fallacy since *Protagoras*, and he does so primarily by allowing Socrates to contradict himself there as well as by making self-contradiction itself thematic in the discussion of Simonides in that brilliant dialogue (*Prt.* 339b7–10). Characteristically and importantly, it is *speeches* that provide the context for both "the science of deception" (or rather ἡ ἀντιλογικὴ τέχνη at *Phdr.* 261d10–e2) and Socrates' use of deliberate self-contradiction in *Protagoras*. When Socrates declares: "I happen to be a forgetful sort of fellow" (*Prt.* 334c8–9) in the midst of reciting a detailed account of past events, it is not enough that Plato allows him to recite verbatim something Protagoras has just said (cf. *Prt.* 359b2–6 and 349d6–8); he also allows Alcibiades to deny that Socrates is as forgetful as he claims to be (*Prt.* 336d3–4). Nor is this example of self-contradiction unique: having introduced the "say only what you believe" principle (*Prt.* 331c3–d1) that Gregory Vlastos made foundational to his account of the Socratic refutation or ἔλεγχος,[36] Socrates promptly contradicts himself on just this point (*Prt.* 333c5–9). But the breadth of Socratic self-contradiction is so extensive in Plato's *Protagoras* that it risks becoming invisible thanks to its ubiquity, as when Socrates makes a long speech in praise of Spartan brevity (*Prt.* 342a6–343c5)—and note that he ends the speech by asking his audience to consider in common whether or not he is speaking the truth (*Prt.* 343c6–7)—in the midst of what is itself the even longer speech that is the dialogue itself apart from its Frame.[37]

The ubiquity of speeches in the dialogues combined with the Curricular Hypothesis provides internal evidence for the view that Plato was teaching rhetoric; if not Demosthenes, then at least Cicero and Dionysius of Halicarnassus supply external evidence for the same claim (see preface). Socrates himself is learning ῥητορική in *Menexenus* (*Mx.* 236a1) and is sharing his teacher's instruction with Menexenus in that dialogue, and he does so by reciting from memory a speech of Aspasia his teacher has beaten into his head (*Mx.* 236b7–c1). The reference to Aspasia as his distinctively female teacher (ἡ διδάσκαλος at *Mx.* 236c3) prepares us for Diotima, and *Symposium* as a whole is a treasury of eloquence and oratorical variety.[38] An anecdote about Demosthenes is our primary evidence that Isocrates may have written a rhetorical manual,[39] but even if he did, can anyone doubt that he taught rhetoric by making his students study his own carefully written speeches? Phaedrus has concealed a speech of Lysias under his cloak so that he can study it at the beginning of *Phaedrus* (*Phdr.* 228a6–b6) before Socrates supplies two more so that we can, and it is no accident that Plato also makes it obvious that there were other inadequate methods of instruction in this subject in the same dialogue, where he not only discusses Isocrates at length and by name (*Phdr.* 278e4–279b3) but also gives the fullest accounting that has come down to us (*Phdr.* 266c1–273e4) of the limited value of the precepts written down by others in rhetorical manuals (τὰ ἐν τοῖς βιβλίοις τοῖς περὶ λόγων τέχνης γεγραμμένοις at *Phdr.* 266d5–6). Once again, *Phaedrus* offers advanced training in subjects that Plato has been teaching his students from the start.

Of course it is not only rhetoric that Plato is using Socrates and Aspasia to teach his readers in *Menexenus*: it is here that we realize, if we had not realized it already, how much importance he attached to a detailed knowledge of Athenian History.[40] In fact, this knowledge is already presupposed in *Protagoras*, where Pericles is still alive, and in the *Alcibiades* dyad, where Plato chose to build his most elementary instruction around a historical person whose character, accomplishments, and crimes Thucydides and Xenophon had already immortalized. Thanks to the drunken Alcibiades, the disastrous Sicilian Expedition is the uninvited guest to Agathon's banquet in *Symposium*,[41] and it is there we learn, once again from Alcibiades, about Socrates' military service (*Smp.* 219e5–221c1) and thus of his direct involvement in battles already narrated by the historians. Like the play of character, a concern with history increases in the dialogues between *Symposium* and *Republic*,[42] and the two virtues that Alcibiades uses Socrates' heroics at Potidaea and Delium to illustrate promptly reappear as the subjects of *Laches* and *Charmides*. Like the instruction in rhetoric that spans the distance between *Protagoras* and *Phaedrus*, Plato's concern with teaching history will extend all the way to the third book of *Laws*, but its importance will recede after *Critias*; like so much else in Plato's pre-*Republic* dialogues, the reader's detailed knowledge of the Peloponnesian War is intended to prepare the reader to appreciate his masterpiece.[43]

Just as Plato's *Republic* constitutes the center of the Reading Order as constructed or reconstructed in *Plato the Teacher*, so too does the Idea of the Good as enshrined in the Allegory of the Cave constitute the theoretical and practical basis of that centrality (see especially *R*. 534b8–d2). The most important thing I learned while writing about the pre-*Republic* dialogues is why Plato allows Socrates to say so little about the Idea of the Good: thanks to what I call "the Εὖ Πράττειν Fallacy,"[44] it is sufficient to distinguish it from what is merely and ignobly "good for me" or "happiness [εὐδαιμονία]." The fallacy in question depends on the slide made possible between the colloquial and literal meanings of εὖ πράττειν, which means "to fare well" or "to be happy [εὐδαιμονεῖν]" (*Euthd*. 280b6) even though it literally means "to do [things] well." Starting in *Alcibiades Major* (*Alc.1* 115b1–116b13), Socrates uses this equivocation to prove that those who "do nobly [καλῶς πράττειν]" by risking wounds and death in wartime by running to the aid (βοηθεῖν) of others "do well" (which of course they do) and thus are happy because they εὖ πράττειν in the colloquial sense (*Alc.1* 116b5); the Fallacy reappears in *Euthydemus, Charmides, Gorgias*,[45] and at the end of *Republic* 1. Without denying that Plato can make himself *appear* to be a eudaemonist, as Aristotle actually was, it is the transcendent Idea of the Good that grounds the other-benefitting *choice* of philosophers to return to the Cave at the (temporary) cost of their (earthly) happiness; it is only those who choose to do so who are Plato's philosophers, and they are likewise the only trustworthy guardians of his or any other city (*R*. 520e4–521a2).

It was first by making a distinction between the Longer and the Shorter Ways (*R*. 435c9–d4 and 504a4–c3) that Plato began to offer this choice to his students, and it is because a majority of them have interpreted his masterpiece in accordance with the Shorter of these that he appears to be a eudaemonist, and thus primarily concerned with offering us a proof that "justice pays" and is thus self-benefitting. Under the guidance of Aristotle, it has become habitual to separate (the historical) Socrates from Plato only on the basis of the Shorter Way, where the soul's division into three parts restores the possibility of ἀκρασία or incontinence, and thus departs from and indeed rejects the kind of "Socratic intellectualism" that Aristotle had been invited to find in *Protagoras*.[46] Along the Shorter

Way, the tripartite soul is the basis for a proof that those who do well inevitably fare well, and thus gain in happiness and pleasure; this proof reaches a peak in *Republic* 4 and then continues after an intermission in *Republic* 8–10. Meanwhile, and apparently by contrast, the so-called "Socratic dialogues" have been read in accordance with an Aristotle-inspired account of Socratic intellectualism that makes Socrates a eudaemonist, and since he repeatedly employs the Εὖ Πράττειν Fallacy in those dialogues, this is not surprising. Aristotle's error was to make the wrong separation although he makes it for what he regards as a good reason: by making ἀκρασία or "weakness of will" the dividing line, he can prove Socrates wrong while upholding "his" (alleged) position against Plato on "the separation of the forms."[47] But as indicated by this crucial separation, it is not in the Shorter Way that Plato offers us something entirely new— for it too upholds the acquisition of virtue on a eudaemonist basis—but only in the Longer, and that novelty, grounded in the Idea of the Good, is that it is at the expense of self-benefit and for the benefit of others that the true philosopher chooses Justice, and returns to the Cave immediately after leaving the Academy, as Demosthenes did.

But even if Aristotle divided Plato against himself while describing the allegedly historical Socrates, he made an invaluable contribution to the correct interpretation of the Divided Line in *Republic* 6. By distinguishing two classes of intelligible objects[48] on the basis of the methodology suitable for the consideration of each, the Divided Line makes it possible to see the Shorter Way as an inquiry that requires the use of images—in this case, the image of a city—and which depends so heavily on its initial hypotheses that it can never move beyond them.[49] In explaining this hypothetical method to Glaucon, Socrates used arithmetic and geometry as examples; Aristotle took "mathematical things [τὰ μαθηματικά]" alone to be what he called "the intermediates [τὰ μεταξύ]" between the Ideas and sensible things.[50] In fact, the scope of Plato's Intermediates is far wider, and the first step toward realizing this is the recognition that the Shorter Way has depended on the use of hypotheses from the start,[51] explicitly so in making the case for a tripartite soul (R. 437a5; cf. *Phd.* 100b5–6), and replicates the image-based language of shaping and drawing (R. 510e1– 511a2) from the very beginning of the city (R. 368d4 and 374a5).[52] When justice in the city emerges each going the job for which they are by nature suited in *Republic* 4 (R. 433a1–6), this confirms or rather simply returns to the initial hypothesis of the division of labor in *Republic* 2 (369e3–370c7; cf. ἐξ ἀρχῆς at 433a1), a return made predictable and indeed inevitable "from the methods we are presently using in our speeches" (R. 435d1–2; cf. 510d1–3), the words that introduce the Shorter Way.

The discovery that the methods associated with "discursive reason" or διάνοια (R. 511d3–e1) in the (second highest part of the) Divided Line are implemented along the Shorter Way of Plato's *Republic* has three important results, any one of which could plausibly become the theme of a substantial monograph: (1) it creates a textual basis for a Justice-based reading of Plato's masterpiece that moves beyond the alternative that has been dominant since Aristotle focused his criticisms on the city,[53] an approach that regards other matters in the text—and the education of the Guardians in particular[54]—as extraneous to what is still called "Plato's Political Theory,"[55] (2) by extending "the Scope of the Intermediates" to include all intelligible objects that depend on a "one-over-many" relationship between "forms" and sensible particulars (R. 596a5–b2)—none of which can be cognized without an Image and all of which depend on the prior Hypothesis of the One[56]—it confines the true Platonic Ideas to those objects accessed only in the highest part of the Divided Line, and (3) it therefore invites us to search for an alternative account of Justice in accordance with the Longer Way based on that highest part of the Line, and thus in a dependent relation to the Idea of the Good (R. 511b2–c2; cf. 535a5-b2). With respect to the first, the merely didactic use of an imaginary City places Socrates' proposals on an altogether different level from those of the Eleatic Stranger in *Statesman* and especially what the Athenian Stranger proposes for practical implementation on Crete in *Laws*; the second points to Beauty, Justice, and the Idea of the Good as the true basis for "Plato's Theory of Forms,"[57] none of which are susceptible to "the Third Man" in *Parmenides*.[58]

For the third, Plato does not ask us to wait: the Allegory of the Cave immediately follows the Divided Line in Plato's *Republic*. Not only does the existence of the City depend on compelling the philosophers to return to the Cave (R. 519c8-d7) but this compulsion undermines the hypothesis upon which the City has been based from the start and which constitutes "justice" along the Shorter Way: by becoming rulers, philosophers will be performing two jobs.[59] When Glaucon objects that by compelling the Guardians to return to the Cave we will be doing them an injustice (R. 519d8-9), Socrates responds that the creators of the City did not construct it for the well-being of the Guardians alone but for the City as a whole (R. 519e1-520a5) and that philosophers who emerge in any other city are under no obligation to sacrifice their happiness for others because they received no nurture (τροφή) from anybody but themselves and therefore owe the cost of that nurture (τὰ τροφεία) to nobody (R. 520a6-b5). But then, turning to the imaginary Guardians of his hypothetical City, Socrates tells us that he said:

> "But you [ὑμεῖς δ'] we have engendered both for yourselves and for the other city [ἡ ἄλλη πόλις; colloquially, 'for the rest of the city'] as both leaders [ἡγεμόναι] and kings in the beehive, having been both better and more per-

fectly educated than those, and more capable of participating in both [ways of life]. It is therefore necessary to go down [καταβατέον] for each in turn to the cohabitation of the others and necessary to become accustomed to observing the dark things there. For once accustomed, you will see ten thousand better than those there, and you will know those idols [τὰ εἴδωλα] and of what they are [merely idols], on account of having seen the truth about things both beautiful and just and good."[60]

This passage creates what I have called "the crisis of the *Republic*,"[61] for it forces every reader *to make a choice*: is this the speech of a non-existent city's founders, addressed only to its imaginary Guardians, or has Plato found a way to direct this καταβατέον directly at me and all the rest of his students?

At the center of this book is the claim that Demosthenes, along with Dion, Phocion, Lycurgus, and Hyperides, took this speech the second way, and that by transcending the literal and comforting alternative, they made the choice that Plato intended them to make. This passage aligns the Academy's true purpose with the more time-consuming and laborious response to the alternatives preserved in Third Wave of Paradox: by giving young Athenians a better and more perfect education (R. 520b7–8) and challenging them to recognize themselves as ὑμεῖς, Plato was training them to become what at least four of them actually became: the ἡγεμόναι, not the kings, of ἡ ἄλλη πόλις, for it was to him that they owed τὰ τροφεία (R. 520b5). All four of them recognized τὰ εἴδωλα for what they are, and their speeches were aimed not at an illusory ease but at the Just, the Beautiful, and the Good. Without the Academy, the citizens of any democratic polity are naturally inclined to value the free expression of individuality over the common good, the pleasure of the moment over the arduous path of virtue, what's good for me personally over what's absolutely good, relativism to ethical absolutes, and self-fulfillment over self-sacrifice. But Plato seems to have thought that even if only a few Athenians chose the longer and harder way, they could arrest the slide of the democratic city into tyranny, and that's just what I am claiming his best students actually did: they freely chose to return to the Cave of political life, armed with the tools that his dialogues had taught them in the Old Academy: rhetoric, the careful observation of character, and the ability to detect and resist deception prominent among them.

In many ways, it was the traditional choice,[62] but the weight of another tradition has made it difficult to imagine that the Academy's purpose could have been anything as obvious, conventional, and patriotic. Over Plato's eloquent objections (R. 495c8–496a10), we have come to expect that philosophy must be theoretical, cosmological, and arcane. Under Plato's successors, the Academy would justify this image, and as the foregoing account of the Divided Line indicates, there were good grounds for inter-Academic debates about the relationship between Ideas and Numbers described in Aristotle's *Metaphysics*, although scarcely sufficient grounds for ignoring the fact that Plato's *Republic* was built around a more difficult and important choice (*R*. 360d8–361d6). If the hegemony of Macedon had made a patriotic Academy obsolete, there had likewise been no need for such an institution in the Athens that had flourished before the Great War. As long as the tradition of selfless service to the city remained strong, Plato's genius was not needed to keep it alive. But quite apart from what I am claiming that Demosthenes' speeches can teach us about Plato, they clearly teach us about the widespread ethical bankruptcy of fourth-century Athens, and it was to counteract the selfishness and greed of a great city gone astray that first Socrates and now his students would take their stand. *Memorabilia* 3 repeatedly depicts Xenophon's Socrates teaching civic virtue, and the decision Glaucon renders after "the crisis of the *Republic*" (*R*. 520e1) shows that it was only after receiving the kind of political instruction that Socrates offered him that he could overcome the selfishness (*R*. 520e4–521a2) and ignorance he displayed at nineteen.[63] Moreover, it is no accident that Charmides, the youngster Xenophon's Socrates fails to persuade to offer his advice to the city in the next chapter,[64] would end up among the Thirty.

Led beyond the Shorter Way by the Divided Line to the Allegory of the Cave, I argued in *Plato the Teacher* that on the Longer Way, Justice is best understood as a *choice*,[65] made by the reader at "the crisis of the *Republic*." Glaucon's speech at the beginning of *Republic* 2 offered a textual basis for the centrality of κρίσις as "decision, judgment" (LSJ; cf. *R*. 360d8 and 361d5) along with the related verbs κρίνειν (*R*. 360e2) and κρίνεσθαι (*R*. 361d3); the choice of lives was likewise emphasized in Xenophon,[66] also in a political context.[67] But Danielle Allen's research suggests the possibility that Plato's unwritten word for this "decision" may have been προαίρεσις, for even though he uses it only once in the dialogues (*Prm*. 143c3), it thereafter flourishes in the writings of his students beginning with Aristotle,[68] coming to mean not only "choosing" but "purpose," "resolution," "course of life," "policy," and "principle of action" (LSJ). In arguing that the use of προαίρεσις indicates an important paradigm shift,[69] Allen finds her most compelling evidence in Lycurgus' *Against Leocrates*:

> The speech is itself an education in choice-making as Lycurgus, in a passage unparalleled in ancient oratory, quotes one after another literary and historical texts, all of which have to do with the climactic moments of choice-making. Lycurgus converts his own rhetorical education in texts about choice-making into a public curriculum; he may be said to be inventing the idea of public education as a sector distinct from the ordinary educative capacities of custom.[70]

Taking Codrus' choice for self-sacrifice as a prominent historical example, and displaying in every literary quotation the enduring influence of Plato's *Ion* on "his own rhetorical education," Lycurgus was rather bringing to the Cave "the idea of public education" he had experienced as a youth in the Academy,[71] and illuminating the choice he had made as a result.

Interpretations of the dialogues have and will always vibrate between an otherworldly theoretical Platonism on the one hand, and a down-to-earth practical skepticism, grounded on Socrates, on the other; at either extreme, Plato disappears. The reason that the Allegory of the Cave occupies the dead center of Platonism—and thus of the curriculum that was designed to teach it—is that the voluntary return of the guardians unites these two poles inseparably: it is on the basis of the ontologically transcendent that the philosopher becomes practical, temporarily sacrificing the joys of theoretical contemplation for the sake of the same public mission that had led to the murder of Socrates.[72] Naturally a project designed to show that practical politicians like Demosthenes and Lycurgus were Plato's students must gravitate toward the down-to-earth rather than the otherworldly, and when the wedding of the One and the Indefinite Dyad of the unwritten teachings,[73] the World Soul in *Timaeus*,[74] or the ὁμοίωσις θεῷ of the *Theaetetus* Digression[75] are taken to be the acme of Platonism, it is easy to regard this gravitation as an irresponsible dumbing down of Plato's richly original and deeply philosophical thought. What needs to be kept in mind is that however traditional might have been the choice Plato was asking his youngsters to make, what Allen calls "the ordinary educative capacities of custom" had by now lost their power, and it was only by aligning Justice inseparably with the transcendence and separation of the Good and the Beautiful as Ideas that Plato grounded the traditional decision for τὸ καλῶς θνήσκειν[76] on a revolutionary ontology that elevated soul over body, Being over Becoming, and doing over faring well.[77]

Plato could not test the degree of any given student's commitment to the choice he was asking them to make directly; he would force them to discover that he was asking them to make it for themselves at "the crisis of the *Republic*." Even if they gave every indication that they had chosen the Longer Way as students, they could only prove it by what they chose to do after leaving the Academy. It was therefore not on the choice itself, but rather on the ontological basis on which he had now grounded it, that Plato tested his students in the post-*Republic* dialogues beginning with *Timaeus*.[78] Beginning with Thales, philosophy had been inseparable from physics and the pleasures of cosmological speculation[79]; thanks to Plato's austere ontology, the realm of Becoming and the visible cosmos, including "the heaven's glorious sun" (cf. R. 509b1-9), was now likened to the fire-cast shadows in the Cave.[80]

Meanwhile, and from the very beginning of the curriculum, Plato had been training his students to recognize both deception and deceivers,[81] and once he had revealed the centrality of the Idea of the Good in *Republic* 6-7 along with the propaedeutic role of διάνοια in turning the student's attention away from Becoming toward unchanging Being (*R.* 525b9–c6 and 526e7–8), this advanced training—commencing with *Timaeus-Critias* and supplemented by the account of ἀπάτη in *Phaedrus*[82]—now takes the form of what I call "basanistic pedagogy,"[83] whereby the student is tested by authoritative characters who undermine the chasm between Being and Becoming even while appearing to uphold it, as Timaeus does (*Ti.* 27d5–28a1; cf. *Phdr.* 262b5–7).[84]

With the entrance of Timaeus "the most astronomical" (*Ti.* 27a3–4; cf. *R.* 529a1–c3), Plato invited those whose thinking remained riveted to the physical and visible (*R.* 518d3-519b5; cf. *Ti.* 47a1–4) to imagine that Socrates, whose neglect of cosmology was notorious,[85] was no longer guiding him, and for them, *Timaeus* would become the paradigmatic Platonic dialogue after Plato's death.[86] Once equated with Timaeus,[87] Plato could plausibly become the neo-Pythagorean Aristotle described in *Metaphysics* A.6 even without the peculiarly un-Socratic Socrates of *Philebus*[88]; only the utterly simple solution of the Problem of the One and the Many introduced in *Republic* 7, made thematic in *Parmenides*, and then reinforced late in *Philebus* itself (*Phlb.* 56d9–e3; cf. 15a1–b2) blocked the path that had already led so many pre-Socratics to believe that "all things are one," and which now inclined many of Plato's students to imagine that the kind of dialectic that collected many into one or divided one into many (*Phdr.* 265d3–266c1; cf. *Sph.* 253d5–e5) could possibly have replaced the dialectical method described in the highest part of the Divided Line (*R.* 511b2–c2).[89] Treating each hypothesis as a mere springboard is an integral part of that method (*R.* 511b4–5), and a willingness to question the hypotheses that every authoritative character in the dialogues speaks for Plato, that the One can be Many or the Many One, and that Socrates believed that everyone who does well fares well, goes a long way toward making even the most difficult Platonic dialogues child's play with respect to delibrate deception.

It was probably considerably more difficult for Plato's first students to believe that their teacher had moved beyond or outgrown Socrates than it has become for us, and since the late nineteenth century, we have discovered a way to disjoin *Euthyphro* and *Apology of Socrates* as "early dialogues" from *Theaetetus, Sophist*, and *Statesman* as compositionally late ones.[90] Joining Timaeus and Critias while anticipating the later arrival of the Athenian Stranger in *Laws-Epinomis*, the Eleatic Stranger enters the picture in the context of Socrates' trial, and despite the fact that *Apology* occupies the place where *Philosopher* isn't,[91] the current reception of Plato has proved itself altogether too comfortable with condemning Socrates to an outgrown phase of Plato's own intellectual development, a sophisticated point of view that is no more consistent with the aims of the Old Academy than the Athenian jury's benighted verdict. Beginning with *Gorgias* and then continuing through *Theages, Meno,* and *Cleitophon,* Plato has prepared the reader for the trial and death of Socrates, but the opening word of the *Republic*—κατέβην or "I went down" (*R.* 327a1)—indicates for the first time that the ultimate cause of his death was his decision to return to the Cave and testify against the shadowy εἴδωλα of happiness, virtue, and justice that prevail there. To this story, there was only one possible ending for the cycle of thirty-five dialogues, for Socrates is absent from only two of them and is the leading speaker in all but seven; unfortunately, *Euthyphro* stands first and the final *Phaedo* fourth in the edition that has come down to us.

By embedding *Sophist* and *Statesman* in what would later become "the First Tetralogy of Thrasyllus," Plato tested his students in three distinct ways, and most simply by challenging them to defend Socrates as self-described in the *Apology* as Plato's *Philosopher*. By having its leading character liken Socrates to a sophist (*Sph.* 230b4–231b8; cf. 229c5–6 and 267e11–a9), refute "the Friends of the Forms" (*Sph.* 248a4–249b4) and ridicule "the Late Learners" (*Sph.* 251b6–252c9), Plato's *Sophist* challenges the student to defend Being as intrinsically unchanging (*Sph.* 250c6–7), a challenge naturally played out in the context of Parmenides (*Tht.* 180e4),[92] whose pedagogical technique Plato has been borrowing since *Timaeus*.[93] But the education the dialogues provide always remains essentially political, and in *Statesman,* the murderous implications of a post-Socratic politics become obvious (*Plt.* 293c5–e2).[94] Perhaps it was from Xenophon that Plato came to realize that the greatest political danger would arise from the myth of a theologized monarch who, posing as a divine shepherd (*Plt.* 275b1–c5; cf. 301d8–e4), would claim to rule men as men rule beasts[95]; more likely, it was from his kinsman Critias (*Criti.* 109b1–c4). But as the cycle of dialogues reaches its finale, it is the contrast between the merely human wisdom of Socrates (*Ap.* 20d8 and 23a5–b4) and the impious pretense to some higher and justifiably despotic knowledge (*Prm.* 134d9–e6; cf. *Plt.* 293c7) to which at least one of Plato's two Strangers will lay claim (*Lg.* 818b9–d1; cf. *Epin.* 986c5–e1) that points to the focal point of his concern for the future, soon to be justified by the theological-political fusion of Philip's power with Aristotle's precepts in Alexander the Great.

In *Gorgias,* Callicles ridicules philosophers because they are ignorant of the laws, inexperienced with the characters of men (*Grg.* 484d2–d6), and perfect strangers to the city's center, where good and noble deeds are done (*Grg.* 485d4–5; cf. 484c8–d2); they would be better advised to learn rhetoric, and thus the power to defend themselves (*Grg.* 486b4–c3). Not one of these charges apply to the philosophers Plato is training if we are willing to reimagine the Academy on the basis of the Curricular Hypothesis. In *Apology of Socrates* and the Speech of the Laws in *Crito*, Plato has given us a thorough education in democratic rhetoric, and thanks to the Allegory of the Cave, every one of his best students will now know how and why to find their way to the city's center. Beginning in the post-*Symposium* dialogues, Plato has been offering us a thorough education in the characters of men and he will test our acumen on this subject with his two Strangers and Timaeus, all three of whom we would naturally be inclined to judge on the basis of reputation rather than substance (*R.* 534c2). As for legal training, Plato devotes his longest dialogue to legislation, and *Laws* requires the advanced student to examine the implications of every word the Athenian Stranger says, especially while legislating. Although often resembling the laws of Athens, the Stranger's legislation repeatedly undermines democratic values, and only our misplaced certainty that Plato despised democracy and sought its undoing has made it possible to read *Laws* sympathetically, a sympathy that not incidentally has required the excision of *Epinomis* to sustain it.[96] As for the Preludes, unquestionably the most attractive aspect of Plato's *Laws*, not one of them possesses a fraction of the grandeur, substance, and rhetorical power of what the Laws of Athens say through Socrates in *Crito*.[97]

It is above all by interpolating three dyads in the interstices of the First Tetralogy that the Reading Order paradigm differs from the reigning ordering by chronology of composition,[98] and it is on the interpretation of *Phaedo* that this difference has the greatest impact. When interpreted as a middle-period dialogue by an author who has not yet written *Republic*, *Phaedrus*, and *Parmenides*, *Phaedo* can easily be consigned to its currently conventional place as the product of an outgrown stage of Plato's development.[99] On the ontological level, this consignment makes all of the following features of the Final Argument constitutive of the Theory of Forms: the forms are (1) causes of becoming (*Phd.* 100c9–e3),[100] (2) they are hypothesized (*Phd.* 100b1-7), (3) they include unitary numbers (*Phd.* 101b10–c5), (4) they include the big (*Phd.* 100b6), and (5) they are therefore susceptible to refutation by "the Third Man" (*Phd.* 100e5–6; cf. *Prm.* 132a1-b2). Best understood as a Final Examination in what it is that the Platonic Ideas really cause (*Phd.* 98e1–99a5), *Phaedo* completes the story of Socrates, and makes his "hero's death" or *Heldentod* the culmination of the Academy's curriculum, preparing its students for the by no means unlikely result of consistently preferring suffering wrong to doing it, and unforgettably illustrating the insouciance with which a Socratic can face what it means to ὑπεραποθνῄσκειν. The theme of Plato's immortal *Phaedo* is purification, but its interpretation is yet to be purified from the distortions of developmentalism. [101]

If we include Cicero, three of the Platonists considered in this book died on behalf of their enduring commitment to democratic or at the very least anti-tyrannical principle, just as the death-scene in *Phaedo* had so long ago inspired them to do. Joining Demosthenes and Cicero in having made the youthful choice, Hyperides perfectly illustrated Allen's point about προαίρεσις when he spoke of the soldiers who had died fighting the Macedonians one last time in what also proved to be the last extent example of Attic oratory: "How noble [καλή] and paradoxical [παράδοξον] was the daring [τόλμη] done by these men, how glorious and magnificent the choice they chose [προαίρεσιν ἥν προείλοντο], how surpassing their virtue [ἀρετή] and manly excellence [ἀνδραγαθία] among dangers, which they offered up for the common freedom of the Greeks!"[102] This is not the rhetoric of flattery; it is the patriotic swansong of Athena's violet-crowned city, with the school of Hellas now preserved in the Academy.[103] More specifically, it was in the Old Academy that freedom and philosophy came together in the student's sovereign choice to prefer what is difficult and noble to what is easy and advantageous. If any sophist could make the advantageous seem good, Plato could make the noble and the good seem advantageous, and both the Εὖ Πράττειν Fallacy and the Shorter Way prove it. Demosthenes proves that Plato the Teacher taught it as well.

4

Demosthenes

Given the vivid complexity of the world preserved for us in the sixty-one speeches that have come down to us under his name,[1] it was always going to be a challenge to make the single chapter dedicated exclusively to Demosthenes commensurable in length with the other four, but despite the fact that all of them revolve around him, his name stands second in this book's title for a reason. The subject of "Demosthenes" cannot be compassed even in a lengthy book, let alone a chapter, and a path-breaking study devoted to him—and it is difficult to see why anyone would wish to write any other kind[2]—would be forced to comprehend not only the richly varied phenomenon of Demosthenes himself, but would need to deal with endlessly discussed and all-too-familiar problems of authenticity,[3] as well as the understudied matter of the order in which the Demosthenic writings have come down to us.[4] On the other hand, even a single-minded emphasis on Demosthenes' debts to Plato must fail to make the subject any more manageable if the hypothesis that he was Plato's student is true, as I am hoping to show here that it is: the connection necessarily impinges on every aspect of his life and output, as well as on methodological questions of order and authenticity. And even though the claim that Demosthenes was Plato's student must not be construed as an excuse for hagiography, his late twentieth-century Anglophone reception, quite apart from its continuing rejection of Plato's influence, has been so relentlessly hostile that an emphasis on his connection with Plato probably has an intrinsically apologetic aspect.

What Socrates said to the Guardians proved to be true in the case of both Demosthenes and Cicero: "For once accustomed, you will see ten thousand better than those there, and you will know those idols [τὰ εἴδωλα] and of what they are" (R. 520c3-4). The speeches, writings, and letters of both these students of Plato have preserved for us two worlds so vividly described and densely populated with their friends and foes that, under the guise of historical balance and verisimilitude, later scholars have been able to use those worlds to attack those who preserved them, exactly as if such "worlds" had some kind of prior and independent existence and thus greater importance than those without whom they would not even exist. In Cicero's case, Sir Ronald Syme led the way for those who have made careers by "biting the hand that feeds them,"[5] and two others stand at the forefront of those who would do very much the same thing to Demosthenes.[6] Without ignoring the greater scholarly impact of George L. Cawkwell,[7] Ernst Badian's 2002 chapter "The Road to Prominence" deserves recognition as "the fourth speech of Aeschines,"[8] for not even Demosthenes' open enemy penned a more devastating jeremiad.[9] Whether by vindicating Aeschines,[10] or palliating Philip,[11] modern scholars have treated Demosthenes' writings as distortions to be seen through rather than precious documents from which can be learned priceless and perennial lessons about democracy, eloquence, and citizenship. In addition to ignoring or annihilating his connection to Plato, such approaches have also made unfortunate choices regarding authenticity and order of presentation in the process of marginalizing and thus misunderstanding Demosthenes himself.

But there are also some encouraging signs from the United Kingdom. In a 2015 doctoral dissertation written under the supervision of Niall Livingstone,[12] Sarah Bremner has moved beyond the apparently historical but in any case ruthlessly revisionist accounts of Demosthenes' battle with Philip associated with Cawkwell and Co.[13] with a new approach to his Assembly speeches that emphasizes the orator's relationship with Athens and the Athenians.[14] An important aspect of what makes Badian's account of the young Demosthenes so damning is that it offers a picture of an ambitious youngster who only came late to the anti-Philip policy that made him powerful and would make him famous[15]; in the run-up to this belated discovery, he treats us to an unprincipled young man ripe for Cawkwell's revisionism.[16] Bremner, by contrast, finds the core of Demosthenes and the essence of his achievement not in any foreign policy but in a consistent and unflagging commitment to making the Athenians better (cf. *Grg*. 515a4-5),[17] exhorting them "to right themselves by abolishing the forms to which they have become accustomed." In this case, it is from indolence, selfishness, and greed that Bremner's Demosthenes summons the Athenians to declare their independence, and identifies Philip not as the instrument of their coming enslavement but as a self-created symptom of what has made them ripe for slavery.

"Demosthenes reminds the Assembly of what can be achieved when they choose to act, and reduces Philip to the product of their inaction."[18]

Because she is not concerned with Plato's influence, Bremner makes no effort to show that Demosthenes can only pose this challenge to the Athenians because he has already made his own Platonic choice. But she is dead right to look past the historical and political circumstances of his call to action against Philip. Just as Philip is a product of the Assembly's inaction, so also is Demosthenes' decision to address, educate, and exhort the Assembly to action a product of his own prior choice to descend to the Cave by ascending the podium, an Academic decision rooted in his own deepest concerns. This decision was made long ago (Greek παλαί), well before he discovered in Philip the perfect vehicle for educating the Athenians in the lessons Plato's Socrates had already educated him. To this extent, Badian is right: In accordance with *Gorgias* and *Republic* 7, Demosthenes was determined to become a leader (cf. *R.* 520c7 and *Grg.* 526a3-5) long before he was granted the chance to discover in the Macedonian menace the means by which he could actually steer the Athenian ship of state away from the shoals of tyranny. That menace proved to be real, and although attempts have been made to make both Demosthenes and Cicero responsible for the success of the enemies they so single-mindedly opposed,[19] such antics prove only that their enemies will always mistake Platonists who return to the Cave, both while living and long dead, as ineffective and short-sighted if not downright unjust (cf. *R.* 361c5-d3), albeit not because they were Platonists. Unfortunately, it is easier to see how the speeches of Aeschines survive for the greater glory of Demosthenes than that the writings of Cawkwell and Co. exist for the same reason.

Considerable attention has been paid to the chronological order of the three *Olynthians*.[20] Easily forgotten is the prior question: why did Callimachus—conventionally regarded as the creator of the collection or τάξις of Demosthenes' writings[21]—begin with the *Olynthians*? It is to Demosthenes that the *Olynthians* introduce the reader, not to the political complexities of fourth century Greece, and Callimachus places the third of them last because it does so best. He followed the *Third Olynthian* with the *First Philippic* because chronological order was not his concern: he not only wants to teach us who Demosthenes is, but just as importantly how he became himself. The sixty-one speeches are not a cadaver whose limbs are to be amputated and then rearranged prior to burial,[22] but rather, like all the classics, a treasure from which to learn and an example of what we too may achieve what has already proved to be achievable (cf. *Grg.* 526a2-3). The ordering of the speeches repeats the pattern again and again: the *First Philippic* follows the *Olynthians* for the same reason that *On the Symmories* follows the *Philippics*, that *Against Leptines* follows *On the Crown* and *On the False Embassy*, and why the series of five speeches on his inheritance spoken by the young Demosthenes follow the series that begins with *Against Meidias* and ends with the late speeches *Against Aristogeiton*. However detrimental in the case of Plato, a concern with "Demosthenes' Development" is therefore a salutary phenomenon, and the studies that Lionel Pearson and Cecil Wooten devoted to the progress of his style complement both Bremner's approach and mine.[23] For me, the τέλος of this development is the fully Platonic Demosthenes, first apparent in the *Third Philippic*, where Bremner's and Wooten's insights likewise coalesce:

> Through the techniques described above Demosthenes created a very different kind of oratory from what he had practiced earlier. In *For the Megalopolitans* he had used a calm, orderly, cerebral approach and had been unsuccessful. In *Philippic I* he devised an approach that was much more energetic and emotional and also failed. In *Philippic III* he would learn to blend these two extremes to create what is probably the finest deliberative speech from the ancient world.[24]

The perfection of his style and the clarity of his message arise from the fact that the *Third Philippic* is the purest expression of Demosthenes' Platonic choice: he finds both his voice and his theme as a direct result of the intersection of that choice with the crisis of the moment.[25] Demosthenes was forty-three at the time (341) and had delivered his *First Philippic* ten years earlier (351); even after finding his foil in Philip, the masterpiece was slow in coming.[26] Quite apart from the battles with his guardians, the early speeches,[27] Meidias, and Aeschines—and long after bellowing at the sea and the mouthful of pebbles—Demosthenes had worked tirelessly and prepared for this moment, just as Cicero had worked and prepared for the consulship, likewise attained when he was forty-three.

Callimachus has prepared us to recognize the perfection of the *Third Philippic* by the late placement of the *Third Olynthian*. As a fully self-realized Platonic orator, Demosthenes must teach (3.4-9), using rhetoric to criticize not to flatter (3.3 and 3.18), he must unmask self-deception (3.19), and emphasize the just choice while describing the just citizen (3.21); he also blames the Athenians for making Philip possible (3.28-29). While borrowing from *Against Leptines* (see below), he moves beyond it: it is rather the discontinuity with the Athens of old that Demosthenes now emphasizes, and it is on the basis of an idealized Athens that he uses shame to remind the Athenians to become "worthy of yourselves" (3.33).[28] This change involves danger, and it is important to realize that it was not because of his *Olynthians* that Demosthenes became the city's leading advisor. As no student of Socrates needs to be reminded, "free speech" in the form of shaming criticism is dangerous to the speaker (3.32), and not since the gadfly harassed the horse (*Ap.* 30e4-5) had the Athenians been asked so directly to recognize and confront their laziness (3.32-34). Although the influence of *Gorgias* is everywhere to be seen, its most obvious sign is the mention of Aristides (3.26); after all, Demosthenes' praise for the Athenian statesmen Aelius Aristides will call "the Four" (3.21-22) might easily cause the careless to overlook the point Socrates had used Aristides to make: that becoming an Athenian statesman "both noble and good" (καλοὶ κἀγαθοί at *Grg.* 527a7) was difficult (*Grg.* 526a3) *but not impossible*. After using the apt image of the inept doctor (3.33),[29] Demosthenes ends the speech not by praising himself but by calling the Athenians to heroism, for the examples are there and the choice others have made is now theirs to make:

> And while I am not blaming the one who is doing some part of his duty [τὰ δέοντα] on your behalf, I am rather also holding you worthy [ἀξιῶ] to do on your own behalf the things for which you honor others, and not to desert the post [τάξις], you men of Athens, the post of virtue [ἡ ἀρετή], which your ancestors [οἱ πρόγονοι] left to you, having attained it through dangers both many and noble.[30]

By the time we reach the *Third Philippic*, we know the necessary vocabulary, and he echoes this passage at the end of it (9.74). Once again, Demosthenes will criticize the Athenians for their willingness to be deceived (9.13), availing himself of "free speech [παρρησία]" (9.3) as Socrates did (*Ap.* 29d2-30c5).[31] He chooses not "to gratify [χαρίζεσθαι]" but rather "to say the best things [τὰ βέλτιστα] (9.2), foremost among which is once again our need to do τὰ δέοντα (9.4)—indeed "to wish to do what is necessary" (9.52)—and even at this late date (καὶ νῦν ἔτι at 9.76), "everything can yet be set right if you decide to do τὰ δέοντα" (9.4). Having failed to secure Olynthus, Athens is now at peace, and while *On the Peace* and the *Second Philippic* have given us an adequate notion of the Peace of Philocles, *On Halonnesus* and *On the Chersonese* have illuminated the humiliations to which that peace has subjected the city.[32] While others have celebrated the eloquence of the *Third Philippic*, it is through a more openly Platonic orientation that Demosthenes really breaks new ground. After starting with *Apology* and *Republic* (9.3), it is *Gorgias* that he repeatedly echoes with the rejection of pleasure (9.4), flattery (9.4), and self-seeking (πλεονεξία at 9.27) all served up with a generous helping of shame (9.24) and a preference for death over flattering Philip (9.65). The noble suicide of Euphraeus gives him a chance to praise another of Plato's students (*Ep.* 321c3-d4) as an enemy of tyranny (9.59-62; cf. 65),[33] and after an image of a ship that can no longer be saved (9.69), he answers Cleitophon's Question (9.70):[34] "what should we do [τί ποιῶμεν]?" He does so by replacing τὰ δέοντα with Plato's favored way to express duty or obligation—the verbal adjective of which καταβατέον (*R.* 520c1) is the paradigm—beginning with "it is necessary for us to compete [ἀγωνιστέον] on behalf of freedom" (9.70; cf. πρακτέον at 9.74). But it is only when he proposes sending forth ambassadors to the rest of Greece by saying "let us now summon the others" to join us [τοὺς ἄλλους ἤδη παρακαλῶμεν]" (9.71; cf. τούς ἄλλους παρακαλεῖν at 9.73)—their mission is "to convoke, to combine, to teach, to correct" (9.73)—that he reveals the Platonic basis of everything he has done and will henceforth do. Echoing *Gorgias* (τοὺς ἄλλους παρακαλῶμεν at *Grg.* 527e5-6), Demosthenes has answered the last call Socrates addressed to Callicles, the same call that Plato himself had answered by creating the Academy.

An attempt must be made to elucidate the intended significance of this "echoing." Demosthenes is not simply or consciously *quoting* Plato's dialogue, and if we could be sure that he echoed *Gorgias* unconsciously, that would only go to show the greater depth of Plato's influence on him. Rather than "quoting" Plato, Demosthenes' words are what in German is called a *Widerhall*, which adds an explicit element of "response" to the possibly merely repetitive nature of our "echo." "Echo" is a Greek word, of course, indeed a purely Greek one, descending to us directly from ἠχώ, and with its long initial vowel and harsher consonant, it better captures the strictly auditory quality of the phenomenon in question and might almost be applied to the thundering of the sea. Whether at the shore or on the βῆμα, the words of Demosthenes are the echo of Plato's, but not in the sense of repeating, parroting, quoting, or even deftly alluding to them. Rather it is Plato's words, too deeply engraved to be merely quoted, that are the baseline-determining *Grundbestimmung* of his own, whereby it is not only his speeches but Demosthenes' life as a whole that is his thoroughly personal and individualized *Widerhall* to his teacher's καταβατέον.[35]

The confluence of Plato's famous critique of "the Democratic Man" (*R.* 558c6-562a3) with Demosthenes' personal circumstances explains how and why it would be Demosthenes of Paeenia who would most eloquently and completely respond to Plato's call. His unflagging discipline, made vivid for us in the stories his enemies preserved about a half-shaved head, a hermit's cave, a weak voice, a lisp, pebbles, and the sea,[36] was his response to Plato's claim—better understood as a challenge—that "the Democratic Man" was an undisciplined and pleasure-seeking shape-shifter, constitutionally unable to dedicate himself to a single goal (*R.* 561c6-d3). The process by which Demosthenes refuted these claims in practice simultaneously confirms them in theory. If Demosthenes had not been susceptible to the foibles of Plato's democratic man to begin with, he would not have needed to take the extreme steps he did to achieve his goals. The first step in achieving them was uniquely personal: he needed to recover his stolen patrimony, and he worked tirelessly and single-mindedly to do so. Had it only been about the money, the young Demosthenes would have confirmed Plato's account of the thrifty "Oligarchic Man" but the sequel proved that it wasn't. Nevertheless, this first step was decisive, because what made the mature Demosthenes so great was that he reminded all Athenians that they too had been cheated of their patrimony just as he had been, and thus needed to recover *their* stolen inheritance. He ably summoned them to acquire the same kind of discipline, commitment, and self-abnegation that had allowed the young Demosthenes to recover his.

In the process, he would save the brilliant speeches of Isaeus from oblivion, for it is just as wrong-headed to deny that Demosthenes had many teachers, as it is to ignore the evidence that Plato was the first of them, in both time and importance. First and foremost, Demosthenes learned from Isaeus the intricacies of inheritance law, and by preserving *Response to Macartatus* and *Response to Leochares*,[37] Callimachus ensured that we would remember that Demosthenes never forgot them. But with respect to rhetoric, Isaeus was not his teacher, and this can be proved not only where Demosthenes excelled him but also where he fell short in comparison, especially with respect to colloquial clarity. The student who comes to Isaeus and Demosthenes after immersion in the dialogues of Plato will find the speeches of the former easier to read and appreciate; the artful simplicity of Lysias is placed in the service of a none too scrupulous ability to play both sides of inheritance disputes.[38] Emphasizing impersonal laws where it suited his client's needs and wills where it didn't, Isaeus adheres to only one fixed principle: nobody acts against their own self-interest.[39] As an Old Academic, Demosthenes would reject this principle in word and deed, and would die in accordance with that rejection. But it was not only or even primarily with respect to ethical principle that Demosthenes excelled Isaeus, but rather in his ability to speak in a variety of different voices and personae: every one of Isaeus' plaintiffs sounds like Isaeus,[40] and to prove it, none of his surviving speeches have been branded inauthentic.[41]

This is hardly true of Plato's student, and of far greater significance than the fact that the character of Sositheus can be distinguished from Aristodemus' even when Demosthenes is channeling Isaeus,[42] there is the colossal problem of Apollodorus.[43] Even if the moderns are right that Demosthenes did not write the seven speeches preserved by Callimachus spoken by Apollodorus, his ability to impersonate him fooled the ancients, and if the ancients were right, we are ones who have been fooled. Nobody who has given despised Platonic dialogues like *Cleitophon* and *Epinomis* any independent reconsideration is likely to accept on faith similar claims about how six of these seven speeches are "unworthy of Demosthenes,"⁴⁴ and an assessment of worthiness should take into consideration their proven success at fooling others into thinking that somebody other than Demosthenes wrote them.⁴⁵ It was clearly the goal of a good logographer (cf. *Phdr.* 258b10-c5) not to be detected *as* a logographer, and Demosthenes would not have been the first to make his obvious ability in this area difficult to spot:

> Plato is in fact a logographer (a writer of speeches for others to deliver) of the first rank. For variety, range, mastery of all the available means of persuasion (in Aristotelian terms ēthos, *pathos*, *logos*) he has no equal.⁴⁶

While Helen North's point is an important one, Demosthenes was at the very least Plato's equal in this respect, but concerning the speeches universally attributed to Apollodorus, only *Against Neaira*, disconnected from the other six by length and position,⁴⁷ deserves defense here.⁴⁸

Crucial for understanding what Apollodorus did for Demosthenes,⁴⁹ *Against Neaira* could not have been written by anyone else precisely because it so obviously seems to have been (see the deposition of Demosthenes at 59.122), much like the even more playful *Against Theocrines* with which Callimachus paired it (more on this speech below). Beyond praise are the seemingly irrelevant hymn to Plataea (59.94-106), the geographical patter-song of 59.108—climaxing with the obscenity—in the midst of the great passage between 107 and 115, a burst of eloquence that includes the interrogation of the returning jurymen by their wives (59.110-111; cf. 48) and culminating with the demand to listen not to Apollodorus but to the personified laws (59.115), the conceit Demosthenes learned from *Crito* and had already used to great effect in *Against Meidias* (21.187). With his skill in making his characters so believable that we have been persuaded to accord them independent existence, Demosthenes may be said to have rivaled if not excelled his teacher, for nobody would be so foolish as to make the parallel claim that the irascible Apollodorus (*Smp.* 172a1-173d3) was the true author of *Symposium* just because Plato places the story in his mouth.⁵⁰

Despite the fact that Isocrates likewise falls short of Platonic and Demosthenic variety with respect to the uniformity and unmistakably Isocratean eloquence of his highly polished style,⁵¹ the problem of Demosthenes' debt to him is infinitely more difficult than the case of Isaeus. To deny that there were many such debts, both direct through reading his writings and indirectly through Isaeus, is senseless. Quite apart from Hubbell's simplistic position (see chapter 3), there are many critical instances of overlap, with the embattled advisor reminding the Athenians of their city's former greatness, and demanding from them a virtuous choice being foremost among them.⁵² Isocrates advises the

Athenians to make the same choice he would later offer to Philip, and the resolutely self-interested character of that choice, even where one might be tempted to find the opposite,[53] is what one would expect from a teacher who traded instruction for a hefty fee.[54] For the present, it is sufficient to supplement the pro-Macedonian *Philippus* (see chapter 2) with the criticisms of Isocrates that can be found in the speeches of Demosthenes. The most sustained attack on him is in *Response to Lacritus*[55]; naturally there were others who saw fit to reject as inauthentic a speech that so strongly suggested Demosthenes' enmity toward Isocrates.[56] But Galen O. Rowe, who was sympathetic to the claim that Demosthenes was Plato's student,[57] also used *Against Androtion* to illustrate Demosthenes' antagonism to Isocrates.[58] Perhaps the clearest proof is furnished by two men named Pytho: whether speaking for himself or as impersonated by Demosthenes in *On Halonnesus*,[59] Hegesippus attacks Philip's spokesman Pytho of Byzantium, reminding the Athenians that he was a student of Isocrates (7.23). Meanwhile, Demosthenes also mentions Pytho of Aenos, a student of Plato's with whom Pytho of Byzantium has been erroneously confused,[60] who assassinated Cotys, and received Athenian citizenship and a crown for doing so (23.119).[61] Were it not for this assassin's subsequent service to Philip, the comparative influence of Isocrates and Plato on Demosthenes might plausibly be measured by the difference between a tyrant's killer and his tongue.

Plato mentions Isocrates by name and praises him for youthful promise in *Phaedrus* (*Phdr.* 279a5-b1).[62] As the unnamed frontiersman between philosophy and politics, he also appears at the end of *Euthydemus* (*Euthd.* 304d4-306d1).[63] By contrast, his Socrates never mentions Herodotus, Thucydides, or Xenophon, while virtually everywhere, but especially in the pre-*Republic* dialogues, Plato is requiring his readers to be familiar with their writings. Even if based on his own dialogues, the Academy's literary curriculum was by no means confined to them—reading them well requires the student to be familiar with a great deal of Greek Literature—and the Curricular Hypothesis explains why Demosthenes drew so heavily on Thucydides in particular.[64] Although there is both internal and external evidence that he did so,[65] Demosthenes no more names Thucydides in his speeches than he does Plato, and although modern scholars have had no reason to explain why he does not name the latter, they have inadvertently provided that explanation by remarking on the way Demosthenes cites information he could only have learned from the historians: "A public speaker who in any obtrusive manner laid claim to being a man of literary research would have been listened to with impatience by an Athenian audience."[66] As already indicated in the introduction, this book's last chapter will consider three waves of suppression regarding the connection between Demosthenes and Plato, but there was also a prior suppression, for which Demosthenes himself was entirely responsible, and the fact that he concealed his debts to Thucydides as well would expedite these later suppressions. But in neither case does he conceal those debts so well that a sympathetic reader cannot detect them, and the passage about Plataea in *Against Neaira*, despite some efforts at concealment,[67] is as eloquent a tribute to Thucydides as the passage about Alcibiades in *Against Meidias* is to Thucydides, Xenophon, and Plato (21.143-45).

Xenophon is a more complicated case, but consideration of his *Ways and Means* is helpful for catching sight of the process by which Demosthenes became himself, explaining at once why he initially failed to recognize the Macedonian threat,[68] and thus only gradually made the transition from Badian's aimless but ambitious young man to Bremner's or rather Plato's physician of the Athenian soul. It probably makes sense to regard the Old Academy's position on current political events as anti-imperial (cf. *Grg.* 518e1-519a7), and thus aligned with the highly civic but resolutely Attica-centered policy proposals of *Ways and Means* (355).[69] The fact that Isocrates' *On the Peace*, likewise written in response to the Social War, also advocated for a post-imperial Athens,[70] indicates why a Philipphobic policy like the one Demosthenes advocated in the 340s would have been neither popular nor plausibly Platonic in the 350s.[71] The extent to which Xenophon influenced Eubulus has been debated,[72] and Cawkwell and Co. have effectively demonstrated that a clear-cut opposition between Demosthenes and a so-called "peace party" is as inconsistent with the vagaries of Demosthenes' early career as it is anachronistic.[73] But however misleading it is to imagine two parties in the 350s,[74] it was Demosthenes' achievement—by sounding the tocsin against him—to create a pro-Philip "peace party" in the next decade (10.55), and for two of Plato's students, the fall of Olynthus in 348 had already begun to clarify matters. Thanks to the resurrection of the *Fourth Philippic*,[75] we can now see that Demosthenes was on one side of the division, Aristotle the other. While Aristotle was enjoying the patronage of Hermias, Demosthenes found his voice in opposition to the Macedonian menace. It was only after he had seen beyond Xenophon's civic but outdated Attica-first quietism that he would discover the truly Platonic position in the just citizen's timeless and eternal political obligation to prevent the victory of tyranny.[76]

By placing *Response to Leptines* (355) after both the retrospective defense of Chaeronea (338) in *On the Crown* (330) and the political complications surrounding the Peace of Philocrates (346) in *On the False Embassy* (343), Callimachus invited us to understand how Demosthenes made this crucial transition.[77] Despite the clarity of *On the Chersonese* and the *Third Philippic*, there is plenty of evidence in the first importantly political lawsuit he brought in his own name that Demosthenes was Plato's student: in addition to the Academic connection with Chabrias (20.1)[78] and the Xenophon-based account of his heroics (20.75-87), the following may be mentioned even if none of them alone is dispositive: the application of αὐτὸ καθ' αὑτό to an object of careful consideration (20.5), the characteristic slide on the slippery εὖ πράττειν (20.110-11; cf. 20.162), the table of opposites (20.10; cf. *Prt.* 332c3-5), the being/seeming distinction (20.10), and the importance of seeing through deception (20.3-4). Having been taught, Demosthenes effortlessly and repeatedly assumes the role of teacher (20.32, 61, 95, 113-14, 141, and 163), and he skillfully uses "the ethos of the city [τὸ τῆς πολέως ἦθος]" (20.13) as a nobility-inspiring analogue for the Idea of the Good. But the Platonism of the speech remains conventional, aristocratic (20.18), and convoluted (20.140-42; cf. 114).[79] While celebrating the Athenian past (20.74), Demosthenes is not yet committed to inducing shame and spiritual regeneration by sharply contrasting it with the Philip-spawning Athens of today (20.164). At its core, the speech is merely echoing Pericles' claim in the *Funeral Oration* that where the rewards of virtue are greatest, there too will be found the best citizens (Thucydides 2.46). In Platonic terms, the speech remains on the Shorter Way, and a virtuous Athens need only continue to *reward* virtue in order to maintain "the dignity of the city" (20.142). It is no accident that he tells the Athenians at the end that he still has much to say (20.163), and it is revealing that he uses imperatives rather than verbal adjectives or hortatory subjunctives to tell them what they should and must do. In short, it is not a difficult self-sacrifice for which he called in 355, and the echo of Isaeus in the last sentence (cf. 20.167 and Isaeus, 7.44) indicates that the speaker, despite the well-chosen theme and the vaguely Platonic political nexus described in the last note, had not yet discovered his own voice.

A number of notes to this chapter have already indicated that at least from the perspective of a Platonist who recognizes Demosthenes as Plato's student, Callimachus has arranged his speeches in an instructive manner, primarily by grouping them in pairs.[80] But the most educational pairing would come from Plutarch, and the writings of Cicero and Demosthenes were preserved for the same reason that Plato's dialogues were. Naturally there have been long periods of darkness when their speeches have been studied merely as rhetorical exemplars, and although this made their reception one-sided, it at least secured their preservation. Especially because Plato himself failed to rise to the challenge of the choice that he summoned others to make, the lives of his best students— those who not only answered his call but who in their turn summoned yet others to answer it—are immeasurably instructive to the Platonist. Putting Platonism into practice by returning to the Cave is a life's work (cf. διαβιῶναι at *Grg.* 526a5), and only after long years of preparatory struggle could the moment meet the man in the *Catilinarians* of Cicero and the *Philippics* of Demosthenes,[81] en route to the even purer public Platonism embodied in *On the Crown* and *Pro Sestio*. Naturally it can be claimed that it was as consummate orators, not as two of Plato's students, that Plutarch paired Demosthenes and Cicero, but despite the efforts of modern scholars to minimize the evidentiary value of Hermippus,[82] there is no evidence in the *Life of Demosthenes* that Plutarch did not regard them as such. Meanwhile, his pairing of Brutus and Dion proves his awareness that both Cicero and Plato had taught the enemies of tyranny. On the other hand, only the missing pair of Augustus and Philip—for Plutarch of Chaeronea would only compare the Macedonian son with the Roman father, not the Roman son with the Macedonian father—would have revealed a truth that had now become too dangerous to speak aloud (see chapter 5), a truth that would have joined Cicero and Demosthenes in a manner that went well beyond their comparably incomparable eloquence.

Second only to rhetoric's role in creating a prejudice against the Academic connection between Demosthenes and Plato is their allegedly irreconcilable difference with respect to democracy, and indeed these alleged disjunctions are two sides of the same coin.[83] Only in a democratic city can a philosopher choose to return to the Cave (cf. *R.* 557e1-2; cf. 520c1-3), and only through rhetoric can a philosopher rise to political prominence in a democratic city.[84] It is no more accidental that the two greatest orators of antiquity were Plato's students than that it was their shared fate to lose their lives in a failed effort to prevent the victory of tyranny. No matter how easy it has become to distinguish Augustus from a tyrant and the Roman Republic from a democracy, it is impossible to deny the parallel between Cicero and Demosthenes. Quite apart from the way both of them illustrated what Platonism in action looks like, the writings of both preserved the memory of democratic and republican institutions in the dark centuries dominated by monarchy that followed their deaths. Under the guise of providing posterity with instruction in rhetorical excellence, their writings more importantly preserved from extinction the eternal desirability of lost freedom, for what had made their unmatchable eloquence possible was the cause of liberty,[85] the threat of tyranny, and the dangerous but noble choice to preserve the one and oppose the other to which they summoned their listeners, and continue to summon them still.

Cicero famously claimed that Socrates had brought philosophy down from the heavens into the cities and into the lives of men.[86] Demosthenes did the same for Plato by actually living out the consequences of the descent for which the Old Academy had prepared him. If the Socratic transformation of philosophy had displaced physics for the sake of ethics, the modification of Plato wrought by Demosthenes used an idealized image of the Athenian past to accomplish the work his teacher had assigned to both the City and the Good.⁸⁷ Like the latter, the idealized Athens of Demosthenes motivated its citizens to look beyond personal happiness and success to the intrinsic nobility of τὸ καλόν,⁸⁸ and this explains why Demosthenes, like Socrates, would achieve the immortal glory of a *Heldentod*.⁸⁹ At the same time, it was "the burden of the Athenian past"⁹⁰ that functioned as the heavenly paradigm to which Socrates had directed our vision at the end of *Republic* 9 (R. 592b1-2).⁹¹ Democratic Athens left the choice to participate in politics to citizens qualified and unqualified alike (R. 557e1-558a3) but the City could not exist without compelling its guardians to serve the others (R. 473b4-c1 and 519c8-d7). Only by applying the laws of the City to herself could a philosopher realize it in practice (R. 592a5-b4), for it would be the political things (τὰ πολιτικά) of this City alone that the Platonist would be willing to do (R. 592a5).⁹² Just as Cicero would later be permitted to do them in Rome, so too "some indeterminate divine chance [θεία τις τύχη]" (R. 592a8) now allowed Demosthenes to do them in Athens. In accordance with what in German is called *Vergegenwärtigung*, both Demosthenes and Cicero would make Plato's timeless challenge applicable to their present circumstances through an idealized version of their now degenerated and dangerously shaken fatherlands.

In short, Demosthenes derived a Platonic obligation to do τὰ πολιτικά from the remade ἦθος of the idealized Athens of Marathon (cf. *Lg.* 698a8-c1), whose greatness depended not on enslavement to law (*Lg.* 698c1-6) but rather on the free choice of its citizens "to encircle Greece with freedom," aware as they were that "dying nobly is the greatest part of virtue."⁹³ Demosthenes' idealization of the Athenian past reached its Platonic peak in the famous "Marathon Oath" in *On the Crown*:

> But it is not, it is not that you erred, O Men of Athens, having risen to danger on behalf of everyone's freedom and salvation [ὑπὲρ τῆς ἁπάντων ἐλευθερίας καὶ σωτηρίας κίνδυνον ἀράμενοι]; by those of our ancestors who went forward out to danger [προκινδυνεύειν] at Marathon I swear it, and by those who stationed themselves alongside [παρατάττεσθαι, i.e., alongside the Spartans and opposite the Persians]⁹⁴ at Plataea, and those fighting by sea at Salamis, and those off Artemisia, and many others, those now lying in our civic memorials: good men, whom all of them alike our city, having deemed them worthy of the same honor laid to rest, Aeschines [ἀγαθοὺς ἄνδρας, οὓς ἅπαντας ὁμοίως ἡ πόλις τῆς αὐτῆς ἀξιώσασα τιμῆς ἔθαψεν, Αἰσχίνη], and not those who proved successful among them nor only those who won. And justly, for by all of them has the work [ἔργον] of good men been done [πράττεσθαι].⁹⁵

It was only when his policy—best understood as his πολιτεία, crafted in response to Plato's—had failed at Chaeronea that the full dimensions of Demosthenes' Platonism would become visible. The youthful *Response to Leptines* had suggested that Athens need only keep its faith with the heroes it had formerly rewarded to maintain its patriotic ἦθος. The passionate eloquence of the *Olynthians* was altogether directed at persuading the Athenians to seize the critical moment or καιρός that might yet protect Olynthus,[96] while the *Third Philippic* depended on the hypothesis that "and even now"[97] it was "perhaps, perhaps" (8.77) possible for Athens to defeat Philip once and for all. In the wreckage of his failed πολιτεία, the retrospective *On the Crown* could no longer point to any hopeful future, pointing instead to the timeless paradigm of selfless service to the city and the Hellenic cause of freedom that Demosthenes located in the Athenian past.

On the Crown is Demosthenes' masterpiece because the circumstances of its delivery required it to be. Delivered halfway between Philip's death (336) and Alexander's (323), he could offer no comforting prospect of ultimate success but instead needed to persuade his audience that they had already succeeded, and he did so by pointing to the Athenian past as paradigm. Eloquence was required to make the burden of that past seem light,[98] to render nobility more important than life itself, and above all to present failure as success:

> And what then of Demosthenes? Has he not surpassed all of those [sc. Attic orators], lean and circumspect, in force, sublimity [*sublimitas*], energy, refinement, and composition? Does he not delight in figures of speech [*figurae*]? Does he not shine with metaphors? Does he not, with made-up speech [*oratio ficta*], give a voice to silent things [*dat tacentibus vocem*]? And isn't that oath sworn in the name of those warriors slain for the city at Marathon and Salamis sufficiently manifest to teach [*satis manifesto docere*] that his preceptor [*praeceptor*] was Plato?[99]

This book echoes and has throughout been attempting to confirm what I will call "Quintilian's Proof."[100]

In support of that confirmation, it is useful to recall (see preface) that Dionysius of Halicarnassus demonstrated Demosthenes' superiority to Plato by comparing the passage from *On the Crown* that includes the Marathon Oath to the part of *Menexenus* where Aspasia "gives a voice to the silent" by reporting (in a "made-up speech") what the dead have said, would say, and indeed are now saying to their sons (*Mx.* 246d1-247c4).[101] To begin with, *Menexenus* proves that Demosthenes was following his *praeceptor* in creating an idealized Athens.[102] Aspasia's Athens selflessly comes to the aid of others for the sake of preserving Hellenic freedom; indeed she criticizes the city for being too generous (*Mx.* 244e1-245a7) while nevertheless exhorting its citizens not to abandon the τάξις of their πρόγονοι (*Mx.* 246b4-5; cf. 3.36).[103] But most importantly, Plato anticipates the conceit that the losers are really the ones who have won:

> *Socrates*: On account of these things, both first and last, and through it all, with full devotion, do completely try [καὶ διὰ παντὸς πᾶσαν πάντως προθυμίαν πειρᾶσθε] so to be that, first and foremost, you surpass us and those who went before in good repute, but if not, know that for us, should we defeat you [νικᾶν] in virtue [ἀρετή], that victory [ἡ νίκη] brings shame [αἰσχύνη], but that our defeat [ἡ δὲ ἧττα], if we should be defeated [ἡττᾶσθαι], brings happiness [εὐδαιμονία].[104]

With the bold succession of initial π's in this passage, one might compare the equally bold series of α's following the Marathon Oath: ἀγαθοὺς ἄνδρας, οὓς ἅπαντας ὁμοίως ἡ πόλις τῆς αὐτῆς ἀξιώσασα τιμῆς ἔθαψεν, Αἰσχίνη. But the crucial point is that happiness is not achieved by winning but by losing the contest of virtue to your offspring, as I am claiming that Plato did thanks to Demosthenes. It is not only those who succeed or "fare well [εὖ πράττειν]" who "do well [εὖ πράττειν]," and it is in the difference between the two meanings of εὖ πράττειν that we discover both the Platonic basis for distinguishing the Idea of the Good from εὐδαιμονία. This is why his *On the Crown* preserves the essence of Demosthenes' Platonism.

Thanks primarily to the widespread promulgation of Christianity, the notion that "greater love hath no man than this, that a man lay down his life for his friends"[105] has been made to seem a hackneyed commonplace, and between the anachronistic insinuation that it must already have been so for the Athenians and an even more misguided effort to preserve Athens as free from Judeo-Christian morality,[106] the revolutionary character of what Demosthenes proves that Plato taught in the Old Academy is easy to overlook:

> But as it were from a single and unchangeable keynote of policy [διάγραμμα τῆς πολιτείας], he [sc. Demosthenes] always continuously held to one tone in the varied circumstances. And of his speeches too Panaetius the philosopher says the majority of them so to have been written that only the Beautiful [τὸ καλόν] for its own sake is to be chosen [ὡς μόνου τοῦ καλοῦ δι' αὑτὸ αἱρετοῦ ὄντος]—*On the Crown, Against Aristocrates*, the one about the tax-exemptions [sc. *In Response to Leptines*], and the *Philippics*—in all of which he guides the citizens not toward the most pleasant [τὸ ἥδιστον], the easiest [τὸ ῥᾷστον], or the most profitable [τὸ λυσιτελέστατον] but often considers it necessary to rank their safety and preservation [ἡ ἀσφάλεια καὶ ἡ σωτηρία] in second place to the Beautiful [τὸ καλόν] and the fitting [τὸ πρέπον].[107]

Plutarch states the case perfectly. But instead of finding the roots of Demosthenes' πολιτεία in Plato, it has now become to identify Platonism with "the unwritten teachings" rather than with what Plato actually wrote in a series of dialogues that naturally culminates with the *Heldentod* of Socrates in *Phaedo*. Instead of recognizing it as such, the current consensus holds that Plato has outgrown *Phaedo* in *Parmenides*, and that serious philosophy will only be found in dialogues like *Timaeus, Sophist*, and *Philebus*. Instead of locating its essence in the unwavering choice for τὸ καλόν that Demosthenes made and called on others to make, "Platonism" will be integrated into a process that finds its natural τέλος in Aristotle.[108] Despite the fact that Socrates lived neither the active nor the contemplative life—he either precedes or obliterates the distinction[109]— it would become possible to believe that the one is more philosophical than the other, forgetting in the process that it was the victory of Macedon that made the choice between them impossible.[110] Instead of a Macedonian τέλος, Greek literature deserves an Athenian one, and in the longer series that begins with Achilles defying Agamemnon in *Iliad* 1, the speeches of Demosthenes constitute its immortal swan song, echoing the one Socrates had already sung in *Phaedo*.

In *Letters*, Plato claimed that the true and the false must be learned together (*Ep.* 344b1-2), and it would give a one-sided picture of the speeches of Demosthenes to concentrate exclusively or even primarily on the moral sublimity made manifest in the Marathon Oath.[111] Properly read, Plato's dialogues offer advanced training in the detection of deception (*Phdr.* 261e3-4; cf. 265b6-8), and it is a skill that Demosthenes would apply throughout the corpus (e.g., 52.1).[112] In *Phaedrus*, Socrates discusses deception and its detection in the context of speeches after supplying some eloquent speeches of his own[113]; even if we can overcome the prejudice that Plato was not teaching his students a subject he allegedly despised (i.e., rhetoric), we will find it difficult to realize that the positive examples of eloquence with which the dialogues abound would be no more useful to Demosthenes than the negative examples of deception, self-contradiction, and deliberate fallacy with which they teem. Where did Demosthenes learn to see through the deceitful promises of Philip, the deceptions of his apologists, and the self-contradictions in the claims of his opponents at law?[114] Throughout the corpus, Demosthenes repeatedly shows that his opponents are testifying against themselves and making his case for him; wielding these techniques came easily to anyone who had realized that Plato's own eloquence had playfully contradicted his deliberately deceptive attack on rhetoric. It is also worth remembering that beginning with *Response to Leptines*, Demosthenes made his public mark by bringing claims of unconstitutionality against decrees presented to or passed by the Assembly; what better way could Plato have trained his students to recognize when a γράφη παρανόμων was in order than by asking them to work their way through the transformative modifications of Athenian legislation in *Laws*?[115] But if it were necessary to identify a single dialogue that exerted the greatest influence on Demosthenes, it would undoubtedly be Plato's *Gorgias*,[116] and the paradox implicated by this claim likewise illuminates the role of deliberate deception in Platonic pedagogy.[117]

Since *Gorgias* appears to be an attack on both rhetoric and Athenian democracy, Demosthenes needed to see through this appearance in order for this great dialogue to teach him how to become the most eloquent of Athenian orators, the foremost defender of his city, and the truly Platonic statesman or πολιτικός.[118] In one way or another, *Gorgias* can be used to illustrate each of the seven areas where an Academic education based on Plato's dialogues left its mark on Demosthenes, beginning with (1) the towering influence of Platonic variety, *varietas*, and ποικίλια (see preface). Blending dialectic with rhetoric, logic with imagery, and refutation with exhortation, *Gorgias* is a dramatic masterpiece, and through Plato's mastery of stylistic variety, (2) the clash of abstract ideas is made vivid by the brilliantly limned characters and personalities of Socrates, Gorgias, Polus, and Callicles. (3) The dialogue is filled with allusions to Thucydides, and requires the student's knowledge of Athenian History.[119] (4) Obviously the rhetorical power of the dialogue's speeches is the central area of influence, but also important was (5) the impact that Plato's use of imagery and storytelling made on his student. (6) Between the exceptional Aristides and the revelation of Socrates as the city's only true πολιτικός, Plato pointed to the role Demosthenes would later play, imaged per "(5)" as the doctor tried by the jury of children. Finally, in order to see that *Gorgias* was summoning him to do what he did, Demosthenes needed (7) to practice a healthy wariness or ἀπιστία (6.24) toward what might seem obvious to others.

The connection between Demosthenes and Plato has become difficult to detect not because it is invisible—for thanks to the play of character, it is virtually ubiquitous—but because we have been persuaded not to look for it. By writing speeches for Socrates, Gorgias, Polus, and Callicles,[120] Plato taught Demosthenes how to become an effective logographer, and it is for this reason that the Academy's influence is not confined to the orations Demosthenes delivered in his own name as a statesman. The case of Apollodorus has already been mentioned, but the narrated dialogue between the crafty Protus and Aristophon in *Response to Zenothemis* (32.15-17), the old seadog of *Response to Apaturias* (33.4-5) who uses an effective thought-experiment (33.32-33), the single personality behind the two alleged speakers in *Response to Phormio*,[121] and the Anytus-like Androcles of *Response to Lacritus* who Demosthenes uses to attack Isocrates (35.40-43), all set the stage for the unforgettable portraits of Apollodorus (36.39-56) and Phormio (36.56-62) as described by the inexperienced speaker of

On Behalf of Phormio (36.1 and 36.28). A well-staged contest between a simpleton and a rogue reappears in *Response to Pantaenetus* (37.41-43 and 37.45) while *Response to Nausimachus* verges on self-parody thanks to the parallel between the young Demosthenes and the rich young man (38.19-20), who must present himself as inept (38.6) if he is to win. It is easy to see why Mantitheus fails in *Response to Boeotus I* but wins in *Against Boeotus II*: by a forthright confession of the sins of his father (40.5, 8, 27, and 45), the young man secured the jury's sympathy at last. *Response to Spudias* is more notable for Demosthenes' use of self-incrimination (41.20), self-contradiction (41.24), and hypothesis (41.26) than for the speech's inexperienced and unnamed speaker (41.2), but in the equally unnamed speaker of *Response to Phaenippus*, Demosthenes has brought a wealthy aristocrat to life (see especially 42.22). *Response to Macartatus* and *Response to Leochares* have already been mentioned in the context of Demosthenes debts to Isaeus (cf. also 42.32 and Isaeus 7.26)

Regardless of how we regard the series of speeches by Apollodorus that follow, Callimachus enlivens it by interpolating the garrulous old man of *Against Euergus and Mnesibulus*, paired with Callistratus—not, of course, the influential speaker of Demosthenes' youth (see introduction)—the repeatedly duped and thus somehow amiable crimial who speaks in *Response to Olympiodorus*.[122] But Callimachus saves the best for last,[123] and following the chronologically problematic *Against Callipus* and *Response to Polycles*,[124] he uses three matched pairs that illustrate the outer limits of Demosthenes' skill as a master of Platonic variety, the play of character, and playful deception. We accept young Ariston's use of obscenity (54.14 and 16) because the upper-class degeneracy of the city's most hubristic young bullies demand it (54.21, 37, and 41); by following *Against Conon* with the speech of an honest farmer from the countryside explaining how to keep a rural road from flooding in *Response to Callicles*, Callimachus introduces the ironic principle that will guide the next pair as well. In the late speech *Against Dionysodorus*, Demosthenes uses the price of food to enlist the jury's sympathy for a wealthy but honest foreign banker duped by a defaulting debtor; in *Response to Eubulides*, it is a poor Athenian who is being accused of being an alien, and who gives Demosthenes the chance to defend poverty as patriotic (57.30-36; with 57.45, cf. 45.67). Nothing in Isocrates, Isaeus, or even Lysias comes close to matching the literary and stylistic variety these paired speeches demand, and even when Antiphon and Isocrates create pairs of opposed speeches,[125] the voices of those who speak them remain the same. But the peak of our author's Platonic playfulness is reached only in the final pair capped by *Against Neaira*, and so effectively drawn is the outraged and betrayed youngster of *Against Theocrines* that the speech as a whole has been attributed to Demosthenes' enemy Dinarchus by critics who fail to realize it would be Demosthenes himself who came forward at last to answer Epichares' call, and thus win the day for his client not once but twice.[126]

But the most important call that Demosthenes answered is the one Socrates addressed to Callicles at the end of *Gorgias*, and the best way to prove the towering influence of this dialogue in particular is to consider the words τοὺς ἄλλους παρακαλῶμεν in context, beginning with the way Plato was already preparing his students for an indignity like the one Demosthenes would experience at the hands of Dinarchus in the Harpalus Affair:

> *Socrates*: And allow whoever it might be to condemn you as a fool and to bespatter you with filth [προπηλακίζειν] if he chooses; yes, by Zeus, and with you, sir, undaunted, to smite you with that dishonorable stroke, for you will suffer nothing terrible if in reality you should be noble and good [καλὸς κἀγαθός], practicing virtue [ἀσκεῖν ἀρετήν].[127]

It was in the Academy that Plato was training his students to practice virtue, and he did so by having them study his dialogues, a course of studies that Demosthenes in particular proves to have been remarkably effective, inspiring him to become the same kind of καλὸς κἀγαθός that Aristides the Just had been (*Grg.* 526b7):

> And after thus having practiced [sc. ἀρετή] together [κοινῇ ἀσκεῖν], then at last [τότε ἤδη], if it should seem to be requisite, we will apply ourselves to political things [τὰ πολιτικά], or whatever kind of thing seems [best] to us, then [τότε] we will consult, being better [able] to consult than now.[128]

Regardless of what their youthful ambitions had been when the entered the Academy, it was only after arduous exercises that they would be prepared to combine ἀρετή with practicing τὰ πολιτικά, and in *Gorgias* Plato was still only preparing his students to choose the life of justice at the crisis of the *Republic*:

> For it is disgraceful for those in such a condition as we now appear to be in, after giving way to youthful insolence as though being something, to whom the same things never seem [to be the case] about the same things, and these things being the greatest ones—to so great a lack of education have we reached—as a guide, then, let us use the account [ὁ λόγος] that has now shown forth, which signifies for us that this is the best way of life [ὁ τρόπος ἄριστος τοῦ βίου]: both to live and to die practicing [ἀσκεῖν] both justice [ἡ δικαιοσύνη] and the rest of virtue [ἡ ἄλλη ἀρετή].[129]

Even before *Phaedo*, the best way of life already anticipates philosophy as the practice of death (introduced at *Phd.* 64a4-6). Meanwhile, the λόγος in question is the central paradox of Plato's *Gorgias*: that it is preferable to suffer an injustice than to do one (introduced at *Grg.* 469c8-d2), and once applied to the Allegory of the Cave, this is the choice that will turn the life of selfishness upside down:

> This then let us follow, and to this let us summon the others [τοὺς ἄλλους παρακαλῶμεν]; not that to which you trust yourself and summon me [παρακαλεῖν], for it is worth nothing, O Callicles.[130]

Although the foremost example of what I have called "double action" (see chapter 2) is the mutual illumination that the Allegory of the Cave gives to and in turn receives from Demosthenes and Co. (including Cicero), this passage is the most important Demosthenes-specific example of the phenomenon.[131] To begin with, the hortatory subjunctive παρακαλῶμεν possesses its own kind of double action: it is used to persuade others to become persuasive, using rhetoric to summon us to become rhetoricians. Naturally these are not the kind of rhetoricians that Plato uses Gorgias and Polus to represent, that Callicles is summoning Socrates to become (hence the second παρακαλεῖν), or that *Gorgias* as a whole is attacking. It is rather the kind of rhetoric that Plato himself is using, that the curriculum of his Academy was designed to teach, and that the example of Demosthenes proves that he successfully taught. Considered in their Platonic context, the words τοὺς ἄλλους παρακαλῶμεν that Demosthenes quotes or echoes in the *Third Philippic* illustrate the Academy's true purpose. Only after the youngsters who enter it have been liberated from the dangerous foolishness that Plato has used Callicles to represent will they be prepared—by an arduous and communal training in ἀρετή that includes being exposed to danger in *Gorgias* and already demands a commitment to that dialogue's λόγος—to do τὰ πολιτικά in accordance with ἡ δικαιοσύνη. "Double action" means that even though it will be impossible to persuade those who take *Gorgias* as proof that Plato rejected rhetoric to accept the evidence that Demosthenes was his student, accepting that evidence may become possible for those who don't.

Encountering *Gorgias* almost halfway between entering the Academy and leaving it,[132] Demosthenes has left behind evidence of that dialogue's continuing influence on him in his *Exordia*,[133] a series of fifty-six preludes or preambles for hypothetical public speeches he must have composed roughly halfway between leaving the Academy (c. 366) and delivering the *Third Philippic* (341). The first of them became the exordium or *prooemium* of the *First Philippic* (351) and the third reappears in the *First Olynthian* (349) thus constituting a characteristically Callimachean prequel for the corpus as a whole. For the most part, however, the preambles are perfectly general, never further specified by subsequent use, and hence timeless.[134] This timelessness makes them unique among the writings of Demosthenes and in some sense the most Platonic of them. The attempt to arrange the writings of Demosthenes in chronological order, despite the fact that Callimachus clearly chose not to do so, is as easy and natural as attempting to do the same for Plato's dialogues is anything but. It is impossible to determine even when *Gorgias* takes place,[135] let alone when it was composed, and what makes an approach based on Reading Order more plausible than ordering the dialogues by dramatic setting or chronology of composition is that Plato has furnished all the information necessary for doing so.[136] Despite the fact that the Peloponnesian War constitutes the necessary and revealing historical backdrop of *Gorgias*,[137] the dialogue's λόγος has proved itself to be timeless, and the *Exordia* of Demosthenes demonstrates that he recognized its timelessness while preparing himself to become one of Plato's καλοὶ κἀγαθοί (*Grg*. 526a7). In turning now to *Exordia* (placed after D61), bear in mind that the parenthetical numbers in the next three paragraphs refer to the fifty-six individual exordia, not to the speeches of Demosthenes.

To begin with, the perfect statement from the introduction to the Loeb edition of the *Exordia* deserves to be quoted:

> Athenian democracy is sharply criticized: members of the Assembly are unwilling to face the facts; they favor speakers who tell them what they like to hear; they shout down unpopular speakers who might have something worthwhile to say; they act impulsively on bad advice and then punish the advisers; they listen to speakers who advocate oligarchy; they submit to being abused from the bema. The speakers, in turn, are inclined to say what is pleasant rather than what is true, to be actuated by partisan motives, and to seek to add to their own reputations at the expense of the common good. The general tone, however, reveals a stubborn faith in democratic government. The faults of the citizen legislators are stressed for the sake of emphasizing their responsibilities.[138]

Plato had used this same strategy while describing the Democratic Man (*R*. 561c6-d8), using criticism as attitude-changing provocation and therapy. This summary clearly echoes Socrates' position in *Gorgias*, and since nobody can doubt Demosthenes' credentials as either a defender of democracy or a practitioner of rhetoric, it may help to dispel the twin notions that Plato could not have taught him rhetoric, and hated the form of government that Demosthenes gave his life to defending.

The details confirm this summary. To speak in terms of an image, a still youthful Demosthenes (13) is preparing himself in the *Exordia* to address the jury of children, defending the doctor's lonely determination (28.1, 38.1) not to gratify (5.1, 19; cf. 9.2, 23.1) nor to deceive (5.1, 46.5) but to persuade his audience to accept the difficult but beneficial medicine (33.3; cf. 53.4).[139] This "medicine" is dangerous to give (38.2) and unpleasant to hear (53.1). He calls it simply "the best" (τὸ βέλτιστον at 12.1-2, 20.1, 40.1, and 47.1; cf. *Grg.* 521d9) as well as "the best things" (τὰ βέλτιστα at 8, 13, 15.1, 37.2, 44.1, 49.1) or "the necessary things" (τὰ δέοντα at 2, 33). Like Socrates and his doctor, he conjures the audience to give his side a hearing (5, 27, 34.2), to listen and learn (47.2, 49.1), not to shout him down (21.4), and thus, by deliberating rationally (44) and at leisure (21.3), to act promptly (21.2; cf. 27, 29.1) while choosing "the just itself" over the profitable (16). In a word, Demosthenes is preparing himself to offer the kind of instruction that will make the Athenians *better* (*Grg.* 514d3-515b2; cf. 15) just as Socrates said that a true πολιτικός would and must do (cf. *Grg.* 521d5-e1). Equally Socratic is the claim that the beginning of sound judgment is to avoid assuming that that you know something before learning about it is (5.3 and 18; cf. 10.1); he also indulges in an irony unparalleled in his speeches (36) while following Xenophon's Socrates on always saying the same things.[140] He also alludes to *Menexenus* (33.2; cf. *Mx.* 235b8-c1), *Republic* 8 on the principal pitfall of democratic freedom (55; cf. *R.* 557e1-2), *Cratylus* on the easy danger of self-deception (9.1; cf. *Cra.* 428d3-5), and demonstrates the limitations of εὖ πράττειν as "to fare well" (24.4) while also shedding light on a deceptive argument in *Euthydemus* (25.2, 39.2, and 43; cf. *Euthd.* 279d6-280b6). But it is above all the influence of *Gorgias*—including an eloquent attack on rhetoric (32; cf. 45)—that is obvious from the start:

> You must not think that the speaker who makes little or no demand on you is right, for you can see how such hopes and advice have caused our present total ruin, but rather it is the speaker who refuses to try to please you and says what must be done and how we may end incurring such shameful losses. To speak truthfully: if a speaker wants to avoid causing you pain and passes over something in a speech that will also be passed over in the course of events, he should speak to please you, but if the allure of words is not fitting for the occasion and causes actual harm, then it is disgraceful to deceive yourselves, and to wait until absolutely compelled before doing what you should willingly have done long before.[141]

In the fifty-six preludes of the *Exordia*, Demosthenes uses the verb for what is advantageous (συμφέρειν) and its related participle fifty-four times, and refers twice simply to "the advantageous [τὸ συμφέρον]" (3.1 and 28.2). Four times he suggests that the advice he intends to give is *both just and advantageous* (18.1, 20.1, 22.1, and 40.1), and the first of these is particularly important: "It seems to me that you would justly [δικαίως] pay attention, men of Athens, if someone should promise to show you that in the matter you are considering that the same things are just [δίκαια] and advantageous [συμφέροντα]" (18.1). This is excellent advice, and readers of Plato's *Alcibiades Major* would be well advised to heed it: it is there that Socrates deploys the Εὖ Πράττειν Fallacy (see chapter 3) in its most ostentatiously fallacious form (*Alc.1* 116b2-5) to prove to Alcibiades that "the just things [τὰ δίκαια]" are the same as "the advantageous things [τὰ συμφέροντα]" (*Alc.1* 113d5-6). The youngster has just split the two on immoralist lines, distinguishing the just as noble from the advantageous as good (*Alc.1* 115a9-16; cf. 50.2): the fact that Alcibiades has never been taught justice nor has discovered what it is for himself—for there never was a time when he thought himself ignorant of it (cf. 5.3 and *Alc.1* 110a4)—is of no consequence since it is not about the just but rather about the advantageous that the Athenians debate in the Assembly. In response, Socrates uses the Fallacy to demonstrate that even an act of heroic self-sacrifice for others in war is advantageous: those who do nobly do well, those who do well necessarily fair well, those who fare well are happy through the acquisition of good things (*Alc.1* 116a6-c8).

The speeches of Demosthenes prove that Alcibiades was correct about the Assembly (*Alc.1* 113d1-8): beginning with the *Olynthians* (cf. 1.1 and 3.36) and ending with the *Exordia*, the stated and uniform purpose of his advice is to secure what will be of advantage to the city and its citizens. Demosthenes is not unique in this respect, not even when it comes to the crucial claim that the just and the advantageous coincide. Isaeus never refers to this coincidence and Lysias does so only once,[142] but Isocrates does so frequently, and discusses the pairing at some length in *Archidamus*.[143] The most interesting case, however, is Aeschines, and in his three surviving speeches, he deploys the pair in three different ways. In *Against Timarchus*, it is used conventionally: with the assumption that he has the law and thus justice on his side, he need only persuade the jury that it is likewise for their own good that they condemn Timarchus.[144] In *On the Embassy*, he deploys it deceptively in the context of the weakest part of his case: despite the fact that Philip's promises proved empty, by relaying them to the Athenians, Aeschines had spoken both what was just and what was advantageous to them,[145] or rather: what would have been advantageous to them had the promises been true, which—through no fault of his own, but solely because of Philip—they were not. But the shoe is on the other foot in *Against Ctesiphon*. To begin with, awarding the crown to Demosthenes is illegal and thus unjust. More importantly, the fact that the advice for which it is being awarded proved to be disadvantageous for the city,[146] it is therefore necessarily both just and advantageous to deny him the crown.[147]

Any accomplished sophist must be able to teach his students how to make what is personally advantageous appear to be both advantageous to the audience and just, but it is considerably more difficult to persuade the city that a course of action that is just is likewise advantageous. There are, of course, examples where doing so is easy: when avenging a wrong or recovering what has been taken away is involved, a retributive or restorative conception of justice is clearly also advantageous to the one that regains what is lost. In the Mytilene Debate immortalized by Thucydides,[148] Cleon has no need to explain why avenging the wrong the rebels have done to Athens is advantageous as well as just; the more difficult task is assigned to Diodotus. Without giving the appearance that he is motivated by pity, philanthropy, or some higher and non-retributive conception of justice, Diodotus must persuade the Athenians that sparing the rebels is advantageous to them.[149] He obviously makes no claim to the effect that the just and the advantageous coincide; as a result, his position can be construed as an amoral one, pursuing the expedient to the exclusion of justice. But sensitive readers have seen through this appearance: Diodotus has disguised the merciful as the advantageous, the self-critical and self-denying as the expedient. This is the single most important thing that Thucydides taught Demosthenes.[150]

But what Plato taught him was even more important and far more difficult to accomplish. Starting from a higher conception of justice that required a choice or προαίρησις for what was absolutely good as opposed to what was personally advantageous—a choice for self-sacrifice at the expense of personal happiness and even life itself—Platonic rhetoric as perfected or rather publicly disseminated by Demosthenes was required to make the audience believe that performing a painful duty was both just and advantageous for the city. Demosthenes proves that he can make this case in the *Olynthians* and he makes it even more effectively in the *Third Philippic*. But precisely because these speeches failed to persuade the Athenians to do τὰ δέοντα in accordance with τὸ βέλτιστον, Demosthenes can still imagine that his painful advice will not only ultimately prove to be advantageous to the city but can also hope or at least pray that giving it will be to his advantage as well.[151] The disaster at Chaeronea, the result of the city's decision to follow his advice at last, opened the door for Aeschines: it was no longer believing Philip's lies but having believed Demosthenes' truths that had proved most disadvantageous to Athens. Without recourse to future events that might yet prove that doing the right thing might also ultimately prove to be advantageous, Demosthenes faced his greatest challenge in *On the Crown*, where he needed to accomplish what only the outer limits of eloquence could possibly achieve: persuading his audience that following disadvantageous advice had been the right thing to do, and that by remaining loyal to what made Athens great, the Athenians had done what was both advantageous and just.

Plato had taught Demosthenes how to make these arguments, and he did so in the *Republic*, thanks to the distinction between the Shorter and Longer Ways. The Shorter Way is designed to persuade the reader that justice pays, and thus that the just and the advantageous coincide.

Thanks to the preliminary struggle with Thrasymachus and the task that Plato's brothers assign to him at the beginning of *Republic* 2, it is obvious that Socrates is defending justice rather than proving that pursuing the personally advantageous is just. But Socrates must nevertheless explicate justice in a way that is compatible with making it advantageous, for this is what Glaucon and Adeimantus are requiring him to do. The proof offered along the Shorter Way anticipates the kind of thing Demosthenes will offer the Athenians in his pre-Chaeronea speeches, but his task in them is both easier and more difficult than the one imposed on Socrates. It is more difficult because doing the right thing already involves both action and self-sacrifice; the just man of the Shorter Way achieves justice internally through self-fulfillment. But Demosthenes' task is easier because the future—even in the desperate form "perhaps, then, perhaps even yet now" (8.77)—takes the place of the rewards of justice, the posthumous ones in particular, to which Plato's brothers would not allow Socrates to appeal. It is therefore only after Chaeronea that Demosthenes is compelled to "ascend the highest heaven of invention," and thus finds himself summoning the Athenians to make the same choice he had made, when he had chosen the Longer Way long ago (παλαί) in the Academy.[152]

Immediately before introducing the distinction between the Longer and the Shorter Ways in *Republic* 4, Socrates explains how Justice will come to light or rather burst into flame in Plato's masterpiece (R. 435a1-4). Only by the friction between the just man of the Shorter Way and the City (R. 434d7-435a1)—which can only come into being when philosophers choose to do a job for which they are not by nature suited, and which does not conduce to their personal happiness—will the flame of Justice flash forth. The proof that Plato never communicated his serious views by the written word depends on the exact same imagery in *Letters* (*Ep.* 341c4-d2),[153] and it is a failure to make this connection that has made it so difficult to realize—and will continue to make it so difficult to accept—that the dialogues were the Old Academy's curriculum. With context supplied by Cleitophon's dissatisfaction with the possibility that Socrates is summoning us to do nothing more than summon others to virtue (*Clt.* 408d5-6), Plato had taught his students what to do in *Republic* 7, thereby making the all-night conversation in the Piraeus the spiritual equivalent of the torch-passing horse race that Adeimantus mentions in *Republic* 1 (R. 328a1-6). With his τοὺς ἄλλους παρακαλῶμεν, Demosthenes demonstrated that he was taking part in this race in both life and death, passing along to the Athenians, the rest of Hellas, and ultimately to us, the torch of justice (cf. R. 435a2-3) that Plato's dialogues—*Gorgias* and *Republic* in particular—had placed in his hand.

Throughout the centuries, students of Demosthenes have been more inclined to shorten the list of authentic speeches that survive than to lament the loss of those that have been lost. Not a single example of a speech that Demosthenes gave as an ambassador survives. What makes their loss all the more significant is that it is to such speeches that the words τοὺς ἄλλους παρακαλῶμεν literally apply: Demosthenes is summoning the Athenians to summon other Greek cities to join in the fight against Philip. Demosthenes himself must have made many such speeches, and it was in gratitude for his embassies to the other Greeks, even while in exile, that Athens brought him home after the Harpalus Affair.[154] But enough of Demosthenes has survived to make it possible to understand why so many conspired over the centuries to assure his survival. Bringing Isaeus, Aeschines, Lycurgus, Hyperides, Dinarchus, and indeed a whole world of Athenian civil procedure and character witnesses along with him, Demosthenes accomplished something far more important than illuminating a turbulent period in Greek History or providing posterity with a comprehensive education in rhetoric. Only after the printing press had assured the survival of Demosthenes would his corpus undergo radical surgery and Plato's influence on him be denied, and the role that "double action" may have played in causing him to survive was once far easier to see than it has now become for us. To what task does Demosthenes continue to summon us? The more insistently we raise this question, the better will we understand the Old Academy, for answering it will simultaneously disclose what Socrates was summoning Callicles to do, and thus why Demosthenes would do what he did.

5

Suppressions

Thanks to creative ingenuity, a wonderful sense of humor, and Platonic inspiration, [Lucian] made a perfect decision: he found a way to make Demosthenes' open enemies praise him, and made the agent sent to capture him tell the story of his heroic death. An imaginary dialogue between Antipater and the agent tasked with bringing Demosthenes to Macedon not only allows the latter to describe how Demosthenes cheated capture by committing suicide but more importantly gives Antipater the opportunity to narrate several speeches of Philip within this dialogue, allowing the latter to describe what made his most dangerous enemy so dangerous, and thus to offer him the kind of praise that only an enemy could. Just as the most devastating and persuasive critique of Demosthenes must come from a self-professed friend of liberty,[1] so too must the highest possible praise come from freedom's open foe. So perfectly Platonic is this *Encomium of Demosthenes* that no Platonist will be surprised to learn that the dialogue's authenticity has been denied, and indeed that "its lack of inspiration"[2] has led to this result.[3] It is better understood as a masterpiece, inspired by Plato's playfulness.[4] The allegedly Macedonian source of this praise is imaginary but the praise itself is Lucian's own.[5] By expressing the highest possible praise for Demosthenes, it leads the sympathetic reader to draw for themselves the only possible conclusion: that [Lucian] knows that Demosthenes was first and foremost Plato's student, and that this explains Antipater's role, Philip's praise, Demosthenes' greatness, and the author's Platonic tricks.

The foregoing account fails to do justice to the complexity of Lucian's dialogue. It revolves around an unnamed narrator and orator who is at a loss about how to properly praise Demosthenes on the anniversary of his death.[6] Conversation begins when a poet named Thersagoras encounters him, determined to make him an audience for his verses, inspired by Homer, composed the night before (1). Lucian does not ask us to join the narrator in listening to these verses (25–26); after reciting them, Thersagoras takes the narrator to his house and gives him a hard-to-find book from the Macedonian archives (27)—of course no such book exists—that contains the dialogue between Antipater and Archias (28-49) that contains within it a narrated dialogue between Philip and Parmenio (33–34), three more speeches about Demosthenes by Philip (35–37, 38, and 39), and a written record of Demosthenes' last words made by the agent Archias (44-49). The second half of the dialogue imagines the narrator, having returned home, reading this book aloud to us; Thersagoras has disappeared. But the poet dominates the dialogue's first half, explaining to the narrator how much easier it is to praise Demosthenes than Homer (9–21). He begins with a comparison of Homer and Demosthenes (5-8), demonstrating a detailed knowledge of both, and emphasizing the orator's variety (6). But what makes praising Demosthenes easier is our detailed knowledge of his life and character, and it is only an embarrassment of riches that makes offering him suitable praise difficult. To prove this important point, Thersagoras lists five themes that might furnish materials for a proper encomium: his speech, his life, his philosophy [φιλοσοφία], his leadership (δημαγωγία), and his death (19). Naturally Lucian or [Lucian] touches on all five in his *Encomium of Demosthenes*.

Lucian entrusts the topic of Demosthenes' education to both Thersagoras and Antipater, and the latter tells how Aristotle often described for him and Alexander the kind of student Demosthenes had been (40). This is an interesting passage because it provides the only evidence that it was Aristotle who had taught both Alexander and Antipater how dangerous Demosthenes was, and thus to demand that the Athenians surrender him.[7] Thersagoras also names Aristotle first among his second catalogue of Demosthenes' teachers: Aristotle, Theophrastus, Xenocrates, and Plato. [Lucian] is our only source for the claim that Demosthenes studied with Theophrastus and Xenocrates, and indeed the claim is impossible on chronological grounds; meanwhile, Dionysius of Halicarnassus had proved that it was not from Aristotle that Demosthenes had learned rhetoric. But whatever its other limitations, this second catalogue has identified Plato as Demosthenes' teacher. In the aggregate, Thersagoras' first catalogue is more plausible: after mentioning Callistratus, he mentions Alcidamus, Isocrates, Isaeus, and Eubulides. These names confirm Lucian's familiarity with Plutarch, Pseudo-Plutarch, Aulus Gellius, and whoever provided information about Eubulides to Diogenes Laertius; as a result of this awareness, he was aware of the evidence that Demosthenes had studied with Plato before hearing Callistratus or turning to Isaeus. Here are the two catalogues in context:

> "About Homer [says Thersagoras], we have received memorial through history neither regarding his education [παίδευσις] nor his practice [ἄσκησις] . . . But for you, there is clearly much here, and not just Callistratus but also the eminent catalogue of Alcidamus, Isocrates, Isaeus, and Eubulides. For with ten thousand pleasures in Athens attracting even those lying under the necessities of paternal control, and with the swift readiness of the age being what it is for adolescents to slip into weaknesses, and this possibility being available to him due to the neglect of his guardians, a yearning [πόθος] for philosophy and political virtue [καί φιλοσοφία καὶ ἡ πολιτικὴ ἀρετή] was constraining him, which led him not to the doors of Phryne but to those of Aristotle, Theophrastus, Xenocrates, and Plato."[8]

Naturally I regard the Academy as the place where a passion for philosophy and a commitment to political virtue became one for the young Demosthenes, making him immune to the democratic equalization of tempting pleasures good and bad that Socrates had described in *Republic* 8; the question, then, is whether [Lucian] or Lucian did so as well? Not only do both catalogues and the words in between them suggest that he did, but the *Encomium of Demosthenes* as a whole, thanks to its playfully dialogic complexity, makes its author's debts to Plato no less obvious than his knowledge of Demosthenes. Dionysius of Halicarnassus praised Demosthenes by presenting him as a greater orator than Plato; Lucian finds a way to use Plato's methods to praise Demosthenes even more highly, for Dionysius, confining his attention to rhetoric, avoids altogether the subjects of φιλοσοφία and ἡ πολιτικὴ ἀρετή. The concealed punch-line is even more obvious in [Lucian] than in Dionysius: just as the most natural explanation for Dionysius' otherwise improbable decision to compare Plato and Demosthenes was that the latter would excel his teacher as an orator, so too it was only through the influence of Plato, not least of all on Lucian himself, that [Lucian] could praise Demosthenes not only for style but for content, indeed for "his speech, his life, his philosophy, his leadership, and his death." The contrast between style and content is mirrored in the dialogue's structure with Thersagoras praising the one, the Macedonians the other. But with respect to both content and style, both parts are equally Platonic.

Platonic parallels abound. The unnamed narrator's first question repeats Socrates' opening question in *Phaedrus* (1; cf. *Phdr.* 227a1), and the unheard Homer-inspired verses that Thersagoras is so eager to recite are analogous to the speech of Lysias that Phaedrus reads aloud in that dialogue (cf. τὸ γραμματεῖον in 2 with *Phdr.* 228d7–8). Particularly with respect to fluency (with εὔροια in 2, cf. *Phdr.* 238c7, poetic inspiration (2; cf. *Phdr.* 238c9–d3) and divine madness (cf. 5 and 13 with *Phdr.* 245a1–8), Lucian thus insures that Plato's *Phaedrus* remains in the reader's mind until the end (cf. ὀπαδός at 49 with *Phdr.* 252c3 and 252e1–3). But Lucian alludes to many other Platonic dialogues as well, and amidst this literary banquet, the most important is when Thersagoras expresses his desire to recompense (ἐκτίνειν) Homer for nurturing his education (τὰ τροφεῖα τῆς παιδεύσεως in 1); the same words that precede "the crisis of the *Republic*" (R. 520b5) when Socrates says that the philosophers who arise in other cities (like Athens) are justified in not repaying anyone for their τὰ τροφεῖα by returning to the Cave, whereas it is Plato whom one repays by doing so.[9] In a broader sense, the dialogue with Thersagoras about Homer and Demosthenes allows [Lucian] to show off his broad knowledge of the latter's speeches, while also emphasizing their literary (6), poetic (8), and indeed inspired character (4; cf. *Lg.* 811c8–9). Both Quintilian and [Longinus] had already identified Homer as a principal source of Plato's inspiration,[10] and while praising Demosthenes in this playful dialogue, [Lucian] leaves no doubt that Plato has inspired him too; in the aggregate, all of this begins to suggest the following analogy: that as Homer is to Plato, so too is Plato to Demosthenes. Of course it can only begin to do so during the dialogue with Thersagoras, for it is with the intersection of φιλοσοφία and ἡ πολιτικὴ ἀρετή that Plato inspired Demosthenes, and it was by returning to the Cave that he repaid his teacher for τὰ τροφεῖα τῆς παιδεύσεως.

The death of Demosthenes allows [Lucian] to channel *Phaedo*, telling the story of how the drug (cf. φάρμακον at 49 with *Phd.* 115a7–8) allowed him to obtain freedom (cf. *Phd.* 115a1) by separating his soul from his body (cf. *Phd.* 114d8–e2). The dialogue's last words are entrusted to Antipater, who refers to Demosthenes' soul as both blessed and unconquerable (ἀήττητος), a word choice that allows Lucian to recall both *On the Crown* (18.247) and *Republic* (R. 375b3). But it is the fiction that Archias has recorded the last words of Demosthenes that gives [Lucian] the fullest opportunities for his encomium. Thanks to the fiction purveyed by Archias that Antipater has no intention to kill him, Demosthenes begins his speech by showing why he would never allow himself to be captured: "'By the fear of torture or death, Archias, I would never have been in Antipater's sight, but if you are telling the truth, all the more is it necessary to be on guard [φυλακτέον] lest having been bribed by Antipater with life itself [ἡ ψυχὴ αὐτή], having left the Hellenic post where I posted myself [ἣν ἐμαυτὸν ἔταξα τάξιν], to change over to the Macedonian side'" (44). This is an interesting text because it not only allows Lucian's Demosthenes to echo Plato's Socrates (*Ap.* 28d9–29a1) but draws a contrast between Demosthenes and the Academy under Speusippus and Xenocrates, which *did* change sides. It is difficult to say how much [Lucian] knew about Speusippus, but his Demosthenes refers directly to *Phaedo* with the words: "And will Demosthenes prefer an unseemly life to a seemly death, completely forgetting the discourses of Xenocrates and Plato about immortality?" (47). As already mentioned, Lucian is our only source for the suggestion that Xenocrates was one of Demosthenes' teachers but it is evident that he believed Plato was, and he makes a compelling case for that belief.

After a brief description of Demosthenes' oratorical power, fittingly expressed in terms of his superiority to Isocrates' student and Philip's spokesman Pytho (32), Antipater uses the word "tool" in a way that recalls a similar passage in Plutarch's *Life of Cicero*:[11]

> 'But I always ranked this secondary, having put it in the place of a tool [ὄργανον]. Demosthenes himself I was admiring exceedingly for both his thought and intelligence, guarding his soul unbent on the straight path amidst all the three waves [τρικυμίαι; cf. R. 472a4] of fortune, and to none of the fearsome things giving in.'[12]

Going further, [Lucian] allows Philip to use passages from *Republic* and *Gorgias* to put Demosthenes' rhetoric in its secondary and properly Platonic place: "But he will rouse his own citizens, made unwilling as though sedated by mandragora [cf. R. 488c5]; employing outspokenness against their laziness as a kind of amputation and cauterization [cf. *Grg.* 480c6–7] and having considered but little in regard to their pleasure [cf. *Grg.* 464e2–465a2]" (36). But it is the juxtaposition of φιλοσοφία, ἡ πολιτεία, and πάλαι ("long ago") in this passage that captures perfectly the Old Academy's impact on the young Demosthenes, and the words λέληθεν ὑμᾶς continue to apply to us:

> "Are you so misled as to believe you will frighten one who long ago made a plan [πάλαι] to expose his soul to the uncertain hazards of his country, and to complain when he assails your deeds? The man who does not shrink before the Assembly of the Athenians has escaped your attention [λέληθεν ὑμᾶς],' he said, 'engaging in politics [πολιτευόμενος] with goodwill toward his country but for himself having put forward his citizenship [ἡ πολιτεία] as exercise for philosophy [γυμνάσιον φιλοσοφίας]."[13]

If his alleged opposition to rhetoric and democracy makes the connection between Plato and Demosthenes improbable on Plato's, it is the absence of philosophy that makes it impossible on Demosthenes' side; [Lucian] is unique among the ancients for stating the crucial point that captures the core of Plato's Πολιτεία: the decision to place a higher good above one's own is ipso facto a γυμνάσιον φιλοσοφίας. The critical word πάλαι will reappear when Archias remarks that Demosthenes "seems to have planned long ago" (43) to die as he did, and the word is apt:[14] it was in response to reading Plato's *Phaedo* as a youth that Demosthenes had done so.[15]

Although the high quality of the *Encomium* might suggest Lucian's authority, this chapter's theme of "suppressions" is even better illustrated if [Lucian] wrote it, and thus that it survived only by a mistaken attribution, like [Plutarch], *Lives of the Ten Orators*.[16] Regardless of who wrote it, and despite the fact that its author states the historical thesis that my book is defending only in the midst of palpable falsehoods, *Encomium of Demosthenes* is the most convincing defense of that thesis in print, and it deserves the reader's attention on that basis. It is a perfect expression of "double action," simultaneously illuminating a civic Plato and a Platonic Demosthenes.[17] Its power resides in the plausibility of its case, not in the authority of its [author], and since the evidence that makes that case elsewhere has so obviously been suppressed—for despite its existence, "it has escaped your attention [λέληθεν ὑμᾶς]"—assigning it to an anonymous author, existing only under erasure, seems fitting and proper. My hypothesis is that it was not safe or at least advisable for a Greek subject of Rome's *imperium* to do so in the second century AD,[18] at a time when any ambitious youngster would have done well to heed Plutarch's advice:

> And when entering upon any office whatsoever, you must not only call to mind those considerations of which Pericles reminded himself when he assumed the cloak of a general: "Take care, Pericles; you are ruling free men, you are ruling Greeks, Athenian citizens," but *you* [emphasis mine] must also say to yourself: "You who rule are a subject, ruling a State controlled by proconsuls, the agents of Caesar; these are not the spearmen of the plain, nor is this ancient Sardis, nor the famed Lydian power." You should arrange your cloak more carefully and from the office of the generals keep your eyes upon the orators' platform, and not have great pride or confidence in your crown, since you see the boots of Roman soldiers just above your head. No, you should imitate the actors, who, while putting into the performance their own passion, character, and reputation, yet listen to the prompter and do not go beyond the degree of liberty in rhythms and meters permitted by those in authority over them [οἱ κρατοῦντες].[19]

The hypothesis of an imperial suppression, building on foundations laid long before, explains some peculiarities already encountered in Dionysius of Halicarnassus (see preface).[20] The pattern will continue: Aelius Aristides (see below), Plutarch, [Lucian], [Dionysius of

Halicarnassus],[21] and [Longinus], will never unequivocally state, but will repeatedly imply, what Cicero had claimed, and Quintilian proved.

Not surprisingly, the "double action" in *Encomium of Demosthenes* begins from the Demosthenes side by describing him in Platonic terms; the anonymous *Letters of Chion of Heraclea* does the opposite, presenting the Old Academy as ideologically committed to tyrannicide, and thus indirectly consistent with Demosthenes' political practice or πολιτεία. Here too we are dealing with a despised and easily dismissed fiction; here too we can discover the suppressed truth. Like the *Encomium of Demosthenes*, *Chion of Heraclea* has a core of historical accuracy: Chion assassinated Clearchus, the tyrant of Heraclea, and he did so after studying at the Academy. But like the book of Macedonian archives that Thersagoras gives to the narrator, the collection of seventeen letters is transparently fictional. Since there is no author from whom authority can be withheld in this case, other expedients are easily found for dismissing the impact of the world's first epistolary novel:[22] Chion's attempt to liberate Heraclea from tyranny failed, the tyrant he assassinated had likewise been a student of Plato's, and the author misunderstood Plato radically.[23] The latter claim, involving the juxtaposition of the last two letters in the collection—to Clearchus (16) and Plato respectively (17)—is the most dialectically useful, and will receive the most attention. But the failure of Chion's attempt is of no value for denying the act's Platonic inspiration—after all, Demosthenes, Dion,[24] and Cicero failed as well—while the evidence that Clearchus was Plato's student, since he unquestionably was the student of Isocrates,[25] will serve to connect *Chion of Heraclea* to larger patterns of misdirection and suppression that implicate Demosthenes as well.

The seventeenth is the only letter in the collection addressed to Plato, and its purpose is to convey that Chion is about to do what his teacher inspired him to do and that he knows in advance that he will be killed for doing it: "I know indeed that I will be done away with, but this I am praying to suffer only having completed the tyrant-killing [ἡ τυραννοκτονία]." A prophetic dream-vision confirms this happy outcome, and with respect to his personal happiness, the choice he has made resonates with a long tradition of dying nobly that goes back to Achilles:

> From this very dream I am hopeful of attaining a noble death [εὔελπις εἰμι καλοῦ θανάτου τυχεῖν]. For I consider in no way counterfeit to be the presaging of the soul since you also repeatedly claim the same. And if the prophecy should prove true, I believe myself about to become most blessed than if a life extending into old age after the τυραννοκτονία is given to me.[26]

Chion's stated willingness to purchase freedom for others at the expense of his own death leads to the clear statement of a truth that every decent person knows but that Plato forced his students to discover or remember for themselves: "For a benefit seems greater to those who are well served in which the one doing it does not share." There are many other aspects that make *Letters* a revealing text, and its depiction of Xenophon's role in bringing Chion to the Academy and the reference to "another five year" period of study there have been considered elsewhere.²⁷ But in the context of Demosthenes' war to the death against Macedon—for despite the persuasive fiction of the *Encomium*, Philip, Antipater, and Archias were his murderers, and Aristotle was their agent²⁸—it is the evidence in the *Letters of Chion* that the Old Academy gave its support to τυραννοκτονία that sets the stage for this text's "double action," for only "a tyrannicide Academy" is compatible with recognizing that it is not Aristotle but Demosthenes who was the Old Academy's paradigmatic product, he for whom ἡ πολιτεία was a γυμνάσιον φιλοσοφίας.

Just as others have suppressed the evidence for a tyrannicide Old Academy,²⁹ so too must Chion deny or suppress its existence *and even possibility* in the collection's penultimate letter to the tyrant Clearchus, a masterpiece of deliberate deception. Chion uses recognizably Platonic rhetoric to assure Clearchus that the philosophy he has imbibed in Plato's Academy has rendered him entirely harmless. In the grand tradition of Diotima and the Athenian Laws in *Crito*, he includes in this letter a speech addressed to himself by the goddess "Tranquility [Ἡσυχία]," who reminds him: "you practiced justice, acquired self-control, and learnt to know God." Having devoted himself to "contemplating the principles of nature," Chion includes an even more specific reference to the "assimilation to God [ὁμοίωσις θεῷ]" in the *Theaetetus* Digression, asking: "What can be more beautiful [κάλλιον] than to devote one's leisure solely to one's immortal self and try to bring that part of oneself into closer contact with that which is akin?"³⁰ To deceive the tyrant he will murder, Chion describes the Academy as altogether committed to the contemplative life, and it is remarkable that only in the sixteenth letter has the most recent editor of the *Letters* found any evidence of its anonymous author's understanding of Platonism.³¹ Between a modern reception that reverses the meaning of this ancient text when not ignoring it entirely, and the noble if ineffective act of tyrannicide at its center, *The Letters of Chion of Heraclea* is a monument in miniature to the suppression of the Old Academy.

Just as an account of Plato that emphasizes Aristotle's account of "the unwritten teachings" justifies Chion's claim that it was "principles of nature [φύσεως ἀρχαί]" that were his primary concern, so too a reading of the dialogues that emphasizes the ὁμοίωσις θεῷ can justify an image of the Academy exclusively devoted to the contemplative as opposed to the active life.[32] It is a historical fact that this image became dominant; my goal is to show why that dominance is best understood as a suppression of an older and more properly Platonic *Platonbild*. The most important evidence for that conception is an image of Plato as a teacher that discovers his teaching not in any alleged oral instruction but in his dialogues as a whole, and orders them in relation to an effective pedagogy in which testing his readers by deliberate deception plays a decisive role. The *Theaetetus* Digression plays an important part in this deception, pointing the reader away from Athens, Socrates, and Socratic piety to the increasingly theological-political concerns of Timaeus, Critias, and Plato's two Strangers. As already indicated, the Third Wave of Paradox in *Republic* 5 is the pivot around which our image of Plato will turn. Beginning with a misreading of *Republic* that takes the City as Plato's theoretical ideal,[33] and which uses Plato's *Letters* to define his political and pedagogical practice in terms of turning kings into philosophers,[34] the increasingly theological and anti-democratic *Timaeus-Critias, Statesman,* and *Laws* can then be used to support an image of the Academy that is anything but tyrannicide,[35] and which will allow it to become increasingly apolitical, arithmetical, cosmological, and contemplative as a result. Although this Academy was well adapted to survive the extinction of Hellenic freedom, first under Macedon and then under Rome, it was no longer Plato's. Aside from living on in the dialogues themselves, the Old Academy would only briefly come back to life when the crisis of his republic led Cicero to read them[36]; after the republic's transformation and his murder, it would survive only in fictional works like the *Encomium of Demosthenes* and *Chion of Heraclea*.[37]

A further investigation of the modern reception of the claim that Clearchus was Plato's student will further illustrate the Plato side of the suppression dynamic and its methods. Consider this recent comment on *The Letters of Chion*: "Now if we try to understand the letters, it seems to me that there is a point behind them which will only be apparent when we take into consideration that Clearchus is supposed to have been a student of Plato, too."[38] The ancient evidence for this claim is weak. The Plato-hating Athenaeus did not include Clearchus is his list of tyrants who emerged from the Academy,[39] and Isocrates apologizes for the fact that Clearchus was *his* student.[40] In this case, Memnon, a second-century AD historian of Heracleia, provides the oldest evidence for the connection, but only as preserved by the late Photius and then repeated in the later Suda: "Clearchus had received an education in philosophy; he was one of the pupils of Plato, and for four years he had been a pupil of the rhetorician Isocrates."[41] Memnon does not mention the much better attested evidence that Chion was Plato's student,[42] and the comparative seriousness with which Demosthenes' connection to the Academy has been taken should surprise nobody, nor is this an isolated case.[43] But Memnon does record the following: "he turned out to be truly savage and bloodthirsty toward his subjects, and reached the peak of arrogance, so that he called himself the son of Zeus, and tinged his face with unnatural dyes, adorning it in all kinds of different ways to make it appears glistening or ruddy to those who saw him."[44] First Xenophon and then Plato were warning their readers against tyranny in precisely this rouged and theologized form: the Athenian Stranger is walking to the same cave on Crete where Zeus taught Minos to be a lawgiver (cf. *Lg.* 625b2 and *Min.* 319d6–e5) and Cyrus overawes the Babylonians with make-up and high heels.[45] But for the same reason that the connection between Demosthenes and Plato was suppressed, it became possible or convenient to imagine Clearchus as his student, and the Academy as the very opposite of tyrannicide.

Through the offices of Athenaeus, Demosthenes' nephew Demochares plays the central and decisive role in creating the image of a tyrant-friendly Academy, and it is equally central to this book's thesis that by the time he did so, Demochares may well have been right. The Old Academy that had educated his uncle was gone, and its connection to Demosthenes had been suppressed in response to Macedonian hegemony. If the political orientation of Speusippus is clear (see chapter 1), the case of Xenocrates has been made to seem debatable, but Polemo became scholarch in 314–313, after Demetrius of Phaleron came to in power (318). Demosthenes never mentions his nephew, and if Demochares was aware of his uncle's connection to Plato, he neither mentioned it nor had any reason to do so. Defending a law against the schools of philosophy that principally attacked Aristotle, Demochares had no interest in considering whether or how the Academy had changed: the important thing was that it, like the Lyceum, was now Macedonian in political orientation. But Athenaeus' motives in using Demochares to present Plato as a tyrant-teacher (cf. τυραννοδιδάσκαλος at *Thg.* 125a2) are obvious,[46] and his use of him is therefore highly selective: Eusebius alone has preserved Demochares' damning indictment of Aristotle.[47] Both the eloquence of Demochares and the motives of Athenaeus are evident in the following passage:

> This is what some representatives of the Academy are like even today, living in an unholy and disgraceful fashion; because they got money through fraud, by acting impiously and unnaturally, and are now prominent people. Chairon of Pellene, for example, who studied not only with Plato, but also with Xenocrates—he was a cruel tyrant of his fatherland, and not only drove the best citizens into exile, but gave their slaves their masters' property, and forced

their wives to live with them, as if they were married. This is how he benefitted from the lovely *Republic* and the lawless *Laws*![48]

Like Clearchus, Chairon of Pellene continues to prove useful for those who prefer a tyrant-friendly Academy.[49] By this point, it should come as no surprise that despite the malice of Demochares as mediated by Athenaeus, and the important role of Hermippus in establishing the fact,[50] the contrast with Demosthenes is patent and predicable: "Chairon's discipleship with Plato and Xenocrates goes undisputed in modern literature."[51] Aside from this amazing contrast, the evidence on which *this* connection rests is weak: Demochares makes both Plato *and Xenocrates* responsible for Chairon's education,[52] thus requiring as it does an unlikely eight-year stay at the Academy. As a result, both the modern reception of the evidence provided by Demochares and the evidence itself points to two of this book's central claims. With respect to the second, the Old Academy that had produced Chion of Heraclea and Demosthenes of Athens had been effectively suppressed beginning with Speusippus, and it would have defeated Demochares' purpose to mention Chion—or Euphraeus, as his uncle had in the *Third Philippic*—let alone Demosthenes himself, Lycurgus, and Hyperides.[53]

Despite the important role of Peripatetic biographers like Hermippus and Aristoxenus, no single source has more decisively shaped our conceptions of the Old Academy than Aristotle, and that includes Plato himself. If the dialogues as opposed to the *Letters* had played a larger role in shaping those conceptions, something like the Curricular Hypothesis would have long since become a commonplace; the reason that it now seems outlandish to claim that it was his own dialogues that Plato taught in the Academy is that a rival conception has long since reigned supreme. Although it depends heavily on a deadpan reading of *Phaedrus* (*Phdr.* 275c5–278d7) and the flame-sparking image of the inefficacy of written instruction in the *Seventh Letter* (*Ep.* 341b5–342a7), Aristotle's *Metaphysics* is primarily responsible for creating a conception of the Old Academy based on "the unwritten teachings."[54] This conception not only ignores and conceals external political realities, but emphasizes internal continuity by focusing on the influence of the Pythagoreans in book A and Number Theory in books M and N, just as if the primary difference between Plato and his successors were to be found there. The Aristotelian distinction between the contemplative and actively political lives has made it easy to misconstrue Plato's purpose radically,[55] quite apart from the corollary error of using that distinction to maintain an Academic preference for contemplation as opposed to political action.[56] Despite the Sicilian fiasco described in Plato's *Letters*, the political action of Academy's founder was assimilated to Aristotle's own practice with Alexander of Macedon and Hermias of Atarneus, thus giving rise to a Macedon-friendly conception of philosophers as the preceptors or advisors to kings and tyrants. This assimilation has rendered virtually invisible the creator of a course in leadership designed for the young men of Athens, and an Academy dedicated to the longer and harder route of turning philosophers into leaders. In the process, it has promoted an image of the Academy that favors foreign students rather than Athenians,[57] enlightened absolutism over chastened democracy, a flight to the ὁμοίωσις θεῷ over the return to the Cave, and tyrants in training rather than tyrant-killers.[58] This book has shown that this conception has prevailed in spite of the fact that evidence contradicting it exists; its purpose has been to show that the external evidence for it—the internal evidence remains intact thanks to the dialogues—has been suppressed.

By juxtaposing Aristotle and Demosthenes, I have used the burning political question of the mid fourth-century to show why one conception ultimately supplanted the other. The fact that Demosthenes and Aristotle have so seldom been compared and contrasted despite their antithetical pro- and anti-Macedonian political orientations and the amazing coincidence of their lifetimes (384–322) is the most compelling evidence for the suppression of the Old Academy, a suppression so complete that even their juxtaposition as two students of Plato has become impossible, and, along with it, what that juxtaposition still has the power to teach us. When Aristotle fled from Athens to Chalcis in 323,[59] he is said to have remarked that he did so lest Athens sin a second time against philosophy,[60] thus configuring himself as Socrates. But thanks to Aristotle's correspondent and supporter Antipater, it was Demosthenes who died a Socratic death, clearly recognized as such, albeit only under erasure, by [Lucian]. The distinction between "the Old Academy" as Aristotle has preserved it, and the alternative conception on offer here, informed by the dialogues and illustrated by Demosthenes, Phocion, Lycurgus, and Hyperides—like the distinction between the Academy that Demochares attacked in 306 and the one his uncle entered at fourteen in 370—is best understood not as either/or but as chronologically conditioned, with the inflection point being the *Letter of Speusippus*, written at around the same time that Alexander was fourteen, and thus ready to receive Aristotle's version of a Platonic education.

Since Martin Heidegger approached the study of Plato's *Sophist* in the context of Aristotle,[61] it would be paradoxical to liken an attempt to recover the Old Academy with a Heideggerian *Destruktion* of a concealing tradition,[62] for it is precisely the Aristotelian tradition that has provided the concealment in Plato's case. Nevertheless, something like a Heideggerian *Destruktion* is being attempted here, likewise in the service of ἀλήθεια, and once again implicating—although to opposite effect—the influence of Aristotle on how we should understand Plato. If it is chronologically and psychologically impossible that a seventeen-year-old from Stagira who showed no sympathy whatsoever for the core idea of Platonism—that is, that the Idea is not of this world, and thus that it is false to say "the world is all that is the case"—exerted an influence on Plato,[63] we have nevertheless allowed him to exert a determinative influence on the way *we* have come to understand him, thus giving Aristotle far more power than he deserves. By the time Plato's dialogues reached the Latin West, Aristotle's influence was already towering, and it remains so today. An influential conception of Socrates created by Gregory Vlastos depends more heavily on Aristotle's account than on either Xenophon or Plato's dialogues as a whole,[64] and the Tübingen school's conception of Plato, like its Plotinian predecessor, is no less dependent on the Stagirite.[65] Aristotle is primarily responsible for reading *Republic* as a misguided political program modified in a more practical direction in *Laws*, and his version of the Allegory of the Cave in *Concerning Philosophy*—preserved by Cicero in *De natura deorum*[66]—leaves no doubt as to "the great gulf fixed" between teacher and student regarding Being and Becoming. While Demosthenes never mentions Plato in his public speeches, he never attacks his views either; the best evidence that he could not have been Plato's student is his lifelong commitment to democratic Athens and his teacher's alleged hostility to both democracy and rhetoric. But the rise of Macedon would simplify things considerably, and even if—as seems probable—the elderly Plato had been inclined to support the post-imperial policy of Xenophon as partially implemented by Eubulus in the late 350s, he might still have been roused to admire Demosthenes' *Olynthians* before his death. As for Aristotle, our best evidence that Plato was sympathetic to Macedon is that a bright young man from Stagira entered the Academy at seventeen and stayed on, and that Euphraeus left it for the court of Perdiccas; as Athenaeus was happy to point out, the attack on Archelaus in *Gorgias* points in the opposite direction.[67]

The first wave of Macedon-inspired suppression seems to have had no effect on Cicero, and without any animus toward either Aristotle or Isocrates, he celebrated the connection between Demosthenes and Plato. It is true that it was his character Antonius who praised Isocrates most highly in *De oratore*,[68] and in reading a skilled writer of philosophical dialogue like Cicero, it is axiomatic that one should not identify the author's views with those of one of his characters, especially one who serves as a foil to Crassus. Unfortunately, this interpretive truism has not been applied to the character named "Cicero"[69] who appears in his later dialogues, and even in the midst of a revival of interest in Cicero, he continues to be confused with this amiable New Academy skeptic who claims to follow Socrates in the deliberately self-contradictory claim that he knows that he knows nothing,⁷⁰ not identified as the writer of philosophical dialogue who created "him." But even before the invention of "Cicero," Cicero had followed Demosthenes by replacing an imaginary City with an idealized Roman Republic in his version of Plato's *Republic*,⁷¹ where Scipio describes a dream that any open-minded reader can see has far more in common with the Allegory of the Cave than the traditionally recognized parallel with the Myth of Er first taught by Chalcidius.⁷² Amidst many other indications that Cicero's understanding of Plato depended on his own careful reading of the dialogues rather than on the competing influences of Philo of Larissa and Antiochus of Ascalon,⁷³ his repeated insistence that Demosthenes had been Plato's student stands out like a ray of Platonic sunshine.⁷⁴ Demosthenes had done what Cicero was now doing; what he was now doing in speech after speech was the same thing Demosthenes had done. He celebrated their common ground in both translations and philosophical dialogues. Both acted in accordance with Plato's τοὺς ἄλλους παρακαλῶμεν, and the Demosthenic core of Ciceronianism, visible in a long series of works between *De inventione* and the *Philippics*, is the ethical use of a philosophy-guided rhetoric, dedicated to combatting the rise and victory of tyranny, and placed in death-defying service to the city, whether in Athens or in Rome.⁷⁵

Picked up by Tacitus, Quintilian, and Aulus Gellius, the Ciceronian connection between Demosthenes and Plato fares differently among the Greek scholars of the imperial age, and I have hypothesized a second or Augustan wave of suppression to explain this difference. Dionysius of Halicarnassus clearly knew that others had connected the two as teacher and student, but even while carefully and emphatically connecting them as rival masters of style, he neither states nor denies their Academic connection (see preface). The fact that he fails to assert it does not prove that he denied it, but even if his did, it was not because he had decided, as modern scholars were the first to do, that the evidentiary value of Hermippus was insufficient to justify the connection. Plutarch cites Hermippus but manages to tell the relevant story less plausibly in his *Life of Demosthenes* than Aulus Gellius had done (see introduction); as for *Lives of the Ten Orators*, if Plutarch didn't write it, then whoever stood behind [Plutarch] evidently ranked being truth's anonymous witness over securing literary immortality for her- or himself. Diogenes Laertius is virtually unique in stating the connection in his compendious *Lives*. But even if he renders Diogenes less than unique, [Lucian] once again illustrates the same curious anonymity, while even if Lucian himself wrote *Encomium of Demosthenes*, he must be said to have suppressed a clear statement of the teacher-student connection even while making it obvious from beginning to end between the lines. Lucian's *Teacher of Orators* may provide a clue: only through parody could a Greek sophist deny the political relevance of Demosthenes' public speeches to the Roman imperial context, and something similar will be gleaned below from Aelius Aristides.[76] And while the author of Chion's *Letters* might perhaps have mistakenly hoped that publishing them anonymously would make them appear to be something more than a work of transparent fiction, he or she may also have recognized the danger of celebrating a tyrannicide Academy for the same reason that aligning Demosthenes with Plato had become imprudent if not dangerous for a Greek subject of Rome to do.[77] Thanks to the dialogue with which *On the Sublime* ends, the identity of [Longinus] may perhaps hold the key for detecting and celebrating a "between the lines" opposition to Rome during the so-called Second Sophistic.

But it is primarily thanks to the achievements of nineteenth-century German philologists that it is no longer easy or even possible *for us* to accept the ancient evidence that Demosthenes was Plato's student. While the results of this "third wave" of suppression are obvious and apparently determinative with respect to their continuing influence, the motives of those responsible for it are, all things considered, virtually impossible to detect or at least synthesize. It is tempting to simplify. Proponents of German unification inevitably valorized Philip as a proto-Bismarck and denigrated Demosthenes as the defender not of liberty but of an obsolete system of independent and outmoded city-states,[78] and if the contrasting views of Drerup and Clemenceau,[79] brought into the open by the First World War, are then read back into the previous century, something with the appearance of national purpose might become visible. On balance, however, it seems more plausible to search elsewhere for an explanation. Although the ancient evidence of a connection between Plato and Demosthenes would tend to valorize rather than diminish the latter at Philip's expense, suppressing it was not the effect of a politically motivated conspiracy. The evidence for it made the story an easy target for two dominant but apolitical aspects of nineteenth-century German philology: *Quellenforschung* and *Echtheitskritik*.[80] The most natural targets of both source-criticism and inauthenticity claims were stories that were regarded as too good to be true, and the fact that a ruthlessly critical and apparently objective skepticism could be set to work confirming traditional conceptions—and suppressing what others had an independent motive to deny—made the "third wave" unstoppable.

In a chronological sense, then, it is the influence of this last wave that has created the intellectual world in which we now find ourselves, and it is doubtless true that if nineteen-century philology had not created a scientifically secure basis for dismissing the ancient evidence, no twenty-first century scholar could get away with denying the connection on the simplistic grounds that because Plato was rhetoric's enemy, he could not have taught Demosthenes. But while it is tempting to depict those simplistic claims as the intellectual fallout of the third wave of suppression, writing this book has persuaded me that they point back to the continuing influence of the first and second waves instead. Thanks to increased attention to Cicero and a growing awareness of Platonic irony, the philosophy vs. rhetoric polarity is becoming indefensible as interpretive bedrock; this can only increase our attention to the second or Augustan wave of suppression. But there are also signs that our collective certainty that Plato was democracy's enemy as well as its critic is weakening,[81] and this shift primarily implicates the first or Macedonian wave, and an image of the Academy handed down to us by Aristotle. In fact, the teacher-student connection unites the apparently opposite targets of the first and second waves: as a Plato-trained democrat, Demosthenes is using rhetoric as purified by a close encounter with *Gorgias*, and both his democratic commitments and rhetorical practices are made equally ancillary to the Academy's impact. Meanwhile, an image of the Academy based on the dialogues as a whole—including Plato's pervasive use of rhetoric in them, and the freedom of interpretation that reading them well demands[82]—is strong enough to withstand the cumulative impact of all three waves, culminating as they do in the oversimplifications of today. If we are willing to take seriously the fact that Plato located his school in an Athens at once still democratic and yet endangered, and can imagine its curriculum—embodied in a series of dialogues replete with rhetoric and deliberate deception—as designed to bring about the wedding of Socratic philosophy and political power in an Athenian context, we will revisit the ancient evidence that Demosthenes was Plato's student with a fresh spirit, and may even be prepared to recognize him as the paradigmatic product of the Old Academy.

Such, of course, is this book's claim, but its principal basis cannot be found within it but rather in a previously published and only recently completed study of the dialogues as a whole. The process was a gradual one. In a previous study of Cicero, it was unnecessary to prove that Demosthenes had actually been Plato's student: it was enough to demonstrate that Cicero's *belief* that he had been was decisive for understanding how Cicero understood himself.[83] But writing about Plato's enigmatic *Menexenus* led to Dionysius of Halicarnassus' hardly less enigmatic comparison of Demosthenes and Plato, and thus reopened the question on a more substantial historical basis that eventually implicated Phocion, Lycurgus, and Hyperides as well.[84] It was thus "with a fresh spirit" that I revisited the ancient evidence, and was immediately impressed with how seemingly single-minded had been the attempt to deny it. In attempting to come to terms with this single-mindedness, I have repeatedly had cause to wonder about the motives of those who so resolutely denied and deny it and have wavered as to whether it was concerted and conspiratorial or merely happenstance and coincidental. To paraphrase the Declaration of Independence, when confronted with "a long train of abuses and usurpations, *pursuing invariably the same object,*" the question was whether or not Jefferson's "evinces a design" was applicable to a virtually unanimous rejection of a connection that a sympathy for Cicero had already made plausible long before encountering Dionysius, "Quintilian's Proof,"[85] the *Letter of Speusippus*, the παρακαλῶμεν in the *Third Philippic*, the story of Codrus in Lycurgus, or the influence of Socrates' last words in the *Funeral Oration* of Hyperides.

It is with Jefferson's words in mind—the "long train" that allegedly "evinces a design" because it is "invariably pursuing the same object"—that the reader is asked to consider another pattern of suppression. This suppression, ancillary to the third wave, was applied not to the external evidence that Demosthenes was Plato's student but to the Demosthenic corpus itself, thus making the move from *Quellenforschung* to *Echtheitskritik*. Consider the *Funeral Oration* of Demosthenes or rather [Demosthenes]. Despite being mentioned in *On the Crown* (18.285), it was pronounced inauthentic by Dionysius in antiquity (see preface), thus setting the pattern for a rejection that dominated the nineteenth-century and came under attack only in the twentieth. Johannes Sykutris, whose research likewise resurrected the letter of Speusippus, led the way here,[86] and the influence of Demosthenes' *Funeral Oration* was thereafter detected in Lycurgus and Hyperides.[87] Important for connecting Demosthenes to the other two members of "the Academic Trio," his *Funeral Oration* also points back to the idealization of Athens already apparent in *Menexenus*. Although Judson Herrman plays down Aspasia's description of the cold reception the sons will receive from their fathers in the afterlife if they have not surpassed them in virtue (see chapter 4), he usefully suggests Plato's influence on both Demosthenes and Hyperides: "the funeral orations of Thucydides, Lysias, and Plato are all silent about the afterlife, while both Demosthenes and Hyperides speculate about the existence of the dead in the underworld or the isles of the blessed."[88] Echoing *Republic* 7 (*R.* 540b6-7), it is Demosthenes who mentions the latter destination (60.34), while the influence of *Menexenus* is also visible when he prepares the way for doing so by calling the dead "happy" (60.33; cf. *Mx.* 247a6).

A *Funeral Oration* following the lost battle of Chaeronea must have been a difficult speech to give, and since it is the only example of epideictic rhetoric in the Demosthenic corpus, there is an easy explanation, at once generic and psychological, for its anomalous features. With the exception of *On the Crown* eight years later, we have very few speeches for the period between 338 and Demosthenes' death in 322, and beginning with the excision of his *Funeral Oration*, nineteenth-century philology is largely responsible for this.[89] Callimachus capped a series of public prosecutions with two speeches that postdate Chaeronea (26.11), and he followed *Against Aristogeiton I* and *II* by returning from the end of his career to the beginning (speeches 27 through 31). Once again, Dionysius got the wrecking ball swinging with the claim that *Against Aristogeiton II* was falsely ascribed to him,[90] and their tone is admittedly peculiar,[91] pervaded at times by a kind of theologized legal mysticism (25.11, 25.16, and 25.97), and opening with the claim that the jurors have already reached the appropriate verdict "from within" (25.2 and 25.81; cf. the internal altars of 25.35). Precisely because both speeches contain hymns to the laws of Athens, they inevitably suggest a familiarity with *Crito* (cf. 25.16 with *Cri.* 52c6–d3). More specifically, the analogy at the end of *Aristogeiton II* between the lawgiver and the doctor (26.26) creates an obvious parallel with *Gorgias* despite replacing δικαιοσύνη with νομοθετική (cf. *Grg.* 464b7–8) in a way that makes the laws rather prescriptive and curative. Further echoes of *Gorgias* include the fact that Aristogeiton is said to be incurable (25.95; cf. *Grg.* 525c1–4)[92]—and Dinarchus tells us that he was convicted in this trial[93]—that Demosthenes invokes the specter of posthumous punishment (25.52; cf. *Grg.* 525c1-8), that he calls on the Athenians to exhort (παρακαλεῖν) each other to come to the aid of their laws (26.27; in addition to *Grg.* 527e5–6, see 526e1–527a4), identifies νόμος with τάξις (cf. 25.19 and 26.27 with *Grg.* 503e4-504d3), links νόμος with φύσις as if they were not opposites (25.65 and 25.81; cf. *Grg.* 483e3),[94] and attacks πλεονεξία (cf. 26.13 and 26.25 with *Grg.* 508a7; see also 483c1-d6). The speeches are also remarkable for the skillful deployment of triads (25.11, 25.16, 25,35, and 25.43), a characteristically Platonic trick (cf. 25.82 and 26.25 with *Grg.* 525a3-6).[95] They also connect [Demosthenes] with the other two members of the Academic trio (25.1 and 26.11).

As already suggested in the last chapter, no single text in the *corpus Demosthenicum* better illustrates the influence of Plato's *Gorgias* on Demosthenes than the *Exordia*, and the rejection of this text by nineteenth-century philologists is yet another indication that suppression is in play. It therefore must count as a counter-indication of better things to come in the twenty-first century that Harvey Yunis, in a 1996 study of "political rhetoric in classical Athens," undertook, in an appendix, the laborious project, all-too-familiar to this author, of investigating the long forgotten nineteenth-century documents that had led to the excision of *Exordia* in order to justify using it to advance his arguments.[96] Although Yunis follows the tradition with respect to the external evidence that Demosthenes was Plato's student,[97] and—despite the timeless, preparatory, and theoretical aspect of *Exordia*[98]—differentiates him as purely practical from Thucydides and Plato,[99] the mere fact of the comparison is telling: "Derived in significant measure from Thucydides and Plato, Demosthenes' model of political rhetoric is tailored to his immediate political purpose."[100] Later efforts,[101] including my own, validate his accurate observation, made without any pretense to self-importance, that: "formerly it was difficult for scholars to fit the collection [sc. *Exordia*] into existing notions of Demosthenes' literary, political, and rhetorical activity."[102] On the other hand, it is likely that even if the restoration of a text like *Exordia* may increasingly compel scholars to admit the influence of dialogues like *Phaedrus* and *Gorgias* on Demosthenes, they will at best follow Schaefer, and thus do so in a way that makes him *Plato's reader*, not his student. It is therefore important to emphasize that in addition to my claim that reading Plato's dialogues *is what it meant to be student in the Old Academy*, there is no external evidence suggesting that Demosthenes did the one as opposed to the other, or that doing so was even possible. Indeed, the crucial passage from Cicero's *Brutus* seems intended to preempt that possibility.

"Demosthenes is said to have read Plato studiously, even to have heard him, and this is apparent from the character and sublimity of his vocabulary; he even says this himself about himself in a certain letter [*in quadam epistula*]."[103] This "certain letter" is the fifth in a collection of six, and with the first four now generally accepted as authentic,[104] it should surprise nobody if the fifth will be the last to join the club or rather will remain the only one never to do so. It has been suggested that the *Fifth Letter* was forged for the express purpose of validating a student-teacher relationship between Demosthenes and Plato.[105] But Cicero merely extrapolates that conclusion from the letter. In the letter, Demosthenes states that his correspondent is behaving in a manner unworthy of the education or παιδεία he received "from Plato's school [ἀπὸ τῆς Πλάτωνος διατριβῆς]" (5.3). Although he does so in terms that indicate his familiarity with the goals of that institution, he never states that he was Plato's student; as a result, Pernot's hypothesis simply won't fit: a forger would easily have found a less indirect way to make the fabricated connection. Thanks to this passage in Cicero, Demosthenes' *Fifth Letter* is cited earlier than any of the other letters in the collection, and even though the prejudice against any epistolary evidence that originated with Bentley and remains dominant in Frede provides its rejection's necessary foundation, it is difficult to doubt that a more specific kind of suppression is in play here. In addition to its uniquely Platonic use of εὖ πράττειν as a greeting, the fact that Demosthenes describes Plato's teaching in relation to "the best [τὸ βέλτιστον]" (5.3) once again indicates the influence of *Gorgias* (cf. *Grg*. 463c4–465a2): "which [sc. παιδεία, i.e., the education which Heracleodorus received ἀπὸ τῆς Πλάτωνος διατριβῆς] is so truly outside the devices by which one gets the better of others [τὰ πλεονεκτήματα] and the sophistries [τὰ σοφίσματα] concerning these [sc. τὰ πλεονεκτήματα], but has rather for the sake of the best [τὸ βέλτιστον] and the most just in all things [καὶ τοῦ δικαιοτάτου πάνθ' ἕνεκα] it been proved by scrutiny and test [LSJ IV on ἐξετάζειν]" (5.3).[106] It would be difficult to come up with a more economical mission statement for the dialogue-based curriculum of the Old Academy, which exposed its students to a wide variety of σοφίσματα for the greater glory of "the best and the most just."

The only other document in the corpus that mentions Plato by name is *The Erotic Essay* or Ἐρωτικός, and the relevant passage indicates Demosthenes' familiarity with Plato's *Letters*. As already mentioned, a Plato scholar is initially shocked by the difference between the way that historians treat the evidence of Plato's *Letters* and the way philosophers do; the latter tend to ignore the collection entirely when not debating about the authenticity of one of its components, the *Seventh Letter* in particular.[107] Demosthenes addresses his chastely erotic speech to a young man named Epicrates, whose name reminds the reader of the speech of Lysias that Phaedrus reads to Socrates in *Phaedrus*.[108] Emphasizing "choice" in the form of προαίρεσις from the start (61.1; cf. 61.2), and preserving the fiction of indirect address—it is to us or some otherwise unnamed audience that he addresses the essay, not Epicrates himself (61.1)—Demosthenes encourages him to take care of himself (with ἡ ἐπιμέλεια ἡ αὑτοῦ at 61.39; cf. 61.43), offers a discourse "concerning philosophy [περὶ τῆς φιλοφίας]" (61.40–47) in the course of which he describes it as providing "knowledge concerning deeds and political discourses [ἡ περὶ τὰς πράξεις καὶ τοὺς πολιτικοὺς λόγους ἐπιστήμη]" (61.44), before recommending Plato as a teacher on the basis of his influence on Archytas: "And Archytas of Tarentum, who as ruler of that city administered affairs so well and philanthropically that his record spread to all and sundry, was at first despised and only gained great distinction after his association with Plato."[109] Within the image of the Academy that has come down to us through Aristotle, Archytas is rather Plato's Pythagorean preceptor than his political pupil; Demosthenes, by contrast, is preserving the true spirit of Plato's *Ninth Letter*, where he admonishes Archytas for chafing about "the lack of leisure [ἡ ἀσχολία]" that arises from concern "regarding the common things [περὶ τὰ κοινά]" (*Ep.* 357e5):

> That it is pleasantest [ἥδιστον] in life to do one's own things [τὸ τὰ αὑτοῦ πράττειν], especially if one should choose to do such things as you; this is clear to almost everyone. But this also it is necessary for you to take to heart [ἐνθυμεῖσθαι]: that each of us has not been born for himself alone, but that our homeland [ἡ πατρίς] has some share of our birth, our parents another, yet another our other friends, and many things too are given over to the critical moments, taking hold of our life. But with the fatherland herself

[ἡ πατρίς αὐτή] calling for the common things [τὰ κοινά], not giving it audience is equally out of place. For at the same time what happens is abandoning a domain to worse people, who enter into the common things [πρὸς τὰ κοινά] not for the sake of the best [τὸ βέλτιστον].[110]

As Cicero would do after him with the immortal words *non nobis solum nati sumus*,[111] Demosthenes also pays tribute to this passage in *On the Crown*:

> The Athenians of that day [sc. during the Persian Wars] did not search for a statesman or a commander who should help them to a servile security: they did not ask to live, unless they could live as free men. Every man of them thought of himself as one born, not to his father and his mother alone, but to his country [ἡ πατρίς]. What is the difference? The man who deems himself born only to his parents will wait for his natural and destined end; the son of his country [ἡ πατρίς] will be willing to die [ἀποθνῄσκειν ἐθελήσει] rather than see her enslaved, and will look upon those outrages and indignities, which the city [ἡ πόλις] in subjection is compelled to endure, as more dreadful than death itself.[112]

What I have called "double action" necessarily works both ways, and as long as our conception of the Old Academy regards Archytas primarily as the intermediary through which Plato was transformed from an ethics-oriented Socratic to a principles-based refiner of Pythagorean physics,[113] it simply won't matter that Demosthenes illuminates and is illuminated in turn by comparing Plato's *Ninth Letter* with the *Erotic Essay*, with this passage in *On the Crown*, or with Cicero's *On Duties*. It is considerably easier and more pleasant to speculate about the genesis and principles of cosmos than to make the difficult choice to die willingly for the sake of your city's freedom and the freedom of other cities as well. But even if the resolutely political emphasis of the dialogues suggests that Demosthenes expressed in words and achieved in action exactly what Plato, through Socrates, was teaching him to do and say, this has been made to seem somehow sub-philosophical in comparison with number theory, cosmology, and the kind of metaphysics that "follows the books on physics." In short, a conception of the Academy based less on the dialogues than on Aristotle's testimony in *Metaphysics*, makes it just as unlikely that Plato is going to be re-recognized as Demosthenes' teacher as that, on the other side, the kind of Demosthenes that Cawkwell and Co. are offering us is likely to be re-recognized as anything even remotely resembling Plato's student.

And with this observation, it is time to complete the project I called "flipping Pernot" in the preface. In response to the *Fifth Letter*, Pernot suggests: "the forger had been inspired precisely [*précisément*] by the tradition according to which Demosthenes had been a student of Plato's."[114] Turning to the *Erotic Essay*, Pernot first remarks, truly—albeit without reference to Plato's *Ninth Letter*—that Archytas is "more often presented in the other sources as Plato's teacher rather than his student,"[115] and then remarks:

> If the *Discourse on Love* is authentic, it constitutes the best evidence for the influence exercised by Plato on Demosthenes. If, on the other hand, it is apocryphal, it loses all value as proof, and by this hypothesis, it is possible that the attribution of this text to Demosthenes, which R. Clavaud considers inexplicable if it was a fake, was inspired precisely [*précisément*] by the link that was commonly established between Demosthenes and Plato.[116]

Having used *précisément* twice to precisely the same effect, Pernot states the hypothesis that it is my intention to flip. Whereas previous treatments of the connection between Demosthenes and Plato have been concerned only with historical truth, Pernot will go farther: "we must go beyond this stage and ask ourselves, whatever the authority of this tradition, why antiquity believed in it and what meaning it gave to it."[117] Without acknowledging that he is begging the question with respect to the historical problem, Pernot returns to Cicero as evidence for a quarrel between philosophy and rhetoric that goes back to the rivalry of Plato and Isocrates, the two great schoolmasters of fourth-century Athens:

> To say that Demosthenes had been Plato's student, in this context, was a good means for a philosopher to demolish the pretensions of the rhetoricians by appropriating their idol [sc. Demosthenes] and that it was philosophy alone that conduced to true eloquence. It was a means of responding to the annexation and usurpation of philosophy performed by some of the orators, like Isocrates or like Aelius Aristides at the end of *For the Four*.[118]

According to Pernot, then, the defenders of philosophy had manufactured the evidence that put rhetoric in its place, thus allowing them to win the quarrel with the orators. While there is no evidence that this evidence was fabricated apart from the question-begging assumption that since such evidence is false, it *must* have been fabricated, there is, by contrast, a great deal of modern evidence that this evidence has been systematically suppressed, albeit not only by those, like Pernot, who are reviving the apparently imperial case for rhetoric that he associates with Aelius Aristides, but also in accordance with an even older wave of suppression.

For Pernot, Aelius Aristides is "Exhibit A" for the quarrel between rhetoric and philosophy,[119] and I am grateful to him for bringing this great author and equally great Platonist to my attention. To address the obvious paradox in a preliminary way: Aelius Aristides does not seem to be a great Platonist for the same reason that Demosthenes does not seem to have been Plato's student, and if the eloquent Plato is—in accordance with traditional conceptions—the enemy of rhetoric, then

Aelius Aristides, the Plato-immersed author of *In Response to Plato: On Behalf of Rhetoric* is at once rhetoric's defender and Plato's enemy. The problem, of course, is that Plato *is* eloquent and Aelius *is* Plato-immersed, and that is only the beginning. Both in *On Behalf of Rhetoric* and even more prominently in *For the Four*,[120] it is primarily on *Gorgias* that Aelius Aristides grounds his defense of rhetoric in opposition to Plato's attack on it. But as already indicated, *Gorgias* is crucial for discovering the influence of Plato on Demosthenes, so the same dialogue that doubtless appears to be a solid basis on which to ground the quarrel between philosophy and rhetoric is also, as Cicero was the first to discover or disclose, the most problematic and even humorous basis on which to do so. Was the author of *For the Four* and *In Response to Plato* aware of this? The answer will depend on whether or not Aelius gives us sufficient reason to believe that he himself subscribes to the traditional view of Plato as rhetoric's enemy, with his *Gorgias* constituting *his* "Exhibit A."[121]

While Aelius Aristides presents himself throughout as the imitator, admirer, and indeed devoted acolyte of Demosthenes,[122] his position toward Plato is nuanced:

> At many points in the *Platonic Orations* Aristides is as loud and insistent in his praise of Plato, and in declarations of his own admiration and affection, as he is in his praise of (the right kind of) philosophy. At the end of *Or. 2* [sc. *In Response to Plato*], he can retrospectively picture the exchange of views between himself and "Plato, the father and teacher of orators" as an exchange of toasts between friends, as if at some banquet of the cultural aristocracy [*In Response to Plato*, 465]. Defending himself in *Or. 4* [sc. *Letter to Capito*] against Capito's criticism of the argument in *Or. 2*, he claims to be at one with his critic in valuing Plato as much as I do my own person" [*Letter to Capito*, 1]. In *Or. 3* [sc. *For the Four*] he declares that he "would rather condemn {him}self to the most extreme punishment than willingly withhold the highest praise from Plato" [*For the Four*, 42], three times characterizes him as "the best of the Greeks" [*For the Four*, 461, 557, and 663], and invokes Aeschylus to underline his refusal to have "anyone who is not a friend to this man and does not honor him as he deserves" as "comrade in arms or anywhere near me" [*For the Four*, 607].[123]

Although I have quoted Michael Trapp at length on the μέν part of his argument, I will not do the same for the much longer δέ part: his thesis is that although Aelius *claims* to be treating Plato "with all due respect," the truth is very different: "Plato, then, is ostensibly praised, but under cover of this token show of respect is relentlessly battered across all three of the Orations."[124] What makes Trapp's article so useful is that he emphasizes Aelius' claim that Plato has repeatedly contradicted himself, and that Aelius will therefore refute him *on the basis of what Plato himself has said*, a method to which Trapp offers a deadpan response: "Detection of inconsistency is a tool of philosophical as well as oratorical polemic."[125] However appropriately this kind of polemic may be applied to other authors, it is rather a friendly method when applied to Plato's deliberate self-contradictions, the palliation or suppression of which has made it easy and natural for so many so-called Platonists to misread Plato.[126] As a result, it has become difficult to imagine how the dialogues themselves constituted an education in political virtue, rhetoric, and the detection of deception, and impossible to see that Demosthenes was Plato's student and deeply influenced by *Gorgias* in particular.

No more than Dionysius or [Longinus] does Aelius Aristides ever state that Plato was Demosthenes' teacher. But as Trapp notes, he concluded *On Behalf of Rhetoric* with the claim that in responding to Plato, he has responded to "the father and teacher of orators," and in that number, he has playfully included himself. While attacking Plato in his *Platonic Orations*, Aelius Aristides tells us that he has really been defending him: "I am running the risk of seeming to contradict Plato, while most of all agreeing with him."[127] Plato has already done the same thing: while appearing to reject rhetoric *tout court*, he has really created a philosophical basis for his own use of it in *Gorgias*, thus preparing the way for an orator like Demosthenes and an astute interpreter like Aelius himself to discover the truth. Another analogy suggests itself: just as Plato appears to reject Homer,[128] Aelius does the same to Plato; both attacks are merely apparent.[129] Thus, without stating the historical connection between Plato and Demosthenes, he joins others in making a good case for it: while Dionysius justifies the connection by a paradoxical and otherwise inexplicable juxtaposition,[130] and [Lucian] does so by using characteristically Platonic tricks to praise Demosthenes, Aelius shows that Plato's attack on rhetoric is self-contradictory, which it is. The core concept is Aelius' claim, most fully developed in *For the Four*,[131] and prepared for him by Plato himself (*Grg.* 517a4–6), that there are really two kinds of rhetoric:[132] the one (ἡ κολακικὴ ῥητορική) that aims at pleasure (ἡδονή) and to gratify (χαρίζεσθαι), and the true one (ἡ ἀληθινὴ ῥητορική) that aims at "the best [τὸ βέλτιστον],"[133] thus recalling Demosthenes' description of Platonic παιδεία in the *Erotic Essay*. This distinction is also doubled, and here he expressly cites Demosthenes to confirm his description of the good form *of philosophy*,[134] while the other he usefully associates with "body lovers,"[135] claiming that it is filled with sophistry,[136] and uses "the small and bald tinker" of *Republic* 6 to describe it (*R*. 495e5).[137]

But it is by means of Aristides the Just that Aelius Aristides most effectively illustrates the deliberately self-contradictory character of Plato's attack on rhetoric and Athenian statesmanship in *Gorgias*. He introduces the passage on Aristides in *On Behalf of Rhetoric* with the words: "still more clearly at the end of the dialogue he has uncovered and revealed everything."[138] In terms of length, most of *For the Four* is devoted to a defense of Pericles, Themistocles, Cimon, and Miltiades, all of whom Plato criticizes through Socrates in *Gorgias*, but here too Aristides the Just plays an important role "at the end."[139] Placing a critique of the Four in Socrates' mouth, Plato prepares us to see that it is already in a certain sense unfair, and he therefore overstates the case before using Aristides to contradict it:

> *Socrates*: True then, as it seems, were our earlier statements: that we know nobody who has been a good man while practicing politics [*Men.* 93a5–6 contradicts this[140]] in our city. And you agree that there is nobody among those of today, but among the previous ones, and you chose these men [sc. "the Four"]. But these shone forth as equal to those today, so that if these were orators, they were neither using the true rhetoric [ἡ ἀληθινὴ ῥητορική]—for they would not then have been tossed out—nor the flattering one [ἡ κολακική].[141]

Since the Athenians will eventually prosecute and murder Socrates, the proof that none of "the Four" aimed to make the Athenians better cannot be that they were ultimately rejected by them (cf. *Grg.* 516c6–517a6).[142] But Socrates' praise for Aristides is even more revealing, not only because of what Plato says that he achieved—while having ample opportunity to be unjust, he lived justly throughout his life (*Grg.* 526a3–5)—or because Aristides the Just was likewise "tossed out,"[143] a fate that Demosthenes would suffer as well, but because his existence contradicts the claim Socrates has just made, as Aelius realized and therefore repeatedly brought to light. By doing so, he recognized Plato's intentions and honored them. Having distinguished the two kinds of rhetoric, he promptly turns to his namesake, naturally associating him with the good kind,[144] and then, after introducing for the first time the two kinds of philosophy,[145] he describes the kind of rhetoric "that is beautiful [καλόν], contriving that the souls of the citizens will best, and fighting through while saying the best things [τὰ βέλτιστα], whether they be pleasanter or less than pleasant for those hearing them."[146] Aelius then imagines someone objecting on the basis of what Socrates had said: "But you have never seen this rhetoric, or if you can name one of the orators of this kind, why have you not told me who it is?" (cf. *Grg.* 517a1-2).[147] To say nothing of Socrates or Plato, this true orator is, of course, Aristides, and Aelius Aristides directs the reader's attention to the crucial text in *Gorgias* (*Grg.* 526a5–b1) that immediately precedes his entrance (*Grg.* 526b1–3):

> And how is it not obviously contradictory to say, on the one hand, that he has never seen this kind of rhetoric, and that no orator of the kind he desires [cf. *Grg.* 504d5–e4] has ever been, and yet again proclaims that Aristides had been such a one? For of these two, it is necessary surely that one or the other is false. And he has reached to such a degree of speaking at variance with

himself [πρὸς τοσοῦτον ἧκε τοῦ διαφωνεῖν αὐτὸς αὑτῷ] that at the same time he claims no citizen of Athens has ever been good [cf. *Grg.* 517a1–2], while at the same time also bearing witness that such there have been elsewhere, and further prophesying indeed that they will also come to be again.[148]

Not only did Demosthenes prove him right but Aelius Aristides knows that he did,[149] and he probably also knew that it was Plato's deepest intention to challenge at least one his students to do so, as Socrates had challenged him. But political realities can make doing so impossible. Soon after Plato's death, the defeat at Chaeronea made the Old Academy's purpose temporarily impracticable. And despite the opportunity or θεία τις τύχη (*R.* 592a8) that allowed Cicero to practice ἡ ἀληθινὴ ῥητορική in Rome—and just as importantly to defend it in theory—the Augustan extinction of republican liberty now made a third Demosthenes temporarily impossible, and this has contributed to making the Plato who had taught both Demosthenes and Cicero invisible. Cicero's Roman admirers did what they could to keep his memory alive, just as some Greek intellectuals under the dominion of Rome preserved and celebrated the remains of the freedom-loving and tyrant-hating Demosthenes. But teaching the lesson of their mutual connection to Plato served the interests neither of the practical rhetoricians of the Imperial Age nor its theoretical philosophers, Platonists included,[150] and aside from a few bright spots, easily misunderstood, the connection was suppressed for a second time. Aelius Aristides is the brightest of those bright spots,[151] and the erudite Pernot has drawn attention to a crucial passage, easily overlooked, that proves this. Near the end of *On Behalf of Rhetoric*, Aelius poses the question: "What then is rhetoric itself, in and of itself, and the orator?"[152] He answers:

> I should not hesitate to say that whoever is the best man is the one who is best with speeches. If therefore there should be anyone and of such quality [εἰ τοίνυν τις καὶ τοιοῦτος ἐγγένοιτο] who, while having rhetoric, can't easily address the people nor debate concerning affairs of state [πολιτεία]—seeing that those affairs are now differently constituted [ἑτέρως ἔχοντα]—and regarding them, being not among the hindmost with respect to reputation, honors, and time-appropriate ambitions, if he alone and for himself should employ such speeches, having honored their nature and the Beautiful [τὸ καλόν] in them, and having inscribed God as guide and overseer of both his life and his speeches, not even for him is it difficult to answer Plato.[153]

One ancient scholiast took the words εἰ τοίνυν τις καὶ τοιοῦτος ἐγγένοιτο to refer to Aelius Aristides himself who, unlike Demosthenes, could not approach the Assembly and discourse "on matters of common concern [περὶ κοινῶν πραγμάτων]."[154] Another ancient scholiast explained the meaning of ἑτέρως ἔχοντα: "since Romans are now holding *imperium* [ἡ ἀρχή]."¹⁵⁵ Roman power made it impossible for Aelius Aristides to put ἡ ἀληθινὴ ῥητορική into practice other than by defending it in a theoretical sense, as he did so platonically and thus playfully in his *Platonic Orations*. While heaping praise on both Plato and Demosthenes without actually connecting them, [Longinus] too found a way to associate the decline of literary loftiness with the extinction of democracy.¹⁵⁶

Increasing attention to *Alcibiades Major* indicates that Plato scholars are becoming more comfortable with restoring evidence rejected since the nineteenth century. But in considering the ancient testimony that the young Demosthenes was Plato's student—and thus may have read this elementary dialogue in the Academy¹⁵⁷—it is less a question of rejection than suppression. It has become comparatively easy for contemporary scholars to recognize the excesses of *Echtheitskritik* and *Quellenforschung*,¹⁵⁸ and thus to apply, however belatedly, the same kind of critical scrutiny to nineteenth-century German philology that it applied, with a single-mindedness that almost "evinces a design," to suppressing the evidence that Plato taught Demosthenes and the other great anti-Macedonian politicians who defended the freedom of "famous Athens" in her democratic twilight. Meanwhile, an increasing sympathy for "reading between the lines" may have the parallel effect of making it easier to see that Dionysius of Halicarnassus, Lucian, Plutarch, Longinus, Aelius Aristides, and the author of *The Letters of Chion*, were simultaneously counteracting and revealing a post-Cicero wave of Roman suppression. But it is the first wave that created and will continue to create the most intractable obstacle to recovering the Old Academy.

The political power of Macedon is long gone, but through Aristotle, its dominion over our understanding of Plato remains generally unchallenged in fact and virtually unchallengeable in principle. Consider the following as an epitaph for the Old Academy: "It is possible, but by no means absolutely certain, that the ideal of 'freedom from disturbance' had pre-Platonic roots; regardless, it was never so effectively integrated into philosophical education until it became philosophy's *purpose* under the first scholarchs of the Early Academy, Speusippus and Xenocrates."¹⁵⁹ Beginning with Speusippus and Xenocrates, the so-called "Old Academy" simultaneously refashioned philosophy itself along imperial lines and initiated this suppression, leaving only Plato's Athens-based dialogues to tell a different story. But it is a decidedly mixed blessing that contemporary political circumstances make telling a more Demosthenes-friendly version of that story both possible and necessary, for today there is another democracy dancing on the edge of tyranny, and only a second Cicero or a third Demosthenes can save it, armed with Plato's ἀληθινὴ ῥητορική, and a whole-souled commitment to live and die in accordance with the transcendent rather than the personal Good.

Notes

INTRODUCTION

1. Plutarch, *Life of Demosthenes*, 5.3–5. For scholarly defiance of common sense, see Friedrich Gebhard, *De Plutarchi in Demosthenis vita fontibus ac fide* (Munich: H. Kutzner, 1880), 11, and Wilhelm Sturm, *De fontibus Demosthenicae historiae quaestiones duae* (Halle: 1881), 58, especially "fingebatur" and "primus."

2. The connection with Plutarch is emphasized from the start, with *Plutarchus* being the first word in Aulus Gellius, *Attic Nights*, 1.1.1.

3. Aulus Gellius, *Attic Nights*, 3.13.

4. Plutarch, *Life of Demosthenes*, 5.1–3 (Bernadotte Perrin translation): "The origin of his [sc. Demosthenes'] eager desire to be an orator, they tell us, was as follows. Callistratus the orator was going to make a plea in court on the question of Oropus, and the trial was eagerly awaited, not only because of the ability of the orator, who was then at the very height of his reputation, but also because of the circumstances of the case, which was notorious. Accordingly, when Demosthenes heard the teachers and tutors agreeing among themselves to be present at the trial, with great importunity he persuaded his own tutor to take him to the hearing. This tutor, having an acquaintance with the public officials who opened the courts, succeeded in procuring a place where the boy could sit unseen and listen to what was said. Callistratus won his case and was extravagantly admired, and Demosthenes conceived a desire to emulate his fame, seeing him escorted on his way by the multitude and congratulated by all; but he had a more wondering appreciation of the power of his oratory, which was naturally adapted to subdue and master all opposition."

5. The writings of Demosthenes will be cited in this form (see Abbreviations), following the standard or received order of his writings.

6. See Paul Kalligas, "Introduction" to Kalligas, Cloe Balla, Effie Baziotopoulou, and Vassilis Karasmanis (eds.), *Plato's Academy: Its Workings and Its History*, 1–10 (Cambridge, UK: Cambridge University Press, 2020), 3: "It has been customary to think that the curriculum for the instruction of the Guardians expounded by Plato in book 7 of his *Republic* must reflect, to some extent at least, the teaching practices employed in the Academy. However, such facile extrapolations about the way in which the Academy actually operated can prove precarious, for we need to take into consideration the social conditions prevailing in fourth-century Athens. One has to be reminded, for instance, that the study of dialectic in the *Republic* is postponed until its prospective practitioners have reached the age of thirty, and then pursued only after they have been subjected to certain strict qualifying tests (*R*. 537d). This does not sit well with the fact that the Academy's students are routinely described as 'youngsters' (νεανίσκοι) in our sources (e.g. Philodemus, Atheneaus, Aelian; cf. [Pl.] *Epin*. 990c4–5)." Cf. Isocrates, 15.289–90, a passage so important that it will be quoted below. For further comment, especially on the use of *R*., see *Ascent to the Beautiful*, Epilogue ("Imagining the Academy"). Alexander was either fourteen or fifteen when Aristotle began teaching him; the princes of Persia begin learning virtue at fourteen in *Alc.1* 121d3–4.

7. Friedrich Leo, *Die griechisch-römische Biographie nach ihrer litterarischen Form* (Leipzig: Teubner, 1901), 126–27.

8. As it was generally taken to be: see Leo, *Die griechisch-römische Biographie*, 124–28.

9. Except where specifically noted, dates and *floruits* of the ancients will be based on Simon Hornblower and Anthony Spawforth (eds.), *The Oxford Classical Dictionary*, fourth edition (Oxford: University Press, 2012), hereafter "OCD," here on 670.

10. See Worthington, *Demosthenes of Athens*, 17, and Douglas M. MacDowell, *Demosthenes the Orator* (Oxford: Oxford University Press, 2009), 20 ("we can believe").

11. See Craig Richard Cooper, "The Development of the Biographical Tradition of the Athenian Orators in the Hellenistic Period" (Doctoral Dissertation, University of British Columbia, 1992), 217–235.

12. See Felix Jacoby, *Fragmente der griechischen Historiker*, no. 1026.

13. Fritz Wehrli, *Die Schule des Aristoteles; Texte und Kommentar: Hermippus der Kalliacheer* (Basel and Stuttgart: Schwabe and Co., 1974).

14. Jan Bollansée, *Hermippos of Smyrna and His Biographical Writings, a Reappraisal* (Louvain: Peeters, 1999); see especially 82-90: "On Isokrates (F 42–44)—On the Pupils of Isokrates (F 45–54)."

15. Bollansée devotes several pages to showing why he should not be called this; see *Hermippos*, 9–14.

16. To avoid multiple citations, I will rely on Wehrli, here *Hermippos der Kallimacheer*, 28–32; fragments 71–75 relate to Demosthenes; fr. 71 is the passage from Plutarch quoted in a note above, fr. 72 is the passage from Aulus Gellius quoted in the text. See also 83-90 for commentary. The key comment, designed to cast doubt on fr. 72, is on 87: "Von Unterricht bei Platon spricht keiner der beiden [sc. Plutarch in fr. 71, and Libanius (fourth-century AD) in his biography of Demosthenes], und mit dem Knabenalter wäre dieser auch schlecht vereinbar." What

Wehrli means here by *Knabenalter* is that Aulus Gellius is making Demosthenes too young to have been Plato's student at eighteen; thus, his conception of Academic *Unterricht* does not imagine Plato as a teacher of youth, as mine does. Note that I take the Curricular Hypothesis and Demosthenes' *Knabenalter* to be *mutually reinforcing*.

17. See Cooper, "Biographical Tradition," 223–24: "Since Hermippus had conceived the history of 4th century prose writing in terms of a school of Isocrates, it was essential for him to establish the scholastic pedigree of the orators treated in his biographies [these include Hyperides; see Wehrli, *Hermippos der Kallimacheer*, fragments 67–68, and Isaeus, fragments 69–70]. Often this meant that he had to alter or refute existing traditions on the scholastic affiliations of these orators. In some cases he departed from earlier Peripatetic tradition that regarded them as students of Plato, either refuting outright that tradition, as in the case of Aeschines (fr. 79) or blending it seamlessly into his own account of the orator's earlier education, as in the case of Demosthenes (fr. 71–2), whereby the orator followed Plato for a time before taking up his study of rhetoric. In either case he is likely responsible for many of the notices found in later souces, which often named the orators as students of both Plato and Isocrates [n709]." The attached note cites Pseudo-Plutarch, *Lives of the Ten Orators*, on Demosthenes, Aeschines, Hyperides, and Lycurgus.

18. Dionysius of Halcarnassus, *Isaeus*, 1 (Usher translation): "Even Hermippus, the biographer of the pupils of Isocrates who is accurate in other matters [ἀκριβὴς ἐν τοῖς ἄλλοις], supplies only two facts about Isaeus, that he studied for some time under Isocrates and was Demosthenes' teacher." This is fr. 69 in Wehrli, *Hermippos der Kallimacheer*; for comment, see 83-84.

19. Schaefer, *Demosthenes*, 1.280.

20. Diogenes Laertius, *Lives of the Eminent Philosophers*, 3.47 (Pamela Mensch translation): "Sabinus adds Demosthenes [sc. as Plato's student], citing Mnesistratus of Thasos as his authority in the fourth book of his *Collected Meditations*. And this is likely." There will be more on the suppression of this testimony below.

21. It is this document that Cicero cites as proof that Demosthenes "heard" and "read studiously" Plato in *Brutus*, 121 and *Orator* 15; naturally pronouncing it inauthentic is a necessary step for those who deny the connection.

22. Schaefer, *Demosthenes*, 1.281; note the "fabrication-suppression dynamic" (see preface) in connection with the previous note.

23. Schaefer, *Demosthenes*, 1.281n4.

24. Karl Hermann Funkhänel, "Dissertatio de Demosthene Platonis discipulo" in Anton Westermann and Karl Hermann Funkhänel (eds.), *Acta Societatis Graecae*, volume 1, 288–306 (Leipzig, Koehler, 1836).

25. Funkhänel, "Dissertatio," 290–92.

26. Funkhänel, "Dissertatio," 291; note that the title of Westermann's essay on *Lives of the Ten Orators* begins with: "On the Author *and the Authority*."

27. See J. H. Scholten, *Disquisitio de Demostheneae Eloquentiae Charactere* (Across the Rhine: Robert Natan, 1835), and Philip Willem van Heusde, *Initia Philosophiae Platonicae*, second revised edition (Leiden: H. W. Hasenberg, 1842), 154–63, 191–93, 207–8, and 520.

28. Karl Hermann Funkhänel, "Isokrates und Demosthenes." *Zeitschrift für die Alterthumswissenschaft* 59-60 (1837), 486–494.

29. See Friedrich Blass, *Die attische Beredsamkeit*, three volumes, second edition (Leipzig: Teubner, 1887-1898), 3.1.iii (for dedication to Schaefer) and 3.1.11–12 (for his rejection of the Plato connection as *ganz unwahrscheinlich*). I will cite the first edition for volume 3, part 2: Friedrich Blass, *Die attische Beredsamkeit*, 3.2 (Leipzig: Teubner, 1880).

30. See Karl Steinhart, *Platon's Leben* (Leipzig: Brockhaus, 1873), 176–78 and 319, notes 78b, 85, and 86.

31. Schaefer, *Demosthenes*, 1.289–92 is the culmination and rhetorical highpoint of a section bookended by Plato that begins on 277.

32. Schaefer, *Demosthenes*, 291.

33. E.g., Steinhart, *Platon's Leben*, 319n8, refers to "den unplatonischen Menexenos."

34. See Trampedach, *Platon, die Akademie* (hereafter simply *Akademie*), 5–7. I am very grateful to the author for making his work available to me. Cf. Ludwig Edelstein, *Plato's Seventh Letter* (Leiden: Brill, 1966), 165: "Plato was greatly interested in questions of politics. But it was the theory of politics, not practical politics that captivated him." For a competing view of the Academy, see Glenn R. Morrow, *Plato's Epistles: A Translation, with Critical essays and Notes* (Indianapolis and New York: Bobbs-Merrill, 1962), 143: "it was intended to serve as a training school for statesmen and public-spirited citizens."

35. Hans-Joachim Gehrke, *Phokion: Studien zur Erfassung seiner historischen Gestalt* (Munich: C. H. Beck, 1976). I am likewise very grateful to this author for making his work available to me. See also the same author's "Das Verhältnis von Politik und Philosophie im Wirken des Demetrios von Phaleron." *Chiron* 8 (1978), 149–193; for making this text available to me and for much else, I am grateful to Matthias Haake.

36. In English, see Matthias Haake, "The Academy in Athenian Politics and Society; Between Disintegration and Integration: The First Eighty Years (387/6-306/5)" in Paul Kalligas, Chloe Balla, Effie Baziotopoulou-Valvani, and Vasilis Karasmanis (eds.), *Plato's Academy: Its Workings and History*, 65–88 (Cambridge, UK: Cambridge University Press, 2020).

37. See Matthias Haake, "'Doing philosophy'—Soziales Kapital versus politischer Mißkredit? Zur Funktionalität und Dysfunktionalität von Philosophie fUur die Elite im sozialen und politischen Raum des klassischen Athen" in C. Mann, M. Haake, and R. von den Hoff (eds.), *Rollenbilder in der athenischen Demokratie: Medien, Gruppen, Räume im politischen und sozialen System. Beiträge zu einem interdisziplinären Kolloquium in Freiburg i. Br., 24. –25. November 2006*, 113–145 (Wiesbaden: Reichert, 2009).

38. See Trampedach, *Akademie*, 125–143.

39. Trampedach, *Akademie*, 136.

40. Plutarch, *Reply to Colotes*, 1126c; cf. Lawrence Trittle, *Phocion the Good* (Oxford and New York: Routledge, 2014), 46.

41. Trampedach, *Akademie*, 127.

42. Trampedach, *Akademie*, 133–4.

43. Diogenes Laertius, *Lives of the Eminent Philosphers*, 3.24, on which see Alice Swift Riginos, *Platonica: The Anecdotes Concerning the Life and Writings of Plato* (Leiden: E. J. Brill, 1976), 153, and Trampedach, *Akademie*, 134n64.

44. This hypothesis may shed some light on the details of Plutarch's version of the Callistratus story; consider especially the role of Demosthenes' teachers and his pedagogue in making it possible for the youth to hear the orator speak at *Life of Demosthenes*, 5.2: "Having therefore heard his teachers and pedagogues agreeing to attend the trial, with importuning and excitement he persuaded his own pedagogue that he might get him into audience."

45. Trampedach, *Akademie*, 126.

46. Trampedach, *Akademie*, 126.

47. Attention turns to Cicero in the other four paragraphs (Trampedach, *Akademie*, 127-29): the first concerns his reliance on Demosthenes' (allegedly spurious) *Fifth Letter*, the second traces Cicero's embrace of the relationship to his self-conception as the synthesizer of Philosophy and Rhetoric, the third identifies this as a species of self-aggrandizement on Cicero's part, and the fifth is both short and pointed: (129): "It should now be clear why Cicero embraced so eagerly the story of the connection between Plato and Demosthenes, which he derived from his sources. What may justify this comparatively detailed discussion of the question is that we also have to consider authors with similar motives, concerning whose knowledge-guiding interests [*erkenntnisleitende Interesse*] we do not know as well as Cicero's." Naturally Trampedach will say nothing regarding his own *erkenntnisleitende Interesse* with respect to the story, least of all in his study's "empirical part," but I hope to have been crystal clear about mine.

48. See Wörle, *Politische Tätigkeit*, 47–52.

49. Wörle, *Politische Tätigkeit*, 52; I have deleted the first four words of this sentence ("Aufgrund dieser Überlegungen und") because they refer to "considerations" that will be explored in chapter 1.

50. P. A. Brunt, "Plato's Academy and Politics" in Brunt, *Studies in Greek History and Thought*, 282–342 (Oxford: Clarendon Press, 1993), 300–301: "They [sc. Plato's students] are indeed said to have included some Athenians in public life: Chabrias, Demosthenes, Hyperides, Lycurgus, Phocion. The testimony, especially for the first two, is unreliable. Zeller observed that there is no trace of Platonic Ideas in the speeches of the orators named. Equally there is none in their policies."

51. C. W. Müller, "Platons Akademiegründung" in Müller, *Kleine Schriften zur antiken Literatur und Geistesgeschichte*, 422–39 (Stuttgart: Teubner, 1999), 433.

52. Trampedach, *Akademie*, 125n2.

53. See Trampedach, *Akademie*, 214–15, beginning with: "Platons Standpunkt läßt sich wie folgt resumieren."

54. Trampedach, *Akademie*, 201n90.

55. Trampedach, *Akademie*, 219.

56. See Altman, *Guardians in Action*, §18.

57. Pernot, *L'Ombre du Tigre*; I am very grateful to the author for giving me a copy of this erudite, fascinating, and beautifully produced book.

58. Pernot, *L'Ombre du Tigre*, 239-298.

59. See Pernot, *L'Ombre du Tigre*, testimonia T1–T38 (239–54).

60. Pernot, *L'Ombre du Tigre*, 22.

61. Pernot, *L'Ombre du Tigre*, 22; partially anodyne to what follows (in the notes) with respect to Mnesistratus is Heinrich Dörrie and Matthias Baltes, *Der Platonismus in der Antike*, volume 2 (Stuttgart-Bad Cannstatt: Frommann-Holzboog, 1990), 375n1.

62. Diogenes Laertius, *Lives of Eminent Philosophers*, 3.47 (Mensch translation).

63. The games begin with Gottlieb Röper, "Conjecturen zu Diogenes Laertius." *Philologus* 3 (1848), 22–65, his most relevant conjecture, embraced as fact by Schaefer, *Demosthenes*, 1.280–81n5, Blass, *Attische Beredsamkeit*, 3.1.12, and Franz Susemihl, *Geschichte der griechischen Litteratur in der Alexendinerzeit*, two volumes (Leipzig: Teubner, 1891–92), 1.499n40b, was to offer an alternative to the then current way of punctuating Diogenes Laertius, *Lives*, 3.46–47: "And some say as well that Theophrastus heard him [sc. Plato], Chaemaeleon says also Hyperides and Lycurgus; similarly Polemo records Demosthenes also. Sabinus says also [καί] Mnesistratus of Thasos." Now instructed by Funkhänel that Demosthenes was not in fact Plato's student (59), Röper refutes the view that Mnesistratus was a student of Plato's himself (58n27) then punctuates the text as we now do: "Polemo records similarly [sc. with respect to Lycurgus]. And Demosthenes Sabinus says—citing [following Isaac Casaubon in deleting the καί] Mnesistratus." For the received text in Röper's time and Casaubon's emendation, see H. G. Hübner (ed.), *Diogenis Laertii de vitis, dogmatis et apophthegmatis clarorum philosophorum libri decem*, volume 1 (Leipzig: Köhler, 1828), 224.

64. Röper's punctuation was promptly embraced, and there is no trace of Hübner's καί in Tiziano Dorandi (ed.), *Diogenes Laertius, Lives of the Eminent Philosophers* (Cambridge, UK: Cambridge University Press, 2013), 268; it reappears in the *apparatus criticus* of Miroslav Marcovich (ed.), *Diogenis Laertii, Vitae philosophorum*, volume 1 (Berlin and New York: De Gruyter, 2008), on 221.

65. The games therefore must continue in Röper, "Conjecturen," 58–60, with the claim that the previously merely insignificant Mnesistratus—his insignificance in comparison with the famous orators proved that the text as received was wrong (59)—should be identified with the Mnesistratus who appears in Diogenes Laertius, *Lives*, 7.177; this allowed Röper to make the new source both late and valueless. Since Diogenes gives no indication that this Mnesistratus was a scholar, Röper resorts to emending the text, claiming that the reference to Peisistratus of Ephesus at 2.60 was a scribal error for "Mnesistratus of Thasos" (58) He goes on to make Polemo the source for Lycurgus, then Mnesistratus the source for the addition of Demosthenes, and finally Sabinus (a contemporary of Lucian) the source not only for Mnesistratus but for Polemo and Chaemaeleon as well (59–60); this last move anticipates later efforts to call into question the evidence for Lycurgus and Hyperides.

66. Pernot, *L'Ombre du Tigre*, 23n3.

67. See Pernot, *L'Ombre du Tigre*, 45–49.

68. Pernot, *L'Ombre du Tigre*, 32.

69. Pernot, *L'Ombre du Tigre*, 31n6.

70. Pernot, *L'Ombre du Tigre*, 49–50.

71. See Pernot, *L'Ombre du Tigre*, 44–46, where we meet in succession *affrontement, rivalité intellectuelle*, and *la querelle*.

72. Pernot, *L'Ombre du Tigre*, 49.

73. Pernot, *L'Ombre du Tigre*, 50.
74. Pernot, *L'Ombre du Tigre*, 50.
75. Pernot, *L'Ombre du Tigre*, 240–41.
76. See Pernot, *L'Ombre du Tigre*, 43–45; before introducing la qurelle (46), he describes Cicero's synthesis, climaxing with *message purement irénique*.
77. Pernot, *L'Ombre du Tigre*, 26–29.
78. Pernot, *L'Ombre du Tigre*, 39–40.
79. See Pernot, *L'Ombre du Tigre*, 28n9.
80. Cf. Blass, *Attische Beredsamkeit*, 3.1.12: "Den Lakedämoniern zeigt er sich [sc. Demosthenes] in seiner Politik in seinen Schriften durchaus abhold." This observation immediately follows the important admission that while in the case of both Lycurgus and Hyperides : "[ist] eine Beeinflussung durch Platon ganz wahrscheinlich, während bei Demosthenes auf eine solche nicht das geringste."
81. Pernot, *L'Ombre du Tigre*, 81–87.
82. Lucian, *Teacher of Orators*, 10.
83. Pernot, *L'Ombre du Tigre*, 88.
84. Pernot, *L'Ombre du Tigre*, 32-33.
85. See *Ascent to the Beautiful*, §5.
86. Pernot, *L'Ombre du Tigre*, 33.
87. See Irene Giaquinta, *Le Epistole di Demostene; Introduzione, traduzione e comment retorico-filologico* (Alessandria: dell'Orso, 2019), especially 463–93. I am very grateful to the author for giving me a copy of this brave, erudite, and beautifully produced book.
88. See Funkhänel, "Dissertatio," 292–93.
89. See Pernot, *L'Ombre du Tigre*, 31–32 on "catalyst."
90. But see André Schott (S. J.), *Vitae comparatae Aristotelis ac Demosthenis, Olympiadibus ac Præturis Atheniensium digeste* (Augsburg: Christopher Mangum, 1603). He mentions only that Demosthenes was the student of Isaeus (preface, 3), but well describes their salient difference while apparently justifying connecting them (preface, 10): "For the Philosopher, in fellowship with Philip, instructed his son in the finest arts; the Orator in his public speeches, strove to redress the injuries of both Kings against the liberty of the Athenians." Unfortunately, Schott thinks that Demosthenes was two years younger than Aristotle.
91. Diogenes Laertius, *Lives of Eminent Philosophers*, 5.1 (R. D. Hicks translation): "Aristotle, son of Nicomachus and Phaestis, was a native of Stagira. His father, Nicomachus, as Hermippus relates in his book *On Aristotle*, traced his descent from Nicomachus who was the son of Machaon and grandson of Asclepius; and he resided with Amyntas, the king of Macedon, in the capacity of physician and friend. Aristotle was Plato's most genuine disciple."
92. For example, many of the ancient *Lives of Aristotle* make him the student of Socrates (d. 399) as well as of Plato; see Ingemar Düring, *Aristotle in the Ancient Biographical Tradition* (Göteborg: Elanders, 1957), 98 and 108, and more accessibly: Jonathan Barnes (ed.), *The Complete Works of Aristotle: The Revised Oxford Translation*, two volumes (Princeton, NJ: Princeton University Press, 1984), 2.2459 (F 652).
93. See Wehrli, *Hermippos*, 22–24 (fragments 44–49) and Bollansée, *Hermippus*, 54–69.
94. Diogenes Laertius, *Lives of Eminent Philosophers*, 5.2.

95. Anton-Hermann Chroust, "Aristotle and Athens: Some Comments on Aristotle's Sojourns in Athens." *Laval théologique et philosophique* 22, no. 2 (1966), 186–196, on 188; cf. W. K. C. Guthrie, *A History of Greek Philosophy*, six volumes (Cambridge, UK: Cambridge University Press, 1967–1981), 26: "Such a man cannot have been happy at Athens just after the fall of Olynthus had shocked the whole city. It was just at this time, in the early part of 347, that Demosthenes began to be acknowledged as a political leader, and with his rousing challenge to the Macedonian peril he soon became the dominant figure in Athens. It was no place for a friend of Macedon."

96. Chroust, "Aristotle and Athens," 188–89: "Athens, it must be admitted, around 349/48 BC was ripe with malicious gossip, corruption, general and ill-concealed ill-feeling towards, and almost paranoid distrust of, everyone 'foreign,' especially of persons who had come from much despised (and feared) Macedonia. In this atmosphere of resentment, anger, and frustration, which thanks to Demosthenes' inflammatory perorations was vented on everything and everyone Macedonian, Aristotle feared that he might suffer 'the fate of Socrates.' Hence, he decided to depart from Athens—probably in the late summer of 348 BC—seeking refuge with Hermias of Atarneus."

97. John Edwin Sandys (ed.), *The First Philippic and the Olynthiacs of Demosthenes with Introduction and Critical and Explanatory Notes* (London: Macmillan, 1897), and *Demosthenes, On the Peace, Second Philippic, On the Chersonesus and Third Philippic; with Introduction and Critical and Explanatory Notes* (London: Macmillan, 1900).

98. Chroust, "Aristotle and Athens," 190.

99. Chroust, "Aristotle and Athens," 194.

100. See Julius Beloch, *Die attische Politik seit Perkles* (Leipzig: Teubner, 1884), 232–64, especially 249–50.

101. See Noriko Sawada, "Allies and Foes (1): Aeschines, Hyperides, Lycurgus" in Gunter Martin (ed.), *The Oxford Handbook of Demosthenes*, 337–51 (Oxford and New York: Oxford University Press, 2019).

102. Chroust, "Aristotle and Athens," 196 (last word): "When Alexander — the only man who could have possibly held together Macedonia and its many conquests—died unexpectedly in June of 323 B.C., Aristotle's position in Athens became utterly untenable. Antipater, to be sure, soon restored Macedonian control over Athens and Greece once more (in the fall of 322 B. C.), but by that time Aristotle was on his deathbed, if not already dead. Otherwise, he might well have returned once more."

103. Also noteworthy in this context is the fact that young Theaetetus, like Demosthenes, has suffered at the hands of his dead father's trustees; see *Tht.* 144d1–2.

104. E.g., Aeschines, 1.22, 2.78-79, and 3.172; note that between calling Phocion and Eubulus as witnesses at 2.84 and the words οἱ τῆς εἰρήνης καὶ τῆς ὑμετέρας ἀδείας συναγωνισταί at 2.183, indicates the existence of the same "Peace Party" that Sawada is at such pains to deny.

105. Guthrie, *History of Greek Philosophy*, 6.36.

106. See Maicon Reus Engler, "Secularização e Practicidade: A *Poética* de Aristóteles em sua Relação com a Teoria da Arte Grego e com a Filosofia Tragica" (Doctoral dissertation, Universidade Federal de Santa Catarina, 2016), 30–31.

107. It was this fiasco in particular that made Plato an easy target for criticism; see J. Geffcken, "Antiplatonika." *Hermes* 64, no. 1 (December 1928), 87–109, especially 92–94 on Aristoxenus, beginning with: "Aber gerade dies bildete das Gebiet des großen Harmonikers Aristoxenos; er hatte u. a. auch von den πυκνώματα, den Verdichtungen der Töne, kundig geredet [he is also our source for the claim that Plato identified the Good with the One]. Darüber aber ergießt Platon seinen vollen Spott. So war der Anlaß zu einem von Aristoxenos mit hochster personlicher Bitterkeit gefuhrten Kampf gegeben, dessen Scharfe auch die Bekanntschaft des Tarentiners mit Platons Feind, dem verbannten Tyrannen Dionysios, nur gesteigert haben wird, eine Polemik, die in höchst unwurdiger Weise auch den Gegner bis in seine Vorlesungen hinein verfolgte." Note the comparison with Hermippus at Leo, *Die griechisch-römische Biographie*, 126 and 102; see also the attempt to whitewash Aristoxenus in A. von Mess, "Die Anfänge der Biographie und der psychologischen Geschichtsschreibung in der griechischen Litteratur." *Rheinisches Museum* 71 (1916), 79–101, especially on 98 (at "so sehen wir").

CHAPTER 1

1. See Plutarch, *Life of Phocion*, first word.
2. Plutarch, *Life of Phocion*, 3.1.
3. Plutarch, *Life of Phocion*, 2.3.
4. Plutarch, *Life of Phocion*, 2.5.
5. Plutarch, *Life of Phocion*, 8.3 (Perrin translation): "And when, as he was once delivering an opinion to the people, he met with their approval, and saw that all alike accepted his argument, he turned to his friends and said: 'Can it possibly be that I am making a bad argument [τι κακὸν λέγων] without knowing it?'" Cf. *Ascent to the Beautiful*, 107n313, on "making a bad argument."
6. Plutarch, *Life of Phocion*, 38.2.
7. Plutarch, *Life of Phocion*, 5.2–4.
8. See Raphael Sealey, "Callistratos of Aphidna and His Contemporaries." *Historia* 5, no. 2 (June 1956), 178–203, on 187: "Callistratos formed political ties with Chabrias. This is illustrated most clearly by the fact that both men were prosecuted in 365 for the loss of Oropos, but the alliance may perhaps be traced earlier." Traced to the Academy on my account.
9. Plutarch, *Life of Phocion*, 6.1. In addition to breaking ground by denying the existence of political parties in Athens on 74 (see introduction), Raphael Sealey, "Athens after the Social War." *Journal of Hellenic Studies* 75 (1955), 74–81, introduced the connection between Callistratus and Chabrias (see previous note) on 79–80.
10. Plutarch, *Life of Phocion*, 8.1.

11. Plutarch, *Life of Phocion*, 7.3; for translation and comment, see Jennifer Tolbert Roberts, *Athens on Trial: The Antidemocratic Tradition in Western Thought* (Princeton, NJ: Princeton University Press, 1994), 117.
12. Demosthenes also compares Lycurgus to Aristides the Just in *Letter 3*, 19.
13. Plutarch, *Life of Phocion*, 16.4.
14. Plutarch, *Life of Phocion*, 17.2.
15. Plutarch, *Life of Phocion*, 17.3.
16. See *Ascent to the Beautiful*, §16.
17. On this embassy, see Dillon, *Heirs to Plato*, 91-94, including the three pertinent questions on 93: "This raises the interesting question of Xenocrates' political position. Was his objection to the pro-Macedonian regime that of a democrat, or simply that of an Athenian nationalist, who objected, for instance, to the Macedonian garrison? Surely, one protests, the head of the Platonic Academy cannot have been a partisan of Athenian democracy? But if one thinks about it carefully, why not?" This is an excellent question.
18. Plutarch, *Life of Phocion*, 27.3.
19. Cf. Plutarch, *Moralia*, 78d, 472e, and 545a.
20. Diogenes Laertius, *Lives of the Eminent Philosophers*, 5.11; on Aristotle's will, see Düring, *Biographical Tradition*, 61–63, noting especially this on 62: "The appointment of Antpater as a kind of Honorary Trustee, corresponding to the Roman *tutor honoris causa*, testifies to the great friendship and intimate relations between the two men, so different in position and in their ways of life." Note that Düring does not assert that they were different in political allegiance, which indeed they were not; cf. "two men who otherwise had very little in common" (386), and 394n92 on Düring, in Anton-Hermann Chroust, "Aristotle and the Foreign Policy of Macedonia." *Review of Politics* 34, no. 3 (July 1972), 367–394.
21. The list of Aristotle's writings includes *nine* books of letters to Antipater; see Diogenes Laertius, *Lives of the Eminent Philosophers*, 5.27, and Barnes (ed.), *Complete Works of Aristotle*, 2458-62, fragments (F) 663–67.
22. See Chroust, "Aristotle and Foreign Policy," 385: "After 335/34 B.C., in particular, the pro-Macedonian party in Athens, feeling secure under the military protection of Alexander and Antipater, brazenly stepped into the open."
23. See Gehrke, *Phokion*, 88.
24. Plutarch, *Life of Phocion*, 27.2.
25. See Paul Kalligas and Voula Tsouna (eds. and trans.), "Philodemus' *History of the Philosophers*; Plato and the Academy (PHerc. 1021 and 164) in Kalligas *et al.*, *Plato's Academy*, 276–383, here on 305–7. The interest in Philodemus displayed in Konrad Gaiser, *Philodems Academica. Die Berichte über Platon und die alte Akademie in zwei herkulanensischen Papyri* (Stuttgart-Ban Cannstatt: Frommann & Holzboog, 1988) has the purpose one would expect from the Tübingen School; see especially 329–38.
26. Diogenes Laertius, *Lives of the Eminent Philosophers*, 4.9.
27. As evidence of the continuing interest generated by this quarrel, see Gianfranco Maddoli, "Senocrate nel clima politico del suo tempo." *Dialoghi di Archeologia* 1 (1967), 304–327; see 308 and 323n15 on Plato and Demosthenes.
28. Jacob Bernays, *Phokion und seine neueren Beurtheiler: Ein Beitrag zur Geschichte der griechischen Philosophie und Politik* (Berlin: Wilhelm Hertz, 1881).

29. See Bernays, *Phokion*, 20–31, climaxing with *Kosmopolitanismus* in the context of Socrates and Anaxagoras; see also 112n10.

30. See Bernays, *Phokion*, 25, on the Phoenician origin of Thales (Herodotus, 1.170), an interesting argument for Bernays, who was Jewish, to make. Indeed, his defense of "cosmopolitanism" supported a common anti-Jewish trope.

31. Bernays, *Phokion*, 35–44.

32. Bernays, *Phokion*, 45–50.

33. See Bernays, *Phokion*, 42–44, including notes 14–16 on 118–23.

34. Theodor Gomperz, "Die Akademie und ihr vermeintlicher Philomacedonismus; Bemerkungen zu Bernays' *Phokion*." *Wiener Studien* 4 (1882), 102–120; the first passage he cites on 102—in order to attack it—is Bernays, *Phokion*, 42: "Gleiche politische Gesinnung wie dem Aristoteles darf einem anderen hervorragenden Mitgliede der Akademie, dem Kalchedonier Xenocrates, dem zweiten Nachfolger Platons in Schulleitung augeschrieben werden."

35. Bernays, *Phokion*, 43; also 121–23n16

36. Gomperz, "Der Akademie," 104.

37. A more friendly reception was given Bernays (see 182n4) in an excursus on "Die philosophenschulen und die politik" (178-234) in Ulrich von Wilamowitz-Moellendorff, *Antigonos von Karystos* (Berlin: Weidmann, 1881), particularly (and appropriately) with respect to Aristotle (182-84).

38. Cf. Hermann Diels, "Review of Jakob Bernays." *Deutsche Litteraturzeitung* 51 (1881), 1955.

39. Arnold Schaefer, "Review of *Phokion und seine neueren Beurtheiler*." *Historische Zeitschrift* 46, no. 3 (1881), 474–476, on 475.

40. Friedrich Blass, "Review of Jakob Bernays." *Göttingische gelehrte Anzeigen* 35 (30 August, 1882), 1089–1097, on 1092.

41. Gehrke, *Phokion*, 213n71.

42. Franz Susemihl, "Bericht über Aristoteles und die ältesten Akademiker und Peripatetiker für 1880–1882." *Jahresbericht für Alterthumswissenschaft* 30 (1882), 1–20. The review of Bernays is on 11–18, the specific claim about Aristotle, directed against both Wilamowitz, *Antigonos* (9–11), and Bernays, is on 11: "indem beide mit Unrecht den Aristoteles für einen einfachen makedonischen Parteigänger halten, wie es Theophrastos in gewisser Weise ja ohne Zweifel war."

43. Bernays, *Phokion*, 40; cf. Düring, *Biographical Tradition*, 284–99, for the *testimonia* relevant to "Relations with Philip and Alexander," but curiously not Antipater. Düring's analogy, quoted earlier, between Antipater as executor and t the Roman *tutor honoris causa* should be recognized as apologetic in tendency; cf. Carlo Natali, *Aristotle: His Life and His School*, edited by D. S. Hutchinson (Princeton, NJ and Oxford: Princeton University Press, 2013), 135–144; see especially 136 on Bernays, 137 on Gomperz, and 141–44 on Düring.

44. Guthrie, *History of Greek Philosophy*, 5.470 and 6.26 (see 26n2 on Düring). See also G. E. L. Owen, "Philosophical Invective." *Oxford Studies in Ancient Philosophy* 1 (1983), 1–25, on 6–10.

45. Bernays, *Phokion*, 41; cf. Chroust, "Aristotle and Foreign Policy," 373: "bridgehead," and the same word in Philip Merlan, "Isocrates, Aristotle and Alexander the Great." *Historia* 3, no. 1 (1954), 60–81, on 61.

46. Bernays, *Phokion*, 43; cf. Diogenes Laertius, *Lives of the Eminent Philosophers*, 8–9.
47. Bernays, *Phokion*, 43; see Plutarch, *Reply to Colotes*, 1125c-d, and Diogenes Laertius, *Lives of the Eminent Philosophers*, 14.
48. Bernays, *Phokion*, 44; cf. Düring, *Biographical Tradition*, 272–83.
49. Plutarch, *Life of Phocion*, 4.1.
50. Bernays, *Phokion*, 44–45.
51. Bernays, *Phokion*, 44: "Ein Männerbund nun, in dem vier so namhaften Mitgliedern wie Plato, Aristoteles, Hermias, und Xenokrates." Note the absence of Speusippus, with whom I would replace Plato.
52. See Bernays, *Phokion*, 37–38.
53. D. R. W. Wormell, "The Literary Tradition Concerning Hermias of Atarneus," *Yale Classical Studies* 5 (1935), 57–92, on 60: "The Sixth Letter illustrates, then, in a striking way what in Plato's view was the educational purpose of the Academy; it was to be a training-ground for rulers." Cf. 59: "It was, however, quite in accordance with Plato's teaching and practice that they [sc. Erastus and Coriscus] should play an active part in politics on their return."
54. See especially Phillip Harding (ed.), *Didymus: On Demosthenes. Translated with Introduction, Text, and Commentary* (Oxford: Clarendon Press, 2006), on 10.32 (56–65) with commentary on 124-162. This text is the first that might be said to compare or at least juxtapose Aristotle and Demosthenes, thus creating an ancient precedent for Schott, *Vitae comparatae Aristotelis ac Demosthenis*, as well as for this book.
55. Blass, "Review of Jakob Bernays, 1090.
56. Bernays, *Phokion*, 39–40.
57. Bernays, *Phokion*, 34.
58. Bernays, *Phokion*, 113.
59. *R.* 473c11–6.
60. See *Plato the Teacher*, §23.
61. Bernays, *Phokion*, 112–13.
62. Bernays, *Phokion*, 33–34.
63. For "intended and was about to do," see *Thg.* 128d2-5, a passage to which Plato guides the reader by the reference to Theages at *R.* 496b6–c3; for discussion, see *Plato the Teacher*, §20. Of course the Sign is also apotreptic—and in relation to political participation—at *Ap.* 31c7–d6.
64. In addition to Xenophon, *Memorabilia*, 3.1-7, see at 1.6.15, where Socrates explains that it is more economical for him to teach others how to be capable politically than to πράττει τὰ πολιτικά himself. Cf. Bernays, *Phokion*, 32: "Athenian politics seemed to them [sc. Socrates and Plato] to be inextricably implicated in such a conflict with morality; they would rather appear to others to be bad citizens on account of their political inactivity—for which Niebuhr had even scolded Plato [the attached note cites '*Kleine Schriften* 1, 467 and 472']—so as not to be judged by their own consciences to be bad men." At B. G. Niebuhr, *Kleine historische und philologische Schriften* 1 (Bonn: Eduard Weber, 1828), 467 we read: "Plato was also no good citizen, worthy of Athens he was not, incomprehensible steps had he taken, he stood as a sinner against the saints, Thucydides and Demosthenes, but he was entirely different from this old fool [sc. Xenophon]."

65. Gomperz, "Der Akademie," 105: "Diogenes' anecdote was twisted so that it will be historically believable, and Plutarch's account will be remodeled so that it confirms the anecdote, now made believable!"
66. Gomperz, "Der Akademie," 116.
67. Theodor Gomperz, "Die herculanischen Rollen." *Zeitschrift für die österreichischen Gymnasien* 16 (1865), 815–826, on 819.
68. Gomperz, "Rollen," 819–22.
69. Gomperz, "Rollen," 821–22: "When a critical historian, after a scientific collection and investigation of all the sources for a report is able to discover in the last analysis no other support than an anonymous text or one of doubtful authorship (Plutarch probably meant the latter with his ambiguous expression [i.e., 'anonymous memoranda'] since it was very easy in antiquity to create a name for an author), so must it be that such a report is very poorly attested indeed. This conclusion is more specious than correct; it is above all completely inapplicable to the present case."
70. Blass, "Review," 1092: "Hermias, Aristotle, Speusippus clearly are not suited to count as representative of the whole Academy so that the political attitude or lack of any in these three men could be advanced as a general mark for the school. There would also immediately be five exceptions to it: the orators Lycurgus and Hyperides, then Xenocrates, Euphraeus, and Leon of Byzantium, about whose membership in the Academy and anti-Macedonian sentiment Plutarch reports in *Phocion* 14."
71. Blass, "Review," 1092.
72. See Anton-Hermann Chroust, "Speusippus succeeds Plato in the Scholarchate of the Academy." *Revue des Études Grecques* 84, no. 401/403 (July-December 1971), 338–341.
73. See Philip Merlan, "The Successor of Speusippus." *Transactions and Proceedings of the American Philological Association* 77 (1946), 103–111.
74. Numbers are unitary (!) Ideas in Leonardo Tarán, "Ideas, Numbers, and Magnitudes: Remarks on Plato, Speusippus, and Aristotle." *Revue de Philosophie Ancienne* 9, no. 2 (1991), 199-231. See more generally Julia Annas, *Aristotle's Metaphysics, Books M and N. Translated with Introduction and Notes* (Oxford: Clarendon Press, 1976), 41–77, beginning with: "Plato's theories about the foundations of mathematics, the derivations of numbers and (later) of geometrical objects do not figure in the dialogues." Appropriately introductory is Werner Jaeger, *Aristotle: Fundamentals of the History of His Development*, translated by Richard Robinson, second edition (Oxford: Oxford University Press, 1948), 11–23; see especially "a closed chapter in the master's life" (14) referring to *Phd.*, *Grg.*, *R.*, and *Smp.*, and "in the *Theaetetus* we have the apotheosis of the un-Socratic philosopher of Plato's later days" (15), the latter claim clearly based on the ὁμοίωσις θεῷ.
75. Bernays, *Phokion*, 40.
76. For the literary remains, see Margherita Isnardi Parente, *Speusippo Frammenti: Edizione, traduzione e commento* (Naples: Bibliopolis, 1980), and Leonardo Tarán, *Speusippus of Athens: A Critical Study, with a Collection of Related Texts and Commentary* (Leiden: Brill, 1981). Philip Merlan, "Zur Biographie des Speusippus." *Philologus* 103 (January 1959), 198–214, is a corrective to Tarán; see especially his useful comments (206–7) on the Bernays/Gomperz debate in the context of the

Letter. For general background, see Guthrie, *History of Greek Philosophy*, 5.457–69, and Dillon, *Heirs of Plato*, 30–88; still useful is Eduard Zeller, *Plato and the Older Academy*, translated by Sarah Alleyne and Alfred Goodwin (London: Longmans, Green, and Co., 1876), 553–580.

77. Bernays cites at Karl Georg Boehncke, *Demosthenes, Lykurgos, Hyperides und ihrer Zeitalter*, volume 1 (Berlin: Georg Reimer, 1864), 442, at *Phokion*, 117.

78. Bernays, *Phokion*, 116-18n13; cf. 39–40.

79. Gomperz, "Der Akademie," 111.

80. E. Bickermann and Joh. Sykutris, *Speusipps Brief an König Philipp: Text, Übersetzung, Untersuchungen* (Berlin: Akademie Verlag: 1928).

81. Cf. Enrico Berti, *Sumphilosophein: La vita nell'Accademia di Platone* (Bari: Laterza, 2010), 235-42 ("La scuola di Platone e i re Macedoni") and Mauro Bonazzi, *Il Platonismo* (Turin: Einaudi, 2015), Appendix I ("I platonici e la politica").

82. Myles Burnyeat and Michael Frede, *The Seventh Letter: A Seminar*. Edited by Dominic Scott (Oxford: Oxford University Press, 2015).

83. See Richard Bentley, *A Dissertation upon the Epistles of Phalaris, Themistocles, Socrates, Euripides, and others, and the Fables of Æsop* (Oxford: University of Oxford, 1697). Cf. Boehncke, *Demosthenes*, 451–52. The *Letter* is no. 30 in the collection called "Socrates" in this title. See Rudolphus Hercher (ed.), ΕΠΙΣΤΟΛΟΓΡΑΦΟΙ ΕΛΛΗΝΙΚΟΙ—*Epistolographi Græci* (Paris: Firman Didot, 1873), 609–635 ("Socratis et Socraticorum Epistolae"); no. 30 ("Philippo"; i.e., "To Philip") is on 629-632.

84. See Natoli, *Letter of Speusippus*; he also argues for the authenticity of no. 31 (Hercher, *Epistolographi Graeci*, 632–33; also "To Philip") in an appendix (161–74).

85. The editor and Carol Atack, who wrote the notes, are not ignorant of Natoli's findings (see Burnyeat and Frede, *Seventh Letter*, 107–8n37) and they make no effort to vindicate Frede's position in response. For some useful observations about the book, likewise skirting the claim relevant here, see Nicholas Denyer, "The Seventh Letter: A Discussion of Myles Burnyeat and Michael Frede, *The Pseudo-Platonic Seventh Letter*." *Oxford Studies in Ancient Philosophy* 51 (2016), 283–92.

86. See William H. F. Altman, "In Defense of Plato's Intermediates." *Plato* 20 (2020), 151-66.

87. See Guthrie, *History of Greek Philosophy*, 5.549 ("Speusippus abandoned the Platonic Forms") and 5.473–74, on Xenocrates' "further lapse into earlier Pythagorean ideas."

88. Cf. Dillon, *Heirs of Plato*, 34 (emphasis mine): "One other incident from this period, however, may be included, the historicity of which has long been under a cloud, but I am now convinced, without adequate cause, and that is the matter of Speusippus' *Letter to King Philip*, which would, if genuine, have to have been composed in 343 or 342. It is a document of some interest, though not one which sheds a very creditable light on Speusippus, trying as it does to ingratiate him and the Academy with Philip, through adducing various mythical, and equally doubtful historical, justifications for the legitimacy of Philip's conquests, while attempting to blacken the reputation of the aged Isocrates and his students, in particular the historian Theopompus, who were basking in Philip's favor at the time. It does, however, constitute an example of the sort of politicking in which a head of school felt that he had to indulge *in the period of the growth of Macedonian power*. It does

not, on the other hand, merit much attention in a study of his philosophy." I beg to differ only with this last judgment; the italicized words are perfect.

89. Following Dillon (see previous note) and Natoli, *Letter of Speusippus*, 64–66, I date the *Letter* to 343–342.

90. Bernays, *Phokion*, 34. This is Aristotle's view; fr. 2 of his *On Kingship* will be quoted in chapter 2.

91. See Dillon, *Heirs of Plato*, 94n14. More importantly, see Matthias Haake, "Warum und zu welchem Ende schreibt man *Peri Basileias*? Überlegungen zum historischen Kontext einer literarische Gattung im Hellenismus" in K. Piepenbrink (ed.), *Philosophie und Lebenswelt in der Antike*, 183–238 (Darmstadt: Wissenschaftliche Buchgesellschaft, 2003), 112–13n23.

92. For a more extensive list, see *Plato the Teacher*, 352–53.

93. For the hypothesis that Plato's *Letters* were forged "to show the character of this strong moral arbiter in the worst light" (646), see Ulrich von Wilamowitz-Moellendorff, *Platon*, second edition, two volumes (Berlin: Weidmannschen Buchhandlung, 1920), 1.645–46 and 653.

94. On Isocrates 5, see S. Perlman, "Isocrates' *Philippus*: A Reinterpretation." *Historia* 6, no. 3 (July 1957), 306–317, noting the use of "body of opinion" and "party" on 312–13; more pertinent to present concerns is Minor M. Markle III, "Support of Athenian Intellectuals for Philip: A Study of Isocrates' Philippus and Speusippus' *Letter to Philip*." *Journal of Hellenic Studies* 96 (1976), 80–99. See also Blass, *Attische Beredsamkeit*, 2.287–92, especially on Aristotle's citations of it (290n6).

95. See Michael Trapp, "Plato in the *Deipnosophistae*" in David Braund and John Wilkins (eds.), *Athenaeus and his World: Reading Greek Culture in the Roman Empire*, 353–363 and 577–578 (Exeter, UK: University of Exeter Press, 2000), especially 357: "*Deipnosophistae* boasts no fewer than three major set-piece discussions in which Plato is either the joint or the sole object of attention, and in which he is treated with disapproval and downright scorn."

96. Athenaeus, *Sophists at Dinner*, 11.506d–e.

97. Cf. Frede, *Seventh Letter*, 33, and Boehncke, *Demosthenes*, 451, with Natoli, *Letter of Speusippus*, 37–38.

98. Blass, "Review of Jakob Bernays, 1090.

99. Bernays, *Phokion*, 117.

100. Athenaeus, *Sophists at Dinner*, 11.506e; cf. Frede, *Seventh Letter*, 31 ("Speusippus has the nerve").

101. See Natoli, *Letter of Speusippus*, 66–100.

102. For background, see R. C. Jebb, *The Attic Orators from Antiphon to Isaeus*, two volumes (London: Macmillan, 1876), 2.150–76, and M. L. W. Laistner (ed.), *Isocrates, De Pace and* Philippus. *Edited with Historical Commentary and Introduction* (Ithaca, NY: Cornell University Press, 1927), 15–24.

103. See Natoli, *Letter of Speusippus*, 50–56.

104. Herodotus, 7.20–21.

105. Thucydides, 4.102–108.

106. Thucydides 4.108.4; as usual, the four bracketed phrases appear in the nominative for ease of discussion, not in the oblique cases found in the text.

107. Zosimus, *Life of Demosthenes*, in Anton Westermann (ed.), ΒΙΟΓΡΑΦΟΙ. *Vitarum scriptores Graeci minores* (Brunschwig: Georg Westermann, 1845), 298–99, lines 44–51. On Zosimus' *Life*, see Brad L. Cook, "The Biographic Tradition" in Gunter Martin (ed.), *The Oxford Handbook of Demosthenes*, 297–308 (Oxford and New York: Oxford University Press, 2019), 303-305.

108. Lucian, *Against an Ignorant Purchaser of Books*, 4.

109. See *Ascent to the Good*, §6.

110. On the request for help the Amphipolitans sent to Athens in 358, see the chilling and insightful sentence in George Grote, *History of Greece; from the Earliest Period to the Close of the Generation Contemporary with Alexander the Great*, twelve volumes (London: John Murray, 1846-1856) 11.328-29: "Much of the future history of Greece turned upon the manner in which Athens dealt with these two conflicting messages."

111. In addition to Sealey, "Athens after the Social War," see Raphael Sealey, *Demosthenes and his Time: A Study in Defeat* (New York and Oxford: Oxford University Press, 1993), chapter 5.

112. Demosthenes 1.8; in the original, Demosthenes refers to the ambassadors by name: Hierax and Stratocles.

113. For the text with English translation, see Natoli, *Letter of Speusippus*, 102–9, here on 103; hereafter the *Letter* will be cited by section numbers, in this case: 2–3.

114. *Letter of Speusippus*, 12.

115. Perlman, "Isocrates' *Philippus*," concludes his reinterpretation on 317 with the claim: "Isocrates was not a tool in the hands of Philip and was not a member of the pro-Macedonian party." Although this assessment is perhaps overly generous, it clearly was Isocrates' intention to be considered a loyal citizen of Athens "and believed that his reputation with posterity depended on that" (I am grateful to Natoli in private correspondence for making this observation). Overly generous or not, Perlman's claim has one important advantage: it leaves room for Speusippus to reveal himself in the *Letter as Just Such a Tool*, thus creating "a race to the bottom." Cf. Markle, "Athenian Intellectuals," 80: "In 343, Speusippus and the Academy saw in the failure of Isocratean mythological warfare over Amphipolis an opportunity for themselves to move into a temporary theological vacuum with a more intense piece of flattery then even Isocrates could bring himself to write, in the hope that they could divert Philip's patronage their way, and that they succeeded, since Aristotle, a former member of the Academy, was appointed as tutor to Alexander."

116. Diogenes Laertius, *Lives of Eminent Philosophers*, 3.40 (Mensch translation).

117. See Schaefer, *Demosthenes*, 2.37n5. But cf. Ulrich von Wilamowitz-Moellendorff, *Antigonos von Karystos* (Berlin: Weidmann, 1881), 339n1, with Wilamowitz, *Platon*, 1.720n2 for a great scholar's change of opinion.

118. See Natoli, *Letter of Speusippus*, 38n87.

119. Aeschines 3.77.

120. While generously commenting on a draft of this book, Natoli wrote: "On the passage from DL [sc. Diogenes Laertius] 3.40: the relative clause beginning ὑφ᾽ οὗ . . . (remarked on by Hicks) interrupts the idea of how Plato died and appears to be an afterthought by Diogenes or more likely an interpolation by someone else. The sentence that follows citing Myronianus continues the idea of

the mode of Plato's death and is strong evidence for interpolation. I missed this. On p. 38 [in Natoli, *Letter of Speusippus*] I took the disputed sentence to be the work of Diogenes and considered the juxtaposition of the two names the reason for the afterthought on the part of Diogenes. If the interpolated sentence was from Theopompus, then my translation would be accurate. See my n.157 for the source of the fragment of Theopompus. You would then not have to 'explain Philip's change of mind.'" For both Natoli's scholarship and his kindness I am most grateful.

121. Isocrates 5.12. Isocrates refers to Plato as a "sophist" elsewhere.

122. For Isocrates' two letters to Philip (2-3), to Antpater (4), and to Alexander (5), see *Isocrates*, translated by George Norlin and LaRue Hook, three volumes (Cambridge. MA: Harvard University Press, 1928-1945), 3.381–429.

123. Athenaeus, *Sophists at Dinner*, 508e.

124. Grote, *History of Greece*, 11.292n2.

125. Athenaeus, *Sophists at Dinner*, 508d-f.

126. See Natoli, *Letter of Speusippus*, 172.

127. Isocrates, 5.12.

128. Isocrates, 5.13 (George Norlin translation); cf. Markle, "Athenian Intellectuals," 87: "Demosthenes later gives precisely the same account of Philip's advantages, but his assessment is given not to explain, as Isocrates, how the Macedonian could benefit the Greeks but why he had been so formidable an enemy. He writes (18.235): 'In the first place, he was the despotic commander of his adherents: and in war that is the most important of all advantages. . . . Then he was well provided with money: he did whatever he chose, without giving notice by publishing decrees, or deliberating in public, without fear of prosecution by informers or indictment for illegal measures. He was responsible to nobody: he was the absolute autocrat, commander, and master of everybody and everything (cf. 19.184–5).' Both Demosthenes and Isocrates understood the advantages in both war and diplomacy enjoyed by Philip as an autocrat, Isocrates stresses much more the power possessed by the Macedonian king and how could be used to bend others to his will."

129. On Euphraeus, see Trampedach, *Akademie*, 93–97; while skeptical about the testimony of Athenaeus via Demochares concerning his farcical "Platonism" in Macedon (96), he writes the following about his death as recorded by Demosthenes on 97: "Euphraios war offenbar gar kein Politiker in engeren Sinne. Er mischte sich ein, als er die Einheit der Polis durch eine bürgerkriegswillige Clique gefährdet sah. Dies und die Zivilcourage, mit der er es tat, könnte man als Ausfluß eines philosophischen Ethos verstehen." There is a closer connection between what Plato called πολιτεία and what Trampedach here calls *Zivilcourage* (although *Tapferkeit* might serve even better) than has heretofore been recognized; this book is an attempt to illustrate and defend that connection.

130. On antiquity, see Schaefer, *Demosthenes* 3.201n3; see also Grote, *History of Greece*, 11.528–30; Ivor Bruns, *Das Litterarische Porträt der Griechen im fünften und vierten Jahrhundert vor Christi Geburt* (Berlin: Wilhelm Hertz, 1896), 580–81; A. W. Pickard-Cambridge, *Demosthenes and the Last Days of Greek Freedom* (New York and London: G P. Putnam's Sons, 1914), 240–45; Thomas Paulsen, *Die Parapresbeia-Reden des Demosthenes und des Aischines. Kommentar und Interpretationen zu Demosthenes, or. XIX, und Aischines, or. II* (Trier: Wissenschaftlicher Verlag Trier, 1999),

247 ("alle Wahrscheinlichkeit spricht für die Korrektheit der Darstellung des Ai."); and Harris, *Aeschines and Athenian Politics*, 57–60, especially 59–60: "Essentially we are left to choose between an account given by a contemporary, which, although hostile, is nonetheless supported by the testimony of several witnesses [none of whom testified, and who were, according to Demosthenes, complicit in 'the false embassy] and another presented by a writer [sc. Plutarch] who was separated from the event in question by several centuries and probably had no other source for the First Embassy than the speeches of Aeschines and Demosthenes. Granting that Aeschines may have exaggerated certain details for the sake of dramatic effect, it would be wrong to question the essentials of his account. Demosthenes' general silence about the First Embassy may therefore be due in part to his reluctance to recall events that had been the cause of great embarrassment to him." Marginally better but unfortunately typical is MacDowell, *Demosthenes the Orator*, 317: "it is unlikely that the description is entirely false."

131. Plutarch, *Life of Demosthenes* 16.1.

132. So often cited as an authority by others, it is Schaefer who offers the authoritative account in *Demosthenes*, 3.197–211.

133. Aeschines 2.31 (Charles Darwin Adams translation, and his note).

134. A point well made by Markle, "Athenian Intellectuals," 97–98.

135. For insight on this passage, see Bernd Steinbock, "A Lesson in Patriotism: Lycurgus' *Against Leocrates*, the Ideology of the Ephebeia, and Athenian Social Memory." *Classical Antiquity* 30, no. 2 (October 2011), 279–317, on 300–301.

136. Xenophon, *Cynegeticus*, 1.14.

CHAPTER 2

1. See Jeff Miller, "Aristotle's Paradox of Monarchy and the Biographical Tradition." *History of Political Thought* 19, no. 4 (Winter, 1998), 501–516, on 505.

2. See J. C. Trevett, "Aristotle's Knowledge of Athenian Oratory." *Classical Quarterly* 46, no. 2 (1996), 371–79.

3. "Anonymous vita Aeschinis" in Ferdinand Schultz (ed.), *Aeschinis orationes* (Leipzig: Teubner, 1865), 5–6.

4. Aeschines, *The Speeches of Aeschines*. Translated by C. D. Adams (London: William Heinemann, 1929).

5. "Anonymous vita Aeschinis," 6.

6. See Nick Fisher (ed.), *Aeschines,* Against Timarchus: *Introduction, Translation, and Commentary* (Oxford: Oxford University Press, 2001), 2–8.

7. See Fisher, *Against Timarchus*, 316–18, and MacDowell, *Demosthenes*, 325-44.

8. Cf. Fisher, *Against Timarchus*, 319: "Despite the efforts of the ancient 'Sokrates industry,'... Aeschines, presumably representing a still living popular tradition, presents Sokrates as a dangerous sophist."

9. For an introduction to Polycrates, see Anton-Hermann Chroust, *Socrates, Man and Myth: The Two Socratic Apologies of Xenophon* (Notre Dame, ID: University of Notre Dame Press, 1957), 69–100.

10. Cf. Fisher, *Against Timarchus*, 320: "if the Athenians were right to condemn Sokrates ... then in consistency, they ought equally to condemn Demosthenes."

11. 1.173, with help from both Adams and Fisher.
12. Cf. Fisher, *Against Timarchus*, 315: "The attack seems totally without relevance to his case against Timarchos, and contrary in spirit to his protestations against Demosthenes' veering off the point."
13. 1.75 (Adams modified).
14. Cf. Fisher, *Against Timarchus*, 322: "Referring to Demosthenes now contemptuously as the 'sophist'... reinforces the idea that he poses a worse threat to the political community even than Sokrates had."
15. See Anton-Hermann Chroust, "Aristotle's Earliest 'Course of Lectures on Rhetoric'." *L'Antiquité Classique* 33, no. 1 (1964), 58–72.
16. See "Vita Marciana" 5, and "Vita Vulgata" 4, in Düring, *Biographical Tradition*, 98, 109, and 132. Cf. Anton-Hermann Chroust, "Aristotle Enters the Academy." *Classical Folia* 19, no. 1 (1965), 21–29, on 25–6, for the implausible parallel claim that "Socrates" was a corruption for Isocrates.
17. "Anonymous Vita Aeschinis," 6. For discussion, see Jan Fredrik Kindstrand, *The Stylistic Evaluation of Aeschines in Antiquity* (Stockholm: Almqvist & Wiksell, 1982), 68–75.
18. See Arnold Hug, "Aeschines und Plato." *Rheinisches Museum* 29 (1874), 434–44,
19. See Geffcken, "Antiplatonica," 96.
20. See Kennedy, *Rhetoric in the Roman World*, 364–69, and Kindstrand, *Aeschines in Antiquity*, 39–41.
21. See William W. Fortenbaugh and Eckart Schütrumpf (eds.), *Demetrius of Phalerum: Text, Translation and Discussion* (London and New York: Routledge, 2000), 247.
22. OCD, 432 (A. B. Bosworth).
23. OCD, 725 (F. W. Walbank and K. S. Sacks).
24. Plutarch, *Life of Demosthenes*, 11.1 (Perrin translation)
25. See Fritz Wehrli, *Demetrios von Phaleron*, second edition (Basel: Schwabe, 1968), 81.
26. Wehrli, *Demetrios*, 82
27. Plutarch, *Life of Demosthenes*, 7.1–3; note the mention of Eunomus at 6.4, who appears in the version in Photius, for which see Roisman and Worthington, *Lives*, 310.
28. Demetrius, fragment 170, is found in Dionysius of Halicarnassus, *Style of Demosthenes* 5: "And he [sc. Plato] is very much the initiate [Stephen Usher translates τελετής as 'hierophant,' which may better capture the essence of religious frenzy] as Demetrius of Phaleron has said somewhere, and a great many others said earlier." This seems to leave room for Aristotle; cf. Wehrli's comment at *Demetrios*, 82: "Peripatetic criticism of Plato's high style ... emerges from the early Aristotelian demand for clear factuality [*Sachlichkeit*] in contrast to the psychagogy of Gorgias." Fragment 163 in from Plutarch, *Life of Demosthenes*, 9 (Perrin): "However, those orations which were spoken off-hand by him had more courage and boldness than those which he wrote out, if we are to put any confidence in Eratosthenes, Demetrius the Phalerian, and the comic poets. Of these, Eratosthenes says that often in his speeches Demosthenes was like one frenzied, and the Phalerean says that once, as if under inspiration [ὥσπερ ἐνθουσιῶντα],

he swore the famous metrical oath to the people: 'By earth, by springs [κρήνας], by rivers [ποταμούς], and by streams [νάματα].'" Cf. *Ion* 534a4–b3.

29. See also Susemihl, *Geschichte der griechischen Litteratur*, 1.135–43. For the role of the Peripatetics in establishing the biography of philosophers as a genre, see von Mess, "Anfänge der Biographie." 340.

30. Cicero, *De legibus*, 3.14 (C. W. Keyes translation).

31. Lara O'Sullivan, *The Regime of Demetrius of Phaleron in Athens, 317–307 BCE: A Philosopher in Politics* (Leiden and Boston: Brill, 2009).

32. After leaving Athens, he "was henceforth no more the politician but rather Demetrius the philosopher" at Gehrke, "Politik und Philosophie," 188; other choice expressions are found on 158 ("nicht das geringste miteinander zu tun") and 181 ("rein politisch"); on *Selbstdarstellung*, see 187.

33. Craig Cooper, "(Re)Making Demosthenes: Demochares and Demetrius of Phaleron on Demosthenes" in Pat Wheatley and Robert Hannah (eds.), *Alexander & His Successors: Essays from the Antipodes*, 310–22 (Claremont, CA: Regina, 2009), 310 (opening words).

34. In addition to Cooper, "(Re)Making Demosthenes," see also Craig Cooper, "Philosophers, Politics, Academics: Demosthenes' Rhetorical Reputation in Antiquity" in Ian Worthington (ed.), *Demosthenes: Statesman and Orator*, 222–45 (London: Routledge, 2001), 226: "This characterization of Demosthenes as a 'practiced rather than natural orator' grew out of Peripatetic discussions on the orator's inability to compete with naturally gifted orators, like Aeschines and Demades."

35. Hence the exceptional misstep at Cooper, "(Re)Making Demosthenrs," 312: "There is a strong possibility that the comments [attributed to Idomenaeus, Hermippus, and Caecilius in the *Vita Aeschinis*], at least in part [true enough] go back to Demetrius of Phaleron. As we have seen [but what follows cannot be attributed to Demetrius], it was held by Peripatetics that Aeschines was self-taught."

36. Cooper, "(Re)Making Demosthenes," 315; he is referring to Aristotle's comments on delivery in *Rhetoric* 3.1.3 and 3.1.5.

37. In general, see Anton-Hermann Chroust, "The Probable Dates of Some of Aristotle's Lost Works." *Rivista Critica di Storia della Filosofia* 22, no. 1 (January-March, 1967), 3–23, starting with: "Critical consensus recognizes the *Gryllus* to be the first important publication of Aristotle."

38. See Düring, *Biographical Tradition*, 258–59, for an early date for (most of) the first two books of the *Rhetoric* itself.

39. W. D. Ross (ed.), *Aristotelis Fragmenta Selecta* (Oxford: Clarendon Press, 1955), 7–8.

40. Anton-Hermann Chroust, "Aristotle's Earliest Course," 61; the reference is to Cicero, *Tusculan Disputations*, 1.7.

41. See Harry M. Hubbell, *The Rhetorica of Philodemus: Translation and Commentary* (New Haven, CT: Yale University Press, 1920), 329: "Now let us take up the story about Aristotle, that he taught rhetoric in the afternoon, saying, ''Tis a shame to be silent and allow Isocrates to speak.'" For the comparatively recent discovery of these fragments, see Siegfried Sudhaus, "Aristoteles in der Beurtheilung des Epikur und Philodem." *Rheinisches Museum* 48 (1893), 552–64.

42. Anton-Hermann Chroust, "Aristotle's First Literary Effort: The *Gryllus*, a Lost Dialogue on the Nature of Rhetoric." *Revue des Études Grecques* 78, nos. 371/373 (July to December, 1965), 576–591, on 591. The "choice of lives" setting indicates the probable origin of the emphasis of Plato's students on choice or προαίρεσις (see chapter 3 on Danielle Allen).

43. Note that the Peripatetic approach to the Academy was to emphasize instead the easier of the Third Wave's two paths, as in Hans B. Gottschalk, "Demetrius of Phalerum: A Politician among Philosophers and a Philosopher among Politicians" in William W. Fortenbaugh and Eckart Schütrumpf (eds.), *Demetrius of Phalerum: Text, Translation and Discussion*, 367-80 (London and New York: Routledge, 2000), on 367: "Plato himself made several attempts to create a philosopher-king in Syracuse, and while these failed, some of his pupils, notably Hermias of Atarneus, succeeded on a smaller scale, at least for a time [note]. From Plato's school this practice passed to others, notably the Peripatos." The attached note further illustrates the continued existence of the Peripatetic approach; instead of trying to document the teacher-student connection between Plato and Hermias—which it would have been impossible to do—Gottschalk writes: "See I. During, Aristotle in the *Ancient Biographical Tradition* (Goteborg 1957) 272–83, for the sources [naturally these sources document Aristotle's relations with Hermias, not Plato's]. The tradition that Aristotle also gave detailed political advice to Alexander is much less securely based."

44. Hubbell, *Rhetorica*, 347; this is Pernot's T1, followed by the four passages in Cicero. On Eubulides, see Hans Kelsen, "The Philosophy of Aristotle and the Hellenic-Macedonian Policy." *International Journal of Ethics* 48, no. 1 (October 1937), 1–64, on 57n120: "The orator Eubulides, of Milet, under whose influence Demosthenes is said to have been, published a writing against Aristotle in which he reproached the latter with having entered Philip's service (Schäfer, op. cit., I, 328)."

45. Hubbell, *Rhetorica*, 330; for the Greek, see Düring, *Biographical Tradition*, 299-300.

46. See Haake, "Warum und zu welchem Ende schreibt man *Peri Basileias*," 111-12n22

47. See Ross, *Fragmenta*, 61–62, here fr. 2.

48. See Felix Grayeff, *Aristotle and His School: An Inquiry into the History of the Peripatos with a Commentary on* Metaphysics Z, H, Λ and Θ (New York: Barnes & Noble, 1974), 37–40.

49. See Miller, "Paradox of Monarchy," 516: "Aristotle's position in Athens, then, would have been a precarious one, and it is not hard to imagine that in order to maintain public credibility, and perhaps even safety, he would have ensured that his public utterances on the subject of kingship (or democracy) did not appear unequivocally biased in favor of Macedon. The tension in the *Politics* between Aristotle's statements on monarchy and his mixed constitution seem to support this contention."

50. Kelsen, "Philosophy of Aristotle," 20.

51. If my interest in the post-Plato Academy were not confined to distinguishing it from "the Old Academy" in this book's sense of that term, it would have been worth exploring at greater length the hypothesis that Xenocrates modified

the overtly pro-Macedonian position of Speusippus in appearance, but not in substance. Aside from the anecdote in Diogenes Laertius' *Life of Xenocrates* that worked to Bernays' advantage, the *Life* as a whole seems to have but one intent: to establish the independence of Xenocrates from Macedon; this might have been Antipater's and Xenocrates' intention as well.

52. Kelsen, "Philosophy of Aristotle," 56.

53. See Kelsen, "Philosophy of Aristotle," 31, and Miller, "Aristotle's Paradox of Monarchy," 511n37: "It is difficult to imagine an Athenian, or any Greek, reading this passage and *not* thinking of Alexander." For anticipations, see William Scott Ferguson, *Hellenistic Athens: An Historical Essay* (London: Macmillan, 1911), 109.

54. Isocrates, *Second Letter to Philip*, 5; Diodorus Siculus, 16.92.5; Plutarch, *Life of Alexander*, 27.4–28.3.

55. See Anton-Hermann Chroust, "Aristotle's Flight from Athens in the Year 323 B.C." *Historia* 15, no. 2 (April, 1966), 185–92; naturally this was merely a pretext (189): "Aristotle's close relationship with Hermias of Atarneus was of course politically suspect, and his situation in Athens was made most gravely difficult by his connections with the Macedonian royal house and certain leading Macedonian statesmen (especially Antipater)." See also O'Sullivan, *Regime of Demetrius*, 206-13, especially on the subsequent prosecutions of Theophrastus and Demades, the latter for his promotion of Alexander's deification (210), for which our source is Aelian, *Varia Historia*, 5.12.

56. See Jaeger, *Aristotle*, 113-19; cf. 107–109 on an earlier hymn by Aristotle to his teacher: "the last lines praise Plato as the mortal through whom this transcendental Form has been realized."

57. Leo Strauss, "Preface to *Hobbes politische Wissenschaft*" (translated by Donald J. Maletz) in Kenneth Hart Green (ed.), Leo Strauss, *Jewish Philosophy and the Crisis of Modernity: Essays and Lectures in Modern Jewish Thought*, 453-56 (Albany: State University of New York Press, 1997), 453.

58. Wittgenstein, *Tractatus Logico-Philosophicus*, prop. 1.

59. See Gabriele Marasco (ed.), *Democare di Leuconoe. Politica e cultura in Atene fra IV e III sec. a. C.* (Florence: Università degli Studi di Firenze, 1984), 23–48, Lara O'Sullivan, "The Law of Sophocles and the Beginnings of Permanent Philosophical Schools in Athens." *Rheinisches Museum* 145, no. 3/4 (2002), 251–262, and especially Matthias Haake, "Das 'Gesetz des Sopkokles' und die Schliessung der Philosophenschulen in Athen unter Demetrios Polioketes" in H. Hugonnard-Roche (ed.), *L'enseignement supérieur dans les mondes antiques et médiévaux. Aspects institutionnels, juridiques et pédagogiques. Colloque international de l'Institut des Traditions Textuelles (Fédération de recherche 33 du C.N.R.S.)*, 89–113 (Paris: Vrin, 2009).

60. Plutarch, *Life of Demetrius*, 10.3–11.1 and 12.1.

61. See Christian Habicht, "Hellenistic Athens and her Philosophers" in Habicht, *Athen in hellenistischer Zeit; gesammelte Aufsätze*, 231–47 (Munich: C. H. Beck, 1994), 236–7, especially: "The law was phrased to include *all* schools but was aimed specifically at the *Peripatos*." Cf. Tor Korhonen, "Self-Concept and Public Image of Philosophers and Philosophical Schools at the Beginning of the Hellenistic Age" in Jaako Frösén (ed.), *Early Hellenistic Athens; Symptoms of a Change*, 33-101 (Helsinki: Finnish Institute of Athens, 1997), 75: "In 307 B.C. Demetrius of Phaleron

lost his position and had to flee to the court of Ptolemy I. He was generally held to be a member of the Peripatos, and he made it possible for Theophrastus to buy 'a garden' (D.L. 5.39)—for the activities of the school." See also 76: "it is unclear if by οἱ λοιποὶ φιλόσοφοι [sc. 'the other philosophers,' i.e., other than Theophrastus in Diogenes Laertius, *Lives of the Eminent Philosophers*, 5.38] Diogenes means all philosophers, or only the other members of the Peripatetic school."

62. Cf. O'Sullivan, "Law of Sophocles," 252, on "the general thrust of Sophocles' law": "The general thrust of Sophocles' law is well understood. It was an essentially political gesture, prompted by the perceived collaboration of the Peripatos with the hated Macedonian overlords."

63. See O'Sullivan, *Regime of Demetrius*, 307–8 (with transliterated Greek restored): "Echoes of Demochares' rhetoric come through again in a fragment of Alexis' play *Hippeus*, produced in 306 at the height of the controversy over the law of Sophocles. When one of Alexis' characters asks 'So this is what the Academy is, this is Xenocrates?' (τοῦτ' ἔστιν Ἀκαδήμεια, τοῦτο Ξενοκράτης;) it is hard not to hear a comical allusion to the catchcry Demochares seems to have used throughout his speech, as quoted, for example, at Athen. 509a 'some of the Academic philosophers now are like that' (*toioutoi eisi kai nun tôn Akadêmaikôn tines*).'" This "even now [καὶ νῦν]" distinguishes Xenocrates' Academy from Plato's.

64. See Matthias Haake, *Der Philosoph in der Stadt: Untersuchungen zur öffentlichen Rede über Philosophen und Philosophie in den hellenistischen Poleis* (Munich: C. H. Beck, 2007), especially 32–43, but including 24–28 on Xenocrates.

65. Most explicitly in Haake, "Doing philosophy," 118; cf. 128n62 on Demosthenes.

66. Haake, *Philosoph in der Stadt*, 40: "Es geht an diesem Punkt nicht darum, ob die platonische Philosophie hier zutreffend 'interpretiert' wird, sondern um die Frage, wie platonische Texte aufgefaßt werden konnten. Und daran besteht kein Zweifel: zahlreiche Äußerungen Platons in der *Politeia*, im *Politikos* und in den *Nomoi* konnten aus der Perspektive des *polites* nur in einer einzigen Weise interpretiert werden - hier redete jemand der Tyrannis das Wort." The attached note cites Trampedach, *Akademie*, 206–15 ("Die Möglichkeit der Philosophenherrschaft"), on which see the introduction.

67. Haake, *Philosoph in der Stadt*, 36: "Weil Chairon nicht allein Schüler Platons, sondern auch von dessen Nachfolger Xenokrates war, bot sich die Möglichkeit, an Hand seiner Person zu verdeutlichen, daß es keineswegs nur der Gründer der Akademie war, der Tyrannen aus seiner Schule hervorbrachte, sondern daß es grundsätzlich zu den Eigenschaften der Akademie gehörte und in ihrer Philosophie begründet lag, Tyrannen zu produzieren."

68. See O'Sullivan, *Regime of Demetrius*, 213–26; note especially 216: "Demochares made further overtly political allegations against Aristotle too in his speech of 307 (see Euseb. *Praep. Evang.* 15.2.6): Aristotle had, he claimed, written letters to the Macedonians against Athens; he had betrayed his native city, Stagira; and, after the fall of Olynthus, he had denounced its wealthiest men to Philip. Demochares' Aristotle, although not a tyrant in his own right, is thus a dangerous political quisling charged with a key rôle in the rise of Macedon: Ephorus had, after all, attributed Philip's conquests in Greece to the wealth gained from the sack of Olynthus (Diod. 16.53.3)."

69. See Haake, "Gesetz des Sopkokles," 106: "Im Anschluß an der *graphe*-Verfahren kehrten die Philosophen wieder nach Athen zurück. Doch es kehrten nicht allein die auf Grund des sophokleiischen Gesetzes in das kurzzeitige Exil gegangenen Philosophen zurück. Im Jahre 305/4 kam Epicur aus Lampsakos in die Stadt und gründete den *Kepos* vor den Mauern der Stadt. Und im Jahre 301/0 nahm Zenon von Kition in der an der Agora gelegenen Stoa Poikile mitten im Herzen der *polis* Athen seine Lehrtätigkeit auf."

70. See Eric Brown, "Contemplative Withdrawal in the Hellenistic Age." *Philosophical Studies* 137, no. 1 (January 2008), 79–89; note, however, that Brown finds the roots of this withdrawal earlier on 80: "Plato and Aristotle insisted that a person in ordinary circumstances could do no better than to withdraw from public affairs and dedicate oneself to the contemplation of eternal truths."

71. Cooper, "(Re)Making Demosthenes," 321.
72. Cooper, "(Re)Making Demosthenes," 319.
73. See Trittle, *Phocion*, 30–31.
74. Cornelius Nepos, *Phocion*, 2.3.
75. See Roisman and Worthington, *Lives*, 269–71.
76. Cooper, "(Re)Making Demosthenes," 311.

77. After contrasting Plato and Demosthenes with respect to their contrasting attitudes toward Sparta (quoted above), Blass strengthens his case for denying their academic connection at *Attische Beredsamkeit*, 3.1.12: "sein [sc. Demosthenes'] Neffe und Nachfolger Demochares war den Philosophen thatsächlich feindlich und schmähte den Aristoteles wie den Sokrates." The implication here, of course, is that if (Demochares knew that) Demosthenes had been Plato's student, Demochares (as not only his nephew but his *Nachfolger* or "successor") would not have attacked Plato and Socrates along with Aristotle. This implication is subject to three objections: (1) our source for this hostility is Athenaeus, whose hostility to Plato is notorious, and who cites it for a polemical purpose, (2) there is no reason to think that Demosthenes told his nephew about his early training, (3) we have no evidence to support the view that Demochares was his uncle's *Nachfolger* in addition to being his *Neffe*; he was rather his relative and admirer, and (4) the thesis of this book is that the Academy that had produced Demosthenes *no longer existed and was long gone by 307*, thanks above all to the fact that Plato's *Nachfolgern*, Speusippus and Xenocrates, had made the Academy eminently worthy of Demochares' anti-Macedonian attack. Even if Demochares really was Demosthenes' own "successor" to the extent that he knew about the connection—*pace* "(2)" and "(3)"—he still had sufficient reason, thanks to "the end of the Old Academy," to tar what now called itself "the Academy" with the same brush he was evidently determined to apply, and with very good reason, to the Lyceum.

78. [Plut.], *Lives of the Ten Orators*, 271 (from the decree of Demochares): "his advice has been the cause of much good for the people, and in general there has been no contemporary statesman who has done more for the cause of freedom and democracy."

79. Cf. "and all the remaining philosophers [καὶ πάντες οἱ λοιποὶ φιλόσοφοι" in Diogenes Laertius, *Lives of the Eminent Philosophers*, 5.38 (Theophrastus).

80. Plutarch, *Life of Phocion*, 9.6.
81. Bernays, *Phokion*, 31.

82. See *Plato the Teacher*, §10, 159, and 348; cf. Charmides in Xenophon, *Memorabilia*, 3.6.
83. Plutarch, *Life of Phocion*, 17.3.
84. Plutarch, *Life of Phocion*, 17.3.
85. On which see Giaquinta, *Epistole di Demostene*, 295–426.
86. See Allen, *Why Plato Wrote*, 90; consider also her list of five on 89–90.
87. In addition to Allen, *Why Plato Wrote*, 90–94, see more specifically Danielle Allen, "Talking about Revolutions: On Political Change in Fourth-century Athens and Historiographic Method" in Simon Goldhill and Robin Osbourne (eds.), *Rethinking Revolutions in Ancient Greece*, 183–217 (Cambridge, UK: Cambridge University Press, 2006).
88. In addition to Allen, *Why Plato Wrote*, 99–141, see Danielle Allen, "Culture War: Plato and Athenian Politics 350–330 BCE" in Claudia Tiersch (ed.), *Die Athenische Deomokratie im 4. Jahrhundert zwischen Modernisierung und Tradition*, 279-292 (Stuttgart: Franz Steiner, 2016).
89. Beginning with Danielle S. Allen, "Changing the Authoritative Voice: Lycurgus' *Against Leocrates*." *Classical Antiquity* 19, no. 1 (April 2000), 5–33.
90. See Allen, "Authoritative Voice," 8n5, and *Why Plato Wrote*, 193n14 and 194n16.
91. Allen, *Why Plato Wrote*, 193n14 and 195n32.
92. See especially Allen, "Culture War," 286–89.
93. Allen, *Why Plato Wrote*, 201n2; this admission is tied to an innocuous claim in the text (123): "Indeed both men [sc. Demosthenes and Lycurgus] maintained their pre-eminence in Athenian politics after Chaeronea [note 2]." In the paragraphs that follow (123–25), she links Lycurgus to Eubulus, doing her best to exploit the traditional "Peace" and "War Party" typology to create the needed opposition.
94. Edmund M. Burke, "*Contra Leocratem* and *de Corona*: Political Collaboration?" *Phoenix* 31, no. 4 (Winter, 1977), 330–340.
95. Allen, *Why Plato Wrote*, 193n14; she attaches importance to the order in which pseudo-Plutarch lists their teachers in *Lives of the Ten Orators*, so the reader might want to consider the opening words of *Demosthenes* (which immediately follows *Lycurgus* and precedes *Hyperides*), noting that placing Plato last strengthens the claim, not weakens it, especially since it is immediately followed by the Callistratus story from Hermippus which has already been shown (see introduction) to presuppose Demosthenes' connection with Plato.
96. Allen, *Why Plato Wrote*, 126: "Aeschines constructs his speech rhetorically so that his account of the kind of citizen Demosthenes has been analogous to the account that Lycurgus gives of Leocrates. Burke's critical error is to think that Demosthenes was acting as an ally of Lycurgus in the political conflict of the 330s. It is instead Lycurgus and Aeschines whose positions align."
97. Burke, "*Contra Leocratem* and *de Corona*," 335; so also 339: "the evidence strongly suggests close collaboration of generally consonant political views for the purpose common political objective: revitalization [cf. Schaefer's *zu verjüngen*, quoted in introduction] of the popular will."
98. See Renehan, "Platonism of Lycurgus."
99. Renehan, "Platonism of Lycurgus," 227–28.
100. Lycurgus, *Against Leocrates*, 132 (translation Burtt).

101. *Lg.* 814b2–4: "just as birds [cf. τὰ πτηνά at 207a9] fighting for their children, even against the strongest [cf. ἰσχυροτάτοις at 207b4] predators, are both willing to die [ἐθέλειν ἀποθνῄσκειν] and to undergo the danger of all dangers [πάντας κινδύνους κινδυνεύειν]."

102. For Allen on Renehan, see "Authoritative Voice," 8n5: "The article is a relatively peculiar compilation of phrases and comments found in Lycurgus' speech for which parallels can also be found somewhere in the Platonic corpus, preferably in the *Laws*. The major flaw with Renehan's article is that many of the parallels that he draws between Lycurgus and Plato might as easily be drawn between the other orators and Plato . . . Renehan was right to think that some of Lycurgus' vocabulary reflects Platonic influence but chose the wrong examples." I agree.

103. *Smp.* 208d2-6.

104. See *Ascent to the Good*, §16.

105. The school's characteristic fight against the light is illuminated when first Leo Strauss and then Stanley Rosen apply Diotima's *post hoc propter hoc* fallacy to the speech of Phaedrus itself: see Leo Strauss, *On Plato's* Symposium, edited with a Foreword by Seth Benardete (Chicago, IL: University of Chicago Press, 2001), 53 and 225, and Stanley Rosen, *Plato's* Symposium, second edition; first published in 1968 (New Haven, CT: Yale University Press, 1987), 55.

106. See *Plato the Teacher*, §9.

107. Cf. Cicero, *De officiis*, 1.28.

108. Wilamowitz, *Platon* 2, 173. Disarmingly personal, Wilamowitz goes on to reject *Ruhmsucht* as the motivating force behind Homer and Lycurgus (174), and he uses the parallel with Aspasia in *Menexenus* to distance Socrates from Diotima on this point; nor does he scruple, when passing over to the climax of the Ascent, to find there "Plato's deepest remarks about his actual inner life [*sein eigenes Innenleben*]."

109. Although he was also fully aware that others would agree with Kenneth Dover (ed.). *Plato,* Symposium (Cambridge, UK: Cambridge University Press, 1990), 152 (on 208b7–209e4): "Perhaps the notion that Alcestis would not have died for Admetus had she not been sure of posthumous fame . . . would not have seemed so grotesque to a Greek as it does to most of us." Diotima's account of ὑπεραποθνῄσκειν was not so much intended to seem grotesque to Plato's readers as "base [αἰσχρόν]," at least in comparison with "the Beautiful itself [αὐτὸ τὸ καλόν]."

110. See William Chase Greene, *Scholia Platonica* (Haverford, PA: American Philological Society, 1938), 63–64 (on '208d Κόδρον').

111. Diogenes Laertius, *Lives*, 3.1.

112. [Aristotle], *Constitution of Athens*, 3.3, is our oldest surviving source that Codrus was considered by οἱ πλείους to be the last king of Athens.

113. Lycurgus, *Against Leocrates*, 86.

114. Steinbock, "Lesson in Patriotism," 287: "Lycurgus' emphasis on the altruistic nature of the kings' self-sacrifice for the deliverance of the entire community is especially noteworthy when contrasted with the reference in Plato's *Symposium*."

115. See *Ascent to the Beautiful*, 437–441.

116. Cf. [Plutarch], *Ten Orators*, 841b–c and 842f. Naturally the bibliography on Lycurgus' political accomplishments, merely sketched here, is extensive. See especially Michele Faraguna, "Lycourgan Athens?" in Vincent Azoulay and Paulin Ismard (eds.), *Clisthène et Lycurge d'Athènes: autour du politique dans la cite classique*, 67–86 (Paris: Sorbonne, 2012), here on 86. For bibliography on *Against Leocrates*, see 73n37; for Plato's influence, see 74n40. For a hatchet-job in the form of background information, see Joseph Roisman (ed.) *Lycurgus: Against Leocrates*, translated by Michael Edwards (Oxford and New York: University Press, 2019), 39–41.

117. [Plutarch], *Ten Orators*, 841d; see also Johannes Engels, "Zur Stellung Lykurgs und zur Aussagekraft seines Militär- und Bauprogramms für die Demokratie vor 322 v. Chr." *Ancient Society* 23 (1992), 5–29.

118. See [Plutarch], *Ten Orators*, for the construction of the theater (841d), laws related to comedy (841e), public copies of the tragedies of Aeschylus, Sophocles, and Euripides, along with statues for them (841e), choral performances in the Piraeus (842a). On all of this, see Johanna Hanink, *Lycurgan Athens and the Making of Classical Tragedy* (Cambridge, UK: Cambridge University Press, 2014), especially 83–89.

119. Stewart Irvin Oost, "Review of *The Ephebic Inscriptions of the Fourth Century B.C.* by O. W. Reinmuth." *Classical Philology* 70, no. 1 (January 1975), 75: "Although the institution is now proved not to have been a creation of the 330's and 320's, it particularly flourished then, in the atmosphere of renascent patriotism at Athens under the leadership of Lycurgus." More importantly, see Steinbock, "Lesson in Patriotism."

120. [Plutarch] begins his account with the fact that the Thirty Tyrants killed Lycurgus' grandfather; see *Ten Orators*, 841b. Cf. 841e (Fowler): "And therefore, when King Alexander demanded his surrender, the people [ὁ δῆμος] did not give him up."

121. Cf. [Plutarch], *Ten Orators*, 842d: "And again when the Athenians were hailing Alexander as a god: 'And what sort of god would he be,' he said, 'when it is necessary for those *leaving* his temple to purify themselves [περιρράνεσθαι]?'"

122. Before quoting the lost biography where a certain Philiscus claimed that "Lycurgus become great and set right [κατορθοῦν] many things which it is not [i.e., which would not be] possible to be set right [passive of κατορθοῦν] for one who had not been an auditor of Plato's speeches [λόγοι]," Olympiodorus has already mentioned that both Lycurgus and Demosthenes were Plato's students (μαθηταί). See Olympiodorus, the Younger of Alexandria, *Commentary on Plato's Gorgias*, edited by Robin Jackson, Kimon Lycos, and Harold Tarrant (Leiden and Boston: Brill, 1998), 268.

123. Lycurgus is often criticized for having recited so many passages from other authors, some of them lengthy, in *Against Leocrates*. See George L. Cawkwell, "Lycurgus," in OCD, 872 (last word): "His disregard of proportion is shown by his inordinately long quotations from the poets."

124. Lycurgus, *Against Leocrates*, 88.

125. See Nicole Loraux, *The Invention of Athens: The Funeral Oration in the Classical City*, translated by Alan Sheridan (Cambridge, MA: Harvard University Press, 1986).

126. [Plutarch], *Ten Orators* (*Hyperides*), 848d–e (Waterfield translation): "After studying under the philosopher Plato, along with Lycurgus, and under the orator Isocrates, Hyperides embarked on a political career in Athens; this was the time when Alexander was involving himself in Greek affairs." Cf. George L. Cawkwell, "Hyperides" in Hornblower and Spawforth, *Oxford Classical Dictionary*, 717 (without apparatus), "(389–322 BC), prominent Athenian statesman, rated second only to Demosthenes amongst the Ten Orators. He studied rhetoric under Isocrates." Once again, we see the curious suppression of Plato's influence.

127. See Judson Herrman (ed.), *Hyperides, Funeral Oration: Edited with Introduction, Translation, and Commentary* (Oxford and New York: Oxford University Press, 2009).

128. For "gallant" as an alternative translation for καλόν, see *Ascent to the Beautiful*, xxvii–ix.

129. For κίνδυνος, see Hyperides, *Funeral Oration*, 40, Lycurgus, *Against Leocrates*, 130, 133, 144, and 147; cf. *Ap.* 28c3 and 28d4. For κινδυνεύειν, Hyperides, *Funeral Oration*, 17, Lycurgus, *Against Leocrates*, 143; cf. *Ap.* 28d7 and context.

130. Hyperides, *Funeral Oration*, 15; cf. Lycurgus, *Against Leocrates*, 129: "for they passed a law concerning all of those who were not willing to undergo danger for the city [τῶν μὴ 'θελόντων ὑπὲρ τῆς πατρίδος κινδυνεύειν]."

131. Lycurgus, *Against Leocrates*, 104 (on the heroes of Marathon) and 107. Cf. *Ap.* 41a8.

132. Hyperides, *Funeral Oration*, 24, Lycurgus, *Against Leocrates*, 130, 133, and 147; cf. *La.* 193a9, *Grg.* 507b8, and *Ap.* 28c4.

133. Hyperides, *Funeral Oration*, 5, Lycurgus, *Against Leocrates*, 133 and 149 (τῇ πατρίδι); cf. *Alc.1* 115b2–3.

134. Hyperides, *Funeral Oration*, 24, 34. Cf. 219d7 and *La.* 192b9.

135. Hyperides, *Funeral Oration*, 40, Lycurgus, *Against Leocrates*, 147; cf. *R.* 561c1–2, on which see *Plato the Teacher*, 352–53.

136. See especially ὑπὲρ καλῶν at Hyperides, *Funeral Oration*, 27, and πρὸ τοῦ καλοῦ at Lycurgus, *Against Leocrates*, 100.30, also καλόν (to die in Tyrtaeus) at 107.1.

137. Hyperides, *Funeral Oration*, 8; all references to Hyperides and Lycurgus are based on *Minor Attic Orators II; Lycurgus, Dinarchus, Demades, Hyperides*, translated by J. O. Burtt (Cambridge, MA: Harvard University Press, 1954).

138. *Palatine Anthology*, 7.253 (Simonides): "If to die gallantly [τὸ καλῶς θνήσκειν] is the greatest part of virtue, Then above all others, chance has allotted this to us; For speeding to encircle Greece with freedom [Ἑλλάδι γὰρ σπεύδοντες ἐλευθερίην περιθεῖναι], We rest here enjoying a fame that won't grow old." Cf. Hyperides, *Funeral Oration*, 16: τῇ Ἑλλάδι [τὴν] ἐλε[υθερ]ίαν περιθεῖναι. Note that the remains of the speech are fragmentary.

139. Hyperides, *Funeral Oration*, 15: οἱ κινδυν[εύειν ἐθ]έλοντες τοῖς σώμασ[ιν].

140. Hyperides, *Funeral Oration*, 26.

141. Hyperides, *Funeral Oration*, 40. This phrase will be revisited in the context of Danielle Allen's emphasis on προαίρεσις in the following chapter; for the present, cf. Steinbock, "Lesson in Patriotism," 287n42: "Lycurgus' phrase προηιροῦντο ἀποθνῄσκειν [*Against Leocrates*, 88] is also reminiscent of the Athenian funeral orations. The emphasis on the fallen soldiers' choice (προαίρησις) to

stand their ground and die is, for instance, used in Demosthenes' funeral oration (Dem. 60.19–21) to celebrate the fallen at Chaeronea as the true victors surpassing the victorious Macedonians."

142. Hyperides, *Funeral Oration*, 42.

143. Dionysius, *Style of Demosthenes*, 25.

144. Hyperides, *Funeral Oration*, 28; cf. Hermann, *Funeral Oration*, 96, notes (emphasis mine): "Hyperides *boldly* describes the soldiers' death as a new birth." Another adverb comes to mind: Platonically.

145. On Hyperides, *Funeral Oration*, 35, see *Minor Attic Orators II*, 534 (Burtt): "There is no surviving parallel to the passage in which the leader [sc. Leosthenes] is depicted in Hades as welcomed by the heroes of old." Without making this erroneous claim, Herrman still does not quote Plato in this connection at Funeral Oration, 102-103. Cf. *Ap.* 40e7–41c7. With *Funeral Oration*, 43, cf. *Ap.* 40c5–e7.

146. *Mx.* 246e7–247a6.

147. See *Ascent to the Beautiful*, §12, §13, and §15.

148. Judson Herrman, "The Authenticity of the Demosthenic *Funeral Oration*." *Acta antiqua Academiae Scientarum Hungaricae* 48 (2008), 171–178. See also Loraux, *The Invention of Athens*, 250–51.

149. Joh. Sykutris, "Der Demosthenische Epitaphios." *Hermes* 63, no. 2 (April 1928), 241–58," especially the argument that it lacks the rhetorical flourishes we could expect from a forger on 251; precisely the kind of thing we do find in Dinarchus, *Against Demosthenes* (see below).

150. See Blass, *Attische Beredsamkeit* 3.2, 3–4, especially "his way of thinking [*Denkweise*] is even less philosophical than Lycurgus' and in his way of life [*Lebenswandel*] he takes Plato as his model even less." This division between *Denkweise* and *Lebenswandel* depends on confining Plato's concerns to the βιός θεωρετικός despite *R.*, *Plt.*, and *Lg.* to say nothing of *Ap.* and Socrates generally.

151. See Trampedach, *Akademie*, 130–31. It is the passage in Olympiodorus that explains the greater length (130); he dismisses Wörle and Renehan in two footnotes (130n43 and 131n44), the latter leading to the claim that such connections "if not entirely random, are yet of little significance and politically meaningless." While admitting "ein allgemeiner Einfluß der platonischen παιδεία erscheint dadegen durchaus möglich," Trampedach explains the possibility of Lycurgus' closer contact with Plato to his aristocratic heritage "und bei seinem politischen Stil" (131).

152. Trampedach, *Akademie*, 131 (emphases mine): "Der Autor einer jüngst erschienen Hypereides-Bigraphie hält einen Unterricht bei Platon *zwar für denkbar*, vermag aber keine Einfüsse der Lerhen Platons auf das Werk *und das politische Leben des Hypereides* zu entdecken."

153. Johannes Engels, *Studien zur politischen Biographie des Hypereides: Athen in der Epoche der lykurgischen Reformen ind des makedonischen Universalreiches*, second edition (Munich: tudov, 1993), 14–18. Naturally the evidence goes back to Hermippus, *On the Students of Isocrates*; see Wehrli, *Hermippos*, 29–30 on frs. 67–68.

154. Engels, *Hypereides*, 16–17.

155. Engels, *Hypereides*, 16; the fragment reads: "and Socrates our ancestors punished for his words." See F. G. Kenyon (ed.), *Hyperidis Orationes et Fragmenta* (Oxford: Clarendon Press, 1906), fr. 55. Had Hyperides, like Aeschines, referred

to "Socrates the sophist," Engels would be justified in writing: "Die fast ironische, kalt-anteilslose Art, in der Hypereides in einem Fragment seiner Rede gegen Autokles 361/60 v.Chr. über die Verurteilung des von Platon immer ehrfurchtsvoll beschriebenen Sokrates spricht, läßt vermuten, daß Hypereides höchstens im Rahmen des gesamten isokrateischen Bildungsganges einige allgemeinbildende Grundstudien der platonischen Philosophie durchlaufen hat."

156. Hyperides, 6.35–40.

157. Engels, *Hypereides*, 15; cf. 15n8 with Blass, *Attische Beredsamkeit* 3.2, 3n4, Herrman, *Funeral Oration*, 108–9 (on 6.43), and Worthington, *Greek Orators II*, 221–25.

158. On which see the perfect comment of Anton Westermann, *Quaestionum Demosthenicarum particular tertia* (Leipzig: Barth, 1834), 112–13; he ends equally well by quoting Pausanias 2.33.3–5.

159. Schaefer, *Demosthenes* 3.1, 310; cf. Ian Worthington, "Demosthenes' (In) Activity during the Reign of Alexander the Great" in Worthington, *Demosthenes: Statesman and Orator*, 90–113; cf. Ian Worthington (ed.), *Greek Orators II; Dinarchus, Hyperides: An Introduction, Text, Translation and Commentary* (Warminster, UK: Aris & Phillips, 1999), 8: "Perhaps it is now that we can detect a split between Demosthenes and the more militant Hyperides."

160. Cf. Worthington, *Greek Orators II*, 190-91 (on 13) and 191–92 (on 14), especially: "I suggest that there could well be some truth in this," and E. Badian, "Harpalus." *Journal of Hellenic Studies* 81 (1961), 16–43, goes much further on 38–39. But note that Worthington's amiable exculpation of Demosthenes on the basis of 5.13, while rejecting Badian's more radical proposal in Ian Worthington, *A Historical Commentary on Dinarchus: Rhetoric and Conspiracy in Later Fourth-Century Athens* (Ann Arbor: University of Michigan Press, 1992), 66–68, maintains that "Hyperides is likely distorting facts in order to point more blame at Demosthenes or to show his ability to switch from one statement to another" (190); for this misconception, his work on Dinarchus had prepared him.

161. Given these later references to Demades and the use of third-person plurals, I take ἐδημηγόρεις and δραπέτης at 5.17 to refer to him, not Demosthenes. Since it was Hyperides who proposed that Demosthenes deliver the Funeral Oration after Chaeronea, he would scarcely recycle the slander of Aeschines that Demosthenes was the δραπέτης who had deserted his post, while Demades fled rather than stand trial (Badian, "Harpalus," 35).

162. Hyperides, *Against Demosthenes*, 14 (Worthington translation for the first sentence): "as if all of did not know that no one destroys the type of man that can be bought, but men plot to get out of the way by any and all means the man who cannot be persuaded or corrupted by bribes. And it seems that there is a danger lest you, Demosthenes, are inexorable [ἀπαραίτητος] and impervious [ἄπειστος] to bribery." The danger was to Demosthenes, and Worthington's comment at *Greek Orators II*, 182 (on Dinarchus 1.113) is preferable to the Badian's two amazing sentences (beginning with "Nor—whether Demosthenes was guilty or innocent") at "Harpalus," 39.

163. See Dionysius of Halicarnassus, *Dinarchus*, 1; why does he begin with this long quotation?

164. Westermann, *Quaestionum Demosthenicarum*, 118–24.

165. Schaefer, *Demosthenes* 3.1, 309.
166. Its authenticity is upheld if not defended in Worthington, *Dinarchus*, 12n28 and 81, ostensibly on the authority of Dionysius.
167. Dionysius of Halicarnassus, *Dinarchus*, 2, and [Plutarch], *Lives of the Ten Orators*, 850b.
168. Schaefer, *Demosthenes* 3.1, 308–310, especially 309: "for the lack of originality and lack of character is characteristic of Dinarchus, and in this speech also he is the representative of a debased eloquence."
169. See especially G. L. Cawkwell, "The Crowning of Demosthenes." *Classical Quarterly* 19, no. 1 (May 1969), 163–180, on 179: "When Agis appealed for help, Demosthenes faced the most important decision of his career, either to urge his country to fight for liberty or merely to continue to hope for a Persian victory. Demosthenes chose the safe course. That is clear enough from what Aeschines and Dinarchus say." Cf. the superior comment of Schaefer, *Demosthenes* 3.1, 193: "How Demosthenes comported himself toward the negotiations about an alliance with Sparta, we can gather only to some extent from the words of his enemies." As the passage quoted first in this note may begin to suggest, Cawkwell is one of the most effective of these.
170. But note that it is Demosthenes who is pro-war, and thus breaks with Lycurgus in Allen, *Why Plato Wrote*, 131–33.
171. Cawkwell, "Crowning," 176 ("Nothing and worse than nothing"); cf. E. Badian, "Agis III." *Hermes* 95, no. 2 (1967), 170-192, on 183: "It is largely Athens that is to blame for the failure of the war, and within Athens Demosthenes—the only man who might have carried the people with him." An authentic *On the Treaty with Alexander* is preferable, and the speech's mixed message is more consistent with the totality of the evidence than the conclusions of Cawkwell and Badian. See Schaefer, *Demosthenes* 3.1, 186–93, especially "kein sicherer Schluß" on 191, and even more so 189: "Und was den Charakter der Rede betreffe, so vermisse man die lautere Offenheit des Demosthenes, die treffende Rüge und den überzeugenden Freimuth; die ganze Rede liege wie unter einem Schleier, sie wolle gerade mit der Sprache heraus und wieder nicht, sie ermuntere zum Kriege und fürchte es rein heraus zu sagen." Cf. Plutarch, *Demosthenes*, 24.1; Diodorus Siculus, 17.62.7; and Blass, *Attische Beredsamkeit* 3.2, 124.
172. Chris Carey, Mike Edwards, Zoltán Farkas, Judson Herrman, László Horváth, Gyula Mayer, Tamás Mészáros, P. J. Rhodes and Natalie Tchernetska, "Fragments of Hyperides' *Against Diondas* from the Archimedes Palimpsest." *Zeitschrift für Papyrologie und Epigraphik* 165 (2008), 1-19.
173. Cf. fr. 96 in Kenyon, *Hyperidis Orationes*, with Carey et al., *Against Diondas*, 18 (on p. 6, 11–12); see also László Horváth (ed.), *Der Neue Hypereides: Textedition, Studien und Erläuterungen* (Berlin: De Gruyter, 2015), 152.
174. Eusebius, *Praeparatio evangelica*, 10.3.14–15, quoted in Horváth, *Neue Hypereides*, 69.
175. Judson Herrman, "Hyperides' *Against Diondas* and the Rhetoric of Revolt." *Bulletin of the Institute of Classical Studies* 52 (2009), 175–185; note especially "the tragic nature of Demosthenes' appeal," "chose to sacrifice themselves for the good of the state," and "an inescapable more obligation" on 177.

176. Herrman, "Rhetoric of Revolt," 180–183, climaxing with: "The complaints expressed by Hyperides in the *Against Diondas* about the Athenian situation in the 330s anticipate the position taken by the speaker of [Demosthenes] 17, who may have been Hyperides himself." For Libanius, see Butcher and Rennie, *Demosthenis Orationes*, 1.211.

177. Carey et al., *Against Diondas*, p. 3, 9–22; for background, see Horváth, *Neue Hypereides*, 24–30; cf. Herrman, "Rhetoric of Revolt," 179: "Diondas' prosecutions, which Hyperides lists at length, were considered above; this information serves as new evidence for political factionalism in the 330s, with some groups of anti-Macedonian politicians, such as Demosthenes, Hyperides, and Lycurgus facing off against those who would advocate a more conciliatory policy, such as Aeschines or Demades."

178. Kenyon, *Hyperidis Orationes*, iii.

179. See Churchill Babington (ed.), *The Oration of Hyperides Against Demosthenes* (London: Parker and Bell, 1850), xv. See also David Whitehead, *Hypereides, The Forensic Speeches: Introduction, Translation, and Commentary* (Oxford: Oxford University Press, 2000).

180. Worthington, *Greek Orators II*, 30.

181. André Laks and Glenn W. Most (eds.), *Early Greek Philosophy*, nine volumes (Cambridge, MA: Harvard University Press, 2016); Gorgias, Socrates, and Prodicus are chapters 32, 33, and 34 in volume 8 ("The Sophists. Part One").

182. Glenn W. Most, "'A Cock for Asclepius.'" *Classical Quarterly* 43, no. 1 (1993), 96-111; cf. Laurence Lampert, *How Socrates Became Socrates: A Study of Plato's Phaedo, Parmenides, and Symposium* (Chicago, IL: University of Chicago Press, 2021), 86 (quoted in chapter 5 below).

183. Hyperides, *Funeral Oration*, 28. Note the orator's refusal to apply the word θάνατος when describing "the virtue *of those who have not been destroyed*," and "who thus for the sake of beautiful things [ὑπὲρ τῶν καλῶν] have departed this life, but they will have the life *of those taking part in an everlasting band* [τάξις]" (27). The Old Academy, along with Achilles (*Ap.* 28b6-29a2), stood at the forefront of this τάξις (cf. *Ap.* 28d6 and 29a2).

184. See Craig Cooper, "A Note on Antipater's Demand of Hyperides and Demosthenes." *Ancient History Bulletin* 7, no. 3 (1993), 130–135.

185. Aristotle, *Metaphysics* 1.9 (991b3–4).

CHAPTER 3

1. See Arlene W. Saxonhouse, *Athenian Democracy: Modern Mythmakers and Ancient Theorists* (Notre Dame, IN: University of Notre Dame Press, 1996), and "Democracy, Equality, and *Eidê*: A Radical View from Book 8 of Plato's *Republic*." *American Political Science Review* 92 no. 2 (1998), 273–83; Monoson, *Plato's Democratic Entanglements*, 165–68; David L. Roochnik, *Beautiful City: The Dialectical Character of Plato's* Republic (Ithaca, NY: Cornell University Press, 2003), Greg Recco, *Athens Victorious; Democracy on Plato's* Republic (Lanham, MD: Lexington

Books, 2007), and Jill Frank, *Poetic Justice: Rereading Plato's* Republic (Chicago, IL: University of Chicago Press, 2018).

2. Cf. Max Pohlenz, *Die Stoa*, two volumes, first edition (Göttingen: Vandenhoeck & Ruprecht, 1949), 1.357, and Barrie Fleet (trans. and ed.), Plotinus, *Ennead IV.8; On the Descent of the Soul into Bodies* (Las Vegas, NV: Parmenides, 2012), 25: "In Plotinus' own case there was clearly little possibility for him or any other philosopher to take part in the government of the Roman world, and we would have to say that the compulsion for him to 'descend into bodies' would be a personal rather than a civic moral compunction." This theme will be considered in a work in progress entitled "Plotinus the Master and the Apotheosis of Imperial Platonism."

3. For the role of equating the pleasant with the good in refuting Protagoras, see *Ascent to the Beautiful*, 71–78.

4. Cf. the three uses of πράττειν τε καὶ λέγειν at Xenophon, *Memorabilia*, 4.2.1–6.

5. For a useful collection of relevant fragments and commentary, see Dörrie and Baltes, *Platonismus*, 111–17 and 369–76.

6. See William L. Benoit, "Isocrates and Plato on Rhetoric and Rhetorical Education." *Rhetoric Society Quarterly* 21, no. 1 (Winter 1991), 60–71, and John Bake (1787–1864), "De aemulatione Platonem inter et Isocratem" in *Scholia Hypomnemata*, volume 3, 27–47 (Leiden: Luchtmans, 1844). More simply, see A. E. Taylor, *Plato: The Man and his Work*, fourth edition (Cleveland, OH: World Publishing, 1956), 5: "Isocrates, like Plato, believed in training young men for public life." Benoit can't seem to believe this (67): despite "the curriculum of Plato's Academy was surely broader than its [Isocratean] counterpart," nevertheless: "Plato's Academy seems to have more in common with graduate education as we envision it today than Isocrates' school."

7. Cf. Bollansée, *Hermippus*, 83: "The school [sc. of Isocrates] became a huge success and would, in the long run, prove to be his most lasting achievement: later tradition even credited him (together with Plato, of all people!) with having taught all the leading figures of the Greek literary and political scene of the fourth century."

8. See especially Isocrates, 2.5–9.

9. Cf. Benoit, "Isocrates and Plato," 67: "Although the *Gorgias* was apparently written about the time the Academy was opened, we have no record that rhetoric was a subject [taught in the Academy] until Aristotle began lecturing on it in the afternoon, at least twenty years later."

10. See Harry Mortimer Hubbell, *The Influence of Isocrates on Cicero, Dionysius, and Aristides* (New Haven: Yale University Press, 1914), xi (will be quoted in the text below).

11. See especially 1.28–33, 4.275, and especially 15.272–77, with particular attention to πλεονεξία (275), the benign profession (276), and the revealing conclusion (277): "to speak well and to think will inevitably accompany those who comport themselves to speeches in a wisdom-loving and honor-loving way." See Hubbell, *Influence of Isocrates*, 37-38 for comment.

12. Hubbell, *Influence of Isocrates*, 52.

13. Hubbell, *Influence of Isocrates*, 54.

14. Hubbell, *Influence of Isocrates*, 61.
15. See David Trapp, "With All Due Respect to Plato: The *Platonic Orations* of Aelius Aristides." *Transactions of the American Philological Association* 150, no. 1 (Spring 2020), 85–113; see especially 104: "both Aristides and Dionysius are in the business of unfavorable comparisons between Plato and Demosthenes, with Aristides again expanding what is for Dionysius a stylistic judgment into a broader assessment of character and motivation."
16. Hubbell, *Influence of Isocrates*, xi–xii.
17. Cf. Demosthenes 21.143–50.
18. For F. D. E. Schleiermacher's excision of *Alc.1*, see the introduction to *Ascent to the Beautiful*.
19. See Friedrich Daniel Ernst Schleiermacher, *Über die Philosophie Platons*, edited by Peter M. Steiner with contributions by Andreas Arndt and Jörg Jantzen (Hamburg: Felix Meiner, 1996), 324–26.
20. See Xenophon, *Memorabilia*, 4.2.1–8; in his pursuit of Euthydemus, Socrates contrives to make himself well known to the young man and too often be in his company before speaking with him for the first time
21. See Edward J. Power, "Class Size and Pedagogy in Isocrates' School." *History of Education Quarterly* 6, no. 4 (Winter 1966), 22–32.
22. See Ross, *Aristotelis Fragmenta Selecta*, 111.
23. For a nice statement of the position, see Zeller, *Plato and the Older Academy*, 25–28, beginning well with "concerning his [sc. Plato's] manner of instruction tradition tells us nothing," and ending poorly with "that friendly life-in-common to which he himself had been accustomed in the Socratic circle and the Pythagorean Society," naturally via "a discourse on the Good, published by Aristotle" (26n33). Preferable is Edelstein, *Plato's Seventh Letter*, 167: "The dialogues are, after all, the only indubitable source of information for a reconstruction of Plato's views."
24. Ross, *Aristotelis Fragmenta Selecta*, 23–24 (from *Nerinthus*), on which see Riginos, *Platonica*, 184-85. Given Aristotle's frequent references to the dialogues, his writings constitute the oldest evidence that they were read outside of the Academy.
25. In addition to Schaefer, *Demosthenes*, 1.292, and Engels, *Hypereides*, 15, see Maurice Croiset, *Des idées morales dans l'eloquence politique de Demosthenes* (Montpellier: J. Martel Ainè, 1874), 32-37, especially 35: "Je me contente de croire que l'autorité de Platon et la beauté de ses idées ont encouragé, dans l'âme du jeune Démosthène, certaines dispositions naturelles. C'est *le sens de l'idéal* [emphasis mine], qui manque le plus aux hommes d'affaires." Cf. Hug, "Aeschines und Plato," 437: "Auch Demosthenes ist von Hermippos an als Schüler Platons bezeichnet worden. Von anderer Seite wurde dies Behauptung dahin ermassigt, dass Demosthenes in bestimmten Reden bestimmte Platonische Vorbilder nachgeahmt habe. So sollte insbesondere die *Kranzrede* in ihrer Anlage der Platonischen *Apologie* nachgebildet sein. Pseudodionys. *Ars rhetor*. 8, anderes bringt Quint. XII, 24, 10. Das Unhaltbare dieser Voraussetzung einer förmlichen Entlehnung oder Nachahmung ist von Funkhänel und Schäfer [citations deleted] hinreichend dargethan worden, womit jetzt auch übereinstimmt Steinhart [citation deleted]. So wahrscheinlich es ist dass Demosthenes die eine oder die andere von den Schriften Platos gelesen hat, so wenig lässt sich dies von irgend einer derselben

genau beweisen. In Demosthenes spiegelt und reproducirt sich in eigenartiger Weise die Ganze Bildung seiner Zeit, und er hat auch diese ganze Bildung, wenn wir von der damals beginnenden Gelehrsamkeit absehen, auf sich wirken lassen."

26. See my *The Relay Race of Virtue: Plato's Debts to Xenophon* (Albany: State University of New York Press, 2022) for the suggestion that *Ap.* and *Grg.* are the two most likely candidates for pre-Academy publication.

27. Themistius also preserves the following anecdote described in Riginos, *Platonica*, 185 (her translation): "The *Apology* brought Zeno from Phoenicia to the Stoa Poikile." Plato had been dead for more than forty years at the time.

28. For this important insight, I am grateful to Dorothea Frede.

29. See *Ascent to the Beautiful*, xiv–xxi.

30. Cf. Guthrie, *History of Greek Philosophy*, 4.235, and *Ascent to the Beautiful*, 34–51.

31. See *Ascent to the Good*, §4.

32. See *Revival of Platonism in Cicero's Late Philosophy*, 95–97 and 138–39.

33. See *Plato the Teacher*, §7.

34. See *Ascent to the Beautiful*,

35. See *Guardians in Action*, §6.

36. See Gregory Vlastos, *Socrates: Ironist and Moral Philosopher* (Cambridge, UK: Cambridge University Press, 1991), 111-13; cf. 111n21 and 113n29. For further discussion, see *Ascent to the Beautiful*, §4.

37. See *Ascent to the Beautiful*, xi-xii, on Plato's use of "performative self-contradiction."

38. See *Ascent to the Beautiful*, §14; *Smp.* immediately follows *Ion* and *Mx.* in the reconstructed Reading Order; for the rhetorical power of the Magnet Speech in *Ion*, see §12.

39. Plutarch, *Life of Demosthenes*, 5.5.

40. See *Ascent to the Beautiful*, 52–53.

41. See *Ascent to the Beautiful*, §15.

42. See *Ascent to the Good*, §7.

43. See *Plato the Teacher*, chapter 1, especially §4.

44. See *Ascent to the Beautiful*, §5.

45. See E. R. Dodds (ed.), *Plato: Gorgias: A Revised Text with Introduction and Commentary* (Oxford: Clarendon Press, 1959), 335–36.

46. See *Ascent to the Good*, introduction.

47. See *Ascent to the Good*, lx–lxi.

48. See Jessica Moss, *Plato's Epistemology: Being and Seeming* (Oxford and New York: Oxford University Press, 2021), especially 181–90.

49. Se *Plato the Teacher*, §11.

50. See Aristotle, *Metaphysics*, 1.6 (987b14–18) and W. D. Ross (ed.), *Aristotle's Metaphysics*, two volumes (Oxford: Clarendon Press, 1924), 1.166–68, in which the initial list of citations outweighs in importance the remainder of the lemma.

51. See *Plato the Teacher*, §12.

52. See *Plato the Teacher*, §13.

53. For a recent defense of the "political" or rather city-oriented reading of *R.*, see Vegetti, "How and why did the *Republic* become apolitical?" in Noburu Notomi and Luc Brisson (eds.), *Dialogues on Plato's* Politeia (*Republic*). *Selected*

Papers from the Ninth Symposium Platonicum, 3–15 (Sankt Augustin: Academia, 2013).

54. See Aristotle, *Politics*, 2.6 (1264b39–1265a1).

55. As in George Klosko, *The Development of Plato's Political Theory*, second edition (Oxford: Oxford University Press, 2006), but standard at least since Ernest Barker, *The Political Thought of Plato and Aristotle* (New York: G. P. Putnam's, 1906).

56. See my "In Defense of Plato's Intermediates"; the crucial text is *Prm.* 143a2-9, which links the One of the arithmetic lesson of *Republic* 7 (*R.* 525d8–526a7) to διάνοια as described in the Divided Line; the "archaic" role of the One is merely implied by "the odd and the even" and "the three kinds of angles" at *R.* 510c3–5. Insofar as it helps the reader to recognize that "One" is not a even a Form—and thus on an altogether lower ontological level than the Idea of the Good—the second part of *Parmenides* constitutes a gymnastic preparation for considering the Good, the Just, and the Beautiful (*Prm.* 135c8–d1).

57. See *Guardians in Action*, §13.

58. See *Guardians on Trial*, §16.

59. See *Plato the Teacher*, §22.

60. *R.* 520b5-c5.

61. See *Plato the Teacher*, §16.

62. In addition to *Plato the Teacher*, 385, see Jeffrey S. Rusten, "Structure, Style, and Sense in Interpreting Thucydides: The Soldier's Choice (Thuc. 2.42.4)." *Harvard Studies in Classical Philology* 90 (1986), 49–76, on 75–76 (last word): "This climactic sentence is written in Thucydides' most ambitious style, with structural repetition to mark emphasis, variation of detail avoid a tedious predictability, and, above all, the insistent superimposing of many contrasting views of the same action onto a single crowded canvas. A simpler account might have been more effective; but the historian-general, who must have seen many deaths in battle, was surely entitled-in the sole section of the epitaphios when he places the dead directly before us-to view them in the process of reaching a complex, dignified, and intensely rational *decision* to offer their lives. Both before and after he does so, it is stressed that Athenians must pay close attention: the city may one day demand from them to the sacrifice of their individuality to its survival."

63. Xenophon, *Memorabilia*, 3.6; Charmides appears in 3.7.

64. See *Relay Race of Virtue*, chapter 1.

65. *Plato the Teacher*, §16, see also 38–42, 95, 100, 181, 236, 351, 368–69, and 358.

66. Xenophon, *Memorabilia*, 2.1.21–34

67. Xenophon, *Memorabilia*, 2.1.8-20.

68. Since Allen begins with Aristotle—who "gave the term *prohairesis* a substantial conceptual structure connected to his theories of agency, responsibility, and character" ("Talking about Revolution," 185)—she does not consider the possibility of a Platonic origin even though she finds her strongest evidence in Demosthenes (210–11, 212–13) and Lycurgus (211–12), and concludes on 216: "In Athens at the end of the fifth and through the mid-fourth century there was a revolutionary change in how leaders were legitimated." The best evidence in Aristotle for the term's Platonic origin is *Metaphysics* 4.2; 1004b22–24 (W. D. Ross translation modified): "For sophistic and dialectic turn on the same class of things

as philosophy, but this differs from dialectic in the nature of the faculty required and from sophistic in respect of the choice [προαίρεσις] of the philosophic life." Ross translated προαίρεσις with "purpose."

69. Kuhn plays a major role in Allen, "Talking about Revolution," 189–95;

70. Allen, "Talking about Revolution," 211; I have corrected typos in the first sentence.

71. Cf. Isocrates 4.289–90 (Norlin translation modified): "For, while in the prime of vigor, when most men of their age are most inclined to indulge their passions, they [although Isocrates is referring to his own students, what he has to say applies at least equally well to Plato's] have disdained a life of pleasure; when they might have saved expense and lived softly, they have elected to pay out money [with this as an exception, of course; see also the role of ὁ ἐπιστατήσων in what follows the quotation] and submit to toil; and, though having emerged only recently from being children [ἄρτι δ' ἐκ παίδων], they have understood what most of their elders do not know: that it is necessary for the one governing his youth rightly and worthily and making a beautiful start in life [καλὴ ἀρχὴ τοῦ βίου], to practice the care of oneself [αὑτοῦ . . . ἡ ἐπιμελεία; cf. *Alc.1* 127e9 and 128d11] rather than of one's things [τὰ αὑτοῦ; cf. *Alc.1* 128d4]."

72. Prevented by his Sign from practicing politics in the traditional way (*Ap.* 31c4–e1; cf. *R.* 496c3–5)—by addressing the Assembly—Socrates regarded himself as the only πολιτικός Athens (*Grg.* 521b6–8; cf. *Men.* 100a1–2), and paid the penalty for being so (*Grg.* 522b3–c3).

73. See *Plato the Teacher*, §28.

74. See *Guardians in Action*, §3.

75. See *Guardians in Action*, §18.

76. *Palatine Anthology*, 7.253 (Simonides): "If to die beautifully [τὸ καλῶς θνῄσκειν] is the greatest part of virtue, Then above all others, chance has allotted this to us; For speeding to encircle Greece with freedom, We rest here enjoying a fame that won't grow old."

77. On *R.* 621d2–3, see *Ascent to the Good*, 77 and 471n55.

78. See *Guardians in Action*, §2.

79. On which, see *Guardians on Trial*, §14.

80. See *Guardians in Action*, §1.

81. See *Ascent to the Beautiful*, §4, and *Ascent to the Good*, §3.

82. See *Guardians in Action*, §7.

83. For βάσανος as "touchstone" (cf. *Grg.* 486d2–7), "the use of this as a test," and "test, trial of genuineness," see LSJ; also *Plato the Teacher*, §8, and *Guardians on Trial*, §7.

84. See *Guardians in Action*, §3, for the role of the Demiurge, the World Soul, and the Chora in this process.

85. Aristotle, *Metaphysics*, 1.6 (987b2); cf. Cicero, *Tusculan Disputations*, 5.10.

86. For Aristotle's references to *Ti.* in comparison with the other Platonic dialogues, see Hermann Bonitz, *Index Aristotelicus* (Berlin: Reimer, 1870), 598–99.

87. Aristotle, *Physics*, (209b11–12).

88. See *Guardians in Action*, chapter 4.

89. See *Guardians in Action*, §8.

90. See *Guardians on Trial*, xiii–iv.

91. See *Guardians on Trial*, chapter 2.
92. See *Guardians on Trial*, §2.
93. See *Guardians in Action*, §2.
94. On which see *Guardians on Trial*, §4.
95. Cf. Xenophon, *Cyropaedia*, 1.1.2–3 and 8.2.14.
96. See *Guardians on Trial*, chapter 4.
97. For the connection between *Lg.* and *Cri.* in the Reading Order, see *Guardians on Trial*, §10.
98. See *Guardians on Trial*, §6.
99. See *Guardians on Trial*, §16.
100. See Aristotle, *Metaphysics*, 1.9 (99ab3–4).
101. See my "Plato's *Phaedo* and 'the Art of Glaucus': Transcending the Distortions of Developmentalism." *Archai* 31 (2021), 1–22.
102. Hyperides, 6.40.
103. Cf. Moses I. Finley, "Plato and Practical Politics" in his *Discoveries and Controversies*, 73–88 (London: Chatto & Windus, 1968), on 82: "it was in the fourth century that Athens really became the 'school of Hellas,' much more so, in a strict sense, than when Pericles used the phrase."

CHAPTER 4

1. For a good example of his ability to create a world, see Sealey, "Callistratus," 195–98; although "Demosthenes" is missing from the text, the notes tell a different story.
2. This observation is intended to be perfectly general, not author-specific and boastful. My incapacity to write such a book must be clearly understood: I came late to the study of Demosthenes, and aside from an attempt to appreciate *De Corona* in Greek in graduate school and an affection for the *Third Philippic* in translation, I first read Demosthenes while writing this book, and did so thanks to *Demosthenes*, eight volumes, translated by J. H. Vince, C. A. Vince, A. T. Murray, N. W. DeWitt, and N.J. DeWitt (Cambridge, MA: Harvard University Press, 1926–1949), hereafter "the Loeb *Demosthenes*," and Judson Herrman (ed.), *Demosthenes, Selected Political Speeches* (Cambridge, UK: Cambridge University Press, 2019), a book that fulfilled its author's admirable purpose in my case (ix): "The primary audience for this book are advanced students who may have little experience with Demosthenic Greek."
3. With respect to authenticity, my prejudice, as already indicated, is to be unashamedly if inconclusively inclusive. In order to keep notes to a minimum, all parenthetical citations in this chapter will refer by number to the sixty-one speeches preserved under the name "Demosthenes." Since the *Exordia* is not included among the sixty-one, references to it—later in the chapter and clearly marked—will be by preamble numbers 1–56.
4. The need to cite Erick Bethe, *Demosthenis scriptorum corpus ubi et qua aetate collectum editumque sunt* (Rostock: Adler, 1897) will justify "understudied." Bringing to the study of the Loeb *Demosthenes* a strong prior interest in a pedagogical

conception of Reading Order, I was repeatedly struck by the felicity with which the ancient editor had arranged these speeches, and in addition to defending (primarily in the notes) as both pedagogically pleasing and instructive the order created by Callimachus or whoever else it was who is responsible for it, I will also reconsider problems of authenticity in the context of that defense.

5. See the author's "Cicero and the Fourth Triumvirate: Gruen, Syme and Strasburger" in Altman (ed.), *Brill's Companion to the Reception of Cicero*, 215–46 (Leiden and Boston: Brill, 2015).

6. Cf. Simon Hornblower, "George Cawkwell's Contribution to Ancient History at Oxford" in Michael A. Flower and Mark Toher (eds.), *Georgica: Greek Studies in Honour of George Cawkwell*, 1–12 (University of London: Institute of Classical Studies, 1991), on 2 ("the allusion to George's fellow New Zealander Sir Ronald Syme is not unique; there are other, perhaps unconscious [!], echoes in George's clipped prose") and W. V. Harris, "Ernst Badian; 1925-2011" in *Biographical Memoirs of Fellows of the British Academy* 16 (2017), 3–17, on 4: "Cawkwell's vigorous personality must also have had a considerable influence. Clearly a third New Zealand scholar, Ronald Syme, who had become Camden Professor of Ancient History at Oxford in 1949, was a powerful inspiration; he suggested the subject of Badian's doctoral thesis and supervised it."

7. Hornblower, "Cawkwell's Contribution," 2: "George's first set of articles was on the Peace of Philokrates. He also dealt with the periods immediately before it ('Defence of Olynthus') and immediately after ('Demosthenes' Policy after the Peace . . .', a period also covered in the piece on Euboia in *Phoenix* 1978). He returned to the subject of the Peace itself in the 1978 book on Philip and in an article in the late 1970's, but his position was, no surprise, unchanged. The message was, crudely, that Demosthenes' policies were mistaken, and his testimony suspect."

8. He has competition, though: Engelbert Drerup, *Aus seiner alten Advokatenrepublik (Demosthenes und seine Zeit)* (Paderborn, 1916) had wrested the crown from Julius Beloch and Eduard Meyer; cf. the latter's "Isokrates' zweiter Brief an Philipp und Demosthenes' zweite Philippika." *Sitzberichte der Preußischen Akademie; philosophisch-historischen Classe* (June 1909), 758–79, on 769–70 (especially 769n1) and Karl Julius Beloch, *Griechische Geschichte*, second edition, volume 3, part 1 (Berlin and Leipzig: De Gruyter, 1922).

9. Ernst Badian, "The Road to Prominence" in Ian Worthington (ed.), *Demosthenes: Statesman and Orator*, 9-44 (London and New York: Routledge, 2000).

10. As in Harris, *Aeschines of Athens*; see especially 114-18, climaxing with "astonishing."

11. George Cawkwell, *Philip of Macedon* (London and Poston: Faber and Faber, 1978).

12. See Niall Livingstone, *A Commentary on Isocrates' Busiris* (Leiden–Boston–Cologne: Brill, 2001); especially 56–66 on the relationship between *Phdr.* and *Busiris*.

13. See Harvey Yunis, "Politics as Literature: Demosthenes and the Burden of the Athenian Past." *Arion* 8, no. 1 (Spring-Summer 2000), 97–118, on 116n9; in addition to J. R. Ellis, G. T. Griffith, and N. G. L. Hammond (cited by Yunis), his students include Badian, Sealey, Hornblower, and Christopher Pelling. Yunis's note is attached to this on 101: "There are other scholars whose work on Demos-

thenes is in the same vein as Cawkwell's ['who produced in the 1960s and 1970s a formidable body of work that completely reversed the traditional assessment of Demosthenes'], but it suffices here to speak only of him, the most prominent among them [note 9]."

14. See Sarah Janet Alexandrina Bremner, "Athenian Ideology in Demosthenes' Deliberative Oratory: Haling the Dēmos" (PhD thesis: University of Birmingham, 2016).

15. See Badian, "Road to Prominence," 33: "a young and ambitious orator's seeking a cause in which he can advocate Athenian activism: against Sparta, against Philip, against Caria or even the King." Note that "good" means "bad" on 23: "Demosthenes had good personal reasons for attacking both Androtion and Timocrates." Note the communion with Sealey.

16. On "revisionist," see Hornblower, "Cawkwell's Contributions," 1–2: "a fashionable word not in the Cawkwell vocabulary."

17. Sarah Bremner, "The Rhetoric of Athenian Identity in Demosthenes' Early Assembly Speeches." *Greek, Roman, and Byzantine Studies* 60 (2020), 565: "Demosthenes presents the Assembly as apathetic, self-interested, and neglectful of their duty as Athenians; in failing to act in a manner worthy of the city they have failed to offer the same protection as their ancestors did to other cities and to their own interests."

18. Bremner, "Athenian Identity," 550.

19. See G. L. Cawkwell, "Demosthenes' Policy after the Peace of Philocrates. I." *Classical Quarterly* 13, no. 1 (May 1963), 120–38, and "Demosthenes' Policy after the Peace of Philocrates. II." *Classical Quarterly* 13, no. 2 (November 1963), 200–213. The comparatively mild version in part I, 121: "In his distrust of Philip Demosthenes was essentially right and no one who believes in liberty will question it. What does requires discussion is whether the means he chose to secure his end were the right ones. This article argues that in 344/3 he chose the wrong means and that the cause of Greek freedom was not best served by its most famous champion." Cf. II, 209: "By insisting that Philip was wholly untrustworthy, Demosthenes and the war-party involved their country in a war which ended in disaster." In Cicero's case, see Ingo Gildenhard, *Creative Eloquence: The Construction of Reality in Cicero's Speeches* (Oxford, UK: Oxford University Press, 2011), 390 (last word): "Cicero conceived of himself as standing in the front line of the war against internal enemies; but, not least by urging the senate into military confrontation with Antony, he may have been one of the gravediggers of the republic."

20. See Christopher Tuplin, "Demosthenes' *Olynthiacs* and the Character of the Demegoric Corpus." *Historia* 47, no. 3 (1998), 276–320.

21. On the evidence for attribution to Callimachus, see Hermann Sauppe, *Epistola critica ad Godofredum Hermannum philologorum princeps* (Leipzig: Weidmann, 1841), 49: "Eum ordinem orationum demosthenicarum, quem nunc habemus, a Callimacho institutum esse docent ea, quae Dionysius [sc. of Halicarnassus; citation deleted] refert." Cf. Schaefer, *Demosthenes*, 3.2.317–22, Blass, *Attische Beredsamkeit*, 3.1.51, and Bethe, *Demosthenis scriptorum corpus*, 3–6. Strictly for the sake of convenience, I will refer to the editor and pedagogue responsible for the τάξις one might call "Demosthenis ordo scriptorum" as "Callimachus."

22. As occurs in the analysis performed in Blass, *Attische Beredsamkeit*, 3.1.52–58.

23. See Lionel Pearson, "The Development of Demosthenes as a Political Orator." *Phoenix* 18, no. 2 (Summer 1964), 95–109, and Cecil Wooten, *A Commentary on Demosthenes' Philippic I: With Rhetorical Analysis of Philippics II and III* (Oxford: Oxford University Press, 2008), 137–66.

24. Wooten, *Philippic I*, 16 (abbreviation expanded); cf. Bremner, "Athenian Identity," 562-66.

25. Cf. Edmund M. Burke, "The Early Political Speeches of Demosthenes: Elite Bias in Response to Economic Crisis." *Classical Antiquity* 21, no. 2 (2002), 165–94, on 189: "adjust his voice, to become less partisan in tone, both prerequisites if he was to lead the city, elite and demos both, against Philip."

26. This is the thesis of T. T. B. Ryder, "Demosthenes and Philip II" in Ian Worthington (ed.), *Demosthenes: Statesman and Orator*, 45–89 (London and New York: Routledge, 2000); note the hint of independence from Cawkwell on 52: "This is not to say that Demosthenes was not right to urge the Athenians to take serious precautions against Philip's threat." Indeed 56–66—up to his compromise with Cawkwellism at the end of this passage—is a clear and balanced account of the most confusing phase of the story of Demosthenes.

27. See especially Pearson's account of *On the Symmories* (14) in "Demosthenes' Development," 96–97, including the role of Thucydides and "slow and careful reading."

28. In 550n23, Bremner, "Athenian Identity," appropriately cites Christina Tarnopolsky, *Prudes, Perverts, and Tyrants: Plato's Gorgias and the Politics of Shame* (Princeton, NJ: Princeton University Press, 2010).

29. See Allison Das, "Medical Imagery in the Speeches of Demosthenes" (Ph.D. dissertation: University of Washington, 2015), starting with 9: "Although Thucydides is arguably the first that we know of to directly compare the politician-orator with the physician, Plato uses this analogy so frequently that it can be considered distinctively Platonic." On 9.33 specifically, cf. 118: "The specific reason that Demosthenes criticizes Hippocratic dietetics is that it keeps the patient in a sort of limbo, for it neither kills nor restores his health" with 26: "The Hippocratics, as Plato (disparagingly) points out, were the first to manipulate diet, sex, sleep, and exercise for both preventive and therapeutic purposes." In general, see 13: "These similarities between Plato and the orators may have contributed to the later biographical tradition that Plato taught some of them."

30. Demosthenes 3.36.

31. See Josiah Ober, *Mass and Elite in Democratic Athens: Rhetoric, Ideology, and the Power of the People* (Princeton, NJ: Princeton University Press, 1989), 318–24; S. Sara Monoson, *Plato's Democratic Entanglements: Athenian Politics and the Practice of Philosophy* (Princeton, NJ: Princeton University Press, 2000), 60–63 and 161–78, especially 164: "Socrates' characterization of true statesmanship in the *Gorgias* has much in common with the political role of speaking with *parrhesia* glorified in the Athenian self-image [note the overlap with Bremner's 'Athenian identity']"; Arlene W. Saxonhouse, "The Practice of Parrhêsia" (85–99) and "The Trial of Socrates" (100–26) in *Free Speech and Democracy in Ancient Athens* (Cambridge, UK: Cambridge University Press, 2006); Elizabeth Markovits, *The Politics of Sincerity: Plato, Frank Speech, and Democratic Judgment* (University Park: Pennsylvania

State University Press, 2008), 65–68; Ryan K. Balot, *Courage in the Democratic Polis: Ideology and Critique in Classical Athens* (Oxford and New York: Oxford University Press, 2014), 47–63; and Daniel J. Kapust, *Flattery and the History of Political Thought: That Glib and Oily Art* (Cambridge, UK: Cambridge University Press, 2018), 32–38.

32. In embryo, the two pairs of speeches in this sentence introduce an important claim about the order in which Callimachus arranged the speeches of Demosthenes that will be developed and defended primarily in the notes: despite the appearance created by the initial triad, they are best understood as arranged *in pairs*. In this and other notes to follow in this chapter—but not in the text—I will refer to the speeches as, for example, D5 for *Concerning the Peace*, so as to discuss this and other aspects of the *Demosthenis ordo scriptorum*. As already hinted above, Callimachus placed D3 after D1 and D2 (the first pair in the corpus) because following D3 with D4 allows him to introduce the use of a prequel, here by pairing the acme of the *Olynthians* in D3 with its (as it were) humble origins in D4. Although the nineteenth-century rejection of D10 (more on this below) made it impossible to see, D9 and D10 are a pair just as first D11–D12, then D13–D14 and D15–D16 obviously are, the latter being a particularly obvious case thanks to being *On Behalf of*. Naturally my claim is not that membership in a pair automatically entitles a document to be considered authentic: D12 does not even pretend to be an authentic work of Demosthenes, and Callimachus included it as ancillary to D11, to which it is, once again, an illuminating prequel; scholarly opinion has also rejected D13. But in order to further emphasize the greatness of D9, Callimachus not only followed it by the chronologically earlier and less consistent D10—and on the cause of this inconsistency, see Alfred Körte, "Zu Didymos' Demosthenes-Commentar." *Rheinishes Museum* 60 (1905), 388–416, on 406—but preceded it with the only slightly less magnificent D8. To D8, D7 plays the role of introduction, just as D1 does to D2 and D5 does to D6. In the first six pairs, then, we have three of the ancillary-prequel model (D3/D4, D9/D10, and D11/D12) and three of the introduction-culmination model (D1/D2, D5/D6, and D7/D8). And to anticipate the two greatest speeches in the corpus (D18 and D19), the two of them, despite appearances, are not a pair: D19/D20 is an ancillary-prequel pair, while D17/D18 is a pair of the introduction-culmination kind, with D17—regardless of authorship—supplying important and indeed necessary information about post-Chaeronea Athens; see Ian Worthington, "Demosthenes' (In)Activity During the Reign of Alexander the Great" in Worthington (ed.), *Demosthenes: Statesman and Orator*, 90-113 (London and New York: Routledge, 2000), on 95–98.

33. See Trampedach, *Akademie*, 96n26: "Das folgende [Euphraeus 'in seiner Heimatstadt Oreos,' 96-7] nach Demosthenes 10.59–62."

34. See *Plato the Teacher*, 29–36, and *Ascent to the Good*, §16.

35. Cf. *Revival of Platonism in Cicero's Late Philosophy*, 3–5

36. See Plutarch, *Life of Demosthenes*, 6.3, 11.1–2, and *Lives of the Ten Orators*, 844d–f.

37. Thanks to Callimachus, in D43 and D44 we have another pair: two speeches concerning inheritance. First, a word on my translation of these speeches' titles: in the Loeb *Demosthenes* and elsewhere, the word "against" is used indiscriminately to translate both κατά and πρός; I will reserve it for speeches whose title begins

with κατά. In a speech like Πρὸς Μακάρτατον, Demosthenes is responding *in the place of a defendant* to the plaintiff's Κατά (which of course we do not have and indeed have no cause to regret not having), in this case, his speech is composed for one Sositheus, who is responding, on behalf of his son, much as Demosthenes is responding on behalf of Sositheus. What makes D43 of interest is that it not only involves the kind of law in which Isaeus was expert and which Demosthenes had needed to learn as a young man, but because it concerns a dispute with which we are already familiar thanks to *Concerning the Estate of Hagnias* (Isaeus 11); indeed, the full title of D43 is *Response to Macartatus concerning the Estate of Hagnias*. In and of themselves, the details of the case are not of importance here; see the Loeb *Isaeus*, with an English translation by Edward Seymour Forster (Cambridge, MA: Harvard University Press, 1927), 381–425. The important matter is that without telling us directly that Demosthenes' was Isaeus' student, Callimachus has made it clear to the reader that he was, announcing the connection first in D43 and then following it with D44, where the connection becomes inheritance law generally. Because of the obvious connection between D43 and Isaeus 11, it is natural to compare them for quality; see especially Schaefer, *Demosthenes*, 3.2.235, where he remarks that while A. G. Becker had thought Demosthenes' treatment superior, he disagrees. But here it must be kept in mind that Schaefer deals with D43 in a supplement to his book ("Beilage VI") that deals with twelve "Trial Speeches of Varied Contents" (200-285), *all of which he regards as inauthentic*. For now, consider the following: all twelve of these speeches are to be spoken by someone other than Demosthenes, who is here writing as a logographer; naturally this makes it difficult to claim that a certain speech does not sound like Demosthenes, or that "its author lacks Demosthenes' customary *fill in the blank*." In this case, Schaefer describes the author's style—but should it not rather be Sositheus' way of speaking that he is describing?—as "schwerfällig und schwülstig" (235), something like "sluggish and bombastic." One might well wonder just how easy it would be to make oneself sound both *schwerfällig* and *schwülstig* when one is not? But the most impressive aspect of D43 is that before "Sositheus" uses an easy to follow Q&A format to review the family tree with utmost clarity (43.48–50), he had said—and here Demosthenes goes beyond Isaeus, who never would have said such a thing—at 43.18 (A. T. Murray translation except for the last sentence): "At the first, men of the jury, it was my intention to write on a board all the kinsfolk of Hagnias, and thus to exhibit them to you one by one; but when I saw plainly that not all the jurymen would have an equally good view, but that those sitting at a distance would be at a disadvantage, it is perhaps necessary to instruct you by word of mouth ['to teach by discourse' would be better], for thus all will be on the same footing [ἀναγκαῖον ἴσως ἐστὶν τῷ λόγῳ διδάσκειν ὑμᾶς: τοῦτο γὰρ ἅπασι κοινόν ἐστιν]. But we will try, yes we will, as most as we're able with utmost brevity, to give a demonstration concerning the family of Hagnias [πειρασόμεθα δὲ καὶ ἡμεῖς ὡς ἂν μάλιστα δυνώμεθα διὰ βραχυτάτων ἐπιδεῖξαι περὶ τοῦ γένους τοῦ Ἁγνίου.]." He then goes on to use an Isaean formula (Isaeus 8.45) at the end (43.84; cf. 27.68 and 28.20) just in case we might be inclined to forget where he learned how to do what he has just done; D27 and D28 are the first two (paired) speeches he gave on his own inheritance.

38. Cf. William Wyse (ed.), *The Speeches of Isaeus, with Critical and Explanatory Notes* (Cambridge, UK: C. F. Clay, 1904), Preface: "The character of Isaeus was regarded with suspicion in antiquity. A rival orator taunted Demosthenes with having 'dieted himself upon Isaeus,' to the detriment of his moral constitution, and in the Augustan age, the judgment of orthodox criticism was summed up by Dionysius of Halicarnassus in these words [*Isaeus*, 3]: πρὸς μὲν τὸν ἀντίδικον διαπονηρεύερται, τοὺς δὲ δικαστὰς καταστρατηγεῖ, τοῖς δὲ πράγμασιν, ὑπὲρ ὧν ὁ λόγος, ἐκ παντὸς πειρᾶται βοηθεῖν ['in response to his opponent he is thoroughly wicked while he out-generals the jurymen; as for the facts his speech concerns, by every means possible he tries to improve them']."

39. Isaeus 3.66: "For none among men hates the profitable [τὸ λυσιτελοῦν] nor makes others worth more than himself." The first two speeches are ordered to illuminate the antinomy, with Isaeus 2 (*Concerning the Estate of Menecles*) upholding a will. For the antinomy, see 6.28; for further attacks on wills, see 4.14–17 and 9.31. In addition to the ten fake wills in this second passage, see also the particularly felicitous oppositions of 9.19, and the doubled opposition at 9.25. Demosthenes mastered this device and used it frequently.

40. Michael Edwards (ed.), *Isaeus, Translated with Introduction and Notes* (Austin: University of Texas Press, 2007), 4: "Isaeus lacks Lysias' supreme ability of characterization (ēthopoiia)."

41. Isaeus, fr. 17 is from a speech whose authenticity Harpocration questioned; see Edwards, *Isaeus*, 203n12.

42. Sosistheus uses his son a prop at the end of D43 at 43.84; in D44 (*Response to Leochares*)—the paired companion to *Response to Macartatus*—Aristodemus is young (44.1) and introduces his father at the start (44.4) as a poor old man, without experience of judicial proceedings.

43. The most detailed treatment in English is Jeremy Trevett, *Apollodorus the Son of Pasion* (Oxford: Clarendon Press, 1992); see also MacDowell, *Demosthenes the Orator*, chapter 5, and more briefly, Worthington, *Demosthenes of Athens*, 28n97.

44. The debated exception is *Against Stephanus I*, which, if by Demosthenes, would place him in so embarrassing an ethical position—he had defended against Apollodorus in D36 the same Phormio he now attacks in D46—that the impulse to denigrate comes into conflict with the will to excise. For the strictly stylistic issues implicated in the debate, see Trevett, *Apollodorus*, 62–73 ("Demosthenes almost certainly wrote 45"). See also his account of the ethical background on 58–62, usefully staged as a debate between Drerup and Pickard-Cambridge. See also Lionel Pearson, "Demosthenes, or Pseudo-Demosthenes, xlv (*In Stephanum* 1)." *Antichthon* 3 (1969), 18-26, directed primarily against Blass.

45. North, "*Summus Orator Plato*," 204: "Plato is in fact a logographer (a writer of speeches for others to deliver) of the first rank." Note also the complaint of Callicles that philosophers will be unfamiliar "with the pleasures, desires, and generally the ἤθοί of men" (*Grg.* 484d5–6).

46. The acutely style-conscious Pearson has elucidated the shortcomings of Apollodorus in a manner that neatly explains what Demosthenes needed to do to make himself sound like Pasion's son; see Lionel Pearson, "Apollodorus the Eleventh Attic Orator" in Luitpold Wallace (ed.), *The Classical Tradition: Studies in Honor of Harry Caplan*, 347-359 (Ithaca, NY: Cornell University Press, 1966), on

348: (1) "speaker's tendency to repeat himself," (2) "lack of proper organization," (3) "lapse into irrelevancy," (4) "untidy and apparently interminable sentences," and (5) "constant restatement." In accordance with a logic explained in *Hp. Mi.* (e.g., 368a4–5) and *Phdr.* 262a5–b1 (cf. *Phdr.* 264c2–e2 on order specifically), only a writer that knows how to arrange material "in such a way that each item is logically connected with the others" is capable of deliberately arranging it incoherently and illogically.

47. Beginning with D45 and D46—*Against Stephanus I* and *Against Stephanus II*—six of the seven speeches spoken by Apollodorus are arranged in pairs, continuing the general pattern (the paired inheritance cases D43 and D44 have been discussed above). Callimachus places D45 first among them for much the same reason he places D43 first among the inheritance twins: just as D43 inevitably recalls Isaues himself, so too does D45 recall D36, thus introducing Apollodorus as a speaker—Demosthenes had already memorably introduced him as a despicable person at 36.39–56—in a manner that deliberately forces upon the reader the ethical dilemma created by D45 and D36. After the initial pair, Callimachus interrupts the series with D47 and D48 (more on this amazing speech below) with D47 joined to D45 and D46 as actions for perjury (ψευδομαρτυρία) and both D47 and D48 joined to D45 and D46 as members of "the *Against* species," that is, written for the plaintiff. Thus D45, D46, D47, and D48 interrupt a series of *Response* speeches that began with D29 and then continues with D49, first of the second pair of Apollodorus-spoken speeches (D49 and D50), these two united by war and politics, especially with regard to triremes, the theme that connects D50 to the singleton D51 (more on this below), which is then followed by the third Apollodorus pair, D52 and D53, neither of which it is conceivable that Demosthenes had written because he was no more than sixteen when they were delivered. I take it that Callimachus placed these last so that we could determine for ourselves the degree to which Demosthenes successfully imitated the style of Apollodorus in the other five speeches, the four that precede them and finally D59, that is, *Against Neaira*, a speech of which all the following are true: (1) it is the last judicial speech in the collection (D60 and D61 belong to a different genre entirely), (2) it is the last speech spoken by Apollodorus, and (3) it contains the only plausible reason for Demosthenes to have switched from attacking Apollodorus in D36 to defending him in D45. See MacDowell, *Demosthenes the Orator*, 121–22; Mogen Herman Hansen, "The Theoric Fund and the *graphe paranomon* against Apollodorus." *Greek, Roman, and Byzantine Studies* 17 (1976), 235–46; Christopher Carey (ed.), *Apollodorus, Against Neaira [Demosthenes] 59 (Greek Orators, 6)* (Warminster: Aris and Phillips, 1992), 152–56, and Konstantinos A. Kapparis (ed.), *Apollodorus, Against Neaira [D59], Edited with Introduction and Commentary* (Berlin and New York: De Gruyter, 1999), 29 and 174–78.

48. For a good overview, see Kapparis, *Against Neaira*, 48–50; for the real reason for its excision, see 402–4, beginning with "oral, vaginal, and anal sex" as implied at 59.108. The words ἀπὸ τριῶν τρυπημάτον [cf. Procopius on Theodora at *Anecdota* 9.18, a passage rendered unforgettable by Edward Gibbon's story of the learned prelate] τὴν ἐργασίον πεποιῆσθαι were suppressed in antiquity; Kapparis comments on 404· "The evidence suggests that the phrase ἀπὸ τριῶν τρυπημάτον (or something similar) was said by Apollodorus, but it was deleted

and eventually removed from the text by a grammarian because he found it too explicit." Dionysius of Halicarnassus denied the speech's authenticity (*On the Style of Demosthenes*, 57) in a passage that begins (Usher translation): "If, however, there are some disgusting, vulgar and crude passages in the speeches that have been falsely ascribed to him."

49. That is, he made the dangerous proposal to divert some of the Theoric Fund to military purposes in accordance with Demosthenes' longstanding policy, but never formally proposed by him. Incidentally, I would explain the critical back-and-forth on the authenticity of D45 by the hypothesis that Demosthenes is deftly imitating Apollodorus ineptly imitating Demosthenes, who had won the day in D36. This hypothesis might also be relevant to Callimachus' decision to include D52 and D53. Finally, it is my hope that nobody will regard such conduct as "unworthy of a student of Plato," especially since Plato himself has frequently been regarded as "unworthy of Plato" (see *Ascent to the Good*, §9).

50. Although in a search for the methods of Callimachus, I will be pairing *Against Neaira* with *Against Theocrines*, the speech that precedes it, it is also true that for the ordering of Demosthenes' speeches to be truly artful and illuminating, there must always be the secondary pairs resulting from the link between the second member of one pair and the first of the next. The perjury link between D44 and D45 has already been mentioned, but even though D59 is the last forensic speech while both D60 and D61 are epideictic in character, the analogy to *Smp.* suggests a subtler link between the secondary pair of D59 and Demosthenes' *Funeral Oration* (D60): Callimachus joined them as comedy to tragedy, for nowhere is Demosthenes more comic than in D59 or more tragic than in D60. Cf. *Smp.* 223c6–d6.

51. See Dionysius of Halicarnassus, *Isocrates*, 20 on ἡ Ἰσοκράτειος ἀγωγή; cf. *On the Style of Demosthenes*, 18: "Not all subjects require the same way of speaking [διάλεκτος]."

52. A complete review of Isocrates' writings would be inappropriate here, but a beginning can be made, for the difference is visible from the start: at 1.5, he eschews "exhortation" and "summoning" or παράκλησις—the noun related to the Platonic-Demosthenic παρακαλῶμεν—for what he calls παραίνεσις, something like "advice" or "counsel." His advice is excellent, but it always aims at self-benefit, and is therefore most promptly offered to kings (2.24, 2.30, and 2.35–37; cf. *Smp.* 208c1–e1), thus revealing the self-interested motives of the advisor (2.53–54). In linking the just and the expedient (2.17, the latter is always the senior partner, and he names his ideal in 3.1 as "gaining advantage [πλεονεξία] through virtue," plausible as good advice for a king (3.60–64). While he praises Athens for disinterested generosity (4.53) and exposing the base consequence of Persian monarchy (4.151), his pitch is τὸ συμφέρον (4.182); when we see him next dispensing the same advice with the same pitch in *Philippus* (5.24) that he gave in *Panegyricus*, it is necessary to measure the sublimity of his advice (5.134–35 and 5.145; cf. *Letter* 2.4) against the power of the man he is advising. See below for the relationship between *Philippus* and *Archdamus*.

53. Isocrates, 8.145 (P. G. Lennox's adaptation of Norlin modified): "But I urge and exhort [παραινῶ καί παρακελεύομαι] those who are younger and more vigorous than I to speak and write the kind of discourses by which they will turn the

greatest states—those which have been wont to oppress the rest—into the paths of virtue and justice, since when the affairs of Hellas are in a happy and prosperous condition, it follows that the situation of the philosophers also becomes much better."

54. Cf. Plutarch, *Life of Demosthenes*, 5.4 and Demosthenes 35.42 (quoted in the following note). More generally, see T. M. Perkins, "Isocrates and Plato: Relativism vs. Idealism." *Southern Speech Communication Journal* 50 (1984), 49–66, and Benoit, "Isocrates and Plato."

55. The explicit connection is made at 35.15 (Murray translation): "Lacritus himself drew up the agreement and joined in sealing it after it was written; for his brothers were still youngish, in fact mere boys, but he was Lacritus, of Phaselis, a personage of note, a pupil of Isocrates." The connection is central (made again at 35.40) to the speech's effectiveness: since the money was borrowed, and since it hasn't been paid back, no eloquence purchased from Isocrates will prove adequate (35.42–43; Murray): "How could there be men baser than the one who teaches such an art, or than those who learn of him? Since, then, he is so clever, and trusts in his power of speaking and in the one thousand drachmae which he has paid to his teacher, bid him show you, either that they did not borrow the money from us, or that, having borrowed it, they have paid it back; or that agreements for overseas trade ought not to be binding; or that it is right for people to use money for some other purpose than that for which they received it under agreement. Let him prove to you whatever one of these propositions he chooses. If he can so prove it to you who sit to decide cases of mercantile contracts, I certainly concede that he is the cleverest of men. But I know well that he would not be able to prove it to you or induce you to believe any one of them." The speech ends with a further attack on sophistry (35.56).

56. In the so-called "Hypothesis" to the speech by Libanius he writes: "Incorrectly have some believed the speech to be inauthentic, deceived by weak proofs." This is an early example of stylistic arguments being deployed for an ulterior purpose, in this case to uphold a direct or at worst indirect connection (through Isaeus) between Demosthenes and Isocrates. Schaefer comments at *Demosthenes*, 3.2.291: "Ob Demosthenes sich so wegwerfend über Isokrates geäußert haben würde, mag ich nicht entscheiden; Benseler hat es bezeifelt." Schaefer himself resorts to the argument's weaknesses, as if the skillful handling of a weak case was disqualifying! Incidentally, Schaefer includes D35 in "Beilage VII" dealing with "Speeches in Business Affairs." These are D35, D32, D33, D34, and D56, all of which he regards as inauthentic; note that with respect to two pairs of these, Callimachus used a similar structuring principle.

57. In a May 13, 2003, obituary in the *Moscow-Pullman Daily News* of Galen R. Rowe (1937-2003), retired from the University of Idaho, it is written: "In his final years, he started a book on the collaboration between Plato and Demosthenes." Efforts to obtain the fruits of this research proved futile, but my guess is that he focused on the connection between *Lg.* and *Against Timocrates* (D24). Note that *Against Androtion* (see following note) is D22.

58. See Galen R. Rowe, "Anti-Isocratean Sentiment in Demosthenes' *Against Androtion.*" *Historia* 49, no. 3 (2000), 278–302; he includes among Isocrates' students not only Androtion but Onetor (cf. D30 and D31)—to whom he connects Meidias

(cf. D21) on 282—and discusses on 287-91 the enmity between Apollodorus and Timotheus ("Isocrates' dearest student" on 286) that resulted in D49, adding D52 to the mix on 288–90. See also his "Two Responses by Isocrates to Demosthenes." *Historia* 51. No. 2 (2002), 149–62, especially 158–59, a passage worth quoting at length in honor of his last efforts (see previous note): "*Against Timocrates* and *The Laws* exhibit some remarkable correspondences of ideas and of style. First with regard to ideas, both documents agree that the laws are supreme; and that all, including officials and leaders, are subject to them (*Laws* 715d; *Against Timocrates* 133–38); that the purpose of the laws is to make people good (*Laws* 707d; *Against Timocrates* 106); that the pursuit of wealth is inimical to this purpose (*Laws* 742d-e; *Against Timocrates* 183-185); that the laws are so interconnected that one must take extreme care to make new laws consistent with the rest (*Laws* 746b-d; *Against Timocrates* 32–33); that once codified a state's laws should be tampered with as little as possible (*Laws* 960d; *Against Timocrates* 139–41); that a division should be made between those laws which pertain to private disputes and those which prescribe the citizens' obligations to the State (*Laws* 767b; *Against Timocrates* 192); and that democracy is preferable to oligarchy (*Laws* 710d–e; *Against Timocrates* 57, 163–164). The corresponding ideas, of course, would have been widely acceptable to Demosthenes' audience and could have come from a variety of sources; however, that Demosthenes selected them for the speech against Timocrates at a time when Plato was emphasizing and developing them in *The Laws* [cf. 158: 'Demosthenes' speech dates to the year 353/2, five or six years before the death of Plato. The latter by this time was working on his last and longest work, *The Laws*'] suggests that Demosthenes' selection of them was inspired by Plato. Further, the points of agreement between him and Plato are of a fundamental sort and in spirit opposed to Isocrates' attitude, as will be seen below, towards laws and constitutions."

59. See John Davies, "Hegesippus of Sounion: An Underrated Politician" in S. D. Lambert (ed.), *Sociable Man: Essays on Ancient Greek social behaviour in honour of Nick Fisher*, 11–24 (Swansea: Classical Press of Wales: 2011).

60. See M. L. W. Laistner, "The Influence of Isocrates's Political Doctrines on some Fourth Century Men of Affairs." *Classical Weekly* 23, no. 17 (March 10, 1930), 129–131, on 131: "Another name is that of Python of Byzantium or Aenus, who entered the service of Philip II, and in due course was sent as Macedonian envoy to Athens. One further disciple of Isocrates is of special interest. Hieronymus was one of the founders of Megalopolis, and subsequently was prominent in the affairs of that town. His policy later was one of friendship toward Philip; this philo-Macedonianism may well have been engendered largely by the political teaching of his former master."

61. See Natoli, *Letter of Speusippus*, 40–41, on disambiguation, and 23.127 on further career of this Pytho.

62. See W. H. Thompson, *The Phaedrus of Plato with English Notes and Dissertations* (London: Wittaker & Co., 1868), appendix 2 ("On the Philosophy of Isocrates, and his Relation to the Socratic Schools"), especially 179–182; cf. Guthrie, *History of Greek Philosophy*, 4.283: "never been presented better than by Thompson."

63. See *Ascent to the Good*, 124n21; cf. Ernst Heitsch, "Der Anonymos im *Euthydem*." *Hermes* 128, no. 4 (2000), 392–404.

64. See especially Brandon David Kosch, "Reading Demosthenes" (PhD dissertation: University of Chicago, 2017), 181–91, beginning with: "Thucydides' profound influence on Demosthenes, with respect to both style and content, was already recognized in antiquity [note 6]." The attached note reads: "There is the famous story told by Zosimus (*Biogr. Gr. W.* 299, 47ss.) that Demosthenes could recite the whole of Thucydides' *Historiae* from memory, and Lucian (*adv. ind.* 4) claims that he copied out the whole text several times. Cf. also D. H. *Thuc.* 53." See also Dionysius of Halicarnassus, *Thucydides*, 53: "Of the orators, Demosthenes alone, just as whosoever of the others seemed to create something great and brilliant in their discourses, so too he also became a devoted admired of Thucydides in many things, and taking them from him, attached them to his political discourses." As for Zosimus, in addition to the anticipation of Fahrenheit 451 to which Kosch refers (47–51), see also 38–39 on Plato.

65. See Michel Nouhaud, *L'Utilisation de l'Histoire par les Orateurs Attiques* (Paris: Les Belles Lettres, 1982).

66. John Edwin Sandys, *The Speech of Demosthenes against the Law of Leptines; A Reivised Text with an Introduction and Explanatory Notes and an autotype Facsimile from the Paris Ms.* (Cambridge, UK: C. J. Clay, 1890), 15.

67. See Kapparis, *Against Neaira*, 375–88; the list of parallels on 380–81 is conclusive, weakening and perhaps disabling the thesis of Mirko Canevaro, "Memory, the Orators, and the Public in Fourth-Century BC Athens" in Luca Catagnoli and Paola Ceccarelli (eds.), *Greek Memories: Theories and Practices*, 136–57 (Cambridge, UK: Cambridge University Press, 2019).

68. See Ryder, "Demosthenes and Philip II," especially his treatment of D16 (48) and D15 (52-53) beginning with: "Demosthenes' thoughts and energies seem not yet to have been focused entirely on the Macedonian menace." On D16, see also G. L. Cawkwell, "The Defense of Olynthus," *Classical Quarterly* 12, no. 1 (May 1962), 122–40, on 124–25.

69. See David Whitehead (ed.), *Xenophon, Poroi (Revenue-Sources)* (Oxford: Oxford University Press, 2019); for Plato's debts to Xenophon, see *Ascent to the Beautiful*, §2 and *Relay Race of Virtue*; they are most obvious in *Menexenus* and *Meno*, on which see *Ascent to the Beautiful*, 403-407, and *Ascent to the Good*, §14.

70. See especially Markle, "Athenian Intellectuals," 81-92.

71. The case is complex and for this author, at least, opaque. For an introduction to the opacity, see Phillip Harding, "Androtion's Political Career." *Historia* 25, no. 2 (1976), 186–200, on 195: the interpretation of D22, D23, and D24 is obviously relevant to any alleged shift in Demosthenes' views relative to Eubulus. Harding sends us to Jaeger and Jaqueline de Romilly, "Les modérés Athéniens vers le milieu du IVe siècle: échos et concordances." *Revue des Études Grecques* 67, no. 316/318 (July–December 1954), 327–354, but it is safest to cite first Burke, "Early Political Speeches," and then MacDowell, *Demosthenes the Orator*, chapter 7, who is content with stating the evident circumstances of D22-24, as well as of D20.

72. Cf. Whitehead, *Poroi*, 42–52, and G. L. Cawkwell, "Eubulus." *Journal of Hellenic Studies* 83 (1963), 47–67, on 63–65.

73. Cf. Badian, "Road to Prominence," 20–22 (on D22) and "The young man in search of a cause" (beginning on 26), especially 26–28 on D20.

74. Sawada, "Allies and Foes," 337–38 deserves some comment: "Although a broad consensus now prevails [primarily thanks to Cawkwell and Co.] that Athens contained no political parties in the modern sense [trivially true], scholars are still tempted to view Athenian politics *in the period of Demosthenes* [emphasis mine; this is an overbroad category, and needs chronological articulation] primarily in the reductivist terms [what allegedly makes such terms inapplicable is that they do not apply, not that they simplify] of pro- and anti-Macedonian division [these terms *came to be applicable*, largely thanks to Demosthenes; they can be shown not to apply in 346 but not in 338 or even 330, although Sawada will try in this latter case]. In fact, it should be remembered, opposition to Demosthenes did not necessarily amount to a pro-Macedonian stance [although this scarcely applies to Aeschines, for whom it did amount to this, the statement is true enough thanks to the overstatement based on 'necessarily' that it rejects], any more than collaboration or friendship with him denoted an anti-Macedonian one [this second clause is false, and will cause Sawada to say of Lycurgus on 346: 'we have little evidence of his political stance towards Macedon or his relations with Demosthenes.' While the strictly quantitative aspect of this statement may stand—we have only one of his speeches—what evidence there is gives no indication of anything other than his collaborative relationship with Demosthenes and his enmity, reciprocated, to Macedon]. Demosthenes did not consistently pursue an active policy of opposition to Macedon [hence the need for a chronological distinction: he did not do so *until he did*; cf. Plutarch, *Life of Demosthenes*, 13.1 (Perrin translation): 'Wherefore I do not know how it occurred to Theopompus to say that Demosthenes was unstable in his character and unable to remain true for any length of time to the same policies or the same men. For it is apparent that after he had at the outset adopted a party and a line of policy in the conduct of the city's affairs, he maintained this to the end, and not only did not change his position while he lived, but actually gave up his life that he might not change it'], and, more importantly, the question of Macedon *was not always* [emphasis mine, and true enough] the key issue in Athenian politics *during his time* [emphasis mine; overbroad once again]." In the passage that follows, she is forced to admit that *for a time* it did become so. See Noriko Sawada, "Athenian Politics in the Age of Alexander the Great: A Reconsideration of the Trial of Ctesiphon." *Chiron* 26 (1996), 57–84, where she cites Raphael Sealey and Ernst Badian as precursors (57n4) while trying to prove, against Burke, "Political Collaboration," that Lycurgus and Demosthenes were not collaborating; so too Allen, "Culture Wars," 286–89.

75. The discovery of Didymus' commentary on the *Fourth Philippic* in 1901 should have been a wakeup call to the practitioners of *Echtheitskritik*, but aside from bringing about a change in attitude toward D10, it did or rather has not. Before its publication in 1904, scholarly opinion was virtually unanimous that D10 was inauthentic, and Schaefer had classified it among "Writings falsified by Rhetoricians" (*Demosthenes*, 3.2.316), along with D11, D12, D13, D25, D26, D29, D60, and D61 (note that Schaefer regarded the forensic speeches considered above as authentically ancient, just not written by Demosthenes). Hence we receive only half of the story in the following true statement in Harding, *Didymos*, 108-109: "His failure to do so here [sc. 'grapple with issues of authenticity'] suggests that, like his contemporary Dionysios of Halikarnassos, Didymos accepted the

authenticity of the *Fourth Philippic*, as do many modern scholars (see e.g. Körte (1905): 388-410; Daitz (1957): 145-62; Pearson (1976):155-57; Worthington (1991): 425-28; Sealey (1993): 232; Hajdu (2002): 44-49; contra Milns (1987): 287-302; the position of Buckler (1994): 106 is confused. Sharply critical of Didymos on this, as on other issues, is Badian (2000): 10–11). It is also probable that he [sc. Didymus] did not find any prior discussion of the topic [i.e., nobody before him suggested that D10 was, as it were, 'forged by rhetoricians']." The date of Körte, "Zu Didymos," should make it obvious: 1904 was a turning point and should have been a wake-up call: to repeat, facts had refuted the certainties of *Echtheitskritik*. But the commentary on D10, and specifically Didymus' lengthy discussion of 10.32, constitutes another turning point: *Didymus is the first scholar to juxtapose Demosthenes and Aristotle* (although Harding comments on 123 that "it would be very strange to introduce a new topic with a quotation from Aristotle, but no reference to a passage in Demosthenes," this seems to have been his intention; see 55), a juxtaposition of considerable impact on this book's attempt to recover the Old Academy. While an ancient *scholium* on 10.32 had identified Hermias of Atarneus as Philip's unnamed agent (Körte, 390), an inauthentic and indeed forged *Fourth Philippic* had made this suggestion easy to ignore; Körte welcomes its confirmation (391) in upholding the authenticity of D10 (410). Here's the text in question (10.32): "Next, he who is doing (and with full consciousness) [ὁ πράττων καὶ συνειδώς] all the things which Philip is preparing against the Persian King, this man has been arrested, and all the deeds [sc. of Philip] the King will now hear not from us as his accusers—who he might well believe to be speaking on behalf of our own private advantage—but from the one [sc. Hermias] having himself done them and setting them in order." In the comments that follows, Didymus makes three points crystal clear: (1) the words ὁ πράττων καὶ συνειδώς apply to Hermias, making him Philip's agent, (2) the character and thus the reputation of Hermias is otherwise a matter of extreme controversy, and Didymus illustrates both the best and the worst things that have been written about him, and (3) Aristotle was closely tied to him (cf. Harding, 144: "The closeness of the relationship between Aristotle and Hermias is nowhere better attested than in Aristotle's own words that are cited later on in the papyrus"), and indeed it is thanks to Didymus that we have the poem or paean Aristotle wrote for Hermias (see 62–63 and 153–56), by far and away the best of such things as were written about him (see also Natali, *Aristotle*, 32–42). Most importantly, since he demonstrates Aristotle's friendship for Hermias in the context of Demosthenes' attack on Philip in D10, Didymus is the first author to draw attention to the political chasm— explored in the present book beginning with its epigraph—between Aristotle and Demosthenes, and regardless of whether anyone else should be regarded "in the reductivist terms of pro- and anti-Macedonian division" (Sawada; see previous note), *these two students of Plato unquestionably should be*. And even though Demosthenes is doubtless referring to Aeschines in the following passage, quoted by Didymus (Harding, 64–65) and imitated by Sallust in the speech he wrote for Cato (*Conspiracy of Catiline*, 52: "if, amid such universal terror, he alone is free from alarm, it the more concerns me to fear for you and myself," J. S. Watson translation), his use of "whoever it might be" leaves room for Aristotle and Isocrates as well (10.34; J. H. Vince translation): "For my part, whenever I see a man afraid of one who dwells at Susa and Ecbatana [sc. the Persian King] and insisting that he is ill-disposed to Athens, though he helped to restore our fortunes in the past and was even now making overtures to us (and if you did not accept them but voted their rejection, the fault is not his; and when I find the same man using very different language about this plunderer of the Greeks [sc. Philip], who is extending his power, as you see, at our very doors and in the heart of Greece, I am astonished, and, whoever he may be [ὅστις ἂν ᾖ ποτ'], it is I that fear him, just because he does not fear Philip." Of course, Aristotle was no longer in Athens at the time, and had commenced the instruction of Alexander.

76. Although I have emphasized the *Third Philippic* (D9) as evidence for Demosthenes' Platonic inspiration, the great passage from *On the Chersonese* about Demosthenes himself beginning at 8.68 deserves comment. It begins with an imaginary objector, an old Socratic device (cf. *Ap.* 20c4–d1 and 28b3–5), who accuses him of cowardice; this gives Demosthenes the chance to point out that no courage is required when you are telling the city what it wants to hear (8.69), creating thereby a contrast with himself: "But whoever on behalf of the best [τὸ βέλτιστον], opposes to your wishes many things, and says nothing for your gratification [πρὸς χάριν] but for the best always [τὸ βέλτιον ἀεί], and chooses that kind of active citizenship [τὴν τοιαύτην πολιτείαν πραιρεῖται] in which chance becomes sovereign over more things than reasoning [a nice description of the Cave] yet offers himself to you as correctable by both of them, this kind of citizen is courageous and useful." The imaginary interrogation continues (8.70), allowing Demosthenes to contrast a desire to make himself great with the intent to make the city great (8.72): "Nor does this seem to me to be the concern of the just citizen to discover the kind of policies by which I will straightway be first among you and you the last of all the others; rather it is necessary to strengthen the city by the policies of the good citizens, and to speak in all things the best always [τὸ βέλτιον ἀεί], not the easiest [τὸ ῥᾷστον]." With the hammered phrase τὸ βέλτιον ἀεί, Demosthenes captures what he regards as Plato's central concern; cf. τὸ βέλτιον at *Letter* 5.3, quoted in the last chapter. For the adumbration of an anti-tyrannical program or πολιτεία in Plato's *Republic*, see *Plato the Teacher*, §30.

77. In fact, the placement of D20 after D19 is problematic, and in many respects D21 would have been a more logical choice. Callimachus' motives are best explained by his intent to arrange the speeches by pairs: D21 begins a three-pair series which are all public speeches of the "Against" type, whereas the title of D20 begins with Πρός. While the reasons for this are technical—he is not formally speaking against Leptines but rather in response and opposition to his law—the fact remains that D20 is a singleton in the *corpus Demosthenicum*, and not easily paired with any speech, *joining D36 and D51 in this respect* (more on this below), while D21, which could usefully and appropriately have followed D19, is also naturally paired with D22. For the technical matters involved, see most recently Christos Kremmydas (ed.), *Commentary on Demosthenes' Against Leptines. With Introduction, Text, and Translation* (Oxford: Oxford University Press, 2012), 25–33; Sandys, *Against Leptines*, xviii–xxiv, and above all, Georg Friedrich Schömann, "De Causa Leptina" in Schömann, *Opuscula Academica*, 237–46 (Berlin: Weidmann, 1866).

78. Thanks to the involvement of both Aristophon and Leodamas on behalf of Leptines (Kremmydas, *Commentary*, 41), it is possible to link Demosthenes once again, as per Hermippus, to Callistratus, following Sandys, *Against Leptines*, xxiv: "Aristophon, who by the overthrow of Callistratus had become the foremost man in Athens." See Jeremy Trevett, "Demosthenes and Thebes." *Historia* 48, no. 2 (1999), 186–202, on Leodamus (187): "He prosecuted Callistratus and Chabrias in 365 over the betrayal of Oropus to the Thebans"; so too MacDowell, *Demosthenes the Orator*, 157–58. It was in response to this prosecution, of course, that Callistratus made the speech that so impressed the young Demosthenes (see introduction), and Sealey, "Callistratos of Aphidna," is particularly useful in explaining the collaboration between Callistratus and Chabrias; see 187–89, especially on their "change of policy," and 195–97 on the trial. Worth quoting is Sealey's comment on Plato's connection, based on *Lives of the Eminent Philosophers*, 3.23–24 on 195: "Chabrias and Callistratos were prosecuted for the loss of Oropus; presumably Chabrias had commanded the expedition of the Athenians in full force and Callistratos had either persuaded them to make this expedition or conducted the negotiations with Themison and the Thebans. The chief prosecutor in both trials was Leodamas and the trial of Chabrias seems to have followed that of Callistratos. Diogenes Laertios (III, 23–24) reports a story that Plato alone of the Athenians pleaded for Chabrias; this is inaccurate, for Lycoleon also pleaded for him [the source is Aristotle, *Rhetoric* 3.10; 1411b6]. Diogenes adds that, when Chabrias and Plato were going together towards the acropolis, Hegesippos met them and tried with threats to dissuade Plato from helping Chabrias." The point here is that there is evidence to support the view that Demosthenes' alleged desertion of the Academy at eighteen in response to Callistratus (as reported by Hermippus) was in fact no such thing, and that in *Response to Leptines* eleven years later, he was opposing Leodamus and Antiphon, the principal opponents of Callistratus and Chabrias, the latter directly connected as to Plato, the former indirectly, albeit twice, i.e., through both Chabrias and Demosthenes. While arguing against Bergk that Plato's involvement in the trial of Chabrias cannot be used to date *Tht.* (636–39), Eduard Zeller, "Über die zeitgeschtlichen Beziehungen des platonischen Theaetet." *Sitzungsberichte der königlich preussischen Akademie der Wissenschaften* 77 (1886), 631–650, having assumed that Plato is the judicially inexperienced philosopher of the Digression (638), goes on to dismiss the evidence in Diogenes entirely (639). On the basis of 638n2, however, one assumes that Zeller wrongly aligns Plato with the oligarchs.

79. Cf. Burke, "Early Political Speeches," 166: "there is detectable in fact a core consistency of perspective in these early years, a guiding bias, evident both in the ecclesia speeches and the forensic orations dealing with political issues, including the logographic addresses. The bias was conservative, grounded in tradition, sympathetic to wealth, essentially elitist in character, though fully aware of the responsibilities to the state that wealth and elite status imposed." There is doubtless an element of *noblesse oblige* in Aristocles the son of Ariston's Platonism.

80. Thanks to the placement of D20, Callimachus reaches D26 in perfectly paired order: regardless of whether D25 and D26 are genuine, the latest of all the speeches in a chronological sense constitute an obvious pair. From them, Callimachus returns to the beginning, and for the first time, the pairing system breaks

down thanks to the triad of inheritance speeches named for Aphobus (D27, D28, and D29). First of all, it was inevitable that the pairing system would need to break down somewhere: there are sixty-one speeches in the corpus. But the Aphobus triad is only *one of three* places where the pairing system is abrogated: as already indicated, both D36 and D51 (on the complexities involved here in relation to D50, see MacDowell, *Demosthenes the Orator*, 133-36) are singletons. Thanks to the odd number of anomalies, the collection as whole will remain odd in number. Note that the transition between *Against*-speeches and *Response*-speeches (with the exception of D20) takes place within the Aphobus triad: like the Onetor pair that follows (D30 and D31), D29 is a *Response*-speech, as are D32, D33, D34, and D35, with the series continuing all the way from D37 to D44, where the Apollodorus speeches begin. D36 (*On Behalf of Phormio*) is the obvious exception, and Callimachus' motives for placing it where he did are mysterious. The paired ordering of the Apollodorus series has already been described, but between D49-D50 and D52-D53, he has interpolated D51. This speech is connected to D50 by trierarchy, so its placement is not as mysterious as that of D36. But I hope by this point to have established that the ordering has an internal logic, and that its structural building block is the pair. The three great pairs that follow D53, the most elegant in the corpus, will be considered below.

81. See Cicero, *De re publica*, 1.10 (David Fott translation): "And, may I ask, who can approve this limitation: they deny that the wise man will undertake any part in the republic beyond what circumstance and necessity compel. As if a greater necessity could happen to anyone than happened to me—in which case, what could I have done if I had not then been consul? And how could I have been consul if I had not maintained this course of life from boyhood, through which I arrived at the most distinguished honor after having been born of equestrian lineage? Therefore, even though the republic may be pressed by dangers, the power to help it does not come at any time or whenever you wish, unless you are in a position where you are allowed to do that."

82. Cf. Rowe, "Anti-Isocratean Sentiment," 293: "Hermippus understood Demosthenes to be the student not of Isocrates but of Plato." Cf. Allen, *Why Plato Wrote*, 195n32.

83. Cf. "Pernot's Triad" at *L'Ombre du Tigre*, 39–40.

84. In his latest book, Pernot adds another triad to explain Plato's hostility to rhetoric of which the one based on his opposition to democracy should be quoted. See Laurent Pernot, *Confluences de la philosophie et de la rhétorique grecque* (Paris: Vrin, 2022), 15: "Or Platon, on le sait, était oppose au régime démocratique, qui lui paraissait incompatible avec la justice et avec la vertu. Il ne pouvait donc que blamer le tout-oratoire qui était un des resorts de ce régime." The other two are his opposition to the rhetoric teaching sophists (15–16) and the victory of vicious over Socratic rhetoric as depicted in *Ap.* (16).

85. Cf. [Longinus], *On the Sublime* 44.2.

86. On Cicero, *Tusculan Disputations*, 5.10, see *Guardians in Action*, §1.

87. Cf. Blair Campbell, "Thought and Political Action in the Athenian Tradition: The Emergence of the 'Alienated" Intellectual." *History of Political Thought* 5, no. 1 (Spring 1984), 17–59, on 47: "For Demosthenes, as for Isocrates, historic Athens provides a timeless model of perfection universal in its appeal; its citizens

alone of mankind have merited a renown that surpasses all detraction [he cites 9.24]. These citizens were exemplars of public-spiritedness and altruism: 'they were careful to obey the spirit of the constitution . . . [and] selfish greed had no place in their statesmanship, but each thought it his duty to further the common weal' [he quotes 9.25–26, and adds: 'see also *Against Leptines*, 91]. So fervent is Demosthenes as guardian of this ideal, indeed, that the role in which he casts himself seems more closely akin to the Old Testament prophet than to Athens' traditional leadership." Campbell's fascinating article deserves careful study, not least of all for opposing this book's thesis in an illuminating manner: more on this below.

88. See *Ascent to the Beautiful*, xxvii–ix, on translating καλόν.

89. Cf. Plutarch, *Life of Demosthenes*, 28.1–30.1, and [Lucian], *Encomium of Demosthenes*, 44–49 (see chapter 5).

90. See Yunis, "Demosthenes and the Burden of the Athenian Past," 104–105: "Demosthenes was faced with the problem of making the argument compelling [sc. an argument that 'rejects the success-oriented model of public discourse,' as in *De Corona*] to a mass audience in a context where it would be unexpected and clash with convention. In theory, he could try either of two strategies. He could, in the manner of a moral philosopher or sophist, attempt to instruct the audience on why success should be rejected as the prevailing measure of worth and some other measure substituted instead. But this strategy, as we know from Plato's Socrates and elsewhere, would leave his popular audience cold [N.B.]. The other strategy, which he did adopt, also stems from an extra-legal context, viz., the heritage of Homeric and tragic poetry. These models offered the great advantage of being familiar to the mass of citizens, indeed of being well-accepted and even cherished by them. In these literary genres, it often occurs that events and human actions are presented and evaluated as admirable or contemptible, noble or base, good or bad, without regard for their success or failure on a scale of advantage and disadvantage. The primary example, of course, is Achilles [Demosthenes never mentions him], whose furious pursuit of his friend's killer would inevitably lead, as he well knew, to his own death." Without denying the role of Plato via Socrates, Yunis minimizes the impact of Plato on Demosthenes through Socrates through Achilles (cf. *Ap.* 28c1–d9; note βέλτιστον at 29d6). For Plato's use of Achilles and Odysseus, see *Ascent to the Beautiful*, §11 and 444–49; *Plato the Teacher*, §35; and *Guardians on Trial*, 154–56 and 321.

91. See *Plato the Teacher*, 199–200 and §31.

92. For the view opposite to mine about this passage, see Vegetti, "How and Why," 14–15: "In the light of these premises, we can better understand what follows [sc. at *R.* 592b3–4], which means literally: 'he would take part in the practical affairs of that city and no other.' Much of the political sense of the *Republic* hangs on this phrase. It contains two meanings that cannot be separated. The first is that obviously the just man (the philosopher) will enter fully into the political activity of the new city [i.e., the City], with a view to its preservation [i.e., once it has been established, which of course it never has been nor will be; thus far, then, simple literalism]. The second is that, if he acts in the historical city [e.g., Athens; i.e., any real city], he will do it *only* with a view to and in function of the advent of the other city." Vegetti is an important interlocutor; he will be revisited in chapter 5.

93. *Palatine Anthology*, 7.253 (Simonides): "If to die gallantly [τὸ καλῶς θνήσκειν] is the greatest part of virtue [ἀρετῆς μέρος ἐστὶ μέγιστον], Then above all others, chance has allotted this to us; For speeding to encircle Greece with freedom [Ἑλλάδι γὰρ σπεύδοντες ἐλευθερίην περιθεῖναι], We rest here enjoying a fame that won't grow old."

94. See *Ascent to the Good*, 191–92.

95. Demosthenes, *On the Crown*, 208.

96. See Herrman, *Political Speeches*, 26 and 78 (on καιρός).

97. The words ἔτι καὶ νῦν undergo a revealing shift in Demosthenes; in Xenophon's *Cyropaedia*, they appears repeatedly, meaning that "and even now" we can still see in the present customs or structures that were created in the past (cf. Isaeus 6.61). In Demosthenes, the phrase points not to the past but to the future: it is not yet too late—we stand at the καιρός (see previous note)—to make the necessary choice "to do the things that are necessary [τὰ δέοντα ποιεῖν]." On this common phrase (first found in the corpus at 1.6), see Herrman, *Political Speeches*, 103 (on προτρέπειν τὰ δέοντα ποιεῖν ὑμᾶς), especially the citation of 18.246.

98. Cf. Yunis, "Burden of the Past," 109: "The burden of the Athenian past—that is, the necessity to confront Philip at Chaeronea in order to remain true to their heritage and therefore to themselves—is clearly not a political argument in the sense that it considers advantage and disadvantage. But, like the response of Thucydides' Melians who spurn the 'reasonable' offer of the plain-speaking Athenian invaders, it is a political argument in that it affects communal action while rejecting the question of advantage." But *pace* Yunis, this does not amount to "a tragic mode of thinking" (110); rather, it is Platonic.

99. Quintilian, *Institutio Oratoria*, 12.10.23–24; he has just named Lysias, Isocrates, Andocides, Hyperides, Lycurgus, Aristgeiton, Isaeus, Antiphon, and Aeschines.

100. To be crystal clear: there is nobody except Plato from whom Demosthenes could have learned to make an argument that looked beyond worldly consequences—that is, the mere shadows of Becoming—towards a transcendent and unchanging Idea of the Good, shining *like the sun* in the realm of Being. It is nevertheless worth adding that our visible sun does indeed very much belong to Becoming or γένεσις; cf. the contrary claim at R. 509b3 with the warning at 507a4–5 and the truth at 517b3.

101. For analysis, see *Ascent to the Beautiful*, §13.

102. Although he separates a political Socrates (42–44) from an "alienated" and politically withdrawn Plato (54–56), Campbell hits the nail on the head in "Thought and Political Action," on 48: "Thus idealist metaphysics and idealized history produce the same result." His equally perfect error is on 58: "Plato's teaching mission is devoid of that sense of duty toward the city characteristic of his teacher." Campbell's basis for this erroneous claim is likewise revelatory: citing Guthrie on Plato's non-Athenian students (58n176), he writes: "Whereas Socrates, according to the *Apology*, preferred to edify his fellow citizen [he should have cited *Tht.* 143d4–6 as well], the Academy readily received pupils from all regions and political persuasions." No claim could more clearly highlight the importance of re-examining (and recovering) the Old Academy on the basis of Phocion, Lycurgus, Hyperides, and Demosthenes. On the first of these, see Zhul-

duz Amangelidyevna Seitkasimova, "May Plato's Academy be considered as the First Academic Institution?" *Open Journal for Studies in History* 2, no. 2 (2019), 35–42, on 40: "Humble, noble and moral, with no hair on the tongue when it was necessary to tell the truth, he [sc. Phocion] had devoted his entire life to Athens like Socrates and the Athenians, and even experienced the same end. Charged and convicted without a clear reason by the Athenian democracy, and sentenced to die by drinking hemlock."

103. See *Ascent to the Beautiful*, 404–408.

104. *Mx.* 247a2–6. Unfortunately Demosthenes plays only a negligible role (25n1) in Pernot, *Confluences*, 25–39 ("Socrate ventriloque ou l'énigme du Ménexène") despite attention to Dionysius of Halicarnassus (31–32).

105. John 15:13; on the relationship between Judeo-Christianity and the reception of Plato, see *Plato the Teacher*, §25.

106. See especially Arthur W. H. Adkins, *Merit and Responsibility* (Oxford: Oxford University Press, 1960).

107. Plutarch, *Life of Demosthenes*, 13.3–4; the passage continues (Perrin translation): "so that, if the loftiness of his principles and the nobility of his speeches had been accompanied by such bravery as becomes a warrior and by incorruptibility in all his dealings, he would have been worthy to be numbered, not with such orators as Moerocles, Polyeuctus, Hypereides, and their contemporaries, but high up with Cimon, Thucydides, and Pericles." The references are to the battlefield at Chaeronea and the Harpalus Affair.

108. See *Guardians in Action*, 424.

109. But see Eric Brown, "False Idles: The Politics of the 'Quiet Life'" in Ryan K. Balot (ed.), *A Companion to Greek and Roman Political Thought*, 485–500 (Chichester: Wiley-Blackwell, 2009), 490: "The contemplative ideal might be Plato's invention. Plato himself and the later tradition attribute the contemplative ideal to some Presocratic philosophers, but it is not clear if the attribution is correct. It is clear, however, that Aristotle retains the contemplative ideal." This gets things muddled: Aristotle *invents*, not retains, the distinction; as for Plato, while distinguishing the kind of philosopher his Socrates isn't from a litigator in *Tht.*, Socrates uses Thales as the prototype of this kind of philosopher, absorbed in the celestial studies (*Tht.* 174a4–8) down from which Socrates called philosophy (Cicero, *Tusculan Disputations*, 5.10).

110. Thus validating much of Brown's "Contemplative Withdrawal in the Hellenistic Age."

111. Cf. [Longinus], *On the Sublime*, 16.2: "But when, just as if suddenly [ἐξαίφνης] inspired by a god, and having become possessed by Apollo [φοιβόληπτος] in prophecy, he speaks out that oath by the best men of Hellas."

112. See Jon Hesk, *Deception and Democracy in Classical Athens* (Cambridge, UK: Cambridge University Press, 2000), 215–19, and especially 218: "But where Plato attempts to carve out a 'true' or 'philosophical' *technē* of rhetoric in the *Phaedrus*, or where (as his detractors gleefully point out) he appropriates the seductive operations of *peithō* for the maintenance of law and social order in his ideal polis, he effectively proposes the same subordination of rhetoric to the articulation and achievement of 'the good' [τὸ βέλτιστον in the case of Demosthenes] which is

implied by the orators' definitions of acceptable *deinotēs* and the good *rhētōr*." Hesk uses Demosthenes and Aeschines to illustrate these definitions on 209–15.

113. See *Guardians in Action*, chapter 2.

114. Primarily but by no means exclusively from Plato; see especially Isaeus 6.46 and 6.58.

115. This is where Rowe's attempt to link D22 to *Lg.* breaks down: there is no γραφή παρανόμων in Magnesia. For a reading of *Lg.* that emphasizes its relevance to Athenian legislation, see Glenn R. Morrow, *Plato's Cretan City: A Historical Interpretation of the* Laws (Princeton, NJ: Princeton University Press, 1960), especially 199–215.

116. See Silvio Accame, *Demostene e l'insegnamento di Platone* (Milan: Carlo Marzorati, 1947), 135–48.

117. See *Ascent to the Beautiful*, xxv–vii. See also R. K. Sprague, *Plato's Use of Fallacy: A Study of the* Euthydemus *and Some Other Dialogues* (New York: Barnes & Noble, 1962).

118. Cf. North, "Summus Orator Plato," 210: "Socrates is able to make this statement [sc. at *Grg.* 521d] because he now admits the theoretical possibility of a noble art of rhetoric, in contrast to the debased kind used by the Athenian rhetors, and the *politikos* who will use the noble rhetoric can be identified with the philosopher, who aims to make the citizens as good as possible, saying what is best, whether pleasant or the reverse (502e, 503a). How such a noble rhetoric would actually operate the *Gorgias* does not reveal, nor does the *Republic* take us much farther." But Demosthenes does.

119. See *Ascent to the Good*, 261–65.

120. Increased attention to Demosthenes' Platonic inheritance should be accompanied by increased attention to Plato's use of rhetoric in speeches like these.

121. See J. O. Lofberg, "The Speakers in the Case of *Chrysippus v. Phormio.*" *Classical Philology* 27, no. 4 (October 1932), 329–35, especially 334: "According to my theory Chrysippus beats his breast in indignation as he recalls the effrontery of Lampis and says, 'He admitted that he had made this statement to this man now addressing you.'"

122. As Blass puts it, Olympiodorus is "the smarter scoundrel [*Schurke*]" at *Attische Beredsamkeit*, 3.1.562; he quotes Hieronymus Wolf (1516–1580) in 559n5, who took the opportunity to echo Cicero's *o tempora, o mores* with: "What astonishing shamelessness [*o mirum impudentiam*] of a man who does not blush to confess his dishonesty!' It is generally quite difficult to find any disagreements between Blass and Schaefer, and instead of viewing their frequent unanimity as signs of "scholarly consensus," it would be better to recognize a student's respect for his influential teacher. Blass follows Schaefer in rejecting D48 as Demosthenes' work as well as by identifying *der Verfasser* with the author of D43; see Schaefer, *Demosthenes*, 3.2.240. Such independence as we can find arises from different assessments of the comparative skill of Apollodorus and *der Verfasser* of D43 and D48; cf. Blass, 561–62, and Schaefer, 241. For honesty, then, Schaefer must be awarded the palm, for he states: "We can assert with certainty that Demosthenes, even given that he was still active as a legal counselor—which is very unlikely—will not have lent his support to such a bad business" (239). In opposition to such simplicities, I would suggest that the place to begin looking for Demosthenes' sense of humor—since

no good student of Plato can be entirely without one (see *Ascent to the Beautiful*, xi)—is in the cases he chose to take up, as here in *Response to Olympiodorus*. We should discard the notion that he became a logographer to make money (cf. Badian, "Road to Prominence," 18) since there is no evidence whatsoever that he ever made any, and plenty to indicate (D21, D30, and D51) that he was independently wealthy. Callimachus seems to have understood Demosthenes' sense of humor and helped sympathetic readers to discover it (see the following note).

123. This is a critical point and will be the occasion for the last long note on "Callimachus" and the *Demothenis ordo scriptorum*. At the end of the "Conclusion [*Schluß*]" of Schaefer's *Demosthenes* (3.2.322), he endorses the suggestion of Karl Rehdantz "that the doubtful speeches stand just at the end of the relevant groups [N.B.; three such groups will be distinguished in {} brackets] of Demosthenic works, as with {1} the *Fourth Philippic* [D10], the reply to Philip's letter [D11] and the letter itself [D12]; then {2} the speeches against *Aristogeiton* [D25 and D26] and finally {3} *Against Theocrines* [D58], *Against Neaera* [D59], the *Funeral Oration* [D60], and the *Erotic Essay* [D61]." Note first that these are the last words of Schaefer's monumental study (it is followed by a chronological table of great value), and this placement should be regarded as significant: the excision of these works has played an important role in "the Third Wave of Suppression," and D25, D26, and D61 will receive attention in the last chapter, as will two other works placed even later in the corpus: *Exordia* and *Letters*. Against the view that Callimachus placed the false works last, a number of objections that could be raised, and the prior division into three groups should be considered first: against "{1}" there is the resurrection of D10 through Didymus and the fact that D12 is merely ancillary to D11. But it is this "group" itself that is objectionable, for even if D13 is inauthentic, D14, D15, and D16 are not so regarded. With regard to "{2}," Rehdantz and Schaefer are on better ground since D21-D26 is an obvious group of three pairs; as already noted, D25 and D26 will be considered further below. But since Schaefer regards none of the Apollodorus speeches as Demosthenic, he fails to note that the placement of D52 and D53 supports his "inauthentic to the rear" ordering hypothesis (unlike the placement of an inauthentic D29 in the midst of the youthful inheritance "group" of D27-D31), since neither could possibly have been spoken by Demosthenes. But since D59 is also spoken by Apollodorus, there really is no such Apollodoran "group," and indeed it is "{3}" that is the crucial case. It is this "group"—once supplemented by *Exordia* and *Letters*—that brings the collection as a whole to a conclusion. In opposition to Schaefer, my claim is that Callimachus "saved the best for last" in the sense that the student who comes to Demosthenes, as I did, in search of Plato's influence on him, is only rewarded explicitly at the very end: the fifth of the six *Letters* mentions Plato by name as does the *Erotic Essay*, while *Exordia* is his most obviously Plato-inspired work (see below). At this point, it should be obvious why scholars who deny that Demosthenes was Plato's students would be willing to accept an "inauthentic to the rear" as opposed to "the best for last" paradigm: it is *necessary* to discard (or suppress) D61 and *Letters* if the connection between Demosthenes and Plato is to be denied. Meanwhile, although not to the extent to which D10 has returned, more scholars have been upholding the authenticity of D60 despite Schaefer and Co.; this will be considered in chapter 5. But given the obvious parallels between D60 and *Mx.*, be-

tween *Exordia* and *Grg.*, and the explicit references to Plato in D61 and *Letters*, the ordering principle looks very different from a Platonic standpoint, and the *ordo scriptorum* suggests that it was this standpoint, not that of Reydantz and Schaefer, that motivated "Callimachus" to place these works at the end. Supporting this view is the placement of D54–D59: with respect to dialogic variety and Platonic playfulness, they are the most Platonic of the forensic speeches. Finally, since no ancient denied that Demosthenes was Plato's student, the notion that "Callimachus" placed the most Plato-friendly texts last because they were considered inauthentic is question-begging anachronism.

124. For the chronology, see Schaefer, *Demosthenes*, 3.2.316, and Trevett, *Apollodorus*, 51. But note that the alteration of *Against* and *Response to* in D52–D53 is then picked up and replicated in the two pairs that follow: D54 and D55, then D56 and D57.

125. See Phillip Harding, "The Purpose of Isokrates' *Archidamos* and *On the Peace*." *California Studies in Classical Antiquity* 6, (1973), 137–149.

126. Libanius came up with the Dinarchus theory; see the Hypothesis to D58. Cf. Schaefer, *Demosthenes*, 3.2.266–80, and Blass, *Attische Beredsamkeit*, 3.1.498–504; the latter's theory that the speech's author was "a student of Demosthenes" (504) echoes a move made against *Hp. Ma.*—see *Ascent to the Beautiful*, §8—and the following passage on the same page is worth quoting: "Strong and bold expressions can be found in it, stronger indeed than Demosthenes is accustomed to use; its figures of speech are in harmony with these in arrangement; individual passages recall Demosthenic ones directly, whether it be in the thoughts themselves or in the method of attack or resistance."

127. *Grg.* 527c6–d2.
128. *Grg.* 527d2–5.
129. *Grg.* 527d5–e5.
130. *Grg.* 527e5–7.

131. But it is also "double action" that a reconsideration of the *ordo scriptorum* brings into view, and which in any case it is this book's purpose to illuminate: readers who take up Demosthenes in the belief that he was Plato's student find themselves confirmed in this belief at the end of the *corpus* as arranged intentionally by Callimachus, and this confirmation in turn illuminates Plato's intentions.

132. Cf. Blass, *Attische Beredsamkeit*, 3.1.322. Plato's students doubtless entered the Academy with political ambitions of the conventional kind, and given Demosthenes' subsequent achievements, it would be silly to confine his to the recovery of his patrimony. Contrary to Hermippus, I regard his attraction to Callistratus as consistent with the Academy's purpose, not an abandonment of it.

133. See Harvey Yunis, *Taming Democracy: Models of Political Rhetoric in Classical Athens* (Ithaca and London: Cornell University Press, 1996), 288n3.

134. See Yunis, *Taming Democracy*, 247–57, especially 255: "Given the great variety of deliberative situations treated in the collection as a whole, it constitutes an extremely flexible tool for the *rhētōr* who wants to be both very active and very prepared. Viewed in this light, the preamble collection is not entirely unrelated to Plato's theoretical edifice of persuasive, instructive speeches proposed in the *Phaedrus* (271b–72a; VII.7 [Yunis is referring to an earlier section of his book]). Plato's ideal *rhētōr*, having recognized what type of auditor each real auditor is,

is to employ the appropriate speech for that auditor out of the universal set of speeches designed to instruct and persuade the types of auditors. Plato's purpose in creating his array of prepared speeches was to turn his rhetorical theory into the basis, at least, of systematic rhetorical practice. The Demosthenic collection is on a far smaller—far more realistic—scale than the improbable, gargantuan project imagined by Plato." The word "realistic" is appropriate: Demosthenes is realizing or better, *instantiating* a Platonic ideal.

135. See Debra Nails, *The People of Plato: A Prosopography of Plato and Other Socratics* (Indianapolis and Cambridge, UK: Hackett, 2002), 326–27 ("throughout the Peloponnesian war").

136. For pertinent examples, see *Ascent to the Good*, 120-25, on *La.* and *Euthd.*, and *Guardians in Action* on *Criti.* and *Phdr.* (126–31).

137. See *Ascent to the Good*, 183–85.

138. Norman W. and Norman J. DeWitt, "Introduction" to the *Exordia* in the Loeb Library's *Demosthenes VII* (Cambridge, MA: Harvard University Press, 1949), 84–85.

139. Cf. Das, "Medical Imagery," 11: "The question that emerges from a brief look at the physician analogy in Plato's *Gorgias* and *Phaedrus* is why would the orators, as Campbell (1982) asks, imitate this analogy when it is so intimately tied to a condemnation of traditional rhetoric, their brand of rhetoric?"

140. Cf. 48.1 and Xenophon, *Memorabilia*, 4.4.6. See also 50.3 for another example of Xenophon's influence.

141. *Exordia* 1.3 (Ian Worthington translation).

142. Lysias, 19.64.

143. Isocrates, 6.34–38.

144. Aeschines, 1.78 and 1.96.

145. Aeschines, 2.118.

146. Aeschines, 3.8 and 3.17.

147. Aeschines, 3.260.

148. Thucyides, 3.36–49.

149. Thucydides, 3.44.1–2 and 3.47.4–48.1.

150. See Yunis, *Taming Democracy*, 256: "Throughout the preambles [sc. *Exordia*] Demosthenes consistently reveals himself a disciple of Diodotus."

151. See *Exordia*, 23.2 and 25.4.

152. Cf. ἐξ ἀρχῆς in Demosthenes, *Letter* 3.45.

153. See *Plato the Teacher*, §21.

154. Plutarch, *Life of Demosthenes*, 27.2–4.

CHAPTER 5

1. Cawkwell, *Philip II*, 10: "In so far as I have criticized Demosthenes as a defender of liberty, it is not because he sought to defend it, but because he did it badly."

2. Lucian, *Lucian, with an English Translation by M. D. Macleod*, eight volumes (Cambridge, MA: Harvard University Press, 1953-1967), 8.237.

3. The best account of these debates, along with a sane response to them is Jennifer Hall, *Lucian's Satire* (New York: Arno Press, 1981), 324–331. Although I was unable to obtain A. Bauer, *Lukians Δημοσθένους ἐγκώμιον* (Paderborn: 1914)—and combined with the date, the absence of information about Bauer online suggests he fell, like so many other gifted young scholars, in the Great War—students of Plato will be amused by what Hall writes about him on 325: "He thinks that the avoidance of hiatus is probably a deliberate parody of rhetorical practice."

4. Cf. Graham Anderson, *The Second Sophistic: A Cultural Phenomenon in the Roman Empire* (London: Routledge, 1993), 117: "The Macedonian memoir seems to set out to be almost a tragic messenger speech in prose—set out in Platonic dialogue, with the naive encomiastic and sophistic reflexes duly smiled upon, true to Platonic tradition, before being superseded by the serious presentation of the last moment of the last of the Greeks."

5. Cf. Hall, *Lucian's Satire*, 330: "The second half of the work (in particular the closing paragraphs) seems too solemn and too elevated in tone to be intended as satire; and at the end of the work Demosthenes has been praised from every angle, as a supreme orator, a fine statesman and a noble patriot." Cf. James Jope, "Review of Adam Bartley, *A Lucian for our Times.*" *Bryn Mawr Classical Reviews* (2010.05.26): "some excellent scholarship about Lucian has likewise been neglected. Jennifer Hall's *Lucian's Satire* (1981), one of the best complete studies of Lucian, is absent from many university libraries and rare on the second-hand market." The Arno Press "book" is a copy of her typescript 1966 dissertation from Cambridge; from first to last (xii and 600–606), her love for Gilbert and Sullivan is evident, and it is a jolly good thing for a Lucian scholar to have.

6. Cf. Lucian, *Encomium of Demosthenes*, 1 with Plutarch, *Life of Demosthenes*, 30.4. In the next six paragraphs, otherwise unidentified parenthetical citations will be to the *Encomium*.

7. See *Ascent to the Beautiful*, 443n300 and 490n31.

8. Lucian, *Encomium of Demosthenes*, 4.

9. See *Plato the Teacher*, 177–78.

10. See Quintilian, *Institutio Oratoria*, 10.81, and [Longinus], *On the Sublime*, 13.3. References to this text are based on D. A. Russell (ed.), *Libellus de sublimitate, Dionysio Longino fere adscriptus* (Oxford: Clarendon Press, 1968).

11. Plutarch, *Life of Cicero*, 32.5: "He himself [sc. Cicero], however, besought his friends not to call him 'orator' but 'philosopher;' for having chosen philosophy as his *métier* [ἔργον], he employed rhetoric as a tool [ὀργάνῳ χρῆσθαι] for the needs of being political [πολιτευόμενος]."

12. Lucian, *Encomium of Demosthenes*, 33.

13. Lucian, *Encomium of Demosthenes*, 41.

14. But Demosthenes himself preferred "from the beginning [ἐξ ἀρχῆς]," as in *Letter* 3.45 (translation by DeWitt and DeWitt): "I have been resolved from the beginning [ἐξ ἀρχῆς] that it is the duty of every man in public life, if only he be a fair-minded citizen, so to feel toward all his fellow-citizens as children ought to feel toward their parents, and, while praying that he may find them perfectly reasonable, yet to bear with them in a spirit of kindliness as they are; because defeat under such circumstances is judged among right-minded men to be an

honorable and befitting victory." Note once again the influence of *Mx.* 247a5–6 and *Ep.* 358a6–8.

15. Cf. Cicero, *Pro Archia* 14: "For unless I had persuaded myself from youth by the precepts of many and by much literature that there exists nothing to be pursued with great effort in life except for praise and the honorable [*honestum*; L. for τὸ καλόν], but that in pursuing them, all tortures of the body, all dangers of death and of exile must be considered of small consequence, I would never have hurled myself into so many and such great battles on your behalf [*pro vestra salutate*; cf. Demosthenes' ὑπὲρ τῆς ἁπάντων ἐλευθερίας καὶ σωτηρίας at 18.208] and against these daily attacks of profligate men."

16. Cf. Rudolf Helm, "Review of A. Bauer, *Lukians* Δημοσθένους ἐγκώμιον." *Berliner Philologische Wochenschaft* 43 (28 October, 1915), 1331–1335, on 1334: "And if genius [*Geist*] alone were the index of Lucian's authorship, one could well attribute it to him. But concerning only the degree of *Geist* one can quarrel, and if someone wanted to maintain that the whole thought-process was too good for Lucian [*zu gut für Lukian*], one could hardly blame him for it."

17. Only in the italicized words does Hall momentarily stumble in *Lucian's Satire*, 563–64n25 (emphasis mine): "The author is, however, making a virtuoso attempt to fit in all the topoi, the στρατιωτικός βίος and φιλόσοφος βίος included, *even though not applicable to Demosthenes.*"

18. Leading the way with a courageous move to Switzerland in 1933 is Harald Fuchs, *Der Geistige Widerstand gegen Rom in der antiken Welt*, second edition, unchanged from 1938 (Berlin: De Gruyter, 1964), but see primarily Ramsay MacMullen, *Enemies of the Roman Order: Treason, Unrest, and Alienation in the Empire* (Cambridge, MA: Harvard University Press, 1966).

19. Plutarch's *Political Advice* [Πολιτικὰ παραγγέλματα], 813d–f (H. N. Fowler translation), on which see Gabba, "Classicistic Revival," 62–63.

20. Bearing in mind that Dionysius of Halicarnassus is the principal focus of Gabba, "Classicistic Revival," see 64: "According to E. L. Bowie, the educated Greek classes in the first two centuries of the empire took refuge in the glories of the fifth and fourth centuries B.C. because they were dissatisfied with their own lack of autonomy and independence; their position therefore can be characterized as anti-Roman." Despite the fact that Gabba's conclusion is expressly denied in E. L. Bowie, "Greeks and their Past in the Second Sophistic." *Past & Present* 46 (February 1970), 3–41, on 41 ("most Greeks were in no real sense *anti*-Roman"), it is accurate about *some* Greeks, and more specifically the ones of concern here.

21. Passages linking Plato and Demosthenes in Pseudo-Dionysius, *Rhetoric*, are usefully collected in Pernot, *Confluences*, 89–90; for discussion, see 76–78.

22. For its priority, see Patricia A. Rosenmeyer, *Ancient Epistolary Fictions: The Letter in Greek Literature* (Cambridge, UK and New York: Cambridge University Press, 2001), 234.

23. See David Konstan and Phillip Mitsis, "Chion of Heraclea: A Philosophical Novel in Letters." *Apeiron* 23, no. 4 (December 1990) 257–79; J. L. Penwill, "Evolution of an Assassin: The Letters of Chion of Heraclea." *Ramus* 39, no. 1 (2010), 24–52; and Pierre-Louis Malosse, *Lettres de Chion d'Héraclée* (Salerno: Helios, 2004).

24. Useful for connecting Dion to the Academy through both tyrants and tyrannicides is Margherita Isnardi Parente, *Studi sull'Accademia platonica antica*

(Florence: Olschki, 1979), 289–99, and F. L. Vatai, *Intellectuals in Politics in the Greek World: From Early Times to the Hellenistic Age* (London: Routledge, 1984), 80–95.

25. See Isocrates, *Letter 7*; cf. Laistner, "Influence of Isocrates," 131: "Clearchus, tyrant of Heraclea Pontica, had been Isocrates's pupil for several years. One wonders whether his tyranny was the perverted outcome of Isocratean teaching on monarchy."

26. *Letters of Chion of Heraclea*, 17.

27. See *Ascent to the Beautiful*, 55–58 and 488–90.

28. Cf. C. M. Wieland, *Lucians von Samosata sämtliche Werke*, eight volumes (Munich, 1788–1799), 6.167 (Jennifer Hall translation): "By the help of Philip he [sc. Lucian] had made a great general of him and now Aristotle must needs make him also a philosopher, a genuine Lucianic trick which at least to me seems to betray unequivocally the stamp of his wit!" Wieland realized that both Philip *and* Aristotle were enemies of Demosthenes.

29. For a balanced overview mentioning Chion and Euphraeus, see Zeller, *Plato and the Older Academy*, 30–32n64, noting the following on Demosthenes (31): "though Demosthenes, his great adversary [sc. Aeschines; Zeller has just rejected the view that he was Plato's student], is variously stated, sometimes with greater and sometimes with less precision, to have been a pupil of Plato, still, however, in his orations no influence of Platonic philosophy appears, significant as may have been Plato's influence on him as a stylist." Note once again the willingness to admit that Demosthenes *read* Plato; but even if there were "no influence of Plato of Platonic philosophy" *in* his orations—and I have tried to show that this is not the case—it is the fact of them that is most relevant in the context of the Cave.

30. *Chion of Heraclea*, 16 (Düring on 75); with the remark that follows—"(For I say that the divine things [τὰ θεῖα] are akin to the divine [τῷ θείῳ])"—cf. *Alc.1* 133c1–6.

31. Pierre-Louis Malosse (ed.), *Lettres de Chion d'Héraclée*, 89: "Curiously, it is in his deceptive letter to Clearchus that Chion reveals himself to be most Platonic; it is there that he discusses subjects of metaphysical order (the divine part of the human soul) and properly philosophical (the necessary conditions for study, the idea philosophy learns first how to search); it is there that he constructs his personification [*prosopopée*] of Ἡσυχία (serenity) modeled on the Laws who appear in *Crito*. But since the text is presented in the previous letter as intended to give the impression that it has been penned by 'a mere windbag,' is it necessary to grasp that the author does not care about Plato? This throws into doubt the sincerity of the Platonism in the work as a whole."

32. As in Brown, "False Idles," 490.

33. The easier or king-based alternative in Third Wave of Paradox should itself be recognized as corollary to the notion, championed most vehemently by Mario Vegetti, that Plato intended the City to be realized. For his programmatic reading of *R.*, see his "How and why did the *Republic* become unpolitical?" While effective against a reading like Leo Strauss's—for Vegetti is correct that *R.* is not intended to prove 'the incompatibility between philosophy and politics' (13)—his reading aligns *R.* with *Plt.* and *Lg.* (see 8 on "cleaning") and maintains the necessity of Aristotle's critique (12): "it is much better to follow the path of refutation, showing, like Aristotle, that it [here, 'the content of the

utopia of the *Republic*'] is 'bad politics,' rather than denying that it is politics *tout court*." For Vegetti, it was "sympathies of a liberal and indeed democratic kind" that had caused a post-Popper revulsion against Plato as "the progenitor of bad totalitarian politics," and "this charitable wishful thinking would have solved the problem, but unfortunately it was quite indefensible" (12). This 2009 De Vogel Lecture is, of course, only the English-language tip of an Italian iceberg, and particularly elegant in structure and argument is Mario Vegetti, *Chi comanda nella città; I Greci e il potere* (Rome: Carocci, 2017); see especially 87 (on the two routes), 98–99 and 121n8 (on Alexander as the masculine queen bee of *Plt*. 301d-e), and 121–22n1 ("con sarcasmo antiliberalle"). More relevant to this book's concerns are Mario Vegetti, *"Un paradigma in cielo"; Platone politico da Aristotele al Novecento* (Rome: Carocci, 2009), where the more difficult, Demosthenic, or Academic route ("l'impiego degli strumenti di una buona retorica per la persuasion delle masse" on 23) is expressly rejected. And even more relevant is Mario Vegetti, "Filosofia e politica: le avventure dell'Accademia" in Francisco Leonardo Lisi (ed.), *The Ways of Life in Classical Political Philosophy; Papers of the 3rd Meeting of the Collegium Politicum, Madrid*, 69–81 (Sankt Augustin: Academia, 2004), which argues for a resolutely and continuously tyrant-friendly Academy on the basis of Plato (70, 72n4, and 73–75), Speusippus' *Letter to Philip* (72), Demochares (78), Chairon of Pellene (Athenaeus 11.509b via Demochares, on 78), and of course Athenaeus (76–81). No enemy of "the young tyrant" in *Lg*. himself—see Klaus Schöpsdau, "Zum 'Tyrannenexkurs' in Platons Nomoi" in Christian Mueller-Goldingen and Kurt Sier (eds.), with assistance from Heike Becker, ΛHNAIKA: Festschrift für Carl Werner Müller zum 65. Geburtstag am Januar 1996, 133-150 (Stuttgart and Leipzig: B. G. Teubner, 1996)—Schöpsdau is accurate and appropriately critical on Vegetti's essay in his "Review of F. L. Lisi (ed.): *The Ways of Life in Classical Political Philosophy.*" *Études platoniciennes* 2 (2006), 363–367, on 364: "Ziel der politischen Aktivitäten [of the Academics] war die Durchsetzung einer egalitären Ordnung mit Hilfe tyrannischer Macht. Leitbild der Akademie war offenbar der 'königliche Mann' des *Politikos*, der das Bild des Philosophen, der durch die *melete thanatou* für seine Seele sorgt (*Phaidon*) oder sich weltfremder Spekulation ergibt (*Theaitet*), weit in den Hintergrund gerückt hatte." And, of course, that's not all that Vegetti has left behind.

34. Cf. Finley, "Plato and Practical Politics," 77 ("embarrassment to some of Plato's most fervent admirers") and 80 ("bad press").

35. See Trampedach, *Akademie*, 89–90n19.

36. For Cicero's independence from both Philo and Antiochus in doing so—except in the sense that it was their differences that compelled him to learn the truth from Plato himself—see *Revival of Platonism*, 225–29.

37. Note that the *Letters of Chion* play a prominent role in MacMullen, *Enemies of the Roman Order*, starting on 11, linked there with Brutus; see especially 52. Cf. Vatai, *Intellectuals in Politics*, 157n144: "For Clearchus substitute Domitian."

38. Frede, *Seventh Letter*, 9; similar are Penwill, "Evolution of an Assassin," and Jason Harris, "Scholarship and Leadership on the Black Sea: Clearchus of Heraclea as (Un)enlightened Tyrant." *Center of Hellenic Studies Research Bulletin* 5, no. 2 (2017).

39. Cf. Trampedach, *Akademie*, 85: "Einigermaßen erstaunlich erscheint es, daß sich die platonfeindliche antike Literatur die person des Klearchos nicht zunutze

hat. Athenaios kennt Klearchos, beschreibt ihn auch als grausamen Tyrannen; doch ist ihm darüber hinaus eine Verbindumg zur Platonschule offenbar unbekannt gewesen."

40. Isocrates, *Letter 7* ("To Timotheus"), 2 and 12–13; cf. Trampedach, *Akademie*, 85: "Klearchos war also viel mehr Isokrates- als Platonschüler." See also Demosthenes, *Against Leptines* (20.84); as mentioned earlier in the context of Galen Rowe (see chapter 4), this Timotheus was Isocrates' prize student (2.241–265).

41. Memnon (Jacoby, *Fragmente der griechischen Historiker*, 434), fr. 1.1.

42. See Trampedach, *Akademie*, 88-90; cf. Wörle, *Politische Tätigkeit*, 139–52.

43. As in Wormell, "Hermias of Atarneus," starting on 58–59; despite the statement in the *Sixth Letter* that Plato does not know Hermias (*Ep.* 322e6-323a1), Wormell attempts to validate Strabo's much later claim "that Hermias studied under Plato" (59); see especially "it is most easily explained," where he offers the theory that Hermias studied at the Academy while Plato was away in Syracuse (contradicted by φύσει at *Ep.* 322e6). But after finding something in Strabo that he does not wish to be accurate, and indeed cannot be, since Aristotle was already in Macedon—that is, that Aristotle fled from Atarneus with his wife when Hermias was captured by the Persians (89)—he writes: "Strabo is also the first witness to the story that Hermias studied under Plato, a statement which, as we have seen, conflicts with the testimony of Plato's Sixth Letter. This is, however, a natural development of the tradition [note that what follows belongs in fact *to an antithetical tradition*, since it aligns the Academy not with tyrants but with the most outspoken opponents of tyranny:], and may be compared with the inclusion of Hypereides, Lycurgus, Aeschines, and even Demosthenes in the list of Plato's pupils [note 72]." 89n72 cites Eduard Zeller, *Die Philosophie der Griechen in ihrer geschichtlichen Entwicklung*, fourth edition (Leipzig: Fues's, 1909), 2.1.420–22n1. While retailing the claim that Clearchus and Chaeron of Pellene were Plato's students, Zeller regards the latter's connection to Chabrias as *sehr unwahrscheinlich* (421).

44. Memnon, fr. 1.1.

45. Xenophon, *Cyropaedia*, 8.1.40–41; cf. 8.3.14.

46. In addition to Trapp, "Plato in the *Deipnosophistae*," see Anton-Herman Chroust, "Charges of Philosophical Plagiarism in Greek Antiquity." *Modern Schoolman*, 38 (1961), 219–37, on 225–27, and the same author's "Plato's Detractors in Antiquity." *Review of Metaphysics* 16, no. 1 (September 1962), 98–118.

47. Eusebius, *Praeparatio evangelica*, 15.2. See also "Early Invectives Against Aristotle" in Düring, *Biographical Tradition*, 373–95

48. Athenaeus, *Sophists at Dinner*, 11.509b.

49. As in Vegetti, "Filosofia e politica," 78, where he cites Margherita Isnardi Parente, "L'Accademia antica e la politica del primo Ellenismo" in Giovanni Casertano (ed.), *I filosofi e el potere nella società e nella cultura antiche*, 89–117 (Naples, Guida, 1988), a more praiseworthy piece of scholarship; in addition to Chairon (103), see 90n1 (praise for Wörle), 104 (on Gomperz and Bernays), 106 (on Phocion), 107 (on Lycurgus), 91–92, 103, and 108 (on Demochares), and finally this continuity-preserving position on 109: "the basic position, that of favor for the moderate-monarchical ideal and the βασιλεία ἔννομος, has not changed at all in the Academy." Chairon creates a hornet's nest of probems for

source-criticism (see following note), deftly negotiated in Gabriele Marasco, "Cherone di Pellene: Un tiranno del IV secolo a.C." in Fulviomario Broilo (ed.), *Xenia: scritti in di Piero Treves*, 111–17 (Rome: "L'Erma" di Bretschneider, 1985); see 115 for an anticipation of a discontinuous "Old Academy" with respect to Speusippus; unfortunately, it is only by taking Gomperz's side on Xenocrates (cf. "l'ostilità di Senocrate verso la politica macedone") that he separates Chairon's Macedon-supported tyranny—a support for which a speech of Demosthenes (D17) is our source—from the Academy's influence.

50. See Wehrli, *Hermippos*, 36–37 (fr. 89) and 95–96; Cf. Gaiser, *Philodems Academica*, 494–501, and Jan Bollansée, "Philodemus on Chairon, Tyrant of Pellene (P. Herc. 1021, Col. 10, 40–12, 41)." *Historia* 51, no. 1 (2002), 32–48; on 41–42; so eager is Gaiser for a Plato-inspired Chairon that he wants Hermippus to have distorted the truth by suggesting "that Chairon's 'desertion' from the Academy and the subsequent establishment of the tyranny in his home town are purely persional decisions, inspired by an unimpeachable thirst for glory" (41); Bollansée responds on 42 by emphazing instead Demochares' unreliability, using Demosthenes 17.10 to do so: "Demochares, on the other hand, whose entire *Oration Against the Philosophers* was conceived as a veritable attack on the Peripatetic school in particular and philosophy in general, had every reason to make the most of all available pieces of evidence which might be helpful to shed unfavorable light on the political views of the leading philosophical movements. In this respect, it would have been wholly in keeping with current rhetorical practice if he had chosen to twist and distort some of the facts, should this have been beneficial to his cause. As a matter of fact, his malicious intentions and his unreliability are abundantly clear when one considers that he does not say a word about the Macedonian help which Chairon is said to have received and which (as has been shown above) is almost certainly historical [referring to 17.10]: in this way attention is focused exclusively on the alleged pernicious effects of Platonic training. Accordingly, the most natural conclusion is that Demochares was responsible for stretching the truth, converting the (probably well-known) case of the renegade Academic and Olympic victor turned tyrant into that of the Academic philosopher who, in accordance with his philosophy, started to oppress the citizenry in his hometown."

51. Bollansée, "Philodemus on Chairon," 35; despite the good sense Bollansée demonstrates elsewhere (see previous note), he does not question a connection for which Demochares is our primary source, despite the fact that the chronology won't work ("he [Chairon] must have stayed in Athens from before 347, the year of Plato's death, until after 339, the year in which Xenocrates became head of the Academy"), and even suggests the possibility that Hermippus' account has been affected by "pro-Academic apologists" on 42. Cf. Geffcken, "Antiplatonika," 87: "Keine schriftstellerische Persönlichket des Altertums hat derartig heftige, durch lange Jahrhunderte tobende Angriffe erfahren wie Platon."

52. See the fragment of *Alexis* at Athenaeus 13.610e.

53. But this is probably giving Athenaeus too much credit for reliability: given his obvious antipathy to Plato, combined with the fact that he is our only source for the passages in Demochares' speech *For Sophocles* that relate to Plato, the fact that no critic has suggested that he was falsifying the evidence by implicating Plato and Socrates in an attack on the Lyceum would be inexplicable if there were

no such thing as what I am calling "suppression." On the other hand, Eusebius wrote: "As to the accusation of Demochares against the philosophers, why need we mention it? For he has reviled not Aristotle only, but all the rest as well."

54. Naturally I am not advocating ignoring the role of either Aristotle's *Physics* or Aristoxenus. For emphasis on the passages just cited from *Phaedrus* and the *Seventh Letter*, see any published product of the Tübingen School.

55. Cf. Brown, "Contemplative Withdrawal in the Hellenistic Age," 80: "The *Republic* says that if you want one of these otherworldly thinkers to help out, you must legislate to compel them. And in my view, Aristotle makes this still plainer. He picks up another of Plato's ways of endorsing contemplative withdrawal and says that the best human life is devoted to being like a god." For Brown on the Cave, see *Plato the Teacher*, 233–34.

56. See Brown, "False Idles," 490 (emphasis mine): "Aristotle *retains* the contemplative ideal."

57. See Grayeff, *Aristotle and His School*, 33–43, from "the Academy, however, supported Athenian and patriotic policies" to "the entire Greek world."

58. This contrast is central to "Plotinus the Master," which will complete a post-*Plato the Teacher* trilogy on Platonism that begins with *Relay Race of Virtue* and the present book.

59. Chroust, "Aristotle's Flight." Note that Chroust's valuable biographical essays are collected in Anton-Herman Chroust, *Aristotle: Some Light on His Life and on some of his Lost Works*, volume 1 (London: Routledge & Kegan Paul, 1973).

60. See *Vita Marciana* 41, in Düring, *Biographical Tradition*, 105; it is translated in Barnes, *Complete Works of Aristotle*, 2.2461: "When the Athenians rose against him, he withdrew to Chalcis, hinting at his reasons: 'I will not allow the Athenians to wrong philosophy twice.' And since citizens and foreigners did not have the same duties to the state of Athens, he writes in a letter to Antipater: 'Life at Athens is difficult.'"

61. Martin Heidegger, *Platon: Sophistes*, "Vorbetrachtung" (§1–§3) and "Einleitender Teil" (§4–§26).

62. Martin Heidegger, *Sein und Zeit*, §6.

63. But see André Laks, "Plato's *Laws*" in Christopher Rowe and Malcolm Schofield (eds.), *The Cambridge History of Greek and Roman Political Thought*, 258–92 (Cambridge, UK: Cambridge University Press, 2000), on 275: "By so resolutely taking into account the human factor, the *Laws*, in its specific and still very Platonic way, opens the path to Aristotle. One might even go so far as to wonder whether there is something truly Aristotelian in the *Laws*."

64. See Vlastos, *Socrates*, 53–106.

65. For the parallel, see *Ascent to the Good*, xlv-vii.

66. Cicero, *De natura deorum*, 2.95–96 (Ross, ΠΕΡΙ ΦΙΛΟΣΟΦΙΑΣ, 13).

67. Athenaeus, *Sophists at Dinner*, 11.506d–e.

68. Cicero, *De oratore*, 2.94.

69. See Altman, *Revival of Platonism*, chapter 2.

70. Cicero, *Academica*, 2.74; cf. 1.16, 1.45, and Altman, *Revival of Platonism*, chapter 3.

71. Cicero, *De re publica*, 2.3.

72. See Altman, *Revival of Platonism*, 3–4.

73. See Altman, *Revival of Platonism*, 224–26.
74. See Altman, *Revival of Platonism*, 281–83.
75. See Altman, *Revival of Platonism*, chapter 11, especially 275–76.
76. See Luciano Canfora, "Afterlife (Antiquity and Byzantine Era)" in Gunter Martin (ed.), *The Oxford Handbook of Demosthenes* 431–51 (Oxford and New York: Oxford University Press, 2019), on 445-46: "We can see how the image of Demosthenes helped to keep a kind of Greek patriotism alive in this period of indisputable (and putatively 'eternal') Roman hegemony, not only from Plutarch and the ironical (?) Lucianic *Encomium*, but also from the explicitly and vibrantly apologetic prose of Aelius Aristides."
77. See Leo Strauss, *Persecution and the Art of Writing* (New York: Free Press, 1952), 24: "For the influence of persecution on literature is precisely that it compels all writers who hold heterodox views to develop a peculiar technique of writing, the technique which we have in mind when speaking of writing between the lines." For the evidence of "persecution" in Strauss's sense, see Fuchs, *Widerstand*, and Macmullen, *Enemies of the Roman Order*; a deflationary approach to the antagonism between the Roman Empire and Greek intellectuals is G. W. Bowersock, *Greek Sophists in the Roman Empire* (Oxford: Clarendon Press, 1969).
78. See Phillip Harding, "Demosthenes in the Underworld: A chapter in the *Nachleben* of a *rhētōr*" in Ian Worthington (ed.), *Demosthenes: Statesman and Orator*, 246–71 (London and New York: Routledge, 2000), on 265: "increasingly through the century, thanks to the influence of Hegel and the rise of Prussian imperialism, German scholars of distinction argued that Demosthenes had been wrong to defend Greek particularism against the rise of the nation state, offered by the unifier, Philip of Macedon. This denigration of Demosthenes culminated in the very Mitfordian vision, 'Demosthenes, that master of the tuneful phrase and the solemn gesture,' of Engelbert Drerup in his polemical tract against democracy ancient and modern, *Aus einer alten Advokatenrepublik* [1916]."
79. See Pernot, *L'Ombre du tigre*, 115–27.
80. Consider, for example, Friedrich Nietzsche, *Beiträge zur Quellenkunde und Kritik bei Laertius Diogenes* (Basel: Carl Schultze, 1870); his proposal to read "Menippus" for "Hermippus" on 28 recalls Röller's earlier excesses (see introduction). Incidentally, there is no justification other than prejudice to assume that "Polemo" at *Lives of the Eminent Philosophers*, 3.47, must be a less authoritative source than the scholarch, aside, that is, from the fact that someone who stated that Lycurgus had been Plato's student would probably not have become the Academy's scholarch when Demetrius of Phaleron was in power. Neither is the scholarch ever given a patronymic.
81. An anonymous referee noted accurately that "Plato's position with regard to democracy has also undergone considerable adjustments in recent years."
82. See *Guardians on Trial*, 357.
83. See Altman, *Revival of Platonism*, 281.
84. See *Ascent to the Beautiful*, §13.
85. For a characteristically erudite discussion of the Marathon Oath and its reception, see Pernot, *L'Ombre du tigre*, 177–238.
86. See Sykutris, "Demosthenische Epitaphios."

87. Herrman, "Demosthenic *Funeral Oration,*" 174; see also Ian Worthington, "The Authorship of the Demosthenic *Epitaphios.*" *Museum Helveticum* 60 (2003), 152–57.

88. Herrman, "Demosthenic *Funeral Oration,*" 177.

89. On *Against Dionysodorus* (56), cf. Schaefer, *Demosthenes,* 3.2.314: "Doch gesetzt auch daß noch im Winter 322/321 das Handelsgericht Klagen annahm und erledigte: so viel steht fest daß damals Demosthenes nicht mehr am Leben war, daß er also der Verfasser der Rede gegen Dionysodoros nicht sein kann." While admitting that Schaefer was wrong about the date (584n1), Blass upholds his verdict at *Attische Beredsamkeit,* 3.586: "Gegen Demosthenes als Verfasser spricht die Zeit und die Composition."

90. Dionysius of Halicarnassus, *On the Style of Demosthenes,* 57.

91. Sympathetic to authenticity are Gunther Martin, *Divine Talk: Religious Argumentation in Demosthenes*; Oxford Classical Monographs (Oxford and New York: Oxford University Press, 2009), 201, and Edward M. Harris, *The Rule of Law in Action in Democratic Athens* (Oxford: Oxford University Press, 2013), 401–402.

92. See Das, "Medical Imagery," 131–38. Note also her discovery of a parallel between 18.307 and *Grg.* 480b2 on 103.

93. See Dinarchus 2.13; cf. Lycurgus, fr. 13.

94. For the self-contradiction or originality involved, see Dodds, *Gorgias,* 268 on κατὰ νόμον γε τὸν τῆς φύσεως: "Callicles is coining a new and paradoxical phrase."

95. See *Ascent to the Beautiful,* 240–41 and 266–67.

96. See Yunis, *Taming Democracy,* appendix II.

97. Yunis, *Taming Democracy,* 247n21: "The ancient accounts of Demosthenes' rhetorical education, which make Demosthenes a student of Isaeus, Isocrates, and Plato among others, are unreliable." He cites Schaefer and Blass to justify this conclusion.

98. Consider the passage in F. Focke, *Demothenesstudien* (Stuttgart: Kohlhammer, 1929), 40, cited by Yunis, *Taming Democracy,* 288n3: "He who entrusts this [sc. *Exordia*] to Demosthenes must have a peculiar conception of him: the man who lectures here about the mischief of negative crowd response [θόρυβος in the original] stands over and above the political contest with academic balance [*mit akademischer Gemessenheit*]." Cf. Yunis on 255: "the preamble collection is not entirely unrelated to Plato's theoretical edifice of persuasive, instructive speeches proposed in the *Phaedrus.*"

99. Yunis, *Taming Democracy,* 20: "The texts of Demosthenes, as published versions of actual speeches, are, or at least purport to be, pure *praxis.*"

100. Yunis, *Taming Democracy,* 20–21. Consider also this gem on 23: "though neither Plato nor Demosthenes ever quotes Thucydides or mentions him by name, there is a palpable train of influence and reaction that links historian to both the philosopher and the politician."

101. See Balot, *Courage in the Democratic Polis,* 48–70.

102. Yunis, *Taming Democracy,* 289.

103. Cicero, *Brutus,* 121; "the character and sublimity of his vocabulary" is the felicitous translation of G. L. Hendrickson.

104. See Jonathan A. Goldstein, *The Letters of Demosthenes* (New York and London: Columbia University Press, 1968).

105. Pernot, *L'Ombre du tigre*, 33.
106. On this passage, see Giaquinta, *Epistole*, 480-81, useful alike for citing parallel passages in Demosthenes and for drawing a contrast with Aristotle.
107. Frede's attack on the *Seventh Letter* is an extreme case, and since the core of his argument is that it must be inauthentic because all ancient collections of letters are, he takes the fact that the *Letter of Speusippus to Philip* refers to information in Plato's *Fifth Letter*, is mentioned in Athenaeus on the authority of Carystius, and refers to information preserved in yet another letter from the same collection—on which see Natoli, *Letter of Speusippus*, Appendix I—as proof of an interlocked web of forgeries rather than as offering each other mutual support.
108. As noted in Harvey Yunis (ed.), *Plato, Phaedrus* (Cambridge, UK: Cambridge University Press, 2011), 107.
109. 61.46 (Ian Worthington translation).
110. *Ep.* 357e6–358b3.
111. "We are not born for ourselves alone" at Cicero, *De officiis*, 1.22.
112. 19.205 (Vince and Vince translation modified).
113. See Guthrie, *History of Greek Philosophy*, 1.333–36, 4.17–33, and 5.447–450.
114. Pernot, *L'Ombre du tigre*, 33.
115. Pernot, *L'Ombre du tigre*, 40.
116. Pernot, *L'Ombre du tigre*, 41.
117. Pernot, *L'Ombre du tigre*, 42.
118. Pernot, *L'Ombre du tigre*, 46.
119. In addition to Pernot, *L'Ombre du tigre*, 46 (quoted above) and 100–15, see Laurent Pernot, "Platon contre Plato: Le problem de la rhétorique dans les *Discours Platoniciens* D'Aelius Aristide" in Monique Dixsaut (ed.), *Contre Platon, vol. 1: Le Platonisme Dévoilé*, 315-338 (Paris: De Vrin, 1993); see especially 327.
120. Recently made available in the Loeb Library; see Michael Trapp (ed. and trans.), *Aelius Aristides, Orations*, volume 2 (Cambridge, MA: Harvard University Press, 2021).
121. He is not alone, of course, and aptly cites Hubbell in "Platon contre Platon," 322n38; cf. Hubbell, *Influence of Isocrates*, 61: "The conflict between rhetoric and philosophy is nowhere plainer than in Aristides."
122. See Procopius Koukoulare, "ΑΙΛΙΟΣ ΑΡΙΣΤΕΙΔΗΣ ΩΣ ΑΠΟΜΙΜΗΤΗΣ ΔΗΜΟΣΘΕΝΟΥΣ ["Aelius Aristides as Imitator of Demosthenes"] (Erlangen: E. Th. Jacob, 1890); this doctoral dissertation for the University of Erlangen was written in classical Greek; a wonder in itself.
123. Trapp, "With All Due Respect," 89. Note that []'s are mine—although three of them cite Trapp's footnotes—while the {}'s are his.
124. Trapp, "With All Due Respect," 104. Curiously, Trapp is more willing to see Athenaeus as (covertly) sympathetic to Plato in his "Plato in the *Deipnosophistae*" than he allows Aelius Aristides to be here, referring on 363 to "Athenaeus' embedding of debates over Plato's quality and value within a Platonic literary frame, which itself defers to and challenges the master's authority."
125. Trapp, "With All Due Respect," 94.
126. See Ryan C. Fowler, "Variations of Receptions of Plato during the Second Sophistic" in Harold Tarrant, Danielle A. Layne, Dirk Baltzly, and François Renaud (eds.), *Brill's Companion to the Reception of Plato in Antiquity*, 223–249 (Boston

and Leiden, Brill, 2018), 236: "Aristides focuses on Plato's inconsistencies in an effort to undermine the primary task of the Platonists: that is, to describe and explain Plato's consistent, unified philosophical doctrine." Cf. "Aristides' attempt, by close examination of individual passages, to divide Plato from himself" at Trapp, "With All Due Respect," 95n25.

127. Aelius Aristides, *On Behalf of Rhetoric*, 462.

128. While appearing to praise Plato, Laurence Lampert reverses Aelius Aristides—who seems to attack him—by aligning Socrates with Odysseus beginning with his "Socrates' Defense of Polytropic Odysseus: Lying and Wrong-Doing in Plato's *Lesser Hippias*." *Review of Politics* 64, no. 2 (Spring 2002), 231–259, and now culminating in Lampert, *How Socrates Became Socrates*, 86: "Socrates' last words share the feature of all his public words: they are Odyssean; with an exoteric ring of edifying piety, they convey the esoteric and deadly content of philosophy."

129. Cf. Aelius Aristides, *On Behalf of Rhetoric*, 12.

130. And note once again that Dionysius never refers to Plato's alleged hostility to rhetoric, which is of course the primary foundation of the *Platonic Orations* of Aelius.

131. Otherwise unidentified citations in this and the following paragraph will be to this text as printed in Trapp, *Aelius Aristides*, following Wilhelm Dindorf (ed.), *Aristides*, three volumes (Leipzig: Weidmann, 1829).

132. Aelius Aristides, *On Behalf of Rhetoric*, 351–55. Cf. Laurent Pernot, "Platon et la rhétorique." *Journal of Greco-Roman Studies* 27, no. 3 (2007), 65–86, on 73: "Cette rhétorique serait 'la vraie rhétorique' ([*Grg.*] 517 a), par opposition à la rhétorique en vigueur, qui est critiquée dans le dialogue. Les orateurs représentant de la vraie rhétorique sont très rares, sauf peut-être Aristide le Juste (526 a–b) et Socrate lui-même (521 d)." To this pair Plato and Demosthenes should be added—as it were on either side of the *Gorgias*—the author who wrote it and the student who reread it carefully.

133. Aelius Aristides, *On Behalf of Rhetoric*, 351.

134. Aelius Aristides, *On Behalf of Rhetoric*, 408.

135. Aelius Aristides, *On Behalf of Rhetoric*, 408.

136. Aelius Aristides, *On Behalf of Rhetoric*, 408–409.

137. Aelius Aristides, *On Behalf of Rhetoric*, 411; cf. Bowersock, *Greek Sophists*, 11: "Aristides' antipathy to philosophers was strong, and his strictures were not altogether just." So too Pernot, "Platon contre Platon," 327: "Aristide n'est pas philosophe."

138. Aelius Aristides, *On Behalf of Rhetoric*, 346 (Michael Trapp translation).

139. Aelius Aristides, *On the Four*, 532–35, 541, 551, 567, and 637–42.

140. See Dodds, *Gorgias*, 359–60.

141. *Grg.* 516e9–517a6.

142. Aelius Aristides, *On the Four*, 444–48.

143. Herodotus 8.79.1.

144. Aelius Aristides, *On Behalf of Rhetoric*, 355–56.

145. Aelius Aristides, *On Behalf of Rhetoric*, 357

146. Aelius Aristides, *On Behalf of Rhetoric*, 358.

147. Aelius Aristides, *On Behalf of Rhetoric*, 358; cf. Gilbert Ryle, *Plato's Progress* (Cambridge, UK: Cambridge University Press, 1966), 187: "If we look at the *Gorgias* more carefully, we find Socrates not only attacking popular oratory, but also contrasting with it an oratory of a quite other and this time valuable sort, namely medicinal and therefore unpopular oratory. The latter should exist, though it virtually does not yet exist." Demosthenes would render this "not yet" obsolete.

148. Aelius Aristides, *On Behalf of Rhetoric*, 358-59.

149. Cf. Hubbell almost seems aware that he is mistaking is author's intentions when he writes in *Influence of Isocrates*, 55 (emphasis mine): "The battle between the philosophers and the rhetoricians was still going on, and Aristides *in spite of all his attempts* to prove Plato supports the sophistical ideal [cf. 'the revival of the sophistical ideal in Cicero' on 54], merely calls attention to the irreconcilable differences between the philosophers and the rhetoricians." The Plato-Demosthenes connection reconciles them, and Aelius Aristides probably knew it. Note that Hubbell follows the section on Aelius Aristides (after admitting in its last paragraph: "he has few actual quotations from Isocrates") with "The Pseudo-Lucianic Laudatio Demosthenis" (64–66), concluding with an astute reading of the text in the first clause, and a dull axe to grind in the second: "He [sc. Demosthenes] is orator, philosopher, statesman and general, and his philosophy is that of Isocrates, the philosophy that is practical."

150. See Friedrich Walter Lenz, "The Quotations from Aelius Aristeides in Olympiodorus' Commentary on Plato's *Gorgias*." *American Journal of Philology* 67, no. 2 (1946), 103–28, and C. A. Behr, "Citations of Porphyry's *Against Aristides* Preserved in Olympiodorus." *American Journal of Philology* 89, no. 2 (April 1968), 186–99. Note that Olympiodorus is late (sixth century AD) which helps to explain his willingness to speak the truth (see following note).

151. All the more so because it was in attempting to refute Aristides that Olympiodorus (see previous note) spoke the truth; see Olympiodorus, the Younger of Alexandria, *Commentary on Plato's Gorgias*, edited by Robin Jackson, Kimon Lycos, and Harold Tarrant (Leiden and Boston: Brill, 1998), 268 on 41.10 ('Then if this is what the good man should,' *Grg*. 515c4–5): "Since what I have said so far is incomplete, I must add this about Plato. There existed the celebrated orators Isocrates and Demosthenes and Lycurgus. But Isocrates was {Plato's} contemporary, whereas Demosthenes and Lycurgus were his students. Now if Demosthenes praised Plato, how should we regard the nonsense of Aristides [an excellent question]? For Demosthenes wrote to Heracleodorus [sc. in the *Fifth Letter*], who had studied with Plato for a short while, but then had fallen by the wayside and come to despise arguments. Demosthenes rebuked him and said: 'Are you not ashamed to despise the teaching and the arguments that you heard from Plato?' And again Philiscus when writing the life of Lycurgus says [Olympiodorus is our only source for this fragment of the fourth-century (B. C.) Philiscus of Miletus; see Trampedach, *Akademie*, 131]: 'Lycurgus was great and set right many things which it would not have been possible for anyone who had not heard the arguments of Plato to set right.' We must also cite the nice remark made by one of the philosophers, that Aristides does not realize that he is contradicting himself [just as Olympiodorus does not realize that Plato is doing so;

thus, he never mentions Aristides the Just in his commentary]. For if Aristides himself says that Demosthenes was the image of Hermes [on this expression, see Pernot, *L'Ombre du tigre*, 129–175] and Demosthenes praises Plato, then all the more divine is Plato [nice to follow this with an all-too-human coda:]. Hence the story that Demosthenes was listening to Plato and praising his style, when one of his companions cuffed him for not attending to the substance of the lessons." He got enough of the substance, nonetheless.

152. Aelius Aristides, *On Behalf of Rhetoric*, 429.

153. Aelius Aristides, *On Behalf of Rhetoric*, 430.

154. See Pernot, *L'Ombre du tigre*, T41 on 255, reproducing Wilhelm Dindorf, *Aristides*, three volumes (Leipzig: Weidmann, 1829), 3.430.

155. See Pernot, *L'Ombre du tigre*, T41 on 255–56, reproducing Dindorf, *Aristides*, 2.146.

156. See the dialogue in [Longinus], *On the Sublime* 44, especially 44.2.

157. See Pernot, *L'Ombre du tigre*, T28; Hermogenes claimed that Demosthenes was borrowing from *Alc.1* 123b4 at 2.17.

158. For a more creative rebirth, see Christopher B. Krebs, "'Making History:' Constructive Wonder (aka *Quellenforschung*) and the Composition of Caesar's *Gallic War* (Thanks to Labienus and Polybius)" in A. D. Poulsen and A. Jönsson (eds.), *Usages of the Past in Roman Historiography*, 91–114 (Leiden and Boston: Brill, 2021).

159. Philip Sidney Horky, "Speusippus and Xenocrates on the Pursuit and Ends of Philosophy" in Harold Tarrant, Danielle A. Layne, Dirk Baltzly and François Renaud (eds.), *Brill's Companion to the Reception of Plato in Antiquity*, 29–44 (Leiden and Boston: Brill, 2018), on 43–44.

Bibliography

Accame, Silvio. *Demostene e l'insegnamento di Platone.* Milan: Carlo Marzorati, 1947.
Adkins, Arthur W. H. *Merit and Responsibility.* Oxford: Oxford University Press, 1960.
Aelius Aristides, volume 1; text and translation by C. A. Behr. Cambridge, MA: Harvard University Press, 1973.
———. *Orations*, volume 2; edited and translated by Michael Trapp. Cambridge, MA: Harvard University Press, 2021.
Aeschines, *The Speeches of Aeschines.* Translated by C. D. Adams. London: William Heinemann, 1929.
Allen, Danielle S. "Changing the Authoritative Voice: Lycurgus' *Against Leocrates.*" *Classical Antiquity* 19, no. 1 (April 2000), 5–33.
———. "Talking about Revolutions: On Political Change in Fourth-century Athens and Historiographic Method" in Simon Goldhill and Robin Osbourne (eds.), *Rethinking Revolutions in Ancient Greece*, 183–217. Cambridge, UK: Cambridge University Press, 2006.
———. *Why Plato Wrote.* Chichester: Blackwell, 2010.
———. "Culture War: Plato and Athenian Politics 350–330 BCE" in Claudia Tiersch (ed.), *Die Athenische Deomokratie im 4. Jahrhundert zwischen Modernisierung und Tradition*, 279–292. Stuttgart: Franz Steiner, 2016.
Altman, William H. F. *Plato the Teacher: The Crisis of the Republic.* Lanham, MD: Lexington Books, 2012.
———. "Cicero and the Fourth Triumvirate: Gruen, Syme and Strasburger" in Altman (ed.), *Brill's Companion to the Reception of Cicero*, 215–246. Leiden and Boston: Brill, 2015.
———. *The Revival of Platonism in Cicero's Late Philosophy:* Platonis aemulus *and the Invention of "Cicero."* Lanham, MD: Lexington Books, 2016.
———. *The Guardians in Action: Plato the Teacher and the Post–Republic Dialogues from* Timaeus *to* Theaetetus. Lanham, MD: Lexington Books, 2016.

———. *The Guardians on Trial: The Reading Order of Plato's Dialogues from* Euthyphro *to* Phaedo. Lanham, MD: Lexington Books, 2016.

———. *Ascent to the Good: The Reading Order of Plato's Dialogues from* Symposium *to* Republic. Lanham, MD: Lexington Books, 2018.

———. *Ascent to the Beautiful: Plato the Teacher and the Pre–Republic Dialogues from* Protagoras *to* Symposium. Lanham, MD: Lexington Books, 2020.

———. "In Defense of Plato's Intermediates." *Plato* 20 (2020), 151–166.

———. "Plato's *Phaedo* and 'the Art of Glaucus': Transcending the Distortions of Developmentalism." *Archai* 31 (2021), 1–22.

———. *The Relay Race of Virtue: Plato's Debts to Xenophon*. Albany: State University of New York Press, 2022.

———. "Plotinus the Master and the Apotheosis of Imperial Platonism" (in progress).

Anderson, Graham. *The Second Sophistic: A Cultural Phenomenon in the Roman Empire*. London: Routledge, 1993.

Annas, Julia. *Aristotle's* Metaphysics, *Books M and N. Translated with Introduction and Notes*. Oxford: Clarendon Press, 1976.

Arnaud, François. "Sur le Style de Platon, en general; et en particulier, sur l'objet que ce philosophe s'est propose dans son dialogue intitulé *Ion*" (1769) in *Oeuvres completes de l'Abbé Arnaud*, volume 2, 157–194. Paris: L. Collin, 1808.

Babington, Churchill (ed.). *The Oration of Hyperides Against Demosthenes*. London: Parker and Bell, 1850.

Badian, Ernst. "Harpalus." *Journal of Hellenic Studies* 81 (1961), 16–43.

———. "Agis III." *Hermes* 95, no. 2 (1967), 170–192.

———. "The Road to Prominence" in Ian Worthington (ed.), *Demosthenes: Statesman and Orator*, 9–44. London and New York: Routledge, 2000.

Bake, John. "De aemulatione Platonem inter et Isocratem" in *Scholia Hypomnemata*, volume 3, 27–47. Leiden: Luchtmans, 1844.

Balot, Ryan K. *Courage in the Democratic Polis: Ideology and Critique in Classical Athens*. Oxford and New York: Oxford University Press, 2014.

Barker, Ernest. *The Political Thought of Plato and Aristotle*. New York: G. P. Putnam's, 1906.

Barnes, Jonathan (ed.). *The Complete Works of Aristotle: The Revised Oxford Translation*, two volumes. Princeton, NJ: Princeton University Press, 1984.

Bauer, A. *Lukians Δημοσθένους ἐγκώμιον*. Paderborn: 1914.

Becker, Albert Gerhard. "Über die Schrift des Plutarchos, *Leben der zehn Redner*" in Becker, *Andokides*, übersetzt *und erklärt*, 111–32. Quedlinburg and Leipzig: Becker, 1833.

Behr, C. A. "Citations of Porphyry's *Against Aristides* Preserved in Olympiodorus." *American Journal of Philology* 89, no. 2 (April 1968), 186–99.

Beloch, Karl Julius. *Die attische Politik seit Perkles*. Leipzig: Teubner, 1884.

———. *Griechische Geschichte*, second edition, volume 3, part 1. Berlin and Leipzig: De Gruyter, 1922.

Benoit, William L. "Isocrates and Plato on Rhetoric and Rhetorical Education." *Rhetoric Society Quarterly* 21, no. 1 (Winter 1991), 60–71.

Bentley, Richard. *A Dissertation upon the Epistles of Phalaris, Themistocles, Socrates, Euripides, and Others, and the Fables of Æsop*. Oxford: University of Oxford, 1697.

Bernays, Jacob. *Phokion und seine neueren Beurtheiler: Ein Beitrag zur Geschichte der griechischen Philosophiu und Politik*. Berlin: Wilhem Hertz, 1881.
Berti, Enrico. *Sumphilosophein: La vita nell'Accademia di Platone*. Bari: Laterza, 2010.
Bethe, Erick. *Demosthenis scriptorum corpus ubi et qua aetate collectum editumque sunt*. Rostock: Adler, 1897.
Bickermann, E. and Joh. Sykutris, *Speusipps Brief an König Philipp: Text, Übersetzung, Untersuchungen*. Berlin: Akademie Verlag: 1928.
Bishop, Caroline. "Roman Plato or Roman Demosthenes? The Bifurcation of Cicero in Ancient Scholarship" in Altman (Ed.), *Brill's Companion to the Reception of Cicero*, 283–306. Leiden and Boston: Brill, 2015.
———. *Cicero, Greek Learning, and the Making of a Roman Classic*. Oxford and New York: Oxford University Press, 2019.
Blass, Friedrich. *Die attische Beredsamkeit*, first edition, volume 3.2. Leipzig: Teubner, 1880.
———. "Review of Jakob Bernays." *Göttingische gelehrte Anzeigen* 35 (30 August, 1882), 1089–97.
———. *Die attische Beredsamkeit*, second edition, three volumes. Leipzig: Teubner, 1887–1898.
Boehncke, Karl Georg. *Demosthenes, Lykurgos, Hyperides und ihrer Zeitalter*, volume 1. Berlin: Georg Reimer, 1864.
Bollansée, Jan. *Hermippos of Smyrna and His Biographical Writings, a Reappraisal*. Louvain: Peeters, 1999.
———. "Philodemus on Chairon, Tyrant of Pellene (P. Herc. 1021, Col. 10, 40–12, 41)." *Historia* 51, no. 1 (2002), 32–48.
Bonazzi, Mauro. *Il Platonismo*. Turin: Einaudi, 2015.
Bonitz, Hermann. *Index Aristotelicus*. Berlin: Reimer, 1870.
Bosworth, A. B. "Demetrius of Phaleron" in Simon Hornblower and Anthony Spawforth (Eds.), *The Oxford Classical Dictionary*, 432, fourth edition. Oxford: University Press, 2012.
Bowersock, G. W. *Greek Sophists in the Roman Empire*. Oxford: Clarendon Press, 1969.
Bowie, E. L. "Greeks and Their Past in the Second Sophistic." *Past & Present* 46 (February 1970), 3–41.
Bremner, Sarah Janet Alexandrina. "Athenian Ideology in Demosthenes' Deliberative Oratory: Haling the Dēmos." PhD thesis: University of Birmingham, 2016.
———. "The Rhetoric of Athenian Identity in Demosthenes' Early Assembly Speeches." *Greek, Roman, and Byzantine Studies* 60 (2020), 544–73.
Brown, Eric. "Contemplative Withdrawal in the Hellenistic Age." *Philosophical Studies* 137, no. 1 (January 2008), 79–89.
———. "False Idles: The Politics of the 'Quiet Life'" in Ryan K. Balot (ed.), *A Companion to Greek and Roman Political Thought*, 485–500. Chichester: Wiley-Blackwell, 2009.
Bruns, Ivor. *Das Litterarische Porträt der Griechen im fünften und vierten Jahrhundert vor Christi Geburt*. Berlin: Wilhelm Hertz, 1896.
Brunt, P. A. "Plato's Academy and Politics" in Brunt, *Studies in Greek History and Thought*, 282–342. Oxford: Clarendon Press, 1993.

Burke, Edmund M. "*Contra Leocratem* and *de Corona*: Political Collaboration?" *Phoenix* 31, no. 4 (Winter, 1977), 330–340.

———. "The Early Political Speeches of Demosthenes: Elite Bias in Response to Economic Crisis." *Classical Antiquity* 21, no. 2 (2002), 165–194.

Burnet, John (ed.). *Platonis Opera*, volumes 2–5. Oxford: Clarendon Press, 1901–1907.

Burnyeat, Myles and Michael Frede, *The Seventh Letter: A Seminar*. Edited by Dominic Scott. Oxford: Oxford University Press, 2015.

Burtt, J. O. (trans.). *Minor Attic Orators II; Lycurgus, Dinarchus, Demades, Hyperides*. Cambridge, MA: Harvard University Press, 1954.

Butcher, S. H. and W. Rennie (eds.). *Demosthenis Orationes*, three volumes. Oxford: Clarendon Press, 1903.

Campbell, Blair. "Thought and Political Action in the Athenian Tradition: The Emergence of the 'Alienated' Intellectual." *History of Political Thought* 5, no. 1 (Spring 1984), 17–59.

Canevaro, Mirko. "Memory, the Orators, and the Public in Fourth–Century BC Athens" in Luca Catagnoli and Paola Ceccarelli (eds.), *Greek Memories: Theories and Practices*, 136–157. Cambridge, UK: Cambridge University Press, 2019.

Canfora, Luciano. "Afterlife (Antiquity and Byzantine Era)" in Gunther Martin (ed.), *The Oxford Handbook of Demosthenes* 431–451. Oxford and New York: Oxford University Press, 2019.

Carey, Christopher (ed.). *Apollodorus, Against Neaira [Demosthenes] 59 (Greek Orators, 6)*. Warminster: Aris and Phillips, 1992.

Carey, Christopher, Mike Edwards, Zoltán Farkas, Judson Herrman, László Horváth, Gyula Mayer, Tamás Mészáros, P. J. Rhodes, and Natalie Tchernetska, "Fragments of Hyperides' *Against Diondas* from the Archimedes Palimpsest." *Zeitschrift für Papyrologie und Epigraphik* 165 (2008), 1–19.

Carey, Earnest. "Introduction" to *The Roman Antiquities of Dionysius of Halicarnassus*, seven volumes. Cambridge, MA: Harvard University Press, 1937.

Cawkwell, G. L. "The Defense of Olynthus," *Classical Quarterly* 12, no. 1 (May 1962), 122–40.

———. "Demosthenes' Policy after the Peace of Philocrates. I." *Classical Quarterly* 13, no. 1 (May 1963), 120–38.

———. "Demosthenes' Policy after the Peace of Philocrates. II." *Classical Quarterly* 13, no. 2 (November 1963), 200–213.

———. "Eubulus." *Journal of Hellenic Studies* 83 (1963), 47–67.

———. "The Crowning of Demosthenes." *Classical Quarterly* 19, no. 1 (May 1969), 163–80.

———. *Philip of Macedon*. London and Poston: Faber and Faber, 1978.

———. "Hyperides" in Simon Hornblower and Anthony Spawforth (eds.), *The Oxford Classical Dictionary*, fourth edition, 717. Oxford: University Press, 2012.

———. "Lycurgus," in Simon Hornblower and Anthony Spawforth (eds.), *The Oxford Classical Dictionary*, fourth edition, 872. Oxford: University Press, 2012.

Chroust, Anton–Herman. *Socrates, Man and Myth: The Two Socratic Apologies of Xenophon*. Notre Dame, ID: University of Notre Dame Press, 1957.

———. "Charges of Philosophical Plagiarism in Greek Antiquity." *Modern Schoolman*, 38 (1961), 219–37.

———. "Plato's Detractors in Antiquity." *Review of Metaphysics* 16, no. 1 (September 1962), 98–118.

———. "Aristotle's Earliest "Course of Lectures on Rhetoric"." *L'Antiquité Classique* 33, no. 1 (1964), 58–72.

———. "Aristotle Enters the Academy." *Classical Folia* 19, no. 1 (1965), 21–29.

———. "Aristotle's First Literary Effort: The *Gryllus*, a Lost Dialogue on the Nature of Rhetoric." *Revue des Études Grecques* 78, nos. 371/373 (July to December, 1965), 576–91.

———. "Aristotle and Athens: Some Comments on Aristotle's Sojourns in Athens." *Laval théologique et philosophique* 22, no. 2 (1966), 186–96.

———. "Aristotle's Flight from Athens in the Year 323 B.C." *Historia* 15, no. 2 (April, 1966), 185–92.

———. "The Probable Dates of Some of Aristotle's Lost Works." *Rivista Critica di Storia della Filosofia* 22, no. 1 (January–March, 1967), 3–23.

———. "Speusippus succeeds Plato in the Scholarchate of the Academy." *Revue des Études Grecques* 84, no. 401/403 (July–December 1971), 338–41.

———. "Aristotle and the Foreign Policy of Macedonia." *Review of Politics* 34, no. 3 (July 1972), 367–94.

———. *Aristotle: Some Light on His Life and on Some of His Lost Works*, volume 1. London: Routledge & Kegan Paul, 1973.

Cook, Brad L. "The *Encomium of Demosthenes*: A Dialogue Worthy of Lucian." Paper delivered to the American Philological Association in Chicago (January 4, 2014).

———. "The Biographic Tradition" in Gunther Martin (ed.), *The Oxford Handbook of Demosthenes*, 297–308. Oxford and New York: Oxford University Press, 2019.

Cooper, Craig Richard. "The Development of the Biographical Tradition of the Athenian Orators in the Hellenistic Period." Doctoral Dissertation, University of British Columbia, 1992.

———. "A Note on Antipater's Demand of Hyperides and Demosthenes." *Ancient History Bulletin* 7, no. 3 (1993), 130–35.

———. "(Re)Making Demosthenes: Demochares and Demetrius of Phaleron on Demosthenes" in Pat Wheatley and Robert Hannah (eds.), *Alexander & His Successors: Essays from the Antipodes*, 310–22. Claremont, CA: Regina, 2009.

———. "Philosophers, Politics, Academics: Demosthenes' Rhetorical Reputation in Antiquity" in Ian Worthington (ed.), *Demosthenes: Statesman and Orator*, 222–245. London: Routledge, 2001.

Croiset, Maurice. *Des idées morales dans l'eloquence politique de Demosthenes*. Montpellier: J. Martel Ainè, 1874.

Das, Allison. "Medical Imagery in the Speeches of Demosthenes." PhD dissertation: University of Washington, 2015.

Davies, John. "Hegesippus of Sounion: An Underrated Politician" in S. D. Lambert (ed.), *Sociable Man: Essays on Ancient Greek Social Behaviour in Honor of Nick Fisher*, 11–24. Swansea: Classical Press of Wales: 2011.

Demosthenes, *Demosthenes*, eight volumes, translated by J. H. Vince, C. A. Vince, A. T. Murray, N. W. DeWitt, and N.J. DeWitt. Cambridge, MA: Harvard University Press, 1926–49.

Denyer, Nicholas. "The Seventh Letter: A Discussion of Myles Burnyeat and Michael Frede, *The Pseudo–Platonic Seventh Letter*." *Oxford Studies in Ancient Philosophy* 51 (2016), 283–92.
de Romilly, Jaqueline. "Les modérés Athéniens vers le milieu du IVe siècle: échos et concordances." *Revue des Études Grecques* 67, no. 316/318 (July–December 1954), 327–354.
DeWitt, Norman W. and Norman J. DeWitt. *Demosthenes VII*. Cambridge, MA: Harvard University Press, 1949.
Diels, Hermann. "Review of Jakob Bernays." *Deutsche Litteraturzeitung* 51 (1881), 1955.
Dillon, John. *The Heirs of Plato: A Study of the Old Academy (347–274 BC)*. Oxford: Oxford University Press, 2003.
Dindorf, Wilhelm (ed.), *Aristides*, three volumes. Leipzig: Weidmann, 1829.
Dionysius of Halicarnassus, *The Critical Essays in Two Volumes*, translated by Stephen Usher. Cambridge, MA: Harvard University Press, 1974 and 1985.
Dodds, E. R. (ed.). *Plato: Gorgias: A Revised Text with Introduction and Commentary*. Oxford: Clarendon Press, 1959.
Dorandi, Tiziano (ed.). *Diogenes Laertius, Lives of the Eminent Philosophers*. Cambridge, UK: Cambridge University Press, 2013.
Dörrie, Heinrich and Matthias Baltes, *Der Platonismus in der Antike*, volume 2. Stuttgart–Bad Cannstatt: Frommann–Holzboog, 1990.
Douglas, A. E. (ed.) *M. Tulli Ciceronis* Brutus. Oxford: Clarendon Press, 1966.
Dover, Kenneth (ed.). *Plato, Symposium*. Cambridge, UK: Cambridge University Press, 1990.
Drerup, Engelbert. *Aus seiner alten Advokatenrepublik (Demosthenes und seine Zeit)*. Paderborn, 1916.
Dugan, John. *Making a New Man: Ciceronian Self–Fashioning in the Rhetorical Works*. Oxford: Oxford University Press, 2005.
Duke, E. A. et al. (eds.), *Platonis Opera*, volume 1. Oxford: Clarendon Press, 1995.
Düring, Ingemar. *Aristotle in the Ancient Biographical Tradition*. Göteborg: Elanders, 1957.
Edelstein, Ludwig. *Plato's Seventh Letter*. Leiden: Brill, 1966.
Edwards, Michael (ed.). *Isaeus, Translated with Introduction and Notes*. Austin: University of Texas Press, 2007.
Egerman, Franz. *Von attischen Menschenbild*. Munich: Filser, 1952.
Engels, Johannes. "Zur Stellung Lykurgs und zur Aussagekraft seines Militär– und Bauprogramms für die Demokratie vor 322 v. Chr." *Ancient Society* 23 (1992), 5–29.
———. *Studien zur politischen Biographie des Hypereides: Athen in der Epoche der lykurgischen Reformen ind des makedonischen Universalreiches*, second edition. Munich: Tudov, 1993.
Engler, Maicon Reus. "Secularização e Practicidade: A *Poética* de Aristóteles em sua Relação com a Teoria da Arte Grego e com a Filosofia Tragica." Doctoral dissertation, Universidade Federal de Santa Catarina, 2016.
Faraguna, Michele. "Lycourgan Athens?" in Vincent Azoulay and Paulin Ismard (eds.), *Clisthène et Lycurge d'Athènes: autour du politique dans la cite classique*, 67–86. Paris: Sorbonne, 2012.

Ferguson, William Scott. *Hellenistic Athens: An Historical Essay*. London: Macmillan, 1911.
Ferrari, G. R. F. "Socratic Irony as Pretense." *Oxford Studies in Ancient Philosophy* 34 (2008), 1–33.
Finley, Moses I. "Plato and Practical Politics" in his *Discoveries and Controversies*, 73–88. London: Chatto & Windus, 1968.
Fisher, Nick (ed.). *Aeschines, Against Timarchus: Introduction, Translation, and Commentary*. Oxford: Oxford University Press, 2001.
Fleet, Barrie (trans. and ed.), Plotinus, *Ennead IV.8; On the Descent of the Soul into Bodies*. Las Vegas, NV: Parmenides, 2012.
Focke, F. *Demothenesstudien*. Stuttgart: Kohlhammer, 1929.
Fortenbaugh, William W. and Eckart Schütrumpf (eds.), *Demetrius of Phalerum: Text, Translation and Discussion*. London and New York: Routledge, 2000.
Fowler, Ryan C. "Variations of Receptions of Plato during the Second Sophistic" in Harold Tarrant, Danielle A. Layne, Dirk Baltzly, and François Renaud (eds.), *Brill's Companion to the Reception of Plato in Antiquity*, 223–49. Boston and Leiden, Brill, 2018.
Frank, Jill. *Poetic Justice: Rereading Plato's* Republic. Chicago, IL: University of Chicago Press, 2018.
Friedrich. Leo. *Die griechisch–römische Biographie nach ihrer litterarischen Form*. Leipzig: Teubner, 1901.
Fuchs, Harald. *Der Geistige Widerstand gegen Rom in der antiken Welt*, second edition, unchanged from 1938. Berlin: De Gruyter, 1964.
Funkhänel, Karl Hermann. "Dissertatio de Demosthene Platonis discipulo" in Anton Westermann and Karl Hermann Funkhänel (eds.), *Acta Societatis Graecae*, volume 1, 288–306. Leipzig, Koehler, 1836.
———. "Isokrates und Demosthenes." *Zeitschrift für die Alterthumswissenschaft* 59–60 (1837), 486–94.
Gabba, Emilio. "Political and Cultural Aspects of the Classicistic Revival in the Augustan Age." *Classical Antiquity* 1, no. 1 (April 1982), 43–65.
Gaiser, Konrad. *Philodems Academica. Die Berichte über Platon und die alte Akademie in zwei herkulanensischen Papyri*. Stuttgart–Ban Cannstatt: Frommann & Holzboog, 1988.
Gebhard, Friedrich. *De Plutarchi in Demosthenis vita fontibus ac fide*. Munich: H. Kutzner, 1880.
Geffcken, J. "Antiplatonika." *Hermes* 64, no. 1 (December 1928), 87–109.
Gehrke, Hans–Joachim. *Phokion: Studien zur Erfassung seiner historischen Gestalt*. Munich: C. H. Beck, 1976.
———. "Das Verhältnis von Politik und Philosophie im Wirken des Demetrios von Phaleron." *Chiron* 8 (1978), 149–93.
Giaquinta, Irene. *Le Epistole di Demostene; Introduzione, traduzione e comment retorico–filologico*. Alessandria: dell'Orso, 2019.
Gildenhard, Ingo. *Creative Eloquence: The Construction of Reality in Cicero's Speeches*. Oxford, UK: Oxford University Press, 2011.
Goldstein, Jonathan A. *The Letters of Demosthenes*. New York and London: Columbia University Press, 1968.

Gomperz, Theodor. "Die herculanischen Rollen." *Zeitschrift* für die österreichischen *Gymnasien* 16 (1865), 815–26.

———. "Die Akademie und ihr vermeintlicher Philomacedonismus; Bemerkungen zu Bernays' *Phokion*." *Wiener Studien* 4 (1882), 102–120.

Gottschalk, Hans B. "Demetrius of Phalerum: A Politician Among Philosophers and a Philosopher among Politicians" in William W. Fortenbaugh and Eckart Schütrumpf (eds.), *Demetrius of Phalerum: Text, Translation and Discussion*, 367–380. London and New York: Routledge, 2000.

Grayeff, Felix. *Aristotle and His School: An Inquiry into the History of the Peripatos with a Commentary on* Metaphysics Z, H, Λ *and* Θ. New York: Barnes & Noble, 1974.

Greene, William Chase. *Scholia Platonica*. Haverford, PA: American Philological Society, 1938.

Grote, George. *History of Greece; from the Earliest Period to the Close of the Generation Contemporary with Alexander the Great*, twelve volumes. London: John Murray, 1846–1856.

Guthrie, W. K. C. *A History of Greek Philosophy*, six volumes. Cambridge, UK: Cambridge University Press, 1967–1981.

Haake, Matthias. "Warum und zu welchem Ende schreibt man *Peri Basileias*? Überlegungen zum historischen Kontext einer literarische Gattung im Hellenismus" in K. Piepenbrink (ed.), *Philosophie und Lebenswelt in der Antike*, 83–138. Darmstadt: Wissenschaftliche Buchgesellschaft, 2003.

———. *Der Philosoph in der Stadt: Untersuchungen zur öffentlichen* Rede *über Philosophen und Philosophie in den hellenistischen Poleis*. Munich: C. H. Beck, 2007.

———. "'Doing philosophy'—Soziales Kapital versus politischer Mißkredit? Zur Funktionalität und Dysfunktionalität von Philosophie fUur die Elite im sozialen und politischen Raum des klassischen Athen" in C. Mann, M. Haake, and R. von den Hoff (eds.), *Rollenbilder in der athenischen Demokratie: Medien, Gruppen, Räume im politischen und sozialen System. Beiträge zu einem interdisziplinären Kolloquium in Freiburg i. Br., 24.–25. November 2006*, 113–45. Wiesbaden: Reichert, 2009.

———. "Das 'Gesetz des Sopkokles' und die Schliessung der Philosophenschulen in Athen unter Demetrios Polioketes" in H. Hugonnard–Roche (ed.), *L'enseignement supérieur dans les mondes antiques et médiévaux. Aspects institutionnels, juridiques et pédagogiques. Colloque international de l'Institut des Traditions Textuelles (Fédération de recherche 33 du C.N.R.S.)*, 89–113. Paris: Vrin, 2009.

———. "The Academy in Athenian Politics and Society; Between Disintegration and Integration: The First Eighty Years (387/6–306/5)" in Paul Kalligas, Chloe Balla, Effie Baziotopoulou–Valvani, and Vasilis Karasmanis (eds.), *Plato's Academy: Its Workings and History*, 65–88. Cambridge, UK: Cambridge University Press, 2020.

Habicht, Christian. "Hellenistic Athens and Her Philosophers" in Habicht, *Athen in hellenistischer Zeit; gesammelte Aufsätze*, 231–47. Munich: C. H. Beck, 1994.

Hall, Jennifer. *Lucian's Satire*. New York: Arno Press, 1981.

Hanink, Johanna. *Lycurgan Athens and the Making of Classical Tragedy*. Cambridge, UK: Cambridge University Press, 2014.

Hansen, Mogen Herman. "The Theoric Fund and the *graphe paranomon* against Apollodorus." *Greek, Roman, and Byzantine Studies* 17 (1976), 235–46.
Harding, Phillip. "The Purpose of Isokrates' *Archidamos* and *On the Peace*." *California Studies in Classical Antiquity* 6, (1973), 137–49.
———. "Androtion's Political Career." *Historia* 25, no. 2 (1976), 186–200.
———. "Demosthenes in the Underworld: A chapter in the *Nachleben* of a *rhētōr*" in Ian Worthington (ed.), *Demosthenes: Statesman and Orator*, 246–71. London and New York: Routledge, 2000.
———. *Didymos*: On Demosthenes. *Translated with Introduction, Text, and Commentary*. Oxford: Clarendon Press, 2006.
Harris, Edward M. *Aeschines and Athenian Politics*. Oxford and New York: Oxford University Press, 1995.
———. *The Rule of Law in Action in Democratic Athens*. Oxford: Oxford University Press, 2013.
Harris, W. V. "Ernst Badian; 1925–2011" in *Biographical Memoirs of Fellows of the British Academy* 16 (2017), 3–17.
Heitsch, Ernst. "Der Anonymos im *Euthydem*." *Hermes* 128, no. 4 (2000), 392–404.
Helm, Rudolf. "Review of A. Bauer, Lukians Δημοσθένους ἐγκώμιον." *Berliner Philologische Wochenschaft* 43 (28 October, 1915), 1331–35.
Hercher, Rudolphus (ed.). ΕΠΙΣΤΟΛΟΓΡΑΦΟΙ ΕΛΛΗΝΙΚΟΙ—*Epistolographi Græci*. Paris: Firman Didot, 1873.
Herrman, Judson. "The Authenticity of the Demosthenic *Funeral Oration*." *Acta antiqua Academiae Scientarum Hungaricae* 48 (2008), 171–78.
———. "Hyperides' *Against Diondas* and the Rhetoric of Revolt." *Bulletin of the Institute of Classical Studies* 52 (2009), 175–85.
———. *Hyperides,* Funeral Oration: *Edited with Introduction, Translation, and Commentary*. Oxford and New York: Oxford University Press, 2009.
———. (ed.). *Demosthenes, Selected Political Speeches*. Cambridge, UK: Cambridge University Press, 2019.
Hesk, Jon. *Deception and Democracy in Classical Athens*. Cambridge, UK: Cambridge University Press, 2000.
Heusde, Philip Willem van. *Initia Philosophiae Platonicae*, second revised edition. Leiden: H. W. Hasenberg, 1842.
Horky, Philip Sidney. "Speusippus and Xenocrates on the Pursuit and Ends of Philosophy" in Harold Tarrant, Danielle A. Layne, Dirk Baltzly and François Renaud (eds.), *Brill's Companion to the Reception of Plato in Antiquity*, 29–44. Boston and Leiden, Brill, 2018.
Hornblower, Simon. "George Cawkwell's Contribution to Ancient History at Oxford" in Michael A. Flower and Mark Toher (eds.), *Georgica: Greek Studies in Honour of George Cawkwell*, 1–12. University of London: Institute of Classical Studies, 1991.
Horváth, László (ed.). *Der Neue Hypereides: Textedition, Studien und Erläuterungen*. Berlin: De Gruyter, 2015.
Hubbell, Harry Mortimer. *The Influence of Isocrates on Cicero, Dionysius, and Aristides*. New Haven: Yale University Press, 1914.
———. *The Rhetorica of Philodemus: Translation and Commentary*. New Haven, CT: Yale University Press, 1920.

Hübner, H. G. (ed.), *Diogenis Laertii de vitis, dogmatis et apophthegmatis clarorum philosophorum libri decem*, volume 1. Leipzig: Köhler, 1828.

Isaeus. With an English translation by Edward Seymour Forster. Cambridge, MA: Harvard University Press, 1927.

Isnardi Parente, Margherita. *Studi sull'Accademia platonica antica*. Florence: Olschki, 1979.

———. *Speusippo Frammenti: Edizione, traduzione e commento*. Naples: Bibliopolis, 1980.

———. "L'Accademia antica e la politica del primo Ellenismo" in Giovanni Casertano (ed.), *I filosofi e el potere nella società e nella cultura antiche*, 89–117. Naples: Guida, 1988.

Isocrates. Translated by George Norlin and LaRue Hook, three volumes. Cambridge. MA: Harvard University Press, 1928–1945.

Jaeger, Werner. *Aristotle: Fundamentals of the History of His Development*. Translated by Richard Robinson, second edition. Oxford: Oxford University Press, 1948.

Jebb, R. C. *The Attic Orators from Antiphon to Isaeus*, two volumes. London: Macmillan, 1876.

Jope, James. "Review of Adam Bartley, *A Lucian* for Our Times." *Bryn Mawr Classical Reviews* (2010.05.26).

Kalligas, Paul. "Introduction" to Kalligas, Cloe Balla, Effie Baziotopoulou, and Vassilis Karasmanis (eds.), *Plato's Academy: Its Workings and Its History*, 1–10. Cambridge, UK: Cambridge University Press, 2020.

Kalligas, Paul, and Voula Tsouna (eds. and trans.), "Philodemus' *History of the Philosophers*; Plato and the Academy (PHerc. 1021 and 164) in in Paul Kalligas, Chloe Balla, Effie Baziotopoulou–Valvani, and Vasilis Karasmanis (eds.), *Plato's Academy: Its Workings and History*, 276–383. Cambridge, UK: Cambridge University Press, 2020.

Kapparis, Konstantinos A. (ed.), *Apollodorus*, Against Neaira *[D59]*, Edited with Introduction and Commentary. Berlin and New York: De Gruyter, 1999.

Kapust, Daniel J. *Flattery and the History of Political Thought: That Glib and Oily Art*. Cambridge, UK: Cambridge University Press, 2018.

Kelsen, Hans. "The Philosophy of Aristotle and the Hellenic–Macedonian Policy." *International Journal of Ethics* 48, no. 1 (October 1937), 1–64.

Kennedy, George A. *The Art of Rhetoric in the Roman World: 300 B.C.–A.D. 300*. Princeton, NJ: Princeton University Press, 1972.

Kenyon, F. G. (ed.). *Hyperidis Orationes et Fragmenta*. Oxford: Clarendon Press, 1906.

Kindstrand, Jan Fredrik. *The Stylistic Evaluation of Aeschines in Antiquity*. Stockholm: Almqvist & Wiksell, 1982.

Klosko, George. *The Development of Plato's Political Theory*, second edition. Oxford: Oxford University Press, 2006.

Konstan, David and Phillip Mitsis, "Chion of Heraclea: A Philosophical Novel in Letters." *Apeiron* 23, no. 4 (December 1990) 257–79.

Korhonen, Tor. "Self–Concept and Public Image of Philosophers and Philosophical Schools at the Beginning of the Hellenistic Age" in Jaako Frösén (ed.), *Early Hellenistic Athens; Symptoms of a Change*, 33–101. Helsinki: Finnish Institute of Athens, 1997.

Körte, Alfred. "Zu Didymos' Demosthenes–Commentar." *Rheinishes Museum* 60 (1905), 388–416.

Kosch, Brandon David. "Reading Demosthenes." Ph.D. dissertation: University of Chicago, 2017.

Koukoulare, Procopius. "ΑΙΛΙΟΣ ΑΡΙΣΤΕΙΔΗΣ ΩΣ ΑΠΟΜΙΜΗΤΗΣ ΔΗΜΟΣΘΕΝΟΥΣ ['Aelius Aristides as Imitator of Demosthenes']. Erlangen: E. Th. Jacob, 1890.

Krebs, Christopher B. "'Making History': Constructive Wonder (aka *Quellenforschung*) and the Composition of Caesar's *Gallic War* (Thanks to Labienus and Polybius)" in A. D. Poulse and A. Jönsson (eds.), *Usages of the Past in Roman Historiography*, 91–114. Leiden and Boston: Brill, 2021.

Kremmydas, Christos (ed.). *Commentary on Demosthenes* Against Leptines. *With Introduction, Text, and Translation*. Oxford: Oxford University Press, 2012.

Laistner, M. L. W. (ed.). *Isocrates*, De Pace *and* Philippus. *Edited with Historical Commentary and Introduction*. Ithaca, NY: Cornell University Press, 1927.

———. "The Influence of Isocrates's Political Doctrines on Some Fourth Century Men of Affairs." *Classical Weekly* 23, no. 17 (March 10, 1930), 129–31.

Laks, André. "Plato's *Laws*" in Christopher Rowe and Malcolm Schofield (eds.), *The Cambridge History of Greek and Roman Political Thought*, 258–92. Cambridge, UK: Cambridge University Press, 2000.

Laks, André, and Glenn W. Most (eds.), *Early Greek Philosophy*, nine volumes. Cambridge, MA: Harvard University Press, 2016.

Lampert, Laurence. "Socrates' Defense of Polytropic Odysseus: Lying and Wrong–Doing in Plato's *Lesser Hippias*." *Review of Politics* 64, no. 2 (Spring 2002), 231–59.

———. *How Socrates Became Socrates: A Study of Plato's* Phaedo, Parmenides, *and* Symposium. Chicago, IL: University of Chicago Press, 2021.

Lenz, Friedrich Walter. "The Quotations from Aelius Aristeides in Olympiodorus' Commentary on Plato's *Gorgias*." *American Journal of Philology* 67, no. 2 (1946), 103–28.

Liddell, Henry George, and Robert Scott, *A Greek–English Lexicon*, revised and augmented throughout by Sir Henry Stuart Jones with the assistance of Roderick MacKenzie and with the co–operation of many scholars, with a Supplement. Oxford: Clarendon Press, 1968.

Livingstone, Niall. *A Commentary on Isocrates'* Busiris. Leiden–Boston–Cologne: Brill, 2001.

Lofberg, J. O. "The Speakers in the Case of *Chrysippus* v. *Phormio*." *Classical Philology* 27, no. 4 (October 1932), 329–35.

Loraux, Nicole. *The Invention of Athens: The Funeral Oration in the Classical City*, translated by Alan Sheridan (Cambridge, MA: Harvard University Press, 1986.

Lucian, *Lucian, with an English Translation by M. D. Macleod*, eight volumes. Cambridge, MA: Harvard University Press, 1953–1967.

MacDowell, Douglas M. (ed.). *Demosthenes, Against Meidias; Edited with Introduction, Translation and Commentary*. Oxford: Oxford University Press, 1990.

———. *Demosthenes the Orator*. Oxford: Oxford University Press, 2009.

MacMullen, Ramsay. *Enemies of the Roman Order: Treason, Unrest, and Alienation in the Empire*. Cambridge, MA: Harvard University Press, 1966.

Maddoli, Gianfranco. "Senocrate nel clima politico del suo tempo." *Dialoghi di Archeologia* 1 (1967), 304–27.

Malosse, Pierre–Louis (ed.). *Lettres de Chion d'Héraclée*. Salerno: Helios, 2004.

Marasco, Gabriele (ed.). *Democare di Leuconoe. Politica e cultura in Atene fra IV e III sec. a. C.*. Florence: Università degli Studi di Firenze, 1984.

———. "Cherone di Pellene: Un tiranno del IV secolo a.C." in Fulviomario Broilo (ed.), *Xenia: scritti in di Piero Treves*, 111–117. Rome: "L'Erma" di Bretschneider, 1985.

Marcovich, Miroslav (ed.). *Diogenis Laertii, Vitae philosophorum*, volume 1. Berlin and New York: De Gruyter, 2008.

Markle, Minor M. III. "Support of Athenian Intellectuals for Philip: A Study of Isocrates' Philippus and Speusippus' *Letter to Philip*." *Journal of Hellenic Studies* 96 (1976), 80–99.

Markovits, Elizabeth. *The Politics of Sincerity: Plato, Frank Speech, and Democratic Judgment*. University Park: Pennsylvania State University Press, 2008.

Martin, Gunther. *Divine Talk: Religious Argumentation in Demosthenes*; Oxford Classical Monographs. Oxford and New York: Oxford University Press, 2009.

———. "Interpreting Instability: Considerations on the *Lives of the Ten Orators*." *Classical Quarterly* 64, no. 1 (2014), 321–36.

———. (ed.). *The Oxford Handbook of Demosthenes* (Oxford and New York: Oxford University Press, 2019.

Merlan, Philip. "The Successor of Speusippus." *Transactions and Proceedings of the American Philological Association* 77 (1946), 103–11.

———. "Isocrates, Aristotle and Alexander the Great." *Historia* 3, no. 1 (1954), 60–81.

———. "Zur Biographie des Speusippus." *Philologus* 103 (January 1959), 198–214.

Mess, A. von. "Die Anfänge der Biographie und der psychologischen Geschictsschreibung in der griechischen Litteratur." *Rheinisches Museum* 70 (1915), 337–57.

Meyer, Eduard. "Isokrates' zweiter Brief an Philipp und Demosthenes' zweite Philippika." *Sitzberichte der Preußischen Akademie; philosophisch–historischen Classe* (June 1909), 758–79.

Miller, Jeff. "Aristotle's Paradox of Monarchy and the Biographical Tradition." *History of Political Thought* 19, no. 4 (Winter 1998), 501–16.

Monoson, S. Sara. *Plato's Democratic Entanglements: Athenian Politics and the Practice of Philosophy*. Princeton, NJ: Princeton University Press, 2000.

Morrow, Glenn R. *Plato's Cretan City: A Historical Interpretation of the Laws*. Princeton, NJ: Princeton University Press, 1960.

———. *Plato's Epistles: A Translation, with Critical essays and Notes*. Indianapolis and New York: Bobbs–Merrill, 1962.

Moss, Jessica. *Plato's Epistemology: Being and Seeming*. Oxford and New York: Oxford University Press, 2021.

Most, Glenn W. "'A Cock for Asclepius.'" *Classical Quarterly* 43, no. 1 (1993), 96–111.

Müller, C. W. "Platons Akademiegründung" in Müller, *Kleine Schriften zur antiken Literatur und Geistesgeschichte*, 422–439. Stuttgart: Teubner, 1999.

Nails, Debra. *The People of Plato: A Prosopography of Plato and Other Socratics*. Indianapolis and Cambridge, UK: Hackett, 2002.
Natali, Carlo. *Aristotle: His Life and His School*, edited by D. S. Hutchinson. Princeton, NJ and Oxford: Princeton University Press, 2013.
Natoli, Anthony Francis. *The Letter of Speusippus to Philip II: Introduction, Text, Translation and Commentary*. Stuttgart: Franz Steiner, 2004.
Niebuhr, B. G. *Kleine historische und philologische Schriften* 1. Bonn: Eduard Weber, 1828.
Nietzsche, Friedrich. *Beiträge zur Quellenkunde und Kritik bei Laertius Diogenes*. Basel: Carl Schultze, 1870.
North, Helen F. "Combing and Curling: *Orator Summus Plato*." *Illinois Classical Studies* 16, no. 1/2 (Spring/Fall 1991), 201–19.
Nouhaud, Michel. *L'Utilisation de l'Histoire par les Orateurs Attiques*. Paris: Les Belles Lettres, 1982.
Ober, Josiah. *Mass and Elite in Democratic Athens: Rhetoric, Ideology, and the Power of the People*. Princeton, NJ: Princeton University Press, 1989.
Olympiodorus the Younger of Alexandria, *Commentary on Plato's Gorgias*, edited by Robin Jackson, Kimon Lycos, and Harold Tarrant. Leiden and Boston: Brill, 1998.
Oost, Irvin. "Review of *The Ephebic Inscriptions of the Fourth Century B.C.* by O. W. Reinmuth." *Classical Philology* 70, no. 1 (January 1975), 75.
O'Sullivan, Lara. "The Law of Sophocles and the Beginnings of Permanent Philosophical Schools in Athens." *Rheinisches Museum* 145, no. 3/4 (2002), 251–62.
———. *The Regime of Demetrius of Phaleron in Athens, 317–307 BCE: A Philosopher in Politics*. Leiden and Boston: Brill, 2009.
Owen, G. E. L. "Philosophical Invective." *Oxford Studies in Ancient Philosophy* 1 (1983), 1–25.
Paulsen, Thomas. *Die Parapresbeia–Reden des Demosthenes und des Aischines. Kommentar und Interpretationen zu Demosthenes, or. XIX, und Aischines, or. II*. Trier: Wissenschaftlicher Verlag Trier, 1999.
Pearson, Lionel. "The Development of Demosthenes as a Political Orator." *Phoenix* 18, no. 2 (Summer 1964), 95–109.
———. "Apollodorus the Eleventh Attic Orator" in Luitpold Wallace (ed.), *The Classical Tradition: Studies in Honor of Harry Caplan*, 347–59. Ithaca, NY: Cornell University Press, 1966.
———. "Demosthenes, or Pseudo–Demosthenes, xlv (*In Stephanum* 1)." *Antichthon* 3 (1969), 18–26.
Penwill, J. L. "Evolution of an Assassin: The Letters of Chion of Heraclea." *Ramus* 39, no. 1 (2010), 24–52.
Perkins, T. M. "Isocrates and Plato: Relativism vs. Idealism." *Southern Speech Communication Journal* 50 (1984), 49–66.
Perlman, S. "Isocrates' *Philippus*: A Reinterpretation." *Historia* 6, no. 3 (July 1957), 306–317.
Pernot, Laurent. "Platon contre Plato: Le problem de la rhétorique dans les *Discours Platoniciens* D'Aelius Aristide" in Monique Dixsaut (ed.), *Contre Platon, vol. 1: Le Platonisme Dévoilé*, 315–38. Paris: De Vrin, 1993.

———. *L'Ombre du tigre: Recherches sur la reception de Démosthène*. Naples: M. DiAuria, 2006.

———. "Platon et la rhétorique." *Journal of Greco–Roman Studies* 27, no. 3 (2007), 65–86.

———. *Confluences de la philosophie et de la rhétorique grecque*. Paris: Vrin, 2022.

Pickard–Cambridge, A. W. *Demosthenes and the Last Days of Greek Freedom*. New York and London: G P. Putnam's Sons, 1914.

Pitcher, L. V. "Narrative Technique in the *Lives of the Ten Orators*." *Classical Quarterly* 55, no. 1 (2005), 217–34.

Pohlenz, Max. *Die Stoa*, two volumes, first edition. Göttingen: Vandenhoeck & Ruprecht, 1948.

Powell J. G. F. (ed.). *M. Tulli Ciceronis, De re publica*, etc. Oxford: Clarendon Press, 2006.

Power, Edward J. "Class Size and Pedagogy in Isocrates' School." *History of Education Quarterly* 6, no. 4 (Winter 1966), 22–32.

Recco, Greg. *Athens Victorious; Democracy on Plato's Republic*. Lanham, MD: Lexington Books, 2007.

Renehan, Robert F. "The Platonism of Lycurgus." *Greek, Roman & Byzantine Studies* 11, no. 3 (1970), 219–31.

Rhys Roberts, W. (ed.). *Dionysius of Halicarnassus, The Three Literary Letters*. Cambridge, UK: At the University Press, 1901.

———. *Dionysius of Halicarnassus, On Literary Composition; Being the Greek Text of De compositione verborum, edited with Introduction, Translation, Notes, Glossary, and Appendices*. London: Macmillan, 1910.

Riginos, Alice Swift. *Platonica: The Anecdotes Concerning the Life and Writings of Plato*. Leiden: E. J. Brill, 1976.

Roberts, Jennifer Tolbert. *Athens on Trial: The Antidemocratic Tradition in Western Thought*. Princeton, NJ: Princeton University Press, 1994.

Roisman, Joseph (ed.) *Lycurgus: Against Leoctrates*, translated by Michael Edwards. Oxford and New York: Oxford University Press, 2019.

Roisman, Joseph and Ian Worthington (ed.) with Robin Waterfield (trans.), *Lives of the Attic Orators*: Texts from Pseudo–Plutarch, Photius, and the Suda. Oxford: Oxford. Oxford University press, 2015.

Roochnik, David L. *Beautiful City: The Dialectical Character of Plato's Republic*. Ithaca, NY: Cornell University Press, 2003.

Röper, Gottlieb. "Conjecturen zu Diogenes Laertius." *Philologus* 3 (1848), 22–65.

Rosen, Stanley. *Plato's Symposium*, second edition; first published in 1968. New Haven, CT: Yale University Press, 1987.

Rosenmeyer, Patricia A. *Ancient Epistolary Fictions: The Letter in Greek Literature*. Cambridge, UK and New York: Cambridge University Press, 2001.

Ross, W. D. (ed.), *Aristotle's Metaphysics*, two volumes. Oxford: Clarendon Press, 1924.

———. *Aristotelis Fragmenta Selecta*. Oxford: Clarendon Press, 1955.

Rowe, Galen R. "Anti–Isocratean Sentiment in Demosthenes' *Against Androtion*." *Historia* 49, no. 3 (2000), 278–302.

Russell, D. A. (ed.) *Libellus de sublimitate, Dionysio Longino fere adscriptus*. Oxford: Clarendon Press, 1968.

Rusten, Jeffrey S. "Structure, Style, and Sense in Interpreting Thucydides: The Soldier's Choice (Thuc. 2.42.4)." *Harvard Studies in Classical Philology* 90 (1986), 49–76.

Ryder, T. T. B. "Demosthenes and Philip II" in Ian Worthington (ed.), *Demosthenes: Statesman and Orator*, 45–89. London and New York: Routledge, 2000.

Ryle, Gilbert. *Plato's Progress*. Cambridge, UK: Cambridge University Press, 1966.

Sandys, John Edwin. *The Speech of Demosthenes against the Law of Leptines; A Reivised Text with an Introduction and Explanatory Notes and an Autotype Facsimile from the Paris Ms*. Cambridge, UK: C. J. Clay, 1890.

———. (ed.). *The First Philippic and the Olynthiacs of Demosthenes with Introduction and Critical and Explanatory Notes*. London: Macmillan, 1897.

———. (ed.). *Demosthenes, On the Peace, Second Philippic, On the Chersonesus and Third Philippic; with Introduction and Critical and Explanatory Notes*. London: Macmillan, 1900.

Sauppe, Hermann. *Epistola critica ad Godofredum Hermannum philologorum princeps*. Leipzig: Weidmann, 1841.

Sawada, Noriko. "Athenian Politics in the Age of Alexander the Great: A Reconsideration of the Trial of Ctesiphon." *Chiron* 26 (1996), 57–84.

———. "Allies and Foes (1): Aeschines, Hyperides, Lycurgus" in Gunther Martin (ed.), *The Oxford Handbook of Demosthenes*, 337–51. Oxford and New York: Oxford University Press, 2019.

Saxonhouse, Arlene W. *Athenian Democracy: Modern Mythmakers and Ancient Theorists*. Notre Dame, IN: University of Notre Dame Press, 1996.

———. "Democracy, Equality, and *Eidê*: A Radical View from Book 8 of Plato's *Republic*." *American Political Science Review* 92 no. 2 (1998), 273–83.

———. "The Practice of Parrhêsia" (85–99) and "The Trial of Socrates" (100–126) in *Free Speech and Democracy in Ancient Athens*. Cambridge, UK: Cambridge University Press, 2006.

Schaefer, Arnold. *Commentatio de libro vitarum decem oratorum*. Dresden: Blochmann, 1844.

———. *Demosthenes und seine Zeit*, three volumes. Leipzig: Teubner, 1856–58.

———. "Review of *Phokion und seine neueren Beurtheiler*." *Historische Zeitschrift* 46, no. 3 (1881), 474–476.

Schleiermacher, Friedrich Daniel Ernst. Über *die Philosophie Platons*, edited by Peter M. Steiner with contributions by Andreas Arndt and Jörg Jantzen. Hamburg: Felix Meiner, 1996.

Scholten, J. H. *Disquisitio de Demostheneae Eloquentiae Charactere*. Across the Rhine: Robert Natan, 1835.

Schömann, Georg Friedrich. "De Causa Leptina" in Schömann, *Opuscula Academica*, 237–246. Berlin: Weidmann, 1866.

Schöpsdau, Klaus. "Zum 'Tyrannenexkurs' in Platons Nomoi" in Christian Mueller–Goldingen and Kurt Sier (eds.), with assistance from Heike Becker, ΛHNAIKA: Festschrift für Carl Werner Müller *zum 65. Geburtstag am Januar 1996*, 133–150, Stuttgart and Leipzig: B. G. Teubner, 1996.

Schott, André (S. J.) *Vitae comparatae Aristotelis ac Demosthenis, Olympiadibus ac Præturis Atheniensium digeste*. Augsburg: Christopher Mangum, 1603.

Schultz, Ferdinand (ed.). *Aeschinis orationes*. Leipzig: Teubner, 1865.

Sealey, Raphael. "Athens after the Social War." *Journal of Hellenic Studies* 75 (1955), 74–81.

———. "Callistratos of Aphidna and His Contemporaries." *Historia* 5, no. 2 (June 1956), 178–203.

———. *Demosthenes and His Time: A Study in Defeat*. New York and Oxford: Oxford University Press, 1993.

Seitkasimova, Zhulduz Amangelidyevna. "May Plato's Academy be considered as the First Academic Institution?" *Open Journal for Studies in History* 2, no. 2 (2019), 35–42.

Slings, S. R. (ed.), *Platonis Rempublicam*. Oxford: Clarendon Press, 2003.

Sprague, R. K. *Plato's Use of Fallacy: A Study of the* Euthydemus *and Some Other Dialogues*. New York: Barnes & Noble, 1962.

Steinbock, Bernd. "A Lesson in Patriotism: Lycurgus' *Against Leocrates*, the Ideology of the Ephebeia, and Athenian Social Memory." *Classical Antiquity* 30, no. 2 (October 2011), 279–317.

Steinhart, Karl. *Platon's Leben*. Leipzig: Brockhaus, 1873.

Strauss, Leo. *Persecution and the Art of Writing*. New York: Free Press, 1952.

———. "Preface to *Hobbes politische Wissenschaft*" (translated by Donald J. Maletz) in Kenneth Hart Green (ed.), Leo Strauss, *Jewish Philosophy and the Crisis of Modernity: Essays and Lectures in Modern Jewish Thought*, 453–56. Albany: State University of New York Press, 1997.

———. *On Plato's* Symposium, edited with a Foreword by Seth Benardete. Chicago, IL: University of Chicago Press, 2001.

Sturm, Wilhelm. *De fontibus Demosthenicae historiae quaestiones duae*. Halle: 1881.

Sudhaus, Siegfried. "Aristoteles in der Beurtheilung des Epikur und Philodem." *Rheinisches Museum* 48 (1893), 552–64.

Susemihl, Franz. "Bericht über Aristoteles und die ältesten Akademiker und Peripatetiker für 1880–1882." *Jahresbericht für Alterthumswissenschaft* 30 (1882), 1–20.

———. *Geschichte der griechischen Litteratur in der Alexandrinerzeit*, two volumes. Leipzig: Teubner, 1891–92.

Swain, Simon. *Hellenism and Empire: Language, Classicism, and Power in the Greek World AD 50–250*. Oxford: Clarendon Press, 1996.

Sykutris, Joh. "Der Demosthenische Epitaphios." *Hermes* 63, no. 2 (April 1928), 241–58.

Tarán, Leonardo. *Speusippus of Athens: A Critical Study, with a Collection of Related Texts and Commentary*. Leiden: Brill, 1981.

———. "Ideas, Numbers, and Magnitudes: Remarks on Plato, Speusippus, and Aristotle." *Revue de Philosophie Ancienne* 9, no. 2 (1991), 199–231.

Tarnopolsky, Christina. *Prudes, Perverts, and Tyrants: Plato's* Gorgias *and the Politics of Shame*. Princeton, NJ: Princeton University Press, 2010.

Taylor, A. E. *Plato: The Man and his Work*, fourth edition. Cleveland, OH: World Publishing, 1956.

Thompson, W. H. *The* Phaedrus *of Plato with English Notes and Dissertations*. London: Wittaker & Co., 1868.

Trampedach, Kai. *Platon, die Akademie und die zeitgenössische Politik*. Stuttgart: Franz Steiner, 1994.

Trapp, Michael. "Plato in the *Deipnosophistae*" in David Braund and John Wilkins (eds.), *Athenaeus and his World: Reading Greek Culture in the Roman Empire,* 353–63 and 577–78. Exeter, UK: University of Exeter Press, 2000.

———. "With All Due Respect to Plato: The Platonic Orations of Aelius Aristides." *Transactions of the American Philological Association* 150 (2020), 85–113.

Trevett, Jeremy C. *Apollodorus the Son of Pasion.* Oxford: Clarendon Press, 1992.

———. "Aristotle's Knowledge of Athenian Oratory." *Classical Quarterly* 46, no. 2 (1996), 371–79.

———. "Demosthenes and Thebes." *Historia* 48, no. 2 (1999), 186–202.

Trittle, Lawrence. *Phocion the Good.* London: Croom Helm, 1988.

Tuplin, Christopher. "Demosthenes' *Olynthiacs* and the Character of the Demegoric Corpus." *Historia* 47, no. 3 (1998), 276–320.

Vatai, F. L. *Intellectuals in Politics in the Greek World: From Early Times to the Hellenistic Age.* London: Routledge, 1984.

Vegetti, Mario. "Filosofia e politica: le avventure dell'Accademia" in Francisco Leonardo Lisi (ed.), *The Ways of Life in Classical Political Philosophy; Papers of the 3rd Meeting of the Collegium Politicum, Madrid,* 69–81. Sankt Augustin: Academia, 2004.

———. "Review of F. L. Lisi (ed.): *The Ways of Life in Classical Political Philosophy.*" Études *platoniciennes* 2 (2006), 363–67.

———. "*Un paradigma in cielo*"; Platone politico da Aristotele al Novecento. Rome: Carocci, 2009.

———. "How and Why Did the *Republic* Become Unpolitical?" in Noburu Notomi and Luc Brisson (eds.), *Dialogues on Plato's* Politeia *(Republic): Selected Papers from the Ninth Symposium Platonicum,* 3–15. Sankt Augustin: Academia, 2013.

———. *Chi comanda nella città; I Greci e il potere.* Rome: Carocci, 2017.

Vlastos, Gregory. *Socrates: Ironist and Moral Philosopher.* Cambridge, UK: Cambridge University Press, 1991.

Walbank, F. W., and K. S. Sacks. "Idomeneus" in Simon Hornblower and Anthony Spawforth (eds.), *The Oxford Classical Dictionary,* 725, fourth edition. Oxford: University Press, 2012.

Wehrli, Fritz. *Demetrios von Phaleron,* second edition. Basel: Schwabe, 1968.

———. *Die Schule des Aristoteles; Texte und Kommentar: Hermippus der Kallimacheer.* Basel and Stuttgart: Schwabe & Co., 1974.

Westermann, Anton (ed.). *Plutarchi vitae decem oratorum.* Quedlinburg and Leipzig: Becker, 1833.

———. *Quaestionum Demosthenicarum particula tertia.* Leipzig: Barth, 1834.

———. (ed.). ΒΙΟΓΡΑΦΟΙ. *Vitarum scriptores Graeci minores.* Brunschwig: Georg Westermann, 1845.

Whitehead, David (ed.). *Hypereides, The Forensic Speeches: Introduction, Translation, and Commentary.* Oxford: Oxford University Press, 2000.

———. *Xenophon,* Poroi *(Revenue–Sources).* Oxford: Oxford University Press, 2019.

Whitmarsh, Tim. *The Second Sophistic.* Cambridge, UK: Cambridge University Press, 2005.

Wieland, C. M. *Lucians von Samosata sämtliche Werke,* eight volumes. Munich, 1788–1799.

Wilamowitz-Moellendorff, Ulrich von. *Antigonos von Karystos*. Berlin: Weidmann, 1881.

———. *Platon*, second edition, two volumes. Berlin: Weidmannschen Buchhandlung, 1920.

Wooten, Cecil W. *Hermogenes' On Types of Style*. Chapel Hill and London: University of North Carolina Press, 1987.

———. *A Commentary on Demosthenes' Philippic I: With Rhetorical Analysis of Philippics II and III*. Oxford: Oxford University Press, 2008.

Wörle, Andrea. *Die politische Tätigkeit der Schüler Platons*. Darmstadt: Kümmerle, 1981.

Wormell, D. R. W. "The Literary Tradition concerning Hermias of Atarneus." *Yale Classical Studies* 5 (1935), 57–92.

Worthington, Ian. *A Historical Commentary on Dinarchus: Rhetoric and Conspiracy in Later Fourth-Century Athens*. Ann Arbor: University of Michigan Press, 1992.

———. (ed.). *Greek Orators II; Dinarchus, Hyperides: An Introduction, Text, Translation and Commentary*. Warminster, UK: Aris & Phillips, 1999.

———. "Demosthenes' (In)Activity during the Reign of Alexander the Great" in Worthington (ed.), *Demosthenes: Statesman and Orator*, 90–113. London and New York: Routledge, 2000.

———. "The Authorship of the Demosthenic *Epitaphios*." *Museum Helveticum* 60 (2003), 152–57.

———. *Demosthenes of Athens and the Fall of Classical Greece*. Oxford: Oxford University Press, 2013.

Wyse, William (ed.). *The Speeches of Isaeus, with Critical and Explanatory Notes*. Cambridge, UK: C. F. Clay, 1904.

Yunis, Harvey. *Taming Democracy: Models of Political Rhetoric in Classical Athens*. Ithaca and London: Cornell University Press, 1996.

———. "Politics as Literature: Demosthenes and the Burden of the Athenian Past." *Arion* 8, no. 1 (Spring–Summer 2000), 97–118.

———(ed.). *Plato, Phaedrus*. Cambridge, UK: Cambridge University Press, 2011.

Zeller, Eduard. *Plato and the Older Academy*, translated by Sarah Alleyne and Alfred Goodwin. London: Longmans, Green, and Co., 1876.

———. "Über die zeitgeschichtlichen Beziehungen des platonischen Theaetet." *Sitzungsberichte der königlich preussischen Akademie der Wissenschaften* 77 (1886), 631–50.

———. *Die Philosophie der Griechen in ihrer geschichtlichen Entwicklung*, fourth edition. Leipzig: Fues's, 1909.

Index

"Academic Trio" (Lycurgus, Hyperides, and Demosthenes), 23–24, 127–28
Academy, ix, xii–xv, xxii, xxv–vii, 2–3, 5–8, 10, 16–17, 19–21, 25–31, 33, 36–41, 46, 48, 50–53, 65–67, 69–71, 75, 77, 79, 81–83, 90, 93, 101, 103–4, 109, 115, 117, 122–23, 126, 130–31, 137, 140n6, 142n34, 147n8, 150n53, 151n70, 152n88, 154n115, 159n43, 161n63, 162n77, 171n9, 172n24, 191n78, 194n102, 198n132, 202n24, 204n43, 204–5n49, 205n50, 205n51, 206n57, 207n80; and Philip of Macedon, 29–31, 36–38, 41, 145n90, 151n68; and selfless service to the city, ix, 78; and traditional choice, 77–78; Athenians and foreigners in, ix, xii, xxvii, 19, 122; original curriculum of, ix, 20, 71, 93; see also Curricular Hypothesis; true purpose of, 77, 104, 113; "Academy, Old," see also Academy, Old; new meaning of, iii, vii, xv, xxv, 19–20, 49–51, 53, 77, 80, 96, 99, 110, 117–23, 126, 129–31, 137, 159–60n51, 162n77, 170n183, 189n75, 194n102, 205n49; and Demosthenes, xxv–vi, 96, 126; and dialogues of Plato, xxvii, 59, 129–30; and tyrannicide, 117–19; end of, 21–42, 55; freedom and philosophy in, 83; party of, 19; purpose of, 77; recovery of, xv, xxv, 53, 122–23, 137, 188–89n75; rhetoric, character, and deception in, 77; suppression of, 121–22; what Plato taught in, 99; traditional meaning of, ix, xxv, 20, 65, 77–78, 121–22, 137; and Archytas, 130–31; and Aristotle, Speusippus, and Xenocrates, xxvi, 65, 121–22, 137
Acamas, 36, 40–41
Accame, Silvio, 196n116
Adkins, A. W. H., 195n106
Aelian, 140n6, 160n55
Aelius Aristides, xxviii, 67, 89, 116, 125, 132–37, 172n15, 207n76, 209n124, 210n128, 210n130, 210n132, 211n149
Aeschines, xiii–iv, xxvi–vii, xxxiii, 7, 9, 14, 19, 35–37, 40, 43–48, 52, 56, 62, 86–88, 97, 107–8, 110, 141n17, 146n101, 146n104, 155–56n130, 163n96, 167–68n155, 168n161, 169n169, 170n177, 188n74, 194n99, 195–96n112, 202n29, 204n43; as

231

Plato's student, 45–47, 52; on Socrates, 44–46, 167–68n155; survival of, 87; writings of: *Against Timarchus* (1), 44–46, 107, 146n104; *On the Embassy* (2), 35, 40, 107, 146n104; *Against Ctesiphon* (3), 43, 107, 146n104; "fourth speech of," 86; veracity of, 155–56n130
Aeschines, Life of, 43, 46
Alexander the Great, xxiii, xxv, xxxiii–iv, 14, 18–20, 23–26, 31, 49–50, 53, 59, 62–63, 81, 112, 122, 140n6, 146n102, 148n22, 154n115, 155n122, 159n43, 160n53, 165n120, 165n121, 165–66n126, 188–90n75, 202–203n33
Allen, D. S., xiv, xxvi–vii, 56, 78–79, 159n42, 169n170, 174–75n68, 175n69, 188n74, 192n82
Amphipolis, xxxvi, 33–36, 39–41, 154n110, 154n115
anachronism, question-begging, 197–98n123
Antipater, xxxiv, 13, 18, 24–26, 29, 47, 64, 118, 122, 146n102, 148n21, 148n22, 149n43, 159–60n51, 160n55, 206n60; and Aristotle, 24, 118, 122, 148n21; and Demosthenes, 64, 118
"Antipater" (Lucian's), 111–12, 114–15
Antipater of Magnesia, 36, 40
Antiphon, 102, 194n99
Apollo, 195n111
Apollodorus, 91–92, 101–2, 182n43, 182n44, 182n46, 183n47, 183–84n48, 184n49, 186n58, 192n80, 196–97n122, 197–98n123; colossal problem of, 91
Apology of Socrates, 34, 45, 62, 80–81, 88–89, 114, 150n63, 166n129, 166n131, 166n132, 167n145, 167n150, 170n183, 173n26, 173n27, 175n72, 190n76, 192n84, 193n90, 194–95n102; and Hyperides, 170n183; and *On the Chersonese*, 190n76; as Plato's *Philosopher*, 81
Archytas, 130–32
Aristides the Just, 103, 135, 148n12, 211–12n151

Aristotle, v, xii, xxii–vii, xxxiii–iv, 3–4, 13, 17–20, 24–28, 31, 43, 46–50, 64–65, 69–70, 74–78, 80–81, 94, 100, 112–13, 118, 120–23, 126, 130–31, 137, 140n6, 164n112, 170n185, 172n23, 188–90n75, 204n43; and Academy, xxiii, 122, 126, 130, 154n115, 157n16, 171n9; and Aeschines, 46; and Alexander; see Alexander the Great; and Antipater, 24–25; see also Antipater; and "contemplative ideal," 195n109, 206; and Demochares, 161–62n68, 205–206n53; and Demosthenes, v, xxiii, xxvii, 17–19, 29, 65, 94, 100, 118, 122, 150n54, 188–90n75, 202n28, 209n106; and Didymus, 188–90n75; and Hermias, 189n75; see also Hermias of Atarneus; and Hermippus, 145n91; and Intermediates, 75; and *Laws*, 206n63; and [Lucian], 112–13, 202n28; and Lyceum, 49; and Peripatetic School, 3, 48, 120–21, 157–58n28; and Philip, 18, 161n68; and Plato's *Laws*, 206n63; and προαίρεσις, 78, 174–75n68; and publication of Plato's dialogues, 69–70, 172n24; and *Republic*, 76, 123; and Socrates, 74–75, 145n92, 146n96, 157n16, 206n60; and suppression of "the Old Academy," 122; and Third Man, 64; and Third Wave of Paradox, 19–20, 49, 121–22, 202–203n33; and *Timaeus*, 80, 175n86; and "unwritten teachings," 118, 121; and Xenocrates, 17, 25; as eudaemonist, 74–75; as pro-Macedonian, xxvi, 19, 26, 29, 50, 94, 118, 146n102, 159n44; as Plato's paradigmatic student, xii, 17, 118, 145n91; as responsible for current conceptions of Plato's intentions, xxvi–vii, 20, 69, 74, 121–23, 137; "flights from Athens" of, 18–19, 122, 146n96, 206n60; sense of humor of, xvii; tried for impiety,

Index

50; works of: *Concerning Philosophy*, 123; *Constitution of Athens*, 164n112; *Gryllus*, 48, 158n37; Letters to Antipater, 148n21; *Metaphysics*, 28, 77, 80, 121, 131, 151n74, 173n50, 174–75n68, 176n100, 175n85; *On Kingship*, 49; Physics, 206n54; *Politics*, 50, 159n49, 174n54; *Rhetoric*, xxii, 48, 158n36, 191n78
Aristoxenus, 7, 69, 121, 147n107, 206n54; as critical of Plato, 147n107
Arnaud, François, xx
Athena, ix, 83
Athenaeus, 32, 36–37, 119–21, 123, 140n6, 162n77, 202–203n33, 204n48, 205–206n52–53, 206n67, 209n107, 209n124; as Plato–hating, 119, 205–206n53

Badian, Ernst, 86–87, 94, 168–69, 177–78, 188n73, 189n74, 196–97n122; and fourth speech of Aeschines, 86
Balot, R. K., x, 179–80n31, 195n109, 208n101
Becker, A. G., xiv, 180–182n37
Beloch, K. J., 18, 146n100, 177n8
Bentley, Richard, 30, 129, 152n83
Bernays, Jacob, 25–33, 39, 51, 50, 53–54, 148–53, 159–60n51, 163n81, 204–205n49; anti–Jewish trope, 148n30
Blass, Friedrich, 4, 11, 26, 28, 61, 142n29, 144n63, 145n80, 149n40, 150n55, 151n70–71, 153n94, 153n98, 162n77, 167n150, 168n157, 169n171, 178n21, 179n22, 182n44, 196–97n122, 198n126, 198n132, 208n89, 208n97
Bollansée, Jan, 3, 140n14–15, 145n93, 171n7, 205n50–51
book, this: and "Quintilian's Proof," 98; central claim of, 77
Bowersock, G. W., 207n77, 210n137
Bremner, S. J. A., 86–87, 178n14, 178n17–18, 179n24, 179n28
Brown, Eric, 162n70, 195n109, 202n32, 206n55–56
Brunt, P. A., 8, 143n50

Burke, E. M., 56, 163n94, 163n97, 179n25, 187n71, 188n74, 191n79
Burnyeat, Myles, 30, 152n82, 152n85

Caecilius, 46, 158n35
Callimachus and "Callimachus," 87–88, 91–92, 94–95, 102, 105, 128, 176–77n4, 180n32, 180–81n37, 183n47, 184n49–50, 185n56, 191–92n80, 197–98n123, 198n131; as traditional editor responsible for the order of Demosthenes' writings, 87, 178n21; saves the best for last, 102, 197n123. See also *Demosthenis ordo scriptorium*
Callistratus, xxxiii, 2–4, 7–8, 11, 22, 102, 112–13, 139n4, 143n44, 147n8–9, 191n78
Campbell, Blair, 192–93n87, 199n139; hits the nail on the head, 194n102
Canfora, Luciano, 207n76
Casaubon, Isaac, 144n63
Cave: Allegory of the, ix, xii–iii, xxi, xxvii, 6, 9–10, 12, 24, 27, 31, 49, 52, 54, 59, 61, 65, 74–79, 81–82, 87, 95–96, 104, 114, 122–24, 190n76, 202n29, 206n55; and "Cave–based Platonism," 12; and "Cave–centric" *Platonbild* ("conception of Plato"), 6, 10
Cawkwell, G. L., 86–87, 165n123, 165–66n126, 169n169, 169n171, 177n6, 177n11, 178n19, 179n26, 187n68, 187n72, 199n1; and Co., 86–87, 94, 131; and Ronald Syme, 177n6; verdict on Demosthenes of, 199n1; vocabulary of, 178n16
Chabrias, xiii, 6–7, 22–23, 95, 143n50, 147n8–9, 191n78, 204n43; and collaboration with Callistratus, 7, 191n78; and Plato, 191n78
Chaeronea, xxv, xxxiv, 21, 23, 26, 29, 41–42, 55–56, 59, 62, 72, 94, 96–97, 108–9, 127–28, 136, 163n93, 166n141, 168n161, 180n32, 194n98, 195n107
Chairon of Pellene, 120–21, 161n67, 203n33, 204n49, 205n50–51

Chion of Heraclea, Letters of, xxviii–ix, 117–21, 137, 201–202n23, 202n29–31, 203n37

Chroust, Anton-Herman, 18–19, 48–49, 146, 148–49, 151n72, 156n9, 157n15–16, 160n55, 204n46, 206n59

Clearchus, 117–21, 202n25, 202n31, 203n37–38, 204n43

Cicero, xi, xiii, xvi–xviii, xx, xxii–iv, xxviii, 4, 6, 15, 22, 47–48, 55, 67, 71, 73, 82–83, 85–88, 95–97, 104, 115, 117, 119, 123–24, 126–27, 129, 131–33, 136–38, 143n47, 145n76, 159n44, 178n19, 203n36, 211n149; and "Cicero," 123–24; and Plato-Demosthenes connection, xi, xiii, xvii, xxii–iv, 4, 12, 55, 117, 126, 141n20, 143n47; as philosopher, 200n11; as Platonist, 6, 12, 82; reception of, 177n5; writings of: *Academica*, 206n70; *Brutus*, xi, 129, 131, 141n21, 208n103; *Catilinarians*, 96, 196–97n122; *De inventione*, 124; *De legibus*, 158n30; *De natura deorum*, 123, 206n66; *De officiis*, xviii, 131, 164n107, 209n111; *De optimo genere oratorum*, xviii; *De oratore*, xvi, xviii, xx, 123, 206n68; *De re publica*, xvii, 192n81, 207n71; "Dream of Scipio," xvii, 124; *Orator*, xvii–viii, 141n20; *Philippics*, xviii, 124; *Pro Archia*, 201n15; *Tusculan Disputations*, 71, 96, 158n40, 175n85, 192n86, 195n109

Clemenceau, Georges, 125
Cook, B. L., xvi, xxix, 154n107
Cooper, C. R., 47–48, 52, 140n11, 141n17, 170n184
Croiset, Maurice, 172n25
Curricular Hypothesis, xxvii, 2, 70–71, 73, 81, 93, 121, 140–41n16

Das, Allison, 179n29, 199n139, 208n92
Demades, 21, 47–48, 52, 62, 158n34, 160n55, 168n161, 170n177; as pro-Macedonian scoundrel, 62
Demetrius of Magnesia, 62

Demetrius of Phaleron, xxvi, xxxiv, 6, 46–49, 51, 62, 120, 157n28, 207n80; and Aeschines as Plato's student, xxvi, 46–47, 52; and defaming Demosthenes, 47; and Demosthenes' pebbles, 47–48; as corrupt Macedonian stooge, 52; as Peripatetic, 46–47; as quisling, 47

Demetrius Poliocetes, 51,

Demochares, xxxiv, 38, 51–53, 120–22, 155n129, 161n63, 161n68, 162n77–78, 202–203n33, 204–205n49, 205n50–51, 205–206n53

Demosthenes, *passim*: and Aristotle, v, 188–89n75, 202n28, 209n106; and Athens, 192–93n87; and Athens' stolen patrimony, 91; *see* Callistratus; and "Cawkwell and Co.," 96; *see also* Cawkwell, G. A; and deconstruction of a concealing tradition, 122; *see also* Heidegger, Martin; and "echoing," 90; and *Gorgias*, 133–34; *see also* Gorgias; and Isaeus, 91–92, 180–81n37; *see also* Isaeus; and the Marathon Oath, xxvii, 97–100, 194n100, 207n85; and Plato's Democratic Man, 90–91; and Plato's words, 90, 199n134; and problems of authenticity, 85; and *reading* Plato, 5, 13, 62, 129, 172n25, 202n29; and Thucydides, xv, 34; and youthful determination, 87; as mythologist, 41; as detective of deception, 95, 100–1, 134; as logographer, 92, 101, 181n37, 196n122; development of, 88; impulse to denigrate, 182n44; sense of humor of, xvii, 196–97n122; world preserved by, 85–86, 176n1; writings of, as treasure not cadaver, 87; will to excise, 182n44; *First Olynthian* (D1), 18, 34, 39, 87, 98, 104, 107–8, 123, 180n32; *Second Olynthian* (D2), 18, 39, 87, 98, 108, 123, 180n32; *Third Olynthian* (D3), 18, 39, 87–88, 98, 106, 108, 123, 180n32; *First*

Philippic (D4), 18, 30, 39, 87–88, 99, 104, 180n32; *On the Peace* (D5), 89, 180n32; *Second Philippic* (D6), 30, 89, 99, 180n32; *On Halonnesus* (D7), 89, 180n32; *On the Chersonese* (D8), 89, 94, 180n32, 190n76; *Third Philippic* (D9), 30, 37, 88–89, 94, 98–99, 104, 108, 121, 127, 180n32, 190n76; *Fourth Philippic* (D10), 94, 180n32, 188–89n75, 197n123; *Reply to Philip* (D11), 180n32, 188n75, 197n123; *Philip's Letter* (D12), 180n32, 188–89n75, 197n123; *On the Symmories* (D13), 87, 179n27, 180n32, 188n75, 197n123; *On the Navy* (D14), 180n32, 197n123; *On Behalf of the Liberty of the Rhodians* (D15), 180n32, 187n68, 197n123; *On Behalf of the Megalopolitans* (D16), 187n68, 197n123; *On the Accession of Alexander* (D17), 180n32, 204–205n49; *On the Crown* (D18), xviii, xxi–v, xxvii, xxxiv, 61, 63, 87, 94, 96–99, 106, 108, 114, 127, 131, 180n32; *On the False Embassy* (D19), xxxiv, 87, 94, 180n32; *Response to Leptines* (D20), xxix, xxxiii, 87–88, 94–95, 98–100, 106, 180n32, 190n77, 191n78, 191–92n80, 192–83n87, 204n40; *Against Meidias* (D21), xxxiii, 18, 88, 92, 94, 106, 186n58, 197n123; *Against Androtion* (D22), 93, 178n15, 185n57, 186n58, 187n71, 197n123; *Against Aristocrates* (D23), 99, 187n71, 197n123; *Against Timocrates* (D24), 178n15, 185n57, 186n58, 187n71, 197n123; *Against Aristogeiton I* (D25), 88, 128, 187–88n75, 191–92n80, 197n123; *Against Aristogeiton II* (D26), 88, 128, 188–89n75, 191–92n80, 197n123; *Against Aphobus I* (D27), 191–92n80,197n123; *Against Aphobus II* (D 28), 191–92n80, 197n123; *Response to Aphobus* (D29), 183n47, 188–89n75, 191–92n80, 197n123; *Response to Onetor I* (D30), 186n58, 197n123; *Response to Onetor II* (D31), 186n58, 192n80, 197n123; *Response to Zenothemis* (D32), 101, 192n80; *Response to Apaturius* (D33), 101, 185n56, 192n80; *Response to Phormio* (D34), 101, 192n80; *Response to Lacritus* (D35), 101, 192n80; *On Behalf of Phormio* (D36), 102, 182n44, 183n47, 191–92n80; *Response to Pantaenetus* (D37), 102, 192n80; *Response to Nausimachus and Xenopeithes* (D38), 102, 192n80; *Response to Boeotus I* (D39), 102; *Against Boeotus II* (D40), 102; *Response to Spudias* (D41), 102; *Response to Phaenippus* (D42), 102, 192n80; *Response to Macartatus* (D43), 91, 102, 182n42, 183n47, 192n80; *Response to Leochares* (D44), 91, 102, 182n42, 183n47, 192n80; *Against Stephanus I* (D45), 182n44, 183n47; *Against Stephanus II* (D46), 183n47; *Against Euergus and Mnesibulus* (D47), 102, 183n47; *Response to Olympiodorus* (D48), 102, 183n47, 196–97n122; *Response to Timotheus* (D49), 183n47, 186n58, 192n80; *Response to Polycles* (D50), 183n47, 191–92n80; *On the Trierarchic Crown* (D51), 183n47, 191–92n80; *Against Callippus* (D52), 102, 183n47, 192n80, 197n123, 198n124; *Response to Nicostratus* (D53), 183n47, 192n80, 197n123, 198n124; *Against Conon* (D54), 102, 192n80, 197n123, 198n124; *Response to Callicles* (D55), 102, 192n80, 197n123, 198n124; *Against Dionysodorus* (D56), 102, 192n80, 197n123, 198n124, 208n89; *Response to Eubulides* (D57), 102, 192n80, 197n123, 198n124; *Against Theocrines* (D58), 92, 102, 184n50, 192n80, 197n123; *Against Neaira* (D59), 92, 94, 103, 183n47, 184n50, 187n67, 197n123; *Funeral Oration* (D60), xx, xxxiv, 41, 61, 127–28,

166n141, 167n148, 168n161, 183n47, 184n50, 188–89n75, 197n123; *Erotic Essay* (D61), xvii, 130, 183n47, 188–89n75, 197n123; *Exordia*, xxviii, 104–7, 128–29, 176n3, 197n123, 199n138, 199n150, 208n98; *Letters*, 16, 129–30, 197n123, 200n14, 209n104

Demosthenis ordo scriptorum (the traditional order or τάξις of Demosthenes' writings, traditionally ascribed to Callimachus), 176–77n4, 178n21, 180n32, 197n123, 198n131; based on pairs, 95, 180n32, 180n37, 183n47, 184n50, 185n56, 191–92n80; and "double action," 198n131; as pedagogically pleasing and instructive, 176–77n4; as Plato-inspired, 196–97n122, 198n131; best for last in, 102, 197n123; "inauthentic to the rear" in, 197–98n122; internal logic of, 192n80

DeWitt, Norman W., 105, 176n2, 199n138, 200n14

Dillon, John, xxv, xxvii, 148n17, 151n76, 152n88–89, 153n91; excellent question of, 148n17

Dinarchus, 62, 102–3, 110, 128, 167n149, 168n160, 168n162, 169n168, 169n169, 198n126; *Against Demosthenes* of, as inauthentic, 62, 167n149

Diodorus Siculus, 160n54, 161n68, 169n171

Diodotus (Thucydides), 108; and Demosthenes, 199n150

Diogenes Laertius, xxv, 4, 7, 10, 17, 25, 36, 113, 124, 141n20, 143n43, 154n116, 154–55n120, 159–60n51, 160–61n61, 162–63n79, 164n111

Dion, xxxiii, 77, 96, 117, 202n24; paired with Brutus by Plutarch, 96

Diondas. *See* Hyperides, works of

Dionysius of Halicarnassus, xi, xviii–xxv, xxvii–viii, 3, 60–61, 67–68, 71, 73, 98, 112–13, 116, 124, 126–28, 134, 137, 169n166, 172n15, 178n21, 182n38, 188–89n75, 195n104, 201n20; and *Against Neaira* of Demosthenes, 183–84n48; and Cicero, xviii, xxii–iii; and *Fourth Philippic* of Demosthenes, 188–89n75; and *Funeral Oration* of Demosthenes, xx, 61, 127; and Plato's alleged hostility to rhetoric, xix, 210n130; and pseudo-Dionysius, 172n25, 201n21; and teachers of Demosthenes, xxii–iv, 3, 134; and "suppression," xxiv; works of: *Dinarchus*, 168n163, 169n167; *Isaeus*, 141n18, 182n38; *Isocrates*, 184n51; *Letter to Ammaeus*, xxii–iv; *On the Ancient Orators*, xviii, xxv; *On the Style of Demosthenes*, xviii–xxii, xxiv, 157n28, 184n51, 208n90; *Thucydides*, 187n64

Dionysius of Syracuse, 19, 147n107

"double action," 63–64, 104, 110, 116–18, 131, 198n131; defined 63–64

Douglas, A. E., xi

Drerup, Engelbert, 125, 177n8, 182n44, 207n78

Düring, Ingemar, 145n92, 148n20, 149n43–44, 150n48, 157n16, 158n38, 159n43, 159n45, 202n30, 204n47, 206n60

Engels, Johannes, 61–63, 70, 165n117, 172n25

Engler, M. R., 147n106

Eubulus, 22, 94, 123, 146n104, 163n93, 187n71–72

Euphraeus, 26, 29, 37–39, 41, 89, 121, 123, 151n70, 155n129, 180n33, 202n29

Eusebius, 63, 120, 161n68, 169n174, 204n47, 205–206n53

fabrication/suppression dynamic, xi, xiii–iv, xxiv–v, xxviii, 1, 11, 15–16; and "flipping Pernot," 15–16, 132, 141n22

Ferguson, W. S., 160n53
Finley, M. I., 176n103, 203n34
Fisher, Nick, 156, 186n59
Fowler, R. C., 210n126
Frede, Dorothea, 173n28
Frede, Michael, 30, 129, 203n38
Fuchs, Harald, 201n18, 207n77
Funkhänel, K. H., 4, 11, 13, 16, 61, 141n26–26, 144n63, 145n88, 172n25; and Hermippus, 4; and Isocrates, 4, 142n28; and *Fifth Letter* of Demosthenes, 16

Gabba, Emilio, xviii, xxv, 201n19–20
Gaiser, Konrad, 148n25, 205n50
Gehrke, Hans–Joachim, 6, 47, 142n35, 148n23, 149n41, 158n32; project of, 6; students of, 6, 47
Giaquinta, Irene, x, 16, 145n87, 163n85, 209n106
Gibbon, Edward, obscene story in, 183–84n48
Gilbert and Sullivan, 200n5
Gildenhard, Ingo, 178n19
Goldstein, J. A., 209n104
Gomperz, Theodor, 25–26, 28–30, 149n34, 204–205n49
Gorgias, xvi, xxviii, 13, 19, 22, 25, 27, 32–33, 48, 53–55, 58, 66–67, 69, 74, 81, 86–87, 89–90, 94–95, 101, 103–6, 109, 115, 123, 126, 128–29, 133–36, 151n74, 166n132, 171n9, 173n26, 175n72, 175n83, 179–80n31, 182n45, 196n118, 197n123, 199n139, 208n92, 210n132, 210n141, 211n147, 211n151; and Academy, 81–82; and Aelius Aristides, xxviii, 133–36, 211n147; and Aristides the Just, 22, 89, 103, 135–36; and *Aristogeiton II*, 128; and Cicero, xvi; and Demosthenes, 87, 89, 101, 103–6, 126, 129, 210n132; and *Exordia*, 105–6, 128, 197n123; and *Fifth Letter*, 129; and Macedon, 19, 27, 32, 123; and *On the Crown*, 208n92; and rhetoric purified, 126; and *Third Philippic*, 89–90, 103–4; Corinthian farmer and, 69; famous claim ("*Gorgias* Reversal") in, 25, 53–55, 58, 103–4
Grote, George, 154n110, 155n124, 155–56n130
Guthrie, W. K. C., 146n95, 146n105, 149n44, 151–52n76, 152n87, 173n30, 186n62, 194n102, 209n113

Haake, Matthias, x, 6, 47, 51, 142, 153n91, 159n46, 160n59, 161
Hall, Jennifer, 200n3, 200n5
Harding, Phillip, 150n54, 187n71, 188–89n75, 198n125, 207n78
Harris, E. M., xxvi, 155–56n130, 177n10, 208n91
Harris, W. V., 177n6
Hegesippus, 93, 186n59
Heidegger, Martin, 122, 206n61–62; and *Destruktion*, 122
Heldentod, 64, 82, 97, 100. *See also* Socrates, heroic death of
Hermias of Atarneus, 17–20, 26–27, 49–50, 94, 122, 146n96, 150n51, 151n70, 159n43, 160n55, 189n75, 204n43; and "the closeness of the relationship between Aristotle," 189n75
Herodotus, 93, 149n30, 153n104, 210n143
Herrman, Judson, x, 61, 63, 127, 167–70n148, 176n2, 194n96–97, 208n87–88; debt to, x, 176n2
Hesk, Jon, 195n112
Homer, 44, 112–14, 134, 164n108
Hubbell, H. M., 67–68, 158n41, 159n44–45, 171n10–14, 172n16, 209n121, 211n149
Hyperides, xiii–iv, xxv–viii, xxxiii–iv, 7, 9, 18–25, 28–29, 43–44, 49, 52–56, 59–65, 70, 77, 83, 110, 121–22, 126–27, 141n17, 143n50, 144n63, 144n65, 145n80, 146n101, 151n70, 163n95, 165–66n126, 176n102, 194n99, 194–95n102, 195n107; and choice, 83; and "double action," 63; and end of Attic oratory, 63; and Egypt, 63; and *Menexenus*, 60–61;

and *Phaedo*, 60, 63, 127; Engels on his connection to Plato, 70; Trampedach on his connection to Plato, 167n152; works of: *Against Demosthenes*, 62, 168n160–61; *Against Diondas*, 63, 169; discovery of, 63; *Funeral Oration*, 59–60, 83, 127, 166, 167n144, 170n183, 176n102; authenticity of, 61 ὑπεραποθνῄσκειν ("to die on behalf of"). See *Symposium*

Idomenaeus, 7, 46, 158n35
Isaeus, xxvii, 1–3, 91–92, 95, 102, 107, 109, 112–13, 141n17–18, 145n90, 185n56, 194n97, 194n99, 196n114, 208n97; and self-interest, 91, 182n39
Isocrates, xiv, xix–xx, xxii, xxxiv, 1–4, 11–12, 31–33, 35–39, 46, 48, 50, 62, 66–69, 73, 92–94, 101–2, 107, 112–13, 115, 117, 119, 123, 132, 140n6, 141n17, 152n88, 154n115, 171n7, 184n52, 189n75, 192–93n87, 194n99, 208n97, 211n149, 211n151; and Aristotle, 48, 158n41; and Cicero, 123; and Clearchus, 117, 119, 202n25, 204n40; and Demosthenes' enemies, 186n58, 186n60; and *Euthydemus*, 93; and Funkhänel, 4; and Hermippus, 3–4, 11–12, 141n17, 167n153, 192n82; and Hubbell, 171–72, 209n121, 211n149; and Hyperides, 62, 165–66n126; and Isaeus, 3, 141n18; and Speusippus, 35, 39; and *Phaedrus*, 73, 93, 177n12; and *Response to Lacritus*, 93, 101, 185n55–56; and self-interest, 92; and "Socrates," 46, 157n16; as Plato's rival, xiv, 2, 66–68, 132, 171n6; writings of, 184n52; survival of, 66: *Antidosis*, 140n6; *Archidamus*, 199n143; *Busirus*, 177n12; *On the Peace*, 94, 185n53; *Panegyricus*, 32, 175n71; *Philippus*, xxxiv, 93, 153n94, 154n115, 155n121, 184n52; τέχναι, 1–2, 4, 73; *To Alexander*, 155n122; *To Nicocles*, 66, 171n8, 184n52; *To Philip*, 31, 33, 36–39, 155n122, 160n54; *To Timotheus*, 202n25, 204n40
Isnardi Parente, Margherita, 151n76, 202n24, 204n49

Jacoby, Felix, 3, 140n12, 204n41
Jaeger, Werner, 151n74, 160n56, 187n71
Jebb, R. C., 153n102
Jefferson, Thomas, 86, 127, 137
Judeo–Christianity, 99, 195n105

Kalligas, Paul, 140n6, 142n36, 148n25
Kapparis, K. A., 183n47, 183n48, 187n67
Kapust, D. J., 179–80n31
Kelsen, Hans, v, 50, 158n40, 159n42, 159n44, 160n53
Kennedy, G. A., xviii, 157n20
Kenyon, F. G., 167n155, 169n173, 170n178
Kindstrand, J. F., 157n17, 157n20
Korhonen, Tor, 160n61
Körte, Alfred, 180n32, 188–89n75

Laistner, M. L. W., 153n102, 186n60, 202n25
Lenz, F. W., 211n150
Libanius, 63, 140n16, 169–70n176, 185n56, 198n126
Livingstone, Niall, 86, 177n12
Longinus, 114, 117, 125, 134, 137, 192n85, 195n111, 200n10, 212n156
Loraux, Nicole, 165n125, 167n148
Lucian, xxviii–ix, 13–15, 43, 48, 124, 144, 200n2, 200n5, 201n16, 202n28; and *Against an Ignorant Purchaser of Books*, 34, 154n108, 187n64; and *Teacher of Orators*, 14–15, 43, 48, 116, 145n82
[Lucian], author of *Encomium of Demosthenes*, xxviii–ix, 67, 111–16, 122, 124, 134, 137, 193n89, 202n28, 207n76, 211n149
Lycurgus, xiii–xv, xxvi–ix, xxxiii–iv, 7, 9, 19–25, 28–29, 43, 49, 52–61,

63, 65, 77–79, 110, 121–22, 126–27, 141n17, 143n50, 144n63, 144n65, 145n80, 146n101, 151n70, 156n135, 169n170, 174n68, 188n74, 194n99, 194–95n102, 204n43, 204–205n49, 207n80, 208n93, 211n151; and Aristides the Just, 148n12; and *Ion*, 59–60, 79; and *Symposium*, 57–60
Lysias, xix, 73, 91, 102, 107, 113, 127, 130, 182n40, 194n99, 199n142

MacDowell, D. M., xxiii, 140n10, 156n130, 156n7, 182n43, 183n47, 187n71, 191n78, 192n80
MacMullen, Ramsay, 203n37, 207n77
Maddoli, Gianfranco, 148n27
Marasco, Gabriele, 160n59, 204–205n49
Markle, M. M., 153n94, 154n115, 155n128, 156n134, 187n70
Martin, Gunther, xv–vi, 146n101, 154n107, 207n76, 208n91
Memnon, 119–20, 204n41, 204n44
Menexenus, xx–xxii, xxiv–v, xxxiii, 60–61, 64, 73, 98–99, 106, 126–27, 164n108, 167n146, 173n38, 187n69, 195n104, 197n123, 200–201n14; and *Exordia*, 106; and *Funeral Oration* (Demosthenes), 197n123; and *Funeral Oration* (Hyperides), 60; and idealization of Athens, 127; and *Letter 3*, 200n14; and *On the Crown*, xx–xxii, xxiv–v, 61, 98, 126
Merlan, Philip, 149n45, 151n73, 151n76
Meyer, Eduard, 177n8
Miller, Jeff, 156n1, 159n49, 160n53
Mnesistratus of Thasos, 10–11, 141n20, 144n61, 144n63, 144n65
Morrow, G. R., 142n34, 196n115
Most, G. W., 63, 170n181–82

Natali, Carlo, 149n43, 189n75
Natoli, A. F., x, xxvi, 30, 36–37, 152n84, 153n89, 186n61, 209n107
Niebuhr, B. G., 150n64
Nietzsche, F. W., 207n80

Ober, Josiah, 179–80n31

Olympiodorus, 165n122, 167n151, 211n150, 211–12n151
O'Sullivan, Lara, 47, 158n31, 160n55, 160n59, 160n62, 161n63, 161n68

Pausanias, 168n158
Pearson, Lionel, 88, 179n23, 179n27, 182n44, 182–83n46, 188–89n75
Pernot, Laurent, x, xxviii, 10–12, 14–17, 43, 48, 129, 131–32, 136, 143n57, 159n44, 192n83–84, 195n104; "to flip," 15. *See also* "flipping Pernot"
"Pernot's Triad," 17, 192n83
Phaedo, 20, 60, 63–64, 75, 81–83, 100, 103, 114–16, 151n74, 176n101; and Demosthenes ([Lucian's]), 116; and *Heldentod*, 100; and ὑπεραποθνήσκειν, 82; and Hyperides, 60, 63; and [Lucian], 114; and purification, 82
Philip of Macedon, xxvi, xxxiii–iv, 18, 21, 23, 26, 29–41, 50, 53, 67, 86–89, 93–96, 98, 100, 107, 110, 145n90, 152n88, 155n122, 155n128, 161n68, 177n7, 178n15, 178n19, 179n25, 186n60, 188–90n75, 194n98, 207n78; discovery by that Demosthenes had been Plato's student, 41; valorization of, 125, 177n7, 178n19, 207n78
"Philip of Macedon" (in Lucian), 14, 111–12, 115, 118, 125, 202n28
Philodemus, 25, 28, 48–49, 140n6, 148n25, 158n41
Phocion, xiii, xxvi–vii, xxxiii–iv, 6–7, 20–26, 28–31, 41, 43, 49, 52–55, 62, 65, 77, 122, 126, 142n40, 143n50, 146n104, 151n70, 194–95n102, 204–205n49; and Socrates, 22, 194–95n102
Photius, xiv, 47, 119, 157n27
Pickard-Cambridge, A. W., 155–56n130, 182n44
Plato, *passim*: and avoidance of hiatus, 200n3; and "basanistic pedagogy," 80; *see* Curricular Hypothesis; and democratic

rhetoric, 81–82; and διάνοια,
75–76, 80; and "Εὖ Πράττειν
Fallacy," 74–75; and γραφὴ
παρανόμων, 100–1, 196n115; and
καταβατέον, 76–77, 90; and the
Marathon Oath, 194n100; and
Reading Order, 61, 70, 74, 82, 105,
173n38, 176n97; and "Third Man,"
64, 76, 82; as logographer, 92,
101, 182n45; as teacher of youth,
140–41n16; austere ontology of,
79; Demosthenes' echo of, 90;
what Demosthenes proves that he
taught, 99; writings of, as Funeral
Oration for Socrates, 64: *Protagoras*,
see *Protagoras*; *Alcibiades Major*,
20, 69–70, 74, 106–7, 137, 140n6,
166n133, 172n18, 175n71, 202n30,
212n157; *Alcibiades Minor*, 69, 71;
Hippias Major, 71–72, 198n126;
Hippias Minor, 71, 182–83n46,
210n128; *Ion*, xx, 59–61, 79, 157n28,
173n38; *Menexenus*, see *Menexenus*;
Symposium, see *Symposium*; *Lysis*,
71; *Euthydemus*, 71, 74, 93, 106,
199n136; *Laches*, 71, 73, 166n132,
166n134, 199n136; *Charmides*, 71,
73–74; *Gorgias*, see *Gorgias*; *Meno*, 67,
81, 135, 175n72, 187n69; *Clitophon*,
109; *Republic*, see *Republic*; *Timaeus*,
xxvii, 72, 79–82, 100, 119, 175n86;
Critias, 81, 199n136; *Phaedrus*,
xvii, xix–xx, 72–74, 80, 82, 92–93,
100, 113–14, 121, 129–30, 177n12,
182–83n46, 186n62, 195–96n112,
198–99n134, 199n136, 199n139,
206n54, 208n98; *Parmenides*, 51, 76,
78, 80–82, 100, 174n56; *Philebus*,
80, 100; *Cratylus*, 106; *Theaetetus*, 9,
13, 19, 67, 79–81, 118–19, 146n103,
151n74, 191n78, 194–95n102,
195n109; *Euthyphro*, 80–81; *Sophist*,
80–81, 100, 122; *Statesman*, 80–81,
167n150, 202–203n33; *Apology of
Socrates*, see *Apology of Socrates*;
Minos, 120; *Crito*, 32, 81–82, 92, 118,
128, 176n97, 202n31; *Laws*, 20, 31,
80, 120, 194n97; *Epinomis*, 31, 80–82,
91, 140n6; *Phaedo*, see *Phaedo*; *Letters*,
5, 9, 13, 27, 30, 39, 89, 100, 109, 121,
130, 150n53, 200–201n14, 204n43,
206n54, 209n110, 209n107
Plato-Demosthenes connection, as
Platonic sunshine, 124; three
"tracks" regarding, 17; first
(external evidence for), 5, 10, 16–17,
41; second (internal evidence for), 5,
10, 13, 17, 41; third (new conception
of both that combines first and
second tracks), xxviii, 5, 17, 41;
seven ways *Gorgias* illustrates, 101
Platonbild ("conception of Plato"), 5, 9,
17, 51, 119
Platonism, xvii, 12, 15, 20, 22, 24, 31,
51, 54–55, 57, 60, 72, 79, 95–96,
98–100, 118, 123, 155n129, 191n79,
202n31, 206n58; acme of, 79; and
Aristotle, 31, 123; and Chaeronea,
72; and Chion, 118, 202n31; and
noblesse oblige, 191n79; and Plotinus,
171n2; and "unwritten teachings,"
99; and Wittgenstein, 51, 123;
as "Cave-based," 12, 79, 95; as
"City-based," 22; as cosmological,
54, 100; as difficult, 54; as
"romantic," 20; Cicero's, xvii, 96;
Demosthenes', 95–96, 98–99; heart
of, 31; Hyperides', 60; in Macedon,
155n129; interpretations of, 79;
Lycurgus', 57; trilogy on, 206n58;
tyranny of, 15
Plotinus, 123, 171n2, 206n58
Plutarch, xiii–v, xxviii, 1–4, 6–8, 10, 12,
14, 21–26, 28, 40–41, 43, 47, 53–55,
95–96, 99, 112, 115–16, 124, 137,
140–41n16, 155–56n130, 207n76;
and Aeschines, 40, 155–56n130; and
Augustus, 96; and Aulus Gellius,
139n2; and perfect statement of the
case, 99; and Philip, 96; writings
of: *Life of Alexander*, 160n54; *Life
of Brutus*, 96; *Life of Cato*, 22, 55;
Life of Cicero, 95–96, 115, 200n11;
Life of Demetrius, 160n60; *Life of*

Demosthenes, xv, 1–4, 28, 47, 55, 95–96, 99, 124, 139n1, 139n4, 140–41n16, 143n44, 156n131, 169n171, 173n39, 180n36, 185n54, 188n74, 193n89, 195n107, 199n154, 200n6; *Life of Dion*, 96; *Life of Phocion*, xiii, 21–26, 28, 43, 53–55, 147–51, 162; *Moralia*, 148n19; *Political Advice*, 116, 201n19; *Reply to Colotes*, xiii, 7, 23, 142n40, 150n47
[Plutarch], author of *Lives of the Ten Orators*, xiv–vi, xxiii, xxvii–ix, 4, 23, 52, 55–56, 112, 116, 124, 141n17, 163n95, 165n116, 169n167
Polemo, xxv, xxxiv, 11, 28, 51, 53, 120, 144n63, 144n65, 207n80
Porphyry, 63, 211n150
Procopius, 183–84n48
Protagoras, 20, 66–74, 95, 171n3; and Academy's purpose, 66–67; and *Alcibiades Major*, 69–70

Quintilian, xxv, xxvii, 48, 98, 114, 117, 124, 127, 194n99, 194n100, 200n10
"Quintilian's Proof," xxvii, 98, 127; confirmed, 194n100

Rehdantz, K. O. A., 197n123
Renehan, R. F., xiv, 57, 163n98, 164n99, 164n102, 167n151
Republic, ix, xvii, xix, xxi, xxvii–viii, 5, 9, 13, 19, 22, 27–28, 31–32, 54–55, 58, 65, 71–82, 87–90, 96–97, 93, 97, 103, 105–6, 108–9, 113–15, 119, 121, 123–24, 127, 134, 136, 140n6, 150n59, 150n63, 151n74, 166n135, 174n56, 174n60, 175n72, 175n77, 193n92, 194n100, 196n118, 206n55; *see* Cave, Allegory of the; as central, 5–6, 74; choice in, 65, 74, 77–78; crisis of, 22, 77–79, 103; democracy–democratic man in, 90–91, 106, 170n1; Divided Line in, 75–76, 78, 174n56; dualism in, xvii; Idea of the Good in, 65, 74–76, 80, 95, 174n56, 194n100; Intermediates in, 174n56; Justice in, 78; Longer Way in, 78, 108–9; One and Many in, 80; Shorter Way in, 75, 78, 108–9; sun in, 194n100; *see* Third Wave of Paradox; tyranny in, 190n76
Rhys Roberts, W., xx, xxiv
Roberts, J. T., 148n11
Roisman, Joseph, xiv–xvi, xxviii, 157n27, 162n75, 165n116
Röper, Gottlieb, 144n63, 144n65
Rowe, G. R., 93, 185n57, 186n58, 192n82
Ryder, T. T. B., 179n26, 187n68
Ryle, Gilbert, 211n147

Sandys, J. E., 146n97, 187n66, 190n77, 191n78
Sallust, 188–89n75
Sauppe, Hermann, 178n21
Sawada, Noriko, 146n101, 146n104, 188–89n75; parsed, 188n74
Saxonhouse, Arlene W., 170n1, 179–80n31
Schaefer, Arnold, xiv, xxviii, 4–5, 7–8, 10–11, 13, 26, 28, 40, 62, 70, 129, 141–42, 144n63, 149n39, 154n17, 155n130, 156n132, 159n44, 163n97, 168n159, 169n165, 169n168, 169n171, 172n25, 178n21, 181n37, 185n56, 188n75, 196n122, 197–98n123, 198n124, 198n126, 208n89, 208n97
Schleiermacher, F. D. E., 69, 172n18
Scholten, J. H., 141n27
Schott, André, 145n90, 150n54
Sealey, Raphael, 147n8, 147n9, 154n111, 176n1, 177–78n13, 178n15, 188n74, 188–89n75, 191n78,
Second Sophistic, xxviii, 125, 200n4, 201n20, 210n126; and Leo Strauss, 124–25
Seitkasimova, Z.A., 194–95n102
Shakespeare, xvii, 79, 109
Simonides, 194n93
Socrates, *passim*: and Athens, 194–95n102; and noble rhetoric, 196n118; knows that he knows nothing, 124; sign of, 150n63

Speusippus, xxv–xxvii, xxxiii–iv, 17, 28–42, 51, 53, 61, 72, 115, 120–22, 127, 137, 150n51, 159–60n51, 162n77, 204–205n49, 212n159; abandons the Platonic Forms, 152n87; as inflection point, xxvii, 212n159; *Letter to Philip* by, xxvi, 29–32, 35–41, 51, 53, 61, 72, 122, 127, 152n84, 152n88 153n89, 153–55, 203n33, 209n107;
as sign of the end of the Old Academy, 39; authenticity of, 30, 32, 61, 152n84, 209n107
Sprague, R. K., 196n117
Steinbock, Bernd, 156n135, 164n114, 165n119, 166n141
Steinhart, Karl, 4, 142n30, 142n33, 172n25
Strabo, 204n43
Strauss, Leo, 50, 160n57, 164n105, 207n77; and Second Sophistic, 125
Sturm, Wilhelm, 139n1
"Suppression, Three Waves of," xxix, 93, 126, 132; (1) Macedonian, xxix, 126, 137–38; (2) Roman, Augustan, or imperial, xxix, 124, 126, 132, 136; (3) nineteenth–century philology, xxix, 125–27, 129, 137, 197n123. *See also* fabrication/ suppression dynamic
Susemihl, Franz, 144n63, 149n42, 158n29
Sykutris, Joh., 152n80, 167n149, 208n86
Syme, Ronald, 86, 177n5–6
Symposium, 24, 57–61, 64, 68–69, 71–73, 82, 92, 151n74, 164n103, 164n105, 164n109, 164n114, 173n38, 184n50, 184n52; and Lycurgus, 57–60; and *Protagoras*, 68; and "to die on behalf of" (ὑπεραποθνήσκειν), 23, 41, 57–59, 61, 64

Tarán, Leonardo, 151n74, 151–52n76
Tarnopolsky, Christina, 179n28
Theophrastus, 46–47, 51, 62, 112–13, 144n63, 160n55, 160–61n61, 162n79

Theopompus, 32, 36–37, 152n88, 154–55n120, 188n74
Third Wave of Paradox in, 19, 27, 38, 49, 77, 159n43, 202–203n33; as pivot around which our image of Plato turns, 119; two routes in, 19–20; (1) turn kings into philosophers ("king–based"), 9, 19, 159n43, 202–203n33; (2) train philosophers to be leaders, 9, 20
Third Wave of Suppression. *See* "Suppression, Three Waves of"
Thucydides (historian), xv, xix, 34, 73, 93–95, 101, 108, 127–29, 150n64, 153n105–6, 174n62, 179n27, 179n29, 187n64, 194n98, 199n149, 208n100
Thucydides (statesman), 195n107
Trampedach, Kai, x, xiv, 6–11, 13, 17, 19, 49, 61, 142n34, 155n129, 161n66, 167n151–52, 180n33, 203n35, 204n39, 204n40, 204n42, 211n151
Trapp, Michael, 133–34, 153n95, 172n15, 204n46, 209n120
Trevett, J. C., 156n2, 182n43, 182n44, 191n78, 198n124
Trittle, Lawrence, 142n40, 162n73
Tübingen School, 123, 148n25, 206n54
Tuplin, Christopher, 178n20

Vatai, F. L., 202n24, 203n37
Vegetti, Mario, 193n92, 202–3n33, 204–205n49
Vlastos, Gregory, 72, 123, 173n36, 206n64

Wehrli, Fritz, 3, 47, 140n13, 140–41n16, 141n17–18, 145n93, 157n25–26, 205n50
Westermann, Anton, xiv–xv, 62, 141n24, 141n26, 154n107, 168n158, 168n164
Whitehead, David, 170n179, 187n69, 187n72
Whitmarsh, Tim, xxviii
Wilamowitz–Moellendorff, Ulrich von, 58, 149n37, 149n42, 153n93, 154n117, 164n108

Wittgenstein, 160n58. *See also* Platonism, and Wittgenstein
Wooten, C. W., xviii, xxii, 88, 179n23–24
Wörle, Andrea, xiv, 8, 10, 13, 143n48–49, 167n151, 204n42, 204–205n49
Wormell, D. R. W., 150n53, 204n43
Worthington, Ian, xiv–xvi, xxviii, 140n10, 157n27, 158n34, 162n75, 170n180, 177n9, 179n26, 180n32, 182n43, 188–89n75, 199n141, 207n78, 208n87, 209n109; on "Plato's contempt for rhetoric," xvi

Xenocrates, xxv–vi, xxxiii–iv, 13, 17, 24–29, 31, 50–51, 53–54, 112–13, 115, 120–21, 137, 148n17, 149n34, 151n70, 152n87, 159–60n51, 161n63–64, 162n77, 204–205n49, 205n51, 212n159; hypothesis regarding, 159–60n51
Xenophon, xxxiii, 41, 45, 73, 81, 93–95, 120, 123, 156n136, 163n82, 171n4, 172n20, 173n26, 176n95, 187n69, 199n140, 204n45; and choice of lives, 78; and Demosthenes, 94–95; and Plato, 45, 93, 120; and theologized monarchs, 81, 120; as "old fool," 150n64; as Socratic, 45; post-imperial policy of, 123; writings of: *Cynegeticus*, 156n136; *Cyropaedia*, 81, 120, 176n95, 194n97, 204n45; *Memorabilia*, 41, 150n64; 163n82, 171n4, 172n20, 174n63, 174n66–67, 199n140; *Poroi*, xxxiii, 94, 123, 187n69

Yunis, Harvey, 128, 177–78n13, 193n90, 194n98, 198n133, 198–99n134, 199n150, 208n96–100, 208n102, 209n108; gem in, 208n100; on *Exordia*, 198n134, 208n96

Zeller, Eduard, 8, 143n50, 151n76, 172n23, 191n78, 202n29, 204n43
Zosimus, 34, 153n107, 187n64

About the Author

Having been persuaded by Plato's *Republic* that Justice requires the philosopher to go back down into the Cave, **William Henry Furness Altman** devoted his professional life to the cause of public education; since retiring in 2013, he has been working as an independent scholar. Born in Washington, DC, where he was educated at the Sidwell Friends School, and with degrees in philosophy from Wesleyan University, the University of Toronto, and the Universidade Federal de Santa Catarina, he was a public high school teacher in Vermont, California, Massachusetts, Connecticut, and Virginia; between 1980 and 2013, he taught social studies, history, philosophy, English, drama, and Latin as well as offering extra curricular instruction in Ancient Greek. He began publishing scholarly articles in philosophy, intellectual history, and classics in 2007, and received his doctorate in 2010 with a dissertation on Hegel. Five volumes devoted to the reading order of Plato's dialogues beginning with *Plato the Teacher: The Crisis of the* Republic (2012) have been published by Lexington Books; the series includes *The Guardians in Action: Plato the Teacher and the Post-Republic Dialogues from* Timaeus *to* Theaetetus (2016), *The Guardians on Trial: The reading order of Plato's Dialogues from* Euthyphro *to* Phaedo (2016), *Ascent to the Good: The Reading Order of Plato's Dialogues from* Symposium *to* Republic (2018), and *Ascent to the Beautiful: Plato the Teacher and the Pre-*Republic *Dialogues from* Protagoras *to* Symposium (2020). With the publication of *Friedrich Wilhelm Nietzsche: The Philosopher of the Second Reich* (Lexington, 2013), he completed "A German Trilogy" that includes *Martin Heidegger and the First World War:* Being and Time *as Funeral Oration* (Lexington, 2012) and his first book, *The German Stranger:*

Leo Strauss and National Socialism (Lexington, 2011). He is also the author of *The Revival of Platonism in Cicero's Late Philosophy:* Platonis aemulus *and the Invention of Cicero* (Lexington, 2016), and the editor of *Brill's Companion to the Reception of Cicero* (Brill, 2015). He is presently working on another trilogy about the origins, practice, and deformation of Platonism comprised by *The Relay Race of Virtue: Plato's Debts to Xenophon* (SUNY, 2022), the present book, and a work in progress titled "Plotinus the Master and the Apotheosis of Imperial Platonism." He has two sons, Philip and Elias, two grandchildren, and is married to Zoraide; they currently divide their time between Calais, Vermont, and Florianópolis, the island capital of Santa Catarina (Brasil).

www.ingramcontent.com/pod-product-compliance
Lightning Source LLC
Chambersburg PA
CBHW020112010526
44115CB00008B/802